GROC's CANDID GUIDE TO THE
N.E. AEGEAN
ISLANDS
including
SAMOS, IKARIA, FOURNOI, THIMENA, CHIOS, PSARA, OINOUSSAI, LESBOS, LIMNOS, AG. ESTRATIOS, THASSOS & SAMOTHRAKI
As well as
Athens City, Piraeus & The Mainland Ports
of
Kavala & Alexandroupoli

for the package, villa, backpacker & ferry-boating holiday-maker, whether travelling by air, car, coach or train.

by
Geoffrey O'Connell

Published by

Ashford Press Publishing
1 Church Road
Shedfield
Hampshire
SO3 2HW

Text © Geoffrey O'Connell, 1987
Maps and illustrations © Geoffrey O'Connell and
Ashford Press Publishing, 1987

Printed in Great Britain

British Library Cataloguing in Publication Data

O'Connell, Geoffrey
    Samos and N. E. Aegean Islands, Athens and Piraeus —
    (The Candid guides) — (The Greek islands).
    1. Samos island (Greece) — description and travel — guide-
    books
    I   Title   II   Series
    914.99   DF901.534

ISBN 0-948762-01-2

CONTENTS

SURROUNDS: including Thermae; Xilosirtis & Chrisostomos. The island topography including: ROUTE ONE: Monokampi, Karavostamon, Efdilos, port & onto Kampos, Galiskari, Armenistis & Christos Rachon.
EXCURSION TO FOURNOI island including: Fournoi, main village & port, Chrisomilea. Thimena island & Thimenao port.

CHIOS **including:** Chios, capital & main port. The island topography including: ROUTE ONE: Karyes, The Monasteries of Kourma, Ag. Markou, Nea Moni & Ag Pateron; Avgonyma & Anavatos. ROUTE TWO: Vrondatos, Monastery of Mirtidiotissa, Pantoukios, Langada, Marmaro, Nagos, Amades, Viki, Kambia, Dievcha, Volissos, Limnos, Limnia, Ag. Gala, Agiasmata & Pityos. ROUTE THREE: Karfas, Ag. Ermioni, Thymiana, Ag. Fotinis, Kallimasia, Ag. Aimilianos, Kataraktis, Nenita, Vokaria & Ag. Ioannis. ROUTE FOUR: Vaviloi, Sklavia, Armolia, Emborios, Pirgi, Olympoi, Mesta, Limani Meston, Vessa & Lithi Papori.
EXCURSION TO PSARA island **including:** Psara, main (& only) village & port.
EXCURSION TO OINOUSSAI island **including:** Oinoussai village & port.

LESBOS **including:** Mitilini, capital & main port.
The S.E. island topography including: ROUTE ONE: Akrotiri, Charamida, Ag. Ermogenis, Loutra, Skala Loutron, Koudourouda & Pyrgi. ROUTE TWO: Moria, Panagiouda, Pamfilla, Paralia Thermis, Upper Thermi, Petalidi, Skala Neon Kydonion, Xampelia, Aspropotamos, Manadamados, Kapi, Sikamia & Skala Sikamias. ROUTE THREE: Ntipi, Pigadakia & Kato Tritos, Perama, Tarti, Agios Isidoros, Plomari, Vatera, Vrissa, Polychnitos, Skala Polychnitou, Vassilika & Agiassos. ROUTE FOUR: Lampou Milli, Agia Paraskevi & the:
N.E. island via Kalloni, Myrssiniotissas Convent, Petra & Molivos. ROUTE FIVE: Skala Kallonis, Parakila, Apothikes, Messotopos & Skala Eressou. ROUTE SIX: Anaxos Skoutarou, Skoutaros, Skalachori, Monastery of Perivolis, Gavathas, Antissa, Monastry Ipsilou & Sigri.

LIMNOS **including:** Mirina, capital & main port.
The island topography including: ROUTE ONE: Avlonas, Kaspakas, Skala Kaspakas, Ag. Giannis & Cape Kalogeri. ROUTE TWO: Kornos, Katalako, Karpassi, Varos, Kotsinas, Romanou, Panagia & Plaka. ROUTE THREE: Moudros, Roussopouli & Skandali. ROUTE FOUR: Plati, Plagisos, Thanos & Thanos Beach, Kontias, Diapori, Nea Koutali & Livadohori.
EXCURSION TO AG ESTRATIOS island **including:** Ag. Estratios, main (& only) village & port.

THASSOS **including:** Thassos, capital & second port.
The island topography including: a circular route clockwise to Makryammos Beach, Panagia, Chrysi Ammoudia, Potamia, Skala Potamias, Kinira, Alyki, Monastery of Archangelou, Potos, Theologos, Pefkari, Limenaria, Kastro, Skala Marion, Skala Kallirachis, Skala Sotiros, Skala Prinos (main port), Neos Prinos, Skala Rachoniou & Glyfada.
KAVALA, mainland ferry-boat port.

SAMOTHRAKI **including:** Kamariotisa, capital village & port.
The island topography including: ROUTE ONE: The Chora. ROUTE TWO: Alonia, Xiropotamos, Lakoma & Profitis Ilias. ROUTE THREE: Paleopoli, Museum of the

Sanctuary of the Great Gods, Kariotes & Therma.
ALEXANDROUPOLI, mainland ferry-boat port.

ILLUSTRATIONS

Please do not forget that prices are given as a guide only especially accommodation and restaurant costs which are subject to fluctuation, almost always upwards. In the last year or so transport costs, especially ferry-boat fees, have also escalated dramatically but the increased value of other currencies to the Greek drachmae has compensated, to some extent, for these seemingly inexorably rising charges.

The series is entering its fifth year of publication and I would appreciate continuing to hear from holidaymakers and travellers who have any additions or corrections to bring to my attention. As in the past, all correspondence (except that addressed 'Dear filth' or similar endearments) will be answered.

I hope readers will excuse the odd errors that creep (well gallop) into the welter of detailed information included in the body text. We manage, in order to keep the volumes as up to date as possible, to cut the period down from inception to publication to some six months which does result in the occasional slip up...

INTRODUCTION

This volume is the fifth in the popular and proven series of GROC's Candid Guides to the Greek Islands. The rationale, the *raison d'etre* behind their production is to treat each island grouping on an individual and comprehensive basis, rather than attempt overall coverage of the 100 or so islands usually described in one volume. This obviates attempting to do justice, to, say, Thassos in amongst an aggregation of many other, often disparate islands.

Due to the vast distances involved very few, if any, vacationers can possibly visit more than a number of islands in a particular group, even if spending as much as four weeks in Greece.

It is important for package and villa holiday-makers to have an unbiased and relevant description of their planned holiday surroundings, rather than the usual extravagant hyperbole of the glossy sales brochure. It is vital for backpackers and ferry-boat travellers to have detailed and accurate information at their finger tips, on arrival. With these differing requirements in mind factual, 'straight-from-the-shoulder' location reports have been combined with detailed plans of the major port, town and/or city of each island in the group as well as topographical island maps.

Amongst the guides on offer there are a number of earnest tomes dealing with Ancient and Modern Greece, its mythology and history, there are a number of thumbnail travel booklets and there are some worthy, if rather out-of-date books available. Unfortunately they do not necessarily assuage the various travellers' differing requirements which must include speedy and accurate identification of one's position on arrival; the location of accommodation and the whereabouts of banks, post office and tourist offices. Additional requisites are a swift and easy to read resume of the town's main locations, cafes, tavernas and restaurants; detailed local bus and ferry timetables as well as a full island narrative. Once the traveller has settled in, then and only then, can he or she start to feel at ease, making their own finds and discoveries.

I have chosen to omit lengthy accounts of the relevant, fabulous Greek mythology and history. These aspects of Greece are, for the serious student, very ably related by authors far more erudite than myself. Moreover, most islands have a semi-official tourist guide translated into English, and for that matter, French, German and Scandinavian. They are usually well worth the 200 to 300 drachmae (drs) they cost, are extremely informative in 'matters archaeological' and are quite well produced, if rather out of date, with excellent colour photographs. Admittedly the English translation might seem a litte quaint (try to read Greek, let alone translate it), and the maps are often unreliable but cartography is not a strong Hellenic suit!

Each new Candid Guide is finally researched as close to the publication date as is possible and naturally any new ideas are incorporated but in the main they follow the now well tried formula. Part One deals with the preliminaries and describes in detail the different aspects of travelling and enjoying to the full the unforgettable experience of a Greek island holiday. Part Two gives a full and thoroughly redrafted account of Athens, still the hub for Greek island travel, and the relevant mainland ports for connections to the particular islands. Part Three introduces the North East Aegean islands, followed by a detailed description of each island, the layout being designed to facilitate quick and easy reference.

1

The exchange rate has fluctuated quite violently in recent years and up-to-date information must be sought prior to departure. For instance at the time of writing the final draft, the rate to the English pound (£) was hovering about 210 drs but prices are subject to fluctuation, usually upward. Annual price increases vary between some 10-20% but fortunately the drachma tends to devalue by approximately the same amount.

Recommendations and personalities are almost always based on personal observation and experience, occasionally emphasised by the discerning comments of readers or colleagues and may well not only change from year to year but be subject to different interpretation by other observers.

The series now incorporates a number of innovative ideas and unique services including:

The Decal: Since 1985 some of the accommodation and eating places recommended in the guides may display a specially produced decal to help readers identify the particular establishment.

Addendum: An updating information sheet incorporated, where possible, in the second year which includes, for instance, corrections, alterations as well as the relevant price and fare increases that have come to hand.

The publisher (and author) are very interested in considering ways and means of improving the guides and adding to the back up facilities, so are delighted to hear from readers with their suggestions.

Enjoy yourselves and **Ya Sou** (welcome).

Geoffrey O'Connell 1987

ACKNOWLEDGMENTS

Every year the list of those to be formally thanked grows and this edition shows no dimunition in their number which has forced the original brief entry from the inside front cover to an inside page.

There are those numerous friends and confidants we meet on passage as well as the many correspondents who are kind enough to contact us with useful information, all of who, in the main, remain unnamed. One constructive critic, who I have never met but deserves a mention for oh so gently cajoling me over this or that, is Iain Morris, *Editor of The Camping and Caravanning Club*.

Rosemary who accompanies me, adding her often unwanted, uninformed comments and asides (and who I occasionally threaten not to take next time), requires especial thanks for unrelieved, unstinting (well almost unstinting) support despite being dragged from this or that sun kissed beach.

Parts One and Two of this volume benefit from the judicious advice and comments of Anne Merewood, assisted by her husband Mike Makrigiorgos, when his army duties permitted. Anne, who also proof read a draft of this book, deserves and receives my heartfelt thanks.

Although receiving reward, other than in heaven, some of those who assisted me in the production of this edition require specific acknowledgement for effort far beyond the siren call of vulgar remuneration! These worthies include Linda Fehrenbach, Graham Bishop, Ted Spittles, Viv Hitie and Maureen Burness of *Type Setting*.

Lastly, and as always, I must admonish Richard Joseph for ever encouraging and cajoling me to take up the pen – surely the sword is more fun?

The cover picture of an Aegean island church is reproduced by kind permission of GREEK ISLAND PHOTOS, Willowbridge Enterprises, Bletchley, Milton Keynes, Bucks.

PART ONE
1 Packing, insurance, medical matters, climatic conditions, conversion tables & a starter course in Greek

Leisure nourishes the body and the mind is also fed thereby; on the other hand, immoderate labour exhausts both. Ovid

Vacationing anywhere on an organised tour allows a certain amount of latitude regarding the amount of luggage packed, as this method of holiday does not preclude taking fairly substantial suitcases. On the other hand, ferry-boating and backpacking restricts the amount a traveller is able to carry and the means of conveyance. The usual method is to utilise backpacks and/or roll-bags, both of which are more suitable than suitcases for this mode of travel. The choice between the two does not only depend on which is the more commodious, for at the height of season it can be advantageous to be distinguishable from the hordes of other backpackers. To promote the chances of being offered a room, the selection of roll-bags may help disassociation from the more hippy of 'genus rucksacker'. If roll-bags are selected they should include shoulder straps which help alleviate the discomfort experienced when searching out accommodation on hot afternoons with arms just stretching and stretching and stretching.

In the highly populous, oversubscribed months of July and August, it is advisable to pack a thin, foam bedroll and lightweight sleeping bag, just in case accommodation cannot be located on the occasional night.

Unless camping out, I do not think a sweater is necessary between the months of May and September. A desert jacket or lightweight anorak is a better proposition and a stout pair of sandals or training shoes are obligatory especially if very much walking is contemplated. Leave out the evening suit and cocktail dresses, as the Greeks are very informal. Instead take loose-fitting, casual clothes, and do not forget sunglasses and a floppy hat.

Should there be any doubt about the electric supply (and you shave) include a pack of disposable razors and ladies might consider acquiring one of the small, gas cylinder, portable hair-curlers prior to departure. Take along a supply of toilet rolls. They are useful for tasks other than that with which they are usually associated, including mopping up spilt liquid, wiping off plates, and blowing one's nose. It might be an idea to include a container of washing powder, a few clothes pegs, some string for a washing line and a few wire hangers to hook up washing.

Those visitors contemplating wide ranging travel should consider packing a few plastic, sealed-lid, liquid containers, a plate and a cup, as well as a knife and fork, condiments, an all-purpose cutting/slicing/carving knife and a combination bottle and tin opener. These all facilitate economical dining whilst on the move as food and drink, when available on ferry-boats and trains, can be comparatively expensive. Camping out requires these elementary items to be augmented with simple cooking equipment.

Mosquito coils can be bought in Greece but a preferable device is a small, two prong, electric heater on which a wafer thin tablet is placed. They can be purchased locally for some 1000 drs and come complete with a pack of the capsules. One trade name is *Doker Mat* and almost every room has a suitable electric point. The odourless vapour given off certainly sorts out the mosquitoes and is (hopefully)

3

harmless to humans. Mark you we did hear of a tourist who purchased one and swore by its efficacy, not even aware it was necessary to place a tablet in position!

Consider packing a pair of tweezers, some plasters, calamine lotion, after-sun and insect cream, as well as a bottle of aspirin in addition to any pharmaceuticals usually required. It is worth noting that sun oil and small packets of soap powder are now cheaper in Greece than much of Europe and shampoo and toothpaste cost the same. Including a small phial of disinfectant has meriι, but it is best not to leave the liquid in the original glass bottle. Should it break, the disinfectant and glass mingled with clothing can prove not only messy but will leave a distinctive and lingering odour. Kaolin and morphine is a very reliable stomach settler. Greek chemists dispense medicines and prescriptions that only a doctor would be able to mete out in many other Western European countries, so prior to summoning a doctor, try the local pharmacy.

Insurance & medical matters

While touching upon medical matters, a national of an EEC country should extend their states National Health cover. United Kingdom residents can contact the local *Department of Health and Social Security* requesting form number *E111 UK*. When completed, and returned, this results in a *Certificate of Entitlement to Benefits in Kind during a stay in a Member State*. Well, that's super! In short, it entitles a person to medical treatment in other EEC countries. Do not only rely on this prop, but seriously consider taking out a holiday insurance policy covering loss of baggage and money; personal accident and medical expenses; cancellation of the holiday and personal liability. Check the exclusion clauses carefully. It is no good an insured imagining he or she is covered for 'this or that' only to discover the insurance company has craftily excluded claims under a particular section. Should a reader intend to hire a scooter ensure this form of 'activity' is comprehensively insured. Rather than rely on the rather inadequate standard insurance cover offered by many tour companies, it is best to approach a specialist insurance broker. For instance, bearing in mind the rather rudimentary treatment offered by the average Greek island hospital, it is almost obligatory to include Fly-Home Medicare cover in any policy. A couple of homilies might graphically reinforce the argument. Firstly the Greek hospital system expects the patient's family to minister and feed the inmate 'out-of-hours'. This can result in holiday companions having to camp in the ward for the duration of any internment. Perhaps more thought-provoking is the homespun belief that a patient is best left the first night to survive, if it is God's will, and to pass on if not! After a number of years hearing of the unfortunate experiences of friends and readers, who failed to act on the advice given herein, as well as the inordinate difficulties I experienced in arranging cover for myself, I was prompted to offer readers an all embracing travel insurance scheme. Details are to be found on Page 42. **DON'T DELAY, ACT NOW**.

Most rooms do not have rubbish containers so why not include some plastic bin liners which are also very useful for packing food as well as storing dirty washing. A universal sink plug is almost a necessity. Many Greek sinks do not have one but, as the water usually drains away very slowly, this could be considered an academic point.

Take along a pack of cards, and enough paperback reading to while away sunbathing sojourns and long journeys. Playing cards are subject to a government tax, which makes their price exorbitant, and books are expensive but some shops and lodgings operate a book-swap scheme.

Many flight, bus, ferry-boat and train journeys start off early in the morning so a small battery-operated alarm clock may well help save sleepless, fretful nights. A small hand or wrist compass can be an enormous help orientating in towns and if room and weight allow, a torch is a useful addition to the inventory.

Readers must not forget their passport which is absolutely essential to (1) enter Greece, (2) book into most accommodation as well as campsites, (3) change money and (4) hire a scooter or car.

In the larger, more popular, tourist orientated resorts Diners and American Express (Amex) credit cards are accepted. Personal cheques may be changed as accompanied by a Eurocheque bank card. Americans can use an Amex credit card at their overseas offices to change personal cheques up to $1000. They may also, by prior arrangement, have cable transfers made to overseas banks, allowing 24 hrs from the moment their home bank receives specific instructions.

It is wise to detail separately from the following items the credit card, traveller's cheques and airline ticket numbers in case they should be mislaid. Incidentally this is a piece of advice I always give but rarely, if ever, carry out myself. Visitors are only allowed to import 3000 drs of Greek currency (in notes) and the balance required must be in traveller's cheques and/or foreign currency. It used to be 1500 drs but the decline in the value of the Greek drachma has resulted in the readjustment. With only 3000 drs in hand it is often necessary to change currency quite quickly which becomes a problem if arrival is over the weekend or the banks are on strike, which sometimes occurs. *See* **Banks, Chapter Seven** for further details in respect of banks and money.

Imported spirits are comparatively expensive (except on some of the duty free Dodecanese islands) but the duty free allowance, that can be taken into Greece, is up to one and a half litres of alcohol. So if you are a whisky or gin drinker, and partial to an evening sundowner, acquire a bottle or two before arrival. Cigars are difficult to buy on the islands, so it may well be advantageous to take along the 75 that can be imported. Note the above applies to fellow members of the EEC. Allowances for travellers from other countries are 1 litre of alcohol and 50 cigars. Camera buffs should take as much film as possible as it is more costly in Greece than in most Western European countries.

Officially, the Greek islands enjoy some 3000 hours of sunshine per year, out of an approximate, possible 4250 hours. The prevailing summer wind is the northerly *Meltemi* which can blow very strongly, day in day out during July and August, added to which these months are usually dry and very hot for 24 hours a day. The sea in April is perhaps a little cool for swimming, but May and June are marvellous months, as are September and October.

For the statistically minded:

The monthly average temperatures in the N.E. Aegean include:

Average monthly air temperature

	Jan	Feb	Mar	Apr	May	June	July	Aug	Sept	Oct	Nov	Dec
Thassos C°	6.2	6.9	9.1	14.1	19.1	23.6	26.3	26.2	21.8	16.6	12.4	8.7
F°	43	44.4	48	57	66	74.5	79	79	71	62	54	47.7
Samos C°	10.9	11.2	12.8	16.3	20.4	24.4	26.5	26.4	23.8	19.7	16.9	12.8
F°	51.6	52	55	61	68.7	76	79.7	79.5	74.8	67.5	61	55

Sea surface temperature
(at 1400 hrs)

	Jan	Feb	Mar	Apr	May	June	July	Aug	Sept	Oct	Nov	Dec
Lesbos C°	14.3	14.3	15.0	17.0	21.4	24.5	26.0	25.2	23.6	19.3	16.8	14.9
F°	57.7	57.7	59	62.6	70.5	76	78.8	77.4	74.5	66.7	62	58.8

The best time of year to holiday

The above charts indicate that probably the best months to vacation are May, June, September and October, July and August being too hot. Additionally, the most crowded months, when accommodation is at a premium, are also July and August and the first two weeks of September. Taking everything into account, it does not need an Einstein to work the matter out.

Conversion tables & equivalent

Units	Approximate Conversion	Equivalent
Miles to kilometres	Divide by 5, multiply by 8	5 miles = 8 km
Kilometres to miles	Divide by 8, multiply by 5	
Feet to metres	Divide by 10, multiply by 3	10 ft = 3 m
Metres to feet	Divide by 3, multiply by 10	
Inches to centimetres	Divide by 2, multiply by 5	1 inch = 2.5 cm
Centimetres to inches	Divide by 5, multiply by 2	
Fahrenheit to centigrade	Deduct 32, divide by 9 and multiply by 5	77°F = 25°C
Centigrade to fahrenheit	Divide by 5, multiply by 9 and add 32	
Gallons to litres	Divide by 2, multiply by 9	2 gal = 9 litres
Litres to gallons	Divide by 9, multiply by 2	

Note: 1 pint = 0.6 of a litre and 1 litre = 1.8 pints

Pounds (weight) to kilos	Divide by 11, multiply by 5	5 k = 11 lb
Kilos to pounds	Divide by 5, multiply by 11	

Note: 16 oz = 1 lb; 1000 g = 1 kg and 100 g = 3.5 oz

Tyre pressures
Pounds per square inch to kilometres per square centimetre

lb/sq.in	kg/cm	lb/sq.in.	kg/cm
10	0.7	26	1.8
15	1.1	28	2.0
20	1.4	30	2.1
24	1.7	40	2.8

The Greeks use the metric system but most 'unreasonably' sell liquid (i.e. wine, spirits and beer) by weight. Take my word for it, a 640g bottle of wine is approximately 0.7 of a litre or 1.1 pints. Proprietory wines such as *Demestika* are sold in bottles holding as much as 950g, which is 1000 ml or 1¾ pints and represents good value.

Electric points in the larger towns, smarter hotels and holiday resorts are 220 volts AC and power any American or British appliance. Older buildings in out of the way places might still have 110 DC supply. Remote pensions may not have any electricity, other than that supplied by a generator and even then the rooms might not be wired up. More correctly they may well be wired but not connected!

Greek time is 2 hours ahead of GMT, as it is during British Summer Time, and 7 hours ahead of United States Eastern Time. That is except for a short period when the Greek clocks are corrected for their winter at the end of September, some weeks ahead of the United Kingdom alteration.

Basics & essentials of the language

These notes and subsequent **Useful Greek** at the relevant chapter endings are not, nor could be, intended to substitute for a formal phrase book or three. Accent marks have been omitted.

Whilst in the United Kingdom it is worth noting that the *British Broadcasting Co.* (Marylebone High St, London W1M 4AA) has produced an excellent book, *Greek*

Language and People, accompanied by a cassette and a record.

For the less committed a very useful, pocket-sized phrase book that I always have to hand is *The Greek Travelmate* (Richard Drew Publishing, Glasgow) costing £1.50.

The Alphabet

Capitals	Lower case	Sounds like
A	α	Alpha
B	β	Veeta
Γ	γ	Ghama
Δ	δ	Dhelta
E	ε	Epsilon
Z	ζ	Zeeta
H	η	Eeta
Θ	θ	Theeta
I	ι	Yiota
K	κ	Kapa
Λ	λ	Lamtha
M	μ	Mee
N	ν	Nee
Ξ	ξ	Ksee
O	ο	Omikron
Π	π	Pee
P	ρ	Roh
Σ	σ	Sighma
T	τ	Taf
Y	υ	Eepsilon
Φ	φ	Fee
X	χ	Chi
Ψ	ψ	Psi
Ω	ω	Omegha

Groupings

αι	'e' as in let
αυ	'av/af' as in have/haff
ει/οι	'ee' as in seen
ευ	'ev/ef' as in ever/effort
ου	'oo' as in toot
γγ	'ng' as in ring
γκ	At the beginning of a word 'g' as in go
γχ	'nks' as in rinks
μπ	'b' as in beer
ντ	At the beginning of a word 'd' as in deer In the middle of a word 'nd' as in send
τζ	'ds' as in deeds

Useful Greek

English	Greek	Sounds like
Hello/goodbye	Γειά σου	Yia soo (informal singular said with a smile)
Good morning/day	Καλημέρα	Kalimera
Good afternoon/evening	Καλησπέρα	Kalispera (formal)
Good night	Καληνύχτα	Kalinikta
See you later	Θα σε δω αργοτερα	Tha se tho argotera
See you tomorrow	Θα σε δω αύριο	Tha se tho avrio

Yes	Ναι	Ne (accompanied by a downwards and sideways nod of the head)
No	Οχι	Ochi (accompanied by an upward movement of the head, heavenwards & with a closing of the eyes)
Please	Παρακαλώ	Parakalo
Thank you	(Σαζ) Ευχαριστώ	(sas) Efkaristo
No, thanks	Οχι ζυχαριστώ	Ochi, efkaristo
Thank you very much	Ευχαριστώ πολύ	Efkaristo poli
(After which the reply may well be)		
Thankyou (and please)	Παρακαλώ	Parakalo
Do you speak English?	Μιλάτε Αγγλικά	Milahteh anglikah
How do you say....	Πωσ λενε...	Pos lene...
...in Greek?	...στα Ελληνικά	...sta Ellinika
What is this called?	Πωσ το λένε	Pos to lene
I do not understand	Δεν καταλαβαίνω	Then katahlavehno
Could you speak more slowly (slower?)	Μπορειτε να μιλάτε πιο αργά	Boreete na meelate peeo seegha (arga)
Could you write it down?	Μπορειτε να μου το γράψετε	Boreete na moo to grapsete

Numbers

One	Ενα	enna
Two	Δυο	thio
Three	Τρια	triah
Four	Τεσσερα	tessehra
Five	Πεντε	pendhe
Six	Εξι	exhee
Seven	Επτα	eptah
Eight	Οκτω	ockto
Nine	Εννεα	ennea
Ten	Δεκα	thecca
Eleven	Εντεκα	endekha
Twelve	Δωδεκα	thodhehka
Thirteen	Δεκατρια	thehka triah
Fourteen	Δεκατεσσερα	thehka tessehra
Fifteen	Δεκαπεντε	thehka pendhe
Sixteen	Δεκαεξι	thekaexhee
Seventeen	Δεκαεπτα	thehkaeptah
Eighteen	Δεκαοκτω	thehkaockto
Nineteen	Δεκαεννεα	thehkaennea
Twenty	Εικοσι	eeckossee
Twenty-one	Εικοσι ενα	eeckcossee enna
Twenty-two	Εικοσι δυο	eeckcossee thio
Thirty	Τριαντα	treeandah
Forty	Σαραντα	sarandah
Fifty	Πενηντα	penindah
Sixty	Εξηντα	exhindah
Seventy	Εβδομηντα	evthomeendah
Eighty	Ογδοντα	ogthondah
Ninety	Ενενητα	eneneendah
One hundred	Εκατο	eckato
One hundred and one	Εκατον ενα	eckaton enna
Two hundred	Διακοσια	theeakossia
One thousand	Χιλια	kheelia
Two thousand	Δυο χιλιάδες	thio kheeliathes

2 Getting to & from the N.E. Aegean & Athens

If all the year were playing holidays, to sport would be as tedious as work. William Shakespeare

To start this chapter off, a word of introductory warning. Whatever form of travel is utilised travellers must not pack money or travellers cheques in luggage that will be stowed away, out of sight. Some years ago, almost unbelievably, we met a young lady who had at the last moment, prior to checking-in at the airport, stuffed some drachmae notes in a zipped side pocket of one of her suitcases. On arrival in Greece, surprise, surprise, she was minus the money.

BY AIR
From the United Kingdom
Scheduled flights To get to the N.E. Aegean it is necessary to fly direct to Athens East (international) airport, transfer by bus to Athens West (domestic) airport and then fly Olympic Airways to the islands of Chios, Lesbos, Limnos or Samos. Note both international and domestic Olympic flights use the West airport.

Heathrow to Athens (3¾ hours): daily, non-stop British Airways, Olympic and others. Scheduled airfare options include: 1st class return, economy, excursion, APEX (Advanced Purchase Excursion Fare), PEX (instant purchase, and the cheapest scheduled fare) and Eurobudget.

Charter flights & package tours Some package tour operators keep a number of seats available on each flight for, what is in effect, a charter flight. A nominal charge is made for accommodation (which need not be taken up), the cost being included in the return airfare. These seats are substantially cheaper than the scheduled APEX fares and are known as 'Charter Cheapies'. Apart from the relatively low price, the normal two week holiday period can be extended by a further week or weeks for a small surcharge. There is a variety of United Kingdom departure airports including Birmingham, Gatwick, Glasgow and Manchester. But, as one correspondent has pointed out, the frequency of charter flights tails off dramatically between October and March, as does the choice of airport departure points. Do not forget this when contemplating an out-of-season holiday.

To ascertain what is on offer, scan the travel section of the Sunday papers, as well as the weekly magazine *Time Out* and, possibly, *Private Eye*. There are many, varied package tours with a number of the large tour operators and the smaller, more personal companies, offering a bewildering array of multi-centre, fly-drive, budget-bed, self catering and personally tailored holidays, in addition to the more usual hotel accommodation.

Exceptionally reasonable charter flights, with the necessary accommodation vouchers, are available through *Owners Abroad Ltd*, Ilford, who also have offices in Manchester, Birmingham and Glasgow. Example fares and routes for 1987 include:

Two week return fares	Low Season	Mid-season	High season
Athens leaving Gatwick Thursday, Friday	From £ 93.75	£ 99.75	£126.75
Athens leaving Manchester Thursday	From £106.75	£114.75	£136.75
Athens leaving Birmingham Thursday	From £105.75	£113.75	£135.75
Athens leaving Glasgow Thursday	From £131.75	£149.75	£164.75

These rates are subject to inexcusable surcharges and airport taxes totalling £14.95 per head. The fares for three weeks are those above plus £30, for four weeks £35 and for five to six weeks, an additional 50 per cent is charged. Note that the total number of weeks allowed in Greece for travellers who arrive and depart by charter flights is six, not twelve weeks.

Perhaps the least expensive flights available are *Courier Flights*. These scheduled seats start off at about £65 return to Athens for the low season period. BUT passengers can only take a maximum of 10 kg of hand luggage, one holdall measuring no more than 1 ft x 2 ft – no other baggage. Other restrictions result in only one passenger being able to travel at a time and for a minimum period of ten or fourteen days.

It is a pity, if inevitable, that Olympic Airways subsidiary, *Allsun Holidays* has had to drop their selected island-hopping-holidays. There were too many complaints! I can imagine.

Olympic Airways has joined the charter flight fray with their 'Love-A-Fare' service. (Yes, 'love-a-fare' which is an APEX option in summer dress), the London to Athens return fare costing £166. The booking must be made at least two weeks in advance and allows a maximum of four weeks stay. There are Olympic offices in London as well as Manchester, Birmingham and Glasgow. Amongst companies offering interesting and slightly off-beat holidays are the *Aegina Club Ltd,* and *Ramblers Holidays*. *Aegina* offer a wide range of tours, three different locations in up to three weeks, and, additionally, will tailor a programme to fit in with client's requirements. *Ramblers,* as would be imagined, include walking holidays based on a number of locations with half-board accommodation. More conventional inclusions, some in smaller, more personal hotels, pensions and tavernas than those used by the larger tour companies, are available from *Greek Sun Holidays*. Their brochure covers a number of the more popular N.E. Aegean islands and a few, individual, interesting locations but, in my opinion, their text is subject to a certain amount of hype. As long as this is allowed for in assessing the suitability of a location then no harm can be incurred by potential vacationeers.

Students Young people lucky enough to be under 26 years of age (oh to be 26 again) should consider contacting *World-Wide Student Travel* who market a number of inexpensive charter flights. Students of any age or scholars under 22 years of age (whatever mode of travel is planned) should take their *International Student Identity Card (ISIC)*. This will ensure discounts are available whenever they are applicable, not only in respect of travel but also for entry to museums, archaeological sites and some forms of entertainment.

If under 26 years of age, but not a student, it may be worthwhile applying for membership of *The Federation of International Youth Travel Organization (FIYTO)* which guarantees youth discounts from some ferry and tour operators.

From the United States of America
Scheduled flights

Olympic flights include departures from:
Atlanta (via John F Kennedy (JFK) airport, New York (NY) daily
Boston (via JFK or La Guardia, NY): daily
Chicago (via JFK): daily
Dallas (via JFK): daily
Houston (via JFK): daily
Los Angeles (via JFK): daily
Miami (via JFK; 15 hours): daily
Minneapolis (via JFK): daily
New York (JFK approximately 10½ hours); daily direct

Norfolk (via JFK): daily except Saturday
Philadelphia (via JFK; about 11 hours): daily
Rochester (via JFK): daily
San Francisco (via JFK; about 14½ hours): daily
Seattle (via JFK or London): daily
Tampa (via JFK): daily
Washington DC (via JFK or La Guardia): daily

Note that flights via New York's John F Kennedy airport involve a change of plane from, or to, a domestic American airline.

USA domestic airlines, including *TWA*, also run a number of flights to Greece and the choice of air fares is bewildering including economy, first class return, super APEX, APEX GIT, Excursion, ABC, OTC, ITC, and others, wherein part package costs are incorporated.

Charter/standby flights & secondary airlines As in the United Kingdom, scanning the Sunday national papers' travel section, including the *New York Times,* will disclose various companies offering package tours and charter flights. Another way to make the journey is to take a standby flight to London and then fly, train or bus on to Greece. Alternatively, there are a number of inexpensive, secondary airline companies offering flights to London, and the major Western European capitals.

Useful agencies, especially for students, include *Let's Go Travel Services.*

From Canada
Scheduled Olympic flights include departures from:
Montreal: twice weekly direct
or (via Amsterdam, JFK and/or La Guardia NY): daily except Mondays
Toronto: twice weekly (via Montreal)
or (via Amsterdam, JFK and/or La Guardia NY): daily except Monday and Friday
Winnipeg (via Amsterdam): Thursday and Sunday only.

As for the USA, the above flights involve a change of airline and there is a choice of domestic and package flights and a wide range of differing fares.

Student agencies include *Canadian Universities Travel Service.*

From Australia
There are Australian airline scheduled flights from Adelaide (via Melbourne), Brisbane (via Sydney), Melbourne and Sydney to Athens. Flights via Melbourne and Sydney involve a change of plane from, or to, a domestic airline. Regular as well as excursion fares and affinity groups.

From New Zealand
There are no scheduled flights.
Various connections are available as well as regular and affinity fares.

From South Africa
Scheduled Olympic flights include departures from:
Cape Town (via Johannesburg). Fridays and Sundays only
Johannesburg: direct, Thursday, Friday and Sunday.

Flights via Johannesburg involve a change of plane from, or to, a domestic airline. South African airline flights from Johannesburg to Athens are available as regular, excursion or affinity fares.

From Ireland
Scheduled Olympic flights from:
Dublin: via London which involves a change of airline to Aer Lingus.

Note that when flying from Ireland, Australia, New Zealand, South Africa, Canada and the USA there are sometimes advantages in travelling via London or other European capitals on stopover and taking inexpensive connection flights to Greece.

Scandinavia

including:

Denmark Scheduled Olympic flights from:

Copenhagen (via Frankfurt): daily involving a change of aircraft as well as non-stop flights on Wednesday, Friday, Saturday and Sunday.

Sweden Scheduled Olympic flights from:

Stockholm (via Copenhagen and Frankfurt): Tuesday, Wednesday, Friday, Saturday.

Norway Scheduled Olympic flights from:

Oslo (via Frankfurt or Copenhagen): daily.

All the Scandinavian countries have a large choice of domestic and package flights with a selection of offerings. Contact *SAS Airlines* for Olympic Airways details.

AIRPORTS

United Kingdom Do not forget if intending to stay in Greece longer than two weeks, the long-stay car parking fees tend to mount up – and will the battery last for a 3 or 4 week layover? Incidentally charges at Gatwick are about £31.65 for two weeks, £41.80 for three weeks and £51.15 for four weeks. The difficulty is that most charter flights leave and arrive at rather unsociable hours, so friends and family may not be too keen to act as a taxi service.

Athens Hellinikon airport is split into two parts, West (Olympic domestic and international flights) and East (foreign airlines). There are coaches to make the connection between the two airports, and Olympic buses to Athens centre as well as city buses.

At the Western or domestic airport, city buses pull up alongside the terminal building. Across the road is a pleasant cafe/restaurant but the service becomes fairly chaotic when packed out. To the left of the cafe (facing) is a newspaper kiosk and further on, across a side road, a Post Office is hidden in the depths of the first building.

The Eastern airport is outwardly quite smart but can, in reality, become an expensive, very cramped and uncomfortable location if there are long delays. These occur when, for instance, the air traffic controllers strike elsewhere in Europe. Remember when leaving Greece to have enough money and some food left for an enforced stay, as flight departures are consistently overdue and food and drink in the airport are costly. There are simply no facilities for an overnight sleep and the bench seats are very soon taken up. You have been warned.

BY TRAIN
From the United Kingdom & European countries (Illustration 1).

Recommended only for train buffs and masochists but one of the alternative routes to be considered when a visitor intends to stay in Greece in excess of 6 weeks. The quickest journey of the three, major scheduled overland routes takes about 60 hours, and a second-class return fare costs in the region of £250. One advantage is that travellers may break the journey along the route (a little difficult on an airline flight), and another is that it is possible to travel out on one route and back by an alternative track (if you will excuse the pun). It is important to take along basic provisions, toilet paper and to wear old clothes.

A recent return to the 'day of the train' reinforced my general opinion and introductory remarks in respect of this particular method of travel, bringing sharply

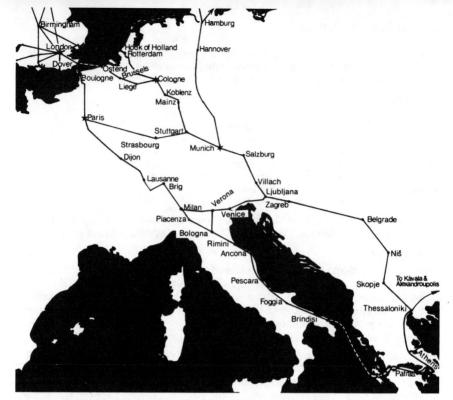

Illustration 1 European Railway Routes

back into focus the disadvantages and difficulties. The list of drawbacks should be enough to deter any but the most determined.

Try not to have a query which involves making use of the overseas information desk at Victoria Station as the facility is undermanned and the wait to get to a counter averages ¾ hr. The staff are very willing but it is of interest that they overcome the intricacies of the official British Rail European timetable ("it's all Greek to me guvnor") by overtly referring to the (infinitely) more managable *Thomas Cook* publication.

The channel crossing is often on craft that would not be pressed into service if we declared war on the Isle of Wight; the sea journey is too short for any cabins to be available; the duty free goods on offer are very limited and there are inordinate delays between train, boat and train.

The French trains that ply between the coast and Paris are of an excellent standard. On the other hand changing trains at the 'black hole' of the Gare du Nord sharply focuses travellers' attention on a whole subculture of human beings who exist in and around a number of European railway stations. My favourite example of this little known branch of the human race is the 'bag-shuffler' – usually a middle-aged lady. The genus is initially recognisable by the multitudinous paper and plastic bags festooned about the person. Once at rest the contents are constantly and interminably shuffled from one bag to another, and back again, the ritual being accompanied by low mutterings.

French railway stations, which are heated to a temperature relating to gentle simmer on a domestic cooker, have perfected a waiting room seating arrangement that precludes any but a drunk contortionist stretching out for a nap. In common with

13

most other railway stations, food and drink are expensive and credit cards impossible to use, even at the swanky station restaurants.

The Metro connection between the railway stations of Gare du Nord and Gare de Lyon is not straightforward and involves a walk. The Gare de Lyon springs a minor trap for the unwary in that the inter-continental trains depart from platforms reached by a long walk up the far left platforms (facing the trains). Don't some of the French trains now resemble children's rocket drawings?

The station's toilet facilities are miniscule and men are charged for other than the use of a urinal and washbasin. Ladies have to pay about 2 Francs (F), a private closet costs 6F and a shower 12F. Potential users must not imagine they will be able to sneak in for a crafty stand-up wash – the toilets are intently watched over by attendants.

Although it may appear to an optional extra, it is obligatory to purchase a couchette ticket for the train journey. This is a Catch 22 situation brought about by the rule that only couchette ticket holders have the right to a seat! Yes, well, not so optional. It is also necessary to pack food and drink, at least for the French part of the journey, as usually there are no refreshment services. In Italy most trains are met, at the various station stops, by trolley pushing vendors of (expensive) sustenance.

Venice station is signed Stazione St Lucia and is most conveniently sited bang-on the edge of the Grand Canal waterfront with shops and restaurants to the left. Some of the cake shops sell slabs of pizza pie for about 800 lira (L) which furnishes good standby nourishment. The scheduled stopover here will have to be adjusted for any (inevitable) delay in arrival. Venice (on the outward journey) is the watershed where Greek, and the occasional Yugoslavian, carriages are coupled up and passengers can be guaranteed to encounter a number of nasties. These replacement compartments are seedier and dirtier than their more Western European counterparts, and the lavatories vary between bad to unspeakable. Faults include toilets that won't flush (sometimes appearing to mysteriously fill up); Greek toilet paper (which apart from other deficiencies lacks body and – please excuse the indelicacy – through which fingers break); no toilet paper at all (which is worst?); no soap dispenser; a lack of coat hooks; water taps that don't and the whole rather grimy.

From Venice the term 'Express' should be ignored as the train's progress becomes slower and slower and slower with long unscheduled stops and quite inordinate delays at the Yugoslavian frontiers. During the Yugoslavian part of the journey it is necessary for passengers to lock themselves into the compartments as some of the locals have an annoying habit of entering and determinedly looting tourists' luggage. There were even totally unsubstantiated rumours, in the 1986 summer, of locals spraying an aerosol knockout gas through the keyholes, breaking in and relieving passengers of their belongings, at their leisure. I must stress I have not actually met victims and the story may be apocryphal. It is inadvisable to leave the train at Belgrade for a stopover as the accommodation available to tourists is extremely expensive, costing in the region of £60 for a double room per night, and it is almost impossible to renegotiate a couchette for the remainder of the onward journey. There are trolley attendants at the major Yugoslavian railway stations but the contents of the rolls proffered are of an 'interesting' nature resembling 'biltong' or 'hardtack' burgers. Certainly when poked by the enthusiastic vendors I'm sure their fingers buckle. Another item of nutriment on offer are large, cheese curd pies and a railway employee wanders round twice a day with a very large aluminium teapot ostensibly containing coffee. Nobody appears to be interested in payment with Yugoslavian dinars, but American dollars or English pounds sterling almost cause a purr of satisfaction. Travellers lucky enough to have the services of a Greek attendant may well find he keeps a cache of alcoholic drinks for sale. An aside is that

Yugoslavians are obsessed by wheel-tapping and at all and every stop, almost at the drop of a sleeper, appear and perform. Much of the journey beyond Belgrade is on a single line track and should, for instance, a cow break into a trot the animal might well overtake the train. At the frontier passengers may be reminded of the rigours of Iron Curtain countries, as they will be subjected to rigorous, lengthy baggage and documents checks by a swamp of officials, whose numbers include stern faced, unsmiling, gun-toting police.

In stark contrast the friendly Greek frontier town of Idomeni is a tonic. Even late at night the station's bank is open as is the taverna/snackbar with a scattering of tables on the platform and a buzz of brightly lit noise and activity.

To avoid the Yugoslavian experience a very pleasant alternative is to opt for the railway route that travels the length of Italy to Brindisi port. Here international ferry-boats can be caught to the mainland Greek port of Igoumenitsa or Patras from either of which buses can be used to make the connection with Athens, whilst Patras offers the possibility of another train journey to Athens.

Brindisi (Italy), contains several traps for the unwary. Unfortunately the railway station and quay for the Italy-Greek ferry-boats are some 200m apart, which on a hot day.... The railway station has no formal ticket office or barrier. It is only necessary to dismount, turn left along the platform, left again, beside the concrete wall supporting the first floor concourse (which stretches over and above the platforms), across the railway lines and left again down the sterile dockland street to the ferry-boat complex. The road, hemmed in by a prefabricated wall on the right, curves parallel to the seawall on the left, from which it is separated by a high chain link fence, a number of railway lines and tarmacadam quay. But, before leaving the station, stop, for all the ticket offices and necessary officials are situated in the referred to upper storey buildings and in the 'Main Street'. My favourite tour office is across the road from the station, alongside a bank on the corner formed by the 'Main St' and the 'Ferry-Boat' street. The staff are very helpful and most informative. Diagonally across the bottom of this end of the 'Main St' is a small, tree edged square which, as it is well endowed with park benches, has become an unofficial waiting room with travellers and backpackers occupying most of the available seating. Do not forget when booking rail tickets to ask for Brindisi Maritime as the town railway station is some kilometres inland.

The international ferry-boats on this route are, in the main, luxurious, beautifully appointed and expensive. Possible trappings include a sea-water swimming pool, a ladies' hairdresser and beauty salon, a number of restaurants and a self-service cafeteria, a coffee bar and a disco. Unfortunately the cafeteria dishes are outrageously expensive with, for instance, a meal for two of veal and potatoes, a spinach pie, lettuce salad and a ½ bottle of emasculated retsina costing about 1750 drs with a coffee hovering on the 100 drs mark. Moral, try not to eat on board. A splendid but expensive two berth cabin with a generous en suite bathroom sets a traveller back some 4000 drs. Prices everywhere are in American dollars and the change desk, even when on the Greece to Italy leg, does not change currency into Italian lira....?

Travellers under 26 years of age can take advantage of British Rail's *Inter-Rail pass* while Americans and Canadians may obtain a *Eurorail pass* prior to reaching Europe by applying to *Victoria Travel Centre*. There is also the *Transalpino ticket* available from the London office of the firm of the same name and all these offers hold out a substantial discount on standard train and ferry fares, but are subject to various terms and conditions. Another student outfit offering cut-price train, coach and airline flights is *London Student Travel (& Eurotrain)*.

Certainly it must be borne in mind that the Greek railway system is not extensive and, unless travelling around other European countries, a concessionary pass might not represent much of a saving. On the other hand discounts in respect of the Greek railways includes travel on some of the state railway buses (OSE).

Examples of the various tickets, costs and conditions are as follows:

Inter-Rail ticket   Under 26 years of age, valid one month for use in 21 countries (and also allows half-fare travel in the UK on Sealink and B+I ships as well as P&O ferries via Southampton and Le Havre).   £139

Transalpino ticket   Under 26, valid for two months, allows stop-over en route to the destination. London to Athens via Brindisi or Yugoslavia   from

	Single	Return
	£99.99	£189.80

Other ticket options include B.I.G.E., Eurotrain and 'Athens Circle'.

Timetables & routes (Illustration 1)

This section caused me as much work as whole chapters on other subjects. *British Rail*, whose timetable I had the greatest difficulty deciphering and *Thomas Cook*, whose timetable I could understand, were both helpful.

Example routes include:

(1) London (Victoria Station), Dover (Western Docks), (jetfoil), Ostend, Brussels, Liege, Aachen, Cologne (change train, ¾ hr delay); Mainz, Mannheim, Ulm, Munich (change train ¾ hr delay), Salzburg, Jesenice, Ljubljana, Zagreb, Belgrade (Beograd), Skopje, Gevgelija, Idomeni, Thessaloniki to Athens.

An example of the journey is as follows:

Departure: 1300 hrs, afternoon sea crossing, evening on the train, late night change of train at Cologne, night on the train, morning change of train at Munich, all day and night on the train arriving Athens very late some 2½ days later at 2314 hrs.

(2) London (Charing Cross/Waterloo East stations), Dover Hoverport, (hovercraft), Boulogne Hoverpoint, Paris (du Nord), change train (and station) to Paris (de Lyon), Strasbourg, Munich, Salzburg, Ljubljana, Zagreb, Belgrade (change train 1¾ hrs delay), Thessaloniki to Athens.

An example:

Departure: 0955 hrs and arrive 2½ days later at 2315 hrs.

Second class single fares from £128 and return fare from £251.30.

(3) London (Victoria), Folkestone Harbour, (ferry-boat), Calais, Paris (du Nord), change train (and station) to Paris (de Lyon), Venice, Ljubljana, Zagreb, Belgrade, Thessaloniki to Athens.

An example:

Departure: 1415 hrs and arrive 2¾ days later at 0840 hrs.

(4) London (Liverpool St), Harwich (Parkeston Quay), ferry-boat, Hook of Holland, Rotterdam, Eindhoven, Venio, Cologne (change train), Mainz, Mannheim, Stuttgart, Ulm, Munich, Salzburg, Jesenice, Ljubljana, Zagreb, Belgrade, Nis, Skopje, Gevgelija, Idomeni, Thessaloniki to Athens.

An example:

Departure: 1940 hrs, night ferry crossing, change train at Cologne between 1048 and 1330 hrs, first and second nights on the train and arrive at Athens middle of the day at 1440 hrs.

An alternative is to take the more pleasurable train journey through Italy and make a ferry-boat connection to Greece:

(5) London (Victoria), Folkestone Harbour, Calais, Boulogne, Amiens, Paris (du Nord), change train and station to Paris (de Lyon), Dijon, Vallorbe, Lausanne, Brig, Domodossala, Milan (Central), Bologna, Rimini, Ancona, Pescara, Bari to Brindisi.

(5a) Brindisi to Patras sea crossing.

(5b) Patras to Athens.

An example:

Departure: 0958 hrs, day ferry crossing, change of train at Paris to the Parthenon Express, one night on the train and arrive at Brindisi at 1850 hrs. Embark on the ferry-boat departing at 2000 hrs, night on the ferry-boat and disembark at 1300 hrs the next day. Take the coach to Athens arriving at 1600 hrs.

The second class single fare costs from £149.90.

On all these services children benefit from reduced fares, depending on their age. Couchettes and sleepers are usually available at extra cost and Jetfoil sea crossings are subject to a surcharge.

Details of fares and timetables are available from *British Rail Europe* or *The Hellenic State Railways (OSE)*. The most cogent, helpful and informative firm through whom to book rail travel must be *Victoria Travel Centre.* I have always found them to be extremely accommodating and it is well worth contacting *Thomas Cook Ltd,* who have a very useful range of literature and timetables available from their Publications Department.

The above are only a guide and up-to-date details must be checked with the relevant offices prior to actually booking.

From the Continent & Scandinavia to Athens

Pick up one of the above main lines by using the appropriate connections detailed in Illustration 1.

Departure terminals from Scandinavia include Helsinki (Finland); Oslo (Norway); Gothenburg, Malmo and Stockholm (Sweden); Fredrikshavn and Copenhagen (Denmark).

BY COACH

This means of travel is for the more hardy voyager and/or young. If the description of the train journey has caused apprehension, the tales of passengers of the less luxurious coach companies should strike terror into the listener/reader. Common 'faults' include lack of 'wash and brush up' stops, smugglers, prolonged border custom investigations, last minute changes of route and breakdowns. All this is on top of the forced intimacy with a number of widely disparate companions, some wildly drunk, in cramped, uncomfortable surroundings.

For details of the scheduled *Euroways Supabus* apply *c/o Victoria Coach Station* or to the *National Express Company*. A single fare costs from £79 and a return ticket from £140. This through service takes 4 days plus, with no overnight layovers but short stops at Cologne, Frankfurt and Munich where there is a change of coach. Fares include ferry costs but exclude refreshments. Arrival and departure in Greece is at the Peloponissou Railway Station, Athens. The timetable is as follows:

Departure from London, Victoria Coach Station, Bay 20: Friday and Saturday at 2030 hrs arriving at 1100 hrs 4½ days later.

Return journey
Departure from Filellinon St, Syntagma Sq, Athens: Wednesday and Friday at 1300 hrs arriving London at 0800 hrs, 4 days later.

Express coach companies include *Consolas Travel*. This well-established company runs daily buses during the summer months, except Sunday, and single fares start at about £35 with a return ticket costing from £69. Other services are run by the various 'pirate' bus companies, the journey time is about the same and, again, prices, which may be slightly cheaper, do not include meals. On a number of islands, travel agents signs still refer to the *Magic Bus*, or as a fellow traveller so aptly put it – the *Tragic Bus*, but the company that ran this renowned and infamous service perished some years ago. Imitators appear to perpetuate the name.

In the United Kingdom it is advisable to obtain a copy of the weekly magazine *Time Out*, wherein the various coach companies advertise. For return trips from Athens, check shop windows in Omonia Sq, the American Express office in Syntagma Sq, or the Students Union in Filellinon St, just off Syntagma Sq. *Eurolines Intercars (Uniroute)* runs a national coach service that shuttles between Athens and Paris on a three day journey. The buses depart twice a week at 1030 hrs, Wednesday and Saturday, at a cost of 12,000 drs but note that baggage costs an extra 200 drs. The French end of the connection is close by the Metro station Porte Vincennes and the Athens terminus is alongside the Stathmos Larissis railway station. Note that travellers wishing to approach the N.E. Aegean islands from northern Greece should disembark at Thessaloniki and catch a bus to the mainland ports of Kavala or Alexandroupoli noting there is a once a week ferry-boat from Thessaloniki to Lesbos and Chios. It is also possible to take the train to Drama for Kavala or on to Alexandroupoli.

These buses are comfortable with air conditioning but no toilet so the leg-stretching stops are absolutely vital, not only to purchase victuals but for passengers to relieve themselves. It is a problem that the standard of the 'way-station' toilets and snackbars varies from absolutely awful to luxurious. And do not forget that the use of the lavatories is usually charged for in Greece and Yugoslavia. To help make the journey acceptable passengers must pack enough food and drink to tide them over the trip.

There are sufficient stops in Greece at, for instance, Livadia, Larissa and Thessaloniki as well as the frontier, which takes up to some 2¾ hrs. The Yugoslavian part of the route passes through Belgrade and at about two-thirds distance there is a lunchtime motorway halt. At this sumptuous establishment even Amex credit cards are accepted and the lavatories are free – a welcome contrast to the previous, mind boggling stop where even the Greeks blanched at the sight of the toilets! The bus and driver change at Trieste which is probably necessary after the rigours of the Yugoslavian roads. Use of the lavatories in the bus station has to be paid for and they are very smelly with a 'lecher' in the ladies. One of the two Italian stops is at a luxurious motorway complex. The route between Italy and France over the Alps takes a tediously long time on winding narrow mountain roads with an early morning change of driver in France. It may well be necessary to 'encourage' the driver on this section to make an unscheduled halt in order to save burst bladders. The bus makes three Paris drop-offs, at about midday three days later, and the best disembarkation point depends on a traveller's plans.

Devotees of the Le Havre channel crossing must make for the Gare St Lazaire railway station. The Metro, with one change, costs about 5 francs (F) each and the coach's arrival time allows passengers to catch a Paris to Le Havre train. This departs on the three hour journey at 1630 hrs and the tickets cost some 100 F each. No information in respect of cross channel ferries is available at the railway station, despite the presence of a number of tourist information desks.

Incidentally the walk from the Le Havre railway terminus to the ferry-boat quay is a long haul but there are reasonably priced taxis between the two points. The superb restaurant *Le Southampton*, conveniently across the street from the dock, may well compensate for the discomfort of the trudge round, especially as they accept payment by Amex.

BY CAR (Illustration 2)
Usually only a worthwhile alternative method of travel if there are at least two adults and travellers are planning to stay for longer than three weeks, as the journey from England is about 1900 miles and takes approximately 50 hrs nonstop driving.

One of the shortest routes from the United Kingdom is via car-ferry to Ostend (Belgium), on to Munich, Salzburg (Germany), Klagenfurt (Austria) and Ljubljana (Yugoslavia). There the Autoput E94 is taken on to Zagreb, Belgrade (Beograd) and Nis on the E5, where the E27 and E55 are taken via Skopje to the frontier town of Gevgelija/Evzonoi. Note that due to major rebuilding works, the Yugoslavian road between Zagreb and Nis can be subject to lengthy delays.

Illustration 2 European Car Routes & Ferry-boat connections

The very large intercontinental lorries are rather more dangerous in Yugoslavia where they appear to regard the middle of the sometimes narrow roads as their own territory.

Drivers through France have a number of possible routes but those choosing to skirt Switzerland will have to cross over into Italy, usually angling down through Lyon and heading in the general direction of Turin. Once over the border into Italy, bypass Turin (Torino) and proceed to Piacenza, Brescia, Verona, Padua (Padova), Venice and cut up to Trieste. I say bypass because the ordinary Italian roads are just 'neat aggravation' and the cities are almost impossible to circumnavigate. Although motorways involve constant toll fees they are much quicker and less wearing on the nerves. Note that Italian petrol stations have a nasty habit of closing for a midday siesta between 1200 and 1500 hrs. An alternative route is via Turin, Milan, Bergamo, Brescia, Verona and on to Trieste which leads around the southern edge of a few of the lakes, in the area of Brescia. Excursions to Padua and Venice are obvious possibilities.

From Trieste the most scenic (and winding) route is to travel the Adriatic coast road via Rijeka, Zadar and Split to Dubrovnik. The lovely medieval inner city of Dubrovnik is well worth a visit. At Petrovac the pain starts as the road swings up to Titograd around to Kosovska Mitrovika, Pristina, Skopje and down to the border at Gevgelija. The stretch from Skopje to the Greek frontier can be rather unnerving. Signposting in Yugoslavia is usually very bad; always obtain petrol when the opportunity crops up and lastly but not least, city lights are often turned off during the hours of darkness (sounds a bit Irish to me!), making night driving extremely hazardous. To save the journey on from Petrovac, it is possible, at the height of the season, to catch a ferry from Dubrovnik (or take the pretty coastal road on to the port of Bar) to Igoumenitsa or Patras on the Greek mainland.

Detailed road reports are available from the *Automobile Association* but I would like to stress that in the Yugoslavian mountains, especially after heavy rain, landslips can (no will!) result in parts of the road disappearing at the odd spot as well as the surface being littered with rocks. There you go!

The main road through Greece, to Athens via Pirgos, Larissa and Lamia, is wide and good but the speed of lorries and their trailer units can still prove disquieting. Vehicles being overtaken are expected to move right over and tuck well into the hard shoulder. From Evzonoi to Athens, via Thessaloniki, is 340 miles (550 kms) and some of the major autoroute is a toll road. Motorists can catch the once-a-week Thessaloniki ferry to Lesbos and/or Chios or turn off here for the northern mainland ports of Kavala and Alexandroupoli. Ferry-boats from Kavala allow passengers to access the N.E. Aegean chain from that end of Greece rather than proceed on to Athens and Piraeus.

Personally my favourite choice of route involves crossing the Channel to Le Havre, cutting down through France, which holds few perils for the traveller, via Evreux, Chartres, Pithiviers, Montargis, Clamecy, Nevers, Lyon and Chambery to the Italian border at Modane. Here the fainthearted can take the tunnel whilst the adventurous wind their way over the Col du Mont Cenis.

In Italy, at say Verona or Padua, it is worth considering, as for the alternative train journey, cutting down the not at all that attractive Adriatic seaboard to one of the international Italian ferry-boat ports of Ancona, Bari, Brindisi or Otranto where boats connect to Igoumenitsa or Patras on the Greek mainland (*See* BY FERRY-BOAT).

General Vehicle & Personal Requirements

Documents required for travel in any European country include an *International Driving Licence,* and a *Carnet de Passages en Douanes* (both issued by the AA and valid for one year) as well as a *Green Insurance Card.* It is recommended to take the vehicle's registration documents as proof of ownership and the vehicle must have a nationality sticker of the approved pattern and design.

Particular countries' requirements include:

Italy Import allowances are as for Greece but the restriction on the importation of Italian currency equals about £100.

All cars entering Italy must possess both right and left hand external driving mirrors.

Switzerland If intending to drive through Switzerland remember that the Swiss require the vehicle and all the necessary documents to be absolutely correct. (They would.) The authorities have a nasty habit of stopping vehicles some distance beyond the frontier posts in order to make thorough checks.

Yugoslavia A valid passport is the only personal document required for citizens of, for example, Denmark, West Germany, Finland, Great Britain and Northern Ireland, Republic of Southern Ireland, Holland and Sweden. Americans and Canadians must have a visa and all formalities should be checked with the relevant Yugoslavian Tourist Office.

It is compulsory to carry a warning triangle, a first aid kit and a set of replacement vehicle light bulbs. The use of spotlights is prohibited and drivers planning to travel during the winter should check the special regulations governing the use of studded tyres.

Visiting motorists cannot obtain fuel without petrol coupons, which are available at the frontier and, supposedly, from travel agents *Kompass* or *Putnik*. Carefully calculate the amount of coupons required for the journey and pay for them in foreign currency at the frontier as the rate allowed is very advantageous compared to that if the coupons are paid for in Yugoslavian dinars. Petrol stations are often far apart, closed or out of petrol, so fill up when possible.

Photographers are only allowed to import five rolls of film; drinkers a bottle of wine and a quarter litre of spirits and smokers 200 cigarettes or 50 cigars. Each person may bring in unlimited foreign currency but only 1500 dinars.

Fines are issued on the spot and the officer collecting one should issue an official receipt.

To obtain assistance in the case of accident or breakdown dial 987 and the *SPI* will come to your assistance.

Greece It is compulsory to carry a first aid kit as well as a fire extinguisher in a vehicle and failure to comply may result in a fine. It is also mandatory to carry a warning triangle and it is forbidden to carry petrol in cans. In Athens the police are empowered to confiscate and detain the number plates of illegally parked vehicles. The use of undipped headlights in towns is strictly prohibited.

Customs allow the importation of 200 cigarettes or 50 cigars, 1 litre of spirits or 2 litres of wine and only 3000 drs but any amount of foreign currency. Visitors from the EEC may import 300 cigarettes or 75 cigars, 1 ½ litres of spirits or 4 litres of wine.

Speed Limits

See table below – all are standard legal limits which may be varied by signs

	Built-up areas	Outside built-up areas	Motorways	Type of vehicle affected
Greece	31 mph (50 kph)	49 mph (80 kph)	62 mph (100 kph)	Private vehicles with or or without trailers
Yugoslavia	37 mph (60 kph) 62 mph* (100 kph)*	49 mph (80 kph)	74 mph (120 kph)	Private vehicles without trailers

*Speed on dual carriageways

BY FERRY-BOAT (Illustration 2)

Some of the descriptive matter under the heading BY TRAIN in this chapter refers to inter-country, ferry-boat travel.

Due to the popularity of the ferry port of Brindisi, height of the season travellers must be prepared for crowds, lengthy delays and the usual ferry-boat scrum (scrum not scum). Other irritants include the exasperating requirement to purchase an embarkation pass, with the attendant formalities which include taking the pass to the police station on the second floor of the port office to have it punched! Oh, by the way, the distance between the railway station and the port is about 200m and it is absolutely necessary to 'clock in' at least 3 hrs before a ferry's departure otherwise passengers may be 'scratched' from the fixture list, have to rebook and pay again. That is why the knowledgeable head for the other departure ports, more especially Otranto.

If making this trip on the return journey from Greece, great care must be taken when purchasing the ferry-boat tickets, especially at Igoumenitsa (Greek mainland). The competition is hot and tickets may well be sold below the published price. If so and a traveller is amongst the 'lucky ones' it is best not to count one's drachmae until on board. The port officials carefully check the tickets and if they find any that have been sold at a discount then they are confiscated and the purchaser is made to buy replacements at the full price. Ouch!

Do not forget that the availability of ferry-boat sailings must be continually checked, as must airline and bus timetables. This is especially necessary during the months of October through to the beginning of May when the services are usually severely curtailed. So be warned.

USEFUL NAMES & ADDRESSES

The Automobile Association, Fanum House, Basingstoke, Hants RG21 2EA   Tel. (0256) 20123

The Greek National Tourist Organization, 195-197 Regent St., London W1R 8DL
Tel. (01)-734 5997
The Italian State Tourist Office, 1 Princes St, London W1R 8AY.   Tel. (01)-408 1254
The Yugoslav National Tourist Office, 143 Regent St, London W1R 8AE.   Tel.(01)-734 5243
British Rail Europe, PO Box 303, London SW1 1JY.   Tel. 01-834 2345 (keep ringing).
The Hellenic State Railways (OSE), 1-3 Karolou St, Athens, Greece   Tel. 01.5222-491
Thomas Cook Ltd, Publications Dept, PO Box 36, Thorpewood, Peterborough PE3 6SB.
Tel. (0733)-63200

Other useful names & addresses mentioned in the text include:
Time Out, Southampton St, London WC2E 7HD.
Courier Flights/Inflight Courier, 45 Church St, Weybridge, Surrey KT13 8DG.   Tel. (0932) 57455/56

Owners Abroad Ltd, Valentine House, Ilford Hill, Ilford, Essex ICI 2DG.   Tel.(01)-514 8844
Olympic Airways, 164 Piccadilly, London W1   Tel. (01)-846 9080
ref. 'Love-a-Fare'   Tel. (01)-846 9966
Aegina Club Ltd, 25A Hills Rd, Cambridge CB2 1NW   Tel. (0223) 63256
Ramblers Holidays, 13 Longcroft House, Fretherne Rd, Welwyn Garden City, Herts AL8 6PQ.
Tel. (07073) 31133
Greek Sun Holidays, 23 Haymarket, London, SW1Y 4DG.   Tel. (01)-839 6055/6
Worldwide Student Travel, 39 Store St, London WC1E 7BZ.   Tel. (01)-580 7733
Victoria Travel Centre, 52 Grosvenor Gdns, London SW1.   Tel. (01)-730 8111
Transalpino, 214 Shaftesbury Ave, London WC2H 8EB.   Tel. (01)-836 0087/8
London Student Travel, (Tel. (01)-730 3402/4473) (& **Eurotrain,**
Tel. (01)-730 6525) both at 52 Grosvenor Gdns, London SW1N 0AG.
Euroways Supabus, c/o Victoria Coach Station, London SW1.   Tel. (01)-730 0202
or c/o National Express Co.
The Greek address is: 1 Karolou St, Athens.   Tel. 5240 519/6
Eurolines Intercars (Uniroute), 102 Cours de Vincennes, 75012 Paris (Metro Porte Vincennes)
National Express Co, Westwood Garage, Margate Rd, Ramsgate CT12 6SI.   Tel.(0843) 581333
Consolas Travel, 29-31 Euston Rd, London NW1   Tel. (01)-278 1931
The Greek address is: 100 Eolou St, Athens.   Tel. 3219 228

Amongst others the agencies and offices listed above have, over the years and in varying degrees, been helpful in the preparation of the guides and I would like to extend my sincere thanks to all those concerned. Some have proved more helpful than others!

Olympic Airways overseas office addresses are as follows:
America: 647 Fifth Ave, New York, NY 10022, USA.   Tel. (0101-212)
(Reservations) 838 3600
(Ticket Office) 735 0290

Canada: 1200 McGill College Ave, Suite 1250, Montreal, Quebec H3B 4G7 Canada.
Tel. (0101 418) 878 9691
: 80 Bloor St West, Suite 406, Toronto ONT M55 2VI, Canada.   Tel. (0101 416) 920 2452
Australia: 44 Pitt St, 1st Floor, Sydney, NSW 2000, Australia.   Tel. (01061 2) 251 2044
South Africa: Bank of Athens Buildings, 116 Marshall St, Johannesburg, S. Africa.
Tel. (01027 11) 836 5951
Denmark: 4 Jernbanegade DK 1608, Copenhagen, Denmark.   Tel. (010451) 126-100
Sweden: 44 Birger Jalsgatan, 11429 Stockholm, Sweden.   Tel. (010468) 113-800

More useful overseas names & addresses include:
Let's Go Travel Services, Harvard Student Agencies, Thayer Hall B, Harvard University, Cambridge, MA02138 USA.   Tel. 617 495 9649
Canadian Universities Travel Service, 187 College St, Toronto ONT M5T 1P7 Canada
Tel. 417 979 2406
Automobile Association & Touring Club of Greece (ELPA), 2 Messogion Street, Athens.
Tel. (01) 7791 615

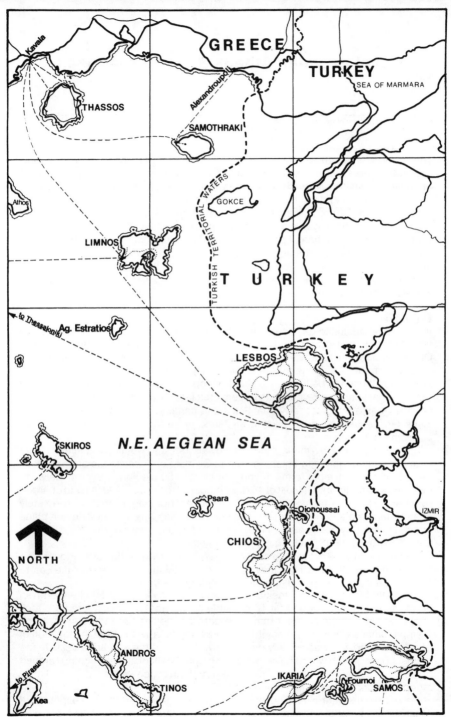

Illustration 3   Islands of the North-Eastern Eagean

3 Travel Between Athens & the N.E. Aegean

I see land. I see the end of my labour. Diogenes

The Greek islands are very thick on the water, numbering between 1000 and 3000, depending upon which authority you wish to believe. Approximately 100 are inhabited of which some 11 are located in the N.E. Aegean islands that I have chosen to agglomerate in the group. (Illustration 3).

Over the years a specialised and efficient system of waterborne travel developed and, in the past, the only way of setting foot on an island was to make for the relevant port and board a ferry-boat. Apart from the advent of international air flights direct to the larger islands, the opening of a number of smaller airfields to take domestic flights has made it possible to fly to Athens and take a flight to the islands of Chios, Lesbos, Limnos and Samos as well as the pivotal mainland ports of Alexandroupoli, Kavala and Thessaloniki.

BY AIR

It can prove difficult to get a seat for domestic flights on the spot, especially at the height of the tourist season, and it may be preferable to forward book through a local Olympic office prior to arrival. Greeks now utilise the services extensively, especially to and from the N.E. Aegean due to the heavy concentration of Armed Services personnel. It used to be true to say that ferry-boat travel was cheaper than airflight but in recent years the reverse has become the fact. In some cases flying was even cheaper than a 3rd class ferry-boat ticket and certainly less expensive than a 2nd class fare. A savage price hike in air fares (in mid 1986) restored the ferries' economic advantage.

Travellers arriving in Athens, other than by aircraft, and wanting a domestic flight from the West airport, can catch one of the Olympic coaches to the airport. These depart from the Olympic terminal and offices, 96-100 (Leoforos) Sygrou, between 0600 hrs and midnight at a cost of 45 drs, compared to the 350/400 drs odd charged by a taxi. An irate reader has taken me to task for not pointing out that approximately an hour must be allowed between catching the airline bus and the relevant plane check-in time. City buses also connect with the Airport, details of which are listed in CHAPTER 9 (ATHENS), amongst the bus timetables.

Many travellers do not wish to stop over in Athens. If this is the case, and arriving other than on an Olympic flight, they can travel directly, after landing, from the East to the domestic, West, airport using the connecting bus service.

The staff of Olympic, the Greek airline, are usually very helpful and their English good, although occasionally it is possible to fall foul of that sporadic Greek characteristic, intransigence. I remember arriving, heavily laden and tired, at the Olympic offices very early one morning. On asking for advice about the location of any suitable hotel, I was politely directed, by the girl at the enquiries desk, to the Tourist police, which would have involved an uphill walk of at least 1½ km weighed down by an assortment of bags. There was a hotel, in which we stayed, immediately around the corner from the terminal!

It is worth considering utilising internal flights on one leg of a journey, especially if Athens is the point of arrival or departure. The possible extra cost of the flight, over and above the overland and ferry fares, must be balanced against the time element.

For instance, Athens to Mitilini (Lesbos) by air takes some 45 mins whilst the ferry takes about 14 hours. One other advantage of domestic air travel is that the fares can be paid for by the use of American Express, Diners or Access Mastercard, possibly saving precious drachmae, especially towards the end of a holiday.

N.E. Aegean island airports include those on Samos, Chios, Lesbos and Limnos and mainland facilities relative to the group are Thessaloniki, Kavala and Alexandroupoli.

NOTE that already in 1987 the cost of domestic flights has risen by a staggering 28% on average.

BY BUS

There are daily scheduled bus services to the mainland ports of Alexandroupoli, Kavala, Piraeus and Thessaloniki (CHAPTER 10) that connect by ferry-boat to the various N.E. Aegean islands.

Please refer to CHAPTER 9 (ATHENS) for full details of bus timetables.

BY FERRY

In the following comments I am calling on my experience of travelling third and tourist class on any number of ferry-boats.

In general, if sleeping arrangements are available they will prove satisfactory if certain basic rules are followed. First claim a bunk by depositing luggage on the chosen berth, it will be quite safe as long as money and passports are removed. The position of a berth is important and despite the labelling of 'Men' and 'Women' sleeping areas, a berth can usually be selected in either. But try to choose one adjacent to stern deck doors to ensure some ventilation as, due to the location of the third and tourist class accommodation, it can get very hot and stuffy beneath decks. A last tip is to lay a towel over plastic bunk covering to alleviate what otherwise would prove to be a sticky, uncomfortable night.

Most of the ferries that service the N.E. Aegean islands only have aircraft type, fold back seats in the 3rd/tourist class decks. Try when possible to find a lounge where the television is muted and as far away as is possible from the large Gypsy entourages that are a feature of these waters. The families spill out over the seats and spread blankets on the floor (sorry sailors, cabin sole) and then settle down to create a 'home from home'. The 'after-mess' is a thought provoking sight, so much so that I can never understand the ship's officers allowing the bivouac to start. During their stay on the vessel the grubby little children half-heartedly beg.

The third class lavatories are often in an unsightly condition even prior to the craft's departure. To help enjoy reasonable surroundings and have the use of a shower, quietly trip into the next class and use their facilities (but don't tell everybody). Both the toilets and the showers suffer from the usual deficiencies listed under Greek bathrooms in CHAPTER 4, so be prepared.

Important points to take into account when interisland ferry-boating include the following:

1. The ferries are owned by individual steamship companies and an employee of one line will be unable or unwilling to give enquirers information in respect of another company's timetable. Incidentally, this individual ownership can lead to a wide disparity in quality of service and general comfort between different ferry-boats.

2. The distances and voyage times are quite often lengthy and tiring. Additionally the duration of the overall passage sometimes (no always) results in the timetable going to the wall, with delays in scheduled departure times on islands well into a ferry's voyage.

3. There are usually four basic fare classes: first, second, tourist and third/deck class. The published fares on scheduled ferries are government controlled and the

third/deck class option represents extremely good value. Purchasers must ensure that they state the fare class required as failure to do so may well result in a more expensive, tourist ticket being bought instead of the cheaper, deck class. Apart from the aforementioned four categories, there can be a variety of first and second-class sleeping accommodation, including private and shared cabins.

There are a number of luxury ferries and tourist trip boats, usually plying a particular island-to-island journey, on which charges are considerably higher. There may also be hydrofoil 'Flying Dolphins', which result in journey times of under half those of the scheduled ferries but at approximately double the cost.

4. Food and drink on the ferries used to be comparatively expensive, but price rises on the land have not been mirrored at sea. On the other hand the service is often discourteous and inefficient so it may be advantageous to pack provisions for a long voyage.

Wholesome and inexpensive ferry-boat picnic food includes: tomatoes, cucumber, bread, salami, ham, Sunfix orange juice and a bottle of wine (or two!). Take some bottled water. Greek chocolate (especially with nuts) is very good but does not keep well in the ambient daytime temperatures.

5. The state of the toilets and the lack of basic supplies makes it mandatory that one or two lavatory rolls are packed, easily to hand as it were. The usualy lack of washroom facilities commends the stowage of a pack of 'wipes'.

Quite frankly, on some occasions it will be necessary to stand on the rim of the toilet bowl as the only way of using the facility. Sorry!

6. Tickets should be purchased from a ticket agency prior to a voyage, as they can cost more when purchased on board. Ticket agency offices vary from 'the plush' to boxed-in back stairs. Clients are advised to check the scheduled prices and they should not go wrong. On the other hand they must be sure their price list is up to date as fare increases over recent years have been very large. For instance the 3rd class Piraeus to Samos (Vathy) charge increased from 1192 drs to 1645 drs between April 1985 and October 1986.

7. At the height of the season, the upper deck seats are extremely hot during the day and uncomfortably chilly at night. It is advisable to stake a claim to a seat as early as possible because the ferries are usually very crowded during the summer months. Voyagers who intend to lay out a sleeping bag and sleep the night away on the deck would do well to remember to occupy a seat, not the deck itself which is more often than not sluiced down in the night hours.

8. Travellers should ensure they have a good, fat book and a pack of cards to while away the longer sea voyages. Despite the awesome beauty of the islands and the azure blue sea, there are often long, unbroken periods of Mediterranean passage to be endured, interrupted only by the occasional passing ship and the dramatic activity and ructions that take place during a port call.

9. Travellers sensitive to discordancy, and who find disagreeable a cacophony, a clamour of sound, may well find unacceptable the usual raucous mix experienced in the average 3rd class lounge. This is made up of two televisions, tuned to different programmes (the picture constantly flickering, suffering a snowstorm or horizontally high jumping in a series of stills) accompanied by an overlaying wail of Greco-Turkish music piped over the ship's tannoy system. Best to fly!

One delight is to keep a weather eye open and hope to observe some dolphins diving and leaping in the ship's wake. Their presence is often made discernible by the loud slapping noise they make when re-entering the water.

Ferry-boaters must take care when checking the connections, schedules and timetables as they can, no do, change during the year, especially outside the inclusive months of May to September, as well as from one year to another. So be warned.

Do not forget, when the information is at it's most confusing, the Port police are totally reliable, but often a little short on English. Their offices are almost always on, or adjacent to the quayside.

For some years the Government, in an effort to promote tourism to selected and 'backwater' islands (who are the lucky ones) have offered free tickets during the out of season months. This offer usually covers the months of April/May and September/October but the only N.E. Aegean passage included in this scheme is between the islands of Chios and Psara.

Please refer to CHAPTER 10 (Mainland Ports) and individual island chapters for full details of ferry-boat timetables.

A few notes will not go amiss in respect of some of the various ferry-boats that ply the N.E. Aegean seas. Local craft are usually covered in the relevant island chapters.

Perhaps the most individual craft that floats in these waters is the **FB Kyklades**, a stable-mate of the 'incredible' **Miaoulis**, about which I have written in GROC's Candid Guide to the Cyclades. This 'African Queen', no, no, the redoubtable **Kyklades** describes a vast semicircular Aegean peregrination setting out from Piraeus to finally dock at Kavala (M) some days later, only to retrace its 'footsteps'. A sort of manned, Flying Dutchman that looms out of the sea only to as mysteriously disappear again. Due to the distances and numbers of ports involved in this weekly schedule, the craft tends to fall behind the official timetable, to say the least. In 1986 the **Kyklades** was out of action for a time and its promises, like those of a reluctant virgin, should be regarded with caution if not disbelief! Well certainly all the information relating to the craft must be regarded with circumspection.

CRUISE SHIPS
Fly/cruise packages on offer are usually rather up-market and in the main are based on seven days or multiples thereof. The cruise ships call in at selected islands for a part or full day, with excursions where applicable.

Other holiday-makers should note that the large influx of this 'genus' of fun loving tourist can have quite an impact on an island, and the *cognoscenti* normally vacate the particular port of call for that day.

GREEK ISLAND PLACE NAMES
This is probably the appropriate place to introduce the forever baffling problem which helps to bedevil the traveller – Greek place names. For instance, the island of Lesbos is often designated Mitilini.

The reason for the apparently haphazard nomenclature lies in the long and complicated territorial ownership of Greece and its islands, more especially the islands. The base root may be Greek, Latin, Turkish or Venetian. Additionally the Greek language has three forms – Demotic (spoken), Katharevousa have each been the official linguistic style. Even as recently as 1967-74 the Colonels made Katharevousa, once again, the authorised form, but Demotic is now the approved language. Help!

Street names can be equally confusing and I have plumped for my personal choice and stated the alternatives, but where this is not possible, well, there you go! I mean how can Athens' main square, Syntagma be spelt Syntagina, Sintagma or Syntagmatos?

Hotel and pension titles give rise to some frustration as can Guides using Greek script names, with two or three alternatives, including a similar meaning, Roman scripted appellation.

Street names are subject to some obscurity as the common noun Odhos (street) is often omitted, whilst Leoforos (avenue) and Plateia (square) are usually kept in the name. The prefix Saint or St is variously written as Agios, Aghios, Ayios, Ag or Ai.

Due to scholastic critical comments I must defend my habit of mixing Roman and Greek script when referring to establishment and street names. For example, I have written the Greek **ΑΚΤΗ ΕΘΝΙΚΗΣ ΑΝΤΙΣΤΑΣΗΣ** which translates to the Roman *Akti Ethnikis Antistasis*. My only defence is that 99.9% of readers will transmit that which they see to the brain without being able to make the mental gymnastics necessary to substitute the different letters, more especially those that have no easy or direct equivalent. Will my more erudite friends excuse the rest of us dyslectic Grecophiles!

A *nome* approximates to a small English county, a number of which make up a province such as the Peloponnese or Thessaly.

At this stage, without apologies, I introduce my own definition to help identify an unspoilt Greek town as follows: *where the town's rubbish is collected by donkey, wooden panniers slung across its back, slowly clip clopping up a stepped hillside street, the driver, not even in sight but probably languishing in a stray taverna!*

Map nomenclature	Greek	Translation
Agios/Ag/Ayios/Aghios	Αγιος	Saint
Akra/Akrotiri	Ακρωτηρι	Cape/Headland
Ano	Ανω	Upper
Archeologikos (horos)	Αρχαιολογικοζ	Ancient (site)
Chora/Horo/Horio/Khorio	Χωριο	Village
Kato	Κατω	Lower
Kolpos	Κολποζ	Gulf
Leoforos	Λεωφοροζ	Avenue
Limni	Λιμνη	Lake/Marsh
Limin	Λιμανι	Port harbour
Moni/Monastiri	Μοναστηρι	Monastery
Naos	Ναοζ	Temple
Nea/Neos	Νεο	New
Nissos	Νησοζ	Island
Odhos/Odos	Δρομοζ (Οδος)	Street
Ormos	Ορμοζ	Bay
Oros	Οροζ	Mountain
Plateia	Πλατεια	Square
Palios/Palaios	Παλιοζ	Old
Potami	Ποταμι	River
Spilia	Σπηλια	Cave
Vuno	Βουνο	Mountain

Useful Greek

English	Greek	Sounds like
Where is...	Που ειναι	Poo eene...
...the Olympic Airways office	τα γραφεια τηζ Ολυμπιακηζ	...ta grafia tis Olimbiakis
...the railway station	ο σιδηροδρομικοζ σταθμοζ	...sidheerothromikos stathmos
...the bus station	ο σταθμοζ των λεωφορειων	...stathmos ton leoforion
...the boat	το πλοιο	...to plio
...the nearest underground station	ο πλησιεοτεροζ σταθμοζ του ηλεκτρικοο	...o pleessiestehros stathmos too eelektrikoo
...the ticket office	το εκδοτηριο των εισιτηριων	...to eckdhoterio ton eessitirion
...the nearest travel agency	το πλησιεστεπο πρακτορεον ταξιδιων	...to pleessiestehro praktorion taxidion
I'd like to reserve...	Θελω να κρατησω	Thelo na kratiso
...seat/seats on the	θεση/θεση για	...thessee/thessis ghia
...to	για	...ghia
...plane	αεροπλανο	...aeroplano
...train	τραινο	...treno
...bus	λεωφορειο	...leoforio
...ferry-boat	πλοιο	...plio

When does it leave/arrive	Ποτε φευγει/φθανει	Poteh fehvghi/fthanee
Is there...	Υπαρχει	Eeparhee...
...from here to	απ εδωστο	...Apetho sto
...to	στον	...ston
Where do we get off	Που κατεβαινομε	Poo katevenomhe
I want to go to	Θελω να παω στουζ	Thelo na pao stoos...
I want to get off at	Θελω να κατεβω στο	Thelo na katevo sto...
Will you tell me when to get off	Θα μου πειτε που να κατεβω	Thah moo peete poo nah kahtevo
I want to go to...	Θελω να παω στουζ	Thelo na pao stoos
Stop here	Σταματα εδω	Stamata etho
How much is it	Ποσο ειναι	Posso eene
How much does it cost	Ποσο κανει η μεταφορα	Posso kani i metafora
...to	στο	...sto
Do we call at	Θα σταματησωμε στην	Tha stamatissome stin

Signs often seen affixed to posts & doors

Greek	English
ΑΦΙΞΙΣ	ARRIVAL
ΑΝΑΧΩΡΗΣΙΣ	DEPARTURE
ΣΤΑΣΙΣ	BUS STOP
ΕΙΣΟΔΟΣ	ENTRANCE
ΕΞΟΔΟΣ	EXIT
ΚΕΝΤΡΟ	CENTRE (as in town centre)
ΕΙΣΟΔΟΣ ΕΛΕΥΘΕΡΑ	FREE ADMISSION
ΑΠΑΓΟΡΕΥΕΤΑΙ Η ΕΙΣΟΔΟΣ	NO ENTRANCE
ΕΙΣΙΤΗΡΙΑ	TICKET
ΠΡΟΣ ΤΑΣ ΑΠΟΒΑΘΡΑΣ	TO THE PLATFORMS
ΤΗΛΕΦΩΝΟΝ	TELEPHONE
ΑΝΔΡΩΝ	GENTLEMEN
ΓΥΝΑΙΚΩΝ	LADIES
ΑΠΑΓΟΡΕΥΕΤΑΙ ΤΟ ΚΑΠΝΙΣΜΑ	NO SMOKING
ΤΑΜΕΙΟΝ	CASH DESK
ΤΟΥΑΛΕΤΕΣ	TOILETS
ΑΝΟΙΚΤΟΝ	OPEN
ΚΛΕΙΣΤΟΝ	CLOSED
ΩΘΗΣΑΤΕ	PUSH
ΣΥΡΑΤΕ	PULL

4 Island Accommodation

How oft doth man by care oppressed, find in an inn a place of rest. Combe

Package, villa and tour organised holiday-makers have accommodation arranged prior to arrival in Greece. If travelling around, then the most important matter is undoubtedly the procurement of lodgings, especially the first overnight stay on a new island or at an untried location.

The choice of accommodation is bewildering, varying from private houses (usually very clean but with basic bathroom facilities) to luxury class hotels able to hold their own with the most modern European counterpart. The deciding factor must be the budget and a person's sensibilities. My comments in respect of standards reflect comparisons with Western European establishments. Those referring to prices are usually in comparison with other Greek options. The standard of accommodation in the N.E. Aegean naturally varies, not only from island to island, but from place to place. For instance, even in the established tourist resort of Samos, accommodation can range from the indecently plush to extremely simple, island Rooms.

Travellers stepping off a ferry-boat are usually part of a swarming throng made up of Greeks, tourists and backpackers engulfed by a quayside mass of Greeks, tourists and backpackers struggling to get aboard the ferry-boat. Visitors may well be approached by men, women and youngsters offering rooms. It is a matter of taking potluck there and then, or searching around the town oneself. The later in the day, the more advisable it is to take an offer, unseen but it is obligatory to establish the price, if the rooms are with or without shower and how far away they are located. It can prove unnerving to be 'picked up' and then commence on an ever-lengthening trudge through the back streets of a strange place, especially as Greek ideas of distance are rather optimistic.

Any accommodation usually requires a traveller's passport to be relinquished. As a passport is also required to change money and to hire a car or a scooter, it is a good idea, if married or travelling with friends, to have separate documents. Then, if necessary, one passport can be left at the abode and another kept for other purposes, as required.

Official sources and many guidebooks lay much emphasis on the role of the Tourist police in finding accommodation, but this cannot be relied upon as the offices may well be closed on arrival. Moreover recent changes in the structure of the various police forces is resulting in the once separate and independent Tourist police being integrated into the offices of the Town police. I regret that this may well be a very retrograde step. Such a pity that the Greeks, the innovators of this excellent service, should now abandon the scheme, more especially in the light of the ever increasing numbers of tourists. Perhaps having achieved their goal of ensuring Greece is a number one holiday spot, the authorities are allowing the tour guides and couriers (that go 'hand in sand' with the ever increasing number of package tourists), to take over the Tourist police role in an *ex officio* capacity? Preposterous! I hope so.

A fruitful source of accommodation leads are convenient tavernas, which, more often than not, result in an introduction to a room or pension owner. Failing that, they usually send out for someone.

BEDROOMS

Greek bedrooms tend to be airy, whitewashed and sparsely furnished. The beds are often hard, as are the small pillows, and unyielding mattresses may well be laid directly on to bed-boards and not springs.

It is advisable to inspect bedroom walls for blood-red splats of flattened, but once gorged, mosquitoes resulting from a previous occupant's night-time vigil. Well designed rooms usually have a top-opening window screened off with gauze so that they can be left ajar without fear of incursions by winged creepy-crawlies. Where no gauze is in evidence, it is best to keep the windows tightly closed at night, however alien this may seem. Those not in possession of a proprietary insect repellent may well have to reconcile themselves to a sleepless night, any tell-tale buzzing echoing in the ears indicating one has already been bitten. It is comparable to being attacked by Lilliputian Stuka night-fighters.

Hanging points are noticeable by their absence. Often there will be no wardrobe but if present, there is unlikely to be any hangers, not even the steel-wire type, and the cupboard doors may be missing. A rather idiosyncratic feature is that clothes hooks, when present, are often very inadequate, looking as if they have been designed, and are only suitable for, hanging coffee mugs by the handles.

Even more maligned and even more misunderstood than Greek food is:

THE GREEK BATHROOM

I use the descriptive word bathroom, rather than refer simply to the toilets, because the total facility requires some elucidation. The following will not apply to Luxury. Class A or B hotels – well, it should not!

The plumbing is quite often totally inadequate and instead of the separate wastes of the bath, shower and sink being plumbed into progressively larger soil pipes, thus achieving a 'venturi' effect, they are usually joined into a similar diameter tube to that of the individual pipes. This inevitably causes considerable back pressure with inescapable consequences. The toilet waste is almost always insufficient in size and even normal, let alone excessive, use of toilet paper results in dreadful things happening, not only to your bathroom, but probably to a number of bathrooms in the building, street and possibly the village. If this were not enough.....the header tank rarely delivers sufficient 'flush'. The Greeks have had, for many years, to be economic in the use of water and some islands ration it, turning off the supply for a number of hours per day, in the height of the summer.

Common faults are to find the lavatory without a seat; flooded to a depth of some inches; the bathroom light not working; no toilet roll; door locks not fitted as well as dirty WC pans and or any combination of the above. Furthermore, the wash basin may well be without a drain plug. Amongst other reasons, the lack of a plug is to stop flooding if a sink tap is accidently left turned on when the mains water is switched off, and not turned off when the water supply is resumed!

The most common type of en suite bathroom is an all purpose lavatory and shower room. Beware! Years of research reveals that the shower head is usually positioned in such a way as to not only wash down the occupant but to drench the (amazingly) absorbent toilet roll as well as the bathers clothes, towel and footwear. Incidentally the drain point is usually located in such a way as to ensure that the bathroom is kept awash to a depth of between 1" and 3".....and the resultant pool invariably lies where a toilet sitter's feet fall – if you read my meaning.

It is not unusual for there to be no hot water, even if a heating system is in evidence. Government energy conservation methods, the comparatively high cost of electricity and the use of moderately sized solar heating panels, all contribute to this state of affairs. Where solar panels are the means of heating the water, remember to beat the rush and shower as early as possible, for the water soon loses its heat. Why not share with a friend? If hot water is available, but it is not heated by solar energy, then it will be necessary to locate the relevant electric switch. This is usually a 4 way position, ceramic knob hidden away behind a translucent panel door. On the other hand.... To be fair to owners of accommodation, it is standard practice to charge for the use of hot water showers so it pays the landlord to have the switch out of sight and reach. Room charges may well be increased by 50 to 100 drs per day for the use of a shower, but this will be detailed on the Government controlled price list that should be displayed, and is usually suspended on the back of the bedroom door.

One stipulation on water-short islands that really offends the West European (and North American?) sense of delicacy, is the oft present, hardly legible sign, requesting guests to put their 'paper' in the wastebin supplied, and not down the pan! I must own up to not always obeying this dictum and have had to make a hurried departure from a number of islands, let alone a pension or village, when the consequences of my profligate use of toilet paper have become apparent.

THE BEACH

Some backpacking youngsters utilise the shore for their night's accommodation. In fact all island ferry-boaters must be prepared to consider the beach as a standby at the more crowded locations during the months of July and August, although I have only had to spend two or three nights on the beach in the eight or nine years of island excursions. Certainly the weather could not be more ideal for sleeping under the stars, the officials are generally not too fussed and may well direct travellers to a suitable spot. Beware of mosquitoes and tar.

CAMPING

In direct contrast to *ad hoc* sleeping out on the beach, camping, except on approved sites, is strictly forbidden, but the law is not always rigorously applied. The restriction comes about from a wish to improve general hygiene, to prohibit and discourage abuse of private property and as a precaution against forest fires. The NTOG operate most of the licensed sites, some of which are spectacularly located, but there are some authorised, privately run camping grounds, which are also price controlled. There are quite a few campsites in the N.E. Aegean. A *Carnet-Camping International*, although not normally requested, affords campers worldwide, third-party liability cover and is available to United Kingdom residents from the AA and other, similar organisations.

If moved on by any official for sleeping out on the beach or illegally camping, it is advisable not to argue and go quietly. The Greek police have fairly wide and autonomous powers and it is preferable not to upset them unnecessarily.

A guide to overnight campsite fees is as follows:
Adults 200-300 drs; children ½ adult rate and tent hire 150-250 drs.

YOUTH HOSTELS (ΞΕΝΩΝΑΣ ΝΕΩΝ)

Establishments include **YMCA** (XAN), **YWCA** (XEN) in Athens as is the **YHA**, which also has one or three outposts on the islands.

Greek Youth Hostels are rather down-at-the-heel and tend to be operated in a somewhat slovenly manner. None of the old get-up-and-go familiar to members of some other countries – morning ablutions in ice-cold water and placing used razor blades in disused tobacco tins nailed to the wall.

It is preferable to have YHA membership, taking the Association's card along. Approximate prices per night at the YMCA and YWCA are 700 drs and in a Youth Hostel 300-350 drs.

ROOMS

The story goes that as soon as a tourist steps off the ferry, he (or she) is surrounded by women crying *Rooms* ('*Dhomatio*'), and whoops, within minutes he is ensconced in some wonderful Greek family's private home.

History may well have been like that, and in truth the ferries are still met at almost every island, the inhabitants offering not only rooms but pensions and the lower category hotels. Rooms are the cheapest accommodation and are generally very clean, sometimes including the option of breakfast, which is ordinarily charged extra. Prices reflect an island's popularity and the season, but usually the mid-season cost in the N.E. Aegean is between 800-1000 drs for a double room, depending upon the classification.

Apart from a prospect being approached leaving the ferry, the Tourist police would, in the past, advise of rooms to let but their role is being drastically reduced in their planned amalgamation with the Town police. The Tourist police offices were signed, if at all, 'ΤΟΥΡΙΣΤΙΚΗ ΑΣΤΥΝΟΜΙΑ'. Householders display the sign 'ΕΝΟΙΚΙΑΖΟΝΤΑΙ ΔΩΜΑΤΙΑ' or simply 'ΔΩΜΑΤΙΑ', when they have a room to rent. Government approved and categorised rooms are subject to an official tariff, and are slightly more expensive than the free-lance householders. A general point relates to a cautionary tale told to us by a delightful French couple. They were in the habit of replying to a room owner's enquiry as to how many nights they wished to stay by saying *"Tonight"*. One lady room owner interpreted this to mean two nights! Beware the inaccurate translation.

At the more tourist popular island resorts a new, unwelcome phenomena has reared 'his' ugly head. This is the long stay, layabout who rents a large double or triple bedroom for the summer season from a hapless, unsuspecting owner of accommodation. The entrepreneur, a species to be avoided, then sublets out the room, cramming in some 5 or 6 a night.

PENSIONS ('PANSION, ΠΑΝΣΙΟΝ')

This type of lodging was a natural progression from *Rooms* and now represents the most easily found and reasonably priced accommodation on offer.

The older type of pension is rather reminiscent of those large Victorian English houses, split up into bed-sits. In the main though they have been purpose built, usually during the Colonels' regime (1967-74) when government grants were freely available for the construction of tourist quarters. The owner often lives on one floor and acts as concierge. The rooms are functional and generally the guests on each level share a bathroom and shower and (a rather nice touch when provided) a communal refrigerator in which visitors can store their various provisions and drinks. Mid-season charges in the N.E. Aegean vary between 1000 and 1500 drs for a double room.

Sometimes a breakfast of coffee, bread and jam, perhaps butter and a boiled egg, is available for about 150 drs and represents fair value compared with the cost of a cafe breakfast.

TAVERNAS (ΤΑΒΕΡΝΑ)

Tavernas are, first and foremost, eating places. Some tavernas, especially those situated by, or near, beaches, have Rooms available. The only drawback is that the more popular the taverna, the less likely guests are to get a full night's sleep, but of course the more involved they will be with the taverna's social life which will often continue on into the small hours. Charges are similar to those of a pension.

HOTELS (ΞΕΝΟΔΟΧΕΙΟΝ)

Shades of difference and interpretation can be given to the nomenclature by variations of the bland, descriptive noun hotel. For instance ΞΕΝΟΔΟΧΕΙΟΝ ΥΠΝΟΥ indicates a hotel that does not serve meals and ΠΑΝΔΟΧΕΙΟΝ a low grade hotel.

Many backpackers don't consider hotels their first choice. The higher classification ones are more expensive than pensions and the lower grade hotels often cost the same, but may well be rather seedy and less desirable than the equivalent class pension. Greek hotels are classified L (Luxury) A, B, C, D and E and the prices charged within these categories (except L) are controlled by the authorities.

It is unfortunately difficult to differentiate between hotels and their charges as each individual category is subject to fairly wide standards, and charges are subject to a multitude of possible percentage supplements and reductions as detailed below:

Shower extra (C, D and E hotels); number of days stayed less than three: plus 10 per cent; air conditioning extra (A and B hotels); out of season deduction (ask); high season extra (ie the months of July, August and the first half of September: plus 20 per cent; single occupancy: about 80 per cent of a double room rate. The higher classification hotels may well insist on guests taking demi-pension terms, especially in high season.

The following table must be treated as a guide only but is based on 1987 prices.

Class	Comments	Indicated mid-season, double-bedroom price
L	All amenities, a very high standard and price. Probably at least one meal in addition to breakfast will have to be purchased. Very clean. Very hot water.	

Note there are no L Class hotels in the N.E. Aegean, that is apart from the Akti-Mirina, *Mirina, Limnos*.

Class	Comments	Indicated mid-season, double-bedroom price
A	High standard and price. Most rooms have en suite shower or bath. Guests may well have to accept demi-pension terms. Clean. Hot water.	6000 drs.
B	Good standard. Many rooms have en suite shower or bath. Clean. Hot water.	3000 drs.
C	Usually an older hotel. Faded elegance, shared bathroom. Cleanish. Possibly hot water.	2500 drs.
D	Older, faded hotel. Shared bathroom, which may well be 'interesting'. A shower, if available will be an 'experience', and the water cold.	2000 drs.
E	Old, faded and unclean. The whole stay will be an 'experience'. Only very cold water.	1500 drs.

The prices indicated include government taxes, service and room occupancy until noon. Where in the text reference is made to 'official rates', these are the prices listed in the *'Guide to the Greek Hotels'*. Generally prices detailed are those applicable to 1986.

THE XENIAS

Originally government owned and promoted to ensure the availability of high-standard accommodation at important tourist centres but now often managed by private enterprise. Only A, B and C rated categories and they are of a better standard than hotels in a similar class.

FLATS & HOUSES

During the summer months this type of accommodation, referred to by travel agents and package tour operators as villas, is best booked prior to arriving in Greece. Not only will pre-booking be easier but, surprisingly, works out cheaper than flying out and snooping around.

The winter is a different matter, but probably not within the scope of most of our readers.

Further useful names & addresses

The Youth Hostel Association, 14 Southampton St, London WC2E 7HY.   Tel. (01) 836 8541.

Useful Greek

English	Greek	Sounds like
I want...	Θελω	Thelo...
...a single room	ενα μονο δωματιο	...enna mono dhomatio
...a double room	ενα διπλο δωματιο	...enna thiplo dhomatio
...with a shower	με ντουζ	...me doosh
We would like a room	Θα θελαμε ενα δωματιο	Tha thelame ena dhomatio
for...	για	ghia...
two/three days/a week/	δυο/τρειζ μερεζ/μια	thio/trees meres/meea
until	εβδομαδα/μεχρι	evthomatha/mekhri
Can you advise of another...	Ξερετε κανενα αλλο...	Xerete kanena alo...
house with rooms	σπιτι με δωματιο	speeti meh dhomatio
pension	πανσιον	panseeon
inn	πανδοχειο	panthokheeo
hotel	ξενοδοχειο	ksenodhokheeo
youth hostel	ξενωναζ νεων	xenonas neon
How much is the room	Ποσο κανει το δωματιο	Poso kanee dho dhomatio ghia
for a night?	για τη νυχτα	ti neektah
That is too expensive	Ειναι πολυ ακριβα	Eene polee akriva
Have you anything cheaper?	Δεν εχετε αλλο πιο φθηνο	Dhen ekhete ahlo pio ftheeno
Is there...	Υπαρχει	Eeparkhee
a shower	ενα ντουζ	doosh
a refrigerator	ενα ψυγειο	psiyeeo
Where is the shower?	Που ειναι το ντουζ	Poo eene dho doosh
I have to leave...	Πρεπει να φυγω	Prepee na feegho...
today	σημερα	simera
tomorrow	αυριο	avrio
very early	πολυ νωρις	polee noris
Thank you for a	Ευχαριστω για την	Efkareesto ghia tin
nice time	συμπαθητικη ωρα*	simpathitiki ora

*This is the exact translation, which would never be used, however, in Greek. An expression meaning rather: 'thanks for the fun' is:

	Ευχαριστω για την	Efkaristo ghia
	διασκεδαση	tin thiaskethasi

5 Travelling around an island

A man is happier for life from having once made an agreeable tour. Anon

A few introductory remarks may well be apposite in respect of holiday-makers' possessions and women in Greece. The matter will also be discussed elsewhere but it is not out of place to reiterate one or two points (Rosemary calls it 'carrying on').

PERSONAL POSSESSIONS

Do not leave airline tickets, money, travellers' cheques and or passports behind at the accommodation. A man can quite easily acquire a wrist-strap handbag in which to conveniently carry these items. The danger does not, even today, lie with the Greeks, but with fellow tourists, down-and-outs and professional thieves working a territory.

WOMEN

There has been, in recent years, a movement towards the 'Spanish-Costa' percentage ploy. Young Greek men, in the more popular tourist areas, have finally succumbed and will now sometimes try it on. It's up to you girls, there is no menace, only opportunities.

Now back to the main theme of the chapter but before expanding on the subject, a few words will not go amiss in respect of:

BEACHES

A surprisingly large number of beaches are polluted in varying degrees, mainly by seaborne plastic and some tar.

Jellyfish and sea urchins can occasionally be a problem in a particular bay, jellyfish increasingly so. One of my Mediterranean correspondents advises me that cures for the jellyfish sting include, ammonia, urine (ugh) and a paste of meat tenderiser (it takes all sorts I suppose).

The biggest headache (literally) to a tourist is the sun, or more accurately, the heat of the sun at the height of the summer season. The islands benefit from the relief of the prevailing wind, the *Meltemi*, but to give an example of the extreme temperatures sometimes experienced, in Athens a few years ago birds were actually falling out of the trees, and they were the feathered variety! Every year dozens of holiday-makers are carted off, suffering from acute sunburn. A little often, (sun that is), must be the watchword.

It is very pleasant to observe more and more middle-aged Greek ladies taking to the sea, often in all enveloping black costumes and straw hats. Some, to preserve their modesty, appear to swim in everyday clothes.

Despite the utterly reasonable condemnation of modern day advances in technology by us geriatrics, one amazing leap forward for all travelling and beach bound mankind is the Walk-Master personal stereo-cassettes. No more the strident, tinny beat of the transistor (or more commonly the 'ghetto-blaster'), now simply the jigging silence of ear-muffed and transfixed faces. Splendid!

It may well be that a reader is a devoted sun worshipper and spends every available minute on the beach, patio or terrace; if so there is no need to read any further. On the other hand when a holiday-maker's interests range beyond conversion of the sun's very strong rays into painful, peeling flesh, and there is a wish to travel around an island, then the question of *modus operandi* must be given some thought.

First, purchase an island map and one of the colourful and extremely informative tourist guides available on the larger islands. It is unfortunate that my old friends **Clyde Surveys** do not produce a map of the N.E. Aegean, only including Samos island in their Dodecanese grouping. It is strange that no one company has made an all inclusive map of the chain but there is a well executed map (No. 6) that includes the islands of Chios, Lesbos and Limnos produced by the **Efstathiadis Group** of Athens.

Having purchased the maps and guides it is necessary to consider the alternative methods of travel and appraise their value.

ON FOOT

Owing to the hilly terrain of the islands and the daytime heat encountered, readers may well have had enough walking without looking for trouble. A quick burst down to the local beach, taverna, shop or restaurant, and the resultant one hundred or so steps back up again, may well go a long way to satiating any desire to go 'walkies'. If needs be, walking is often the only way to negotiate the more rugged donkey tracks and the minimum footwear is a solid pair of sandals or 'trainers'.

HITCHING

The comparative paucity of privately owned cars makes hitchhiking an unsatisfactory mode of travel. On the other hand, if striking out to get to, or return from, a particular village on a dead end road, most Greek drivers stop when thumbed down. It may well be a lift in the back of a Japanese pickup truck, possibly sharing the space with some chickens, a goat or sheep or all three!

DONKEY

Although once a universal 'transportation module', now usually only available for hire on specific journey basis in particular locations. A personal prejudice is to consider donkey rides part of the unacceptable face of tourism, added to which it is now exorbitantly expensive.

BUSES

Buses (and taxis) are the universal method of travel in Greece, so the services are widespread if, naturally enough, a little Greek in operation. Generally they run approximately on time and the fares are, on the whole, extremely reasonable. Passengers must expect to share the available space with fairly bulky loads and, occasionally, live-stock.

The trick is to first find the square on which the buses terminus and then locate the bus office where the tickets are pre-purchased and on the walls or windows of which is stuck the timetable and the fares structure. On some bus routes the fares are collected by a conductor, although this is unusual. Be available well prior to the scheduled departure times as buses have a 'nasty habit' of departing early. Ensure any luggage is placed in the correct storage compartment, otherwise it may go missing.

Buses are often crowded, especially when a journey coincides with a ferry-boat disgorging its passengers. The timetables are usually scheduled so that a bus or buses await a ferry-boat's arrival, except perhaps very early or late arriving craft. A bus rarely leaves a potential client standing, they just encourage everyone in. The real fun starts if the bus is not only 'sardine packed', but fares are collected by the conductor who has to somehow make his way through, round and over the passengers.

Do not fail to observe the decorations, festooned around and enveloping the driver. Often these displays resemble a shrine, which taking account of the way some of the drivers propel their bus, is perhaps not so out of place. Finally do have some change available as coins are always in short supply. It is helpful to know that local buses may be labelled TOPIKO (ΤΟΠΙΧΟ).

A critic recently took me to task for not stressing that the summer bus schedules listed throughout the text are the subject of severe curtailment, if not total termination, during the winter months from October through to May. So, smacked hand Geoffrey and readers please note.

TAXIS

As indicated in the previous sub-heading, taxis are the 'other' mode of island travel. They are usually readily available and can be remarkably modern and plush. On the other hand....

Ports and towns nearly always have a main square on which the taxis rank but come the time of a Ferry-boat's arrival they usually queue on the quayside. Fares are governed by law and, at the main rank, are often displayed giving examples of the cost to various destinations. Charges are reasonable by European standards, but it is essential to establish the cost prior to hiring.

It may come as a shock for a 'fare' to have his halting pidgin Greek answered in 'pure' Australian or American. But this is not surprising when one considers that many island Greeks have spent their youth on merchant ships or emigrated to the New World for 10 to 15 years. On their return home, with a relatively financially secure future, many take to taxi driving to supplement their income (and possibly to keep out of the little woman's way?).

BICYCLE, SCOOTER & CAR HIRE

Be very careful to establish what (if any) insurance cover is included in the rental fee, and that the quoted hire charge includes the various compulsory taxes.

On the whole, bicycles are very hard work and poor value in relation to, say, the cost of hiring a Lambretta or Vespa scooter – an option endorsed when the mountainous nature of most islands, and the midday heat, is taken into consideration. The ubiquitous Italian machines are progressively being replaced by semi-automatic Japanese motorcycles which, although they do away with the necessity to fight the gears and clutch, are not entirely suited to transporting two heavyweights. I have had the frightening experience, when climbing a steep mountainside track, of the bike jumping out of gear, depositing my passenger and I on the ground leaving the scooter whirling round like a crazed mechanical catherine-wheel.

It is amazing how easy it is to get a good tan while scootering. The moderate wind draws the sun's heat, the air is laden with the smell of wild sage and oleanders and with the sun on one's back...marvellous!

Very rarely is a deposit requested when hiring a bike or motorbike but a passport is required. Always shop around to check out various companies' charges: the nearer to a port, town or city centre a hirer is, the more expensive the machines will be. A short walk towards the unfashionable quarters can be very rewarding. Take a close look over the chosen mode of transport before settling up, as maintenance of any mechanical unit in Greece is poor to non-existent. Bicycles and scooters, a few years old, will be 'pretty clapped out'. A client must check the brakes, they will be needed, and should not allow the hirer to fob him off without making sure there is a spare wheel.

Increasingly, the owners of two wheeled vehicles are hiring out dubious looking crash helmets. Flash young Greek motorbike riders usually wear their 'Space Age' headgear on the handlebars, where no doubt it will protect them (that is the handlebars) from damage.

A useful tip when hiring a scooter is to take along a towel! It doubles up as useful additional padding for the pillion passenger's bottom on rocky roads and saves having to sit on the painfully hot plastic seating should a rider forget to raise the squab when parked up. Sunglasses are necessary to protect the rider's eyes from airborne insects. Out of the height-of-season and early evening it becomes very chilly so a sweater or jumper is a good idea and females may well require a head scarf, whatever the time of day or night.

Fuel is served in litres and five litres of two-stroke costs about 320-340 drs. Fill up as soon as possible as fuel stations are in fairly short supply outside the main towns. Increasingly the gap between the scooter and the car is being filled with more sophisticated machinery which include moon-tyred and powerfully engined Japanese motorbikes and beach-buggies.

Typical daily hire rates are: for a bicycle 150 drs; a scooter/Lambretta 1000-1500 drs; a car from 5000 drs including full insurances and taxes but mileage may cost extra, calculated at so much per kilometre. Out of season and period hire for all forms of conveyance can benefit from 'negotiation'.

Car hire companies require a daily deposit, which now starts off at 10,000 drs per day, as well as a hirer's passport and driving licence details. It is noticeable that I and many readers regard car hire as a legalised rip-off. Another subject that causes unpleasant disputes is the increasing habit of the hire companies to charge comparatively expensively for any damage incurred, and I mean any damage however slight. A hirer's detailed reasons for the causes of an accident, the damage and why it should not cost anything falls on deaf ears. Furthermore it is no use threatening to involve the police as they will not be at all interested in the squabble.

Several other words of warning might not go amiss. Taking into account the state of the roads, do not hire a two-wheeled conveyance if not thoroughly used to handling one. There are a number of very nasty accidents every year, involving tourists and hired scooters. Additionally the combination of poor road surfaces and usually inadequate to non-existent lights should preclude any night-time scootering. A hirer must ensure he (or she) is fully covered for medical insurance, including an unscheduled, Medicare flight home, and check, before leaving the homeshores, that a general holiday policy does not exclude accidents incurred on hired transport.

The glass fronted metal framed shrines mounted by the roadside are graphic reminders of a fatal accident at this or that spot. Incidentally, on a less macabre note, if the shrine is a memorial to a man, the picture and bottle often present (more often than not of Sophia Loren and whisky) represent that person's favourite earthbound desires.

But back to finger-wagging. The importance of the correct holiday insurance cover cannot be over-stressed. The tribulations I have encountered in obtaining inclusive insurance, combined with some readers' disastrous experiences, have resulted in the inclusion in the guide of an all embracing scheme. This reminder should be coupled with the strictures in CHAPTER 1 drawing attention to the all-inclusive policy devised for readers of the *Candid Guides*, for details of which *See Page 42. Enough said!*

ROADS

The main roads of most islands are passable but asphalted country lanes often degenerate alarmingly, becoming nothing more than heavily rutted and cratered tracks. Much road building and reconstruction is under way. Beware as not all roads, indicated as being in existence on the official maps, are anything more than, at the best, donkey tracks or are simply non-existent. Evidence of broken lines marking a road on the map must be interpreted as meaning there is no paved highway at all.

Further useful names and addresses
Clyde Surveys Ltd., Reform Road, Maidenhead, Berks SL6 8BU   Tel. (0628) 21371
Efstathiadis Group, 14 Valtetsiou St, Athens.   Tel. 3615 011

Useful Greek

English	Greek	Sounds like
Where can I hire a...	Που μπορω να νοικιασω ενα	Poo boro na neekeeaso enna...
...bicycle	ποδηλατο	...pothilato
...scooter	σκουτερ	...sckooter
...car	αυτοκινητο	...aftokinito
I'd like a...	Θα ηθελα ενα	Tha eethela enna...
I'd like it for...	Θα το ηθελα για	Tha dho eethela ghia...
...a day	μια μερα (or: μια)	...mia mera
...days	μερες	...meres
...a week	μια εβδομαδα	...mia evthomadha
How much is it by the...	Ποσο κανει την	Poso kanee tin...
...day	μερα	...mera
...week	εβδομαδα	...evthomadha
Does that include...	Συμπεριλαμβανονται σαυτο	Simberilamvanonte safto
...mileage	τα χιλιομετρα	...tah hiliometra
...full insurance	μικτη ασφαλεια	...meektee asfaleah
I want some	Θελω	Thelo
...petrol (gas)	βενζινης	...vehnzini
...oil	λαδι	...lathi
...water	νερο	...nero
Fill it up	Γεμιστε το	Yemiste to
...litres of petrol (gas)	λιτρα βενζινης	...litra vehnzinis
How far is it to...	Ποσο απεχει	Poso apechee
Which is the road for...	Ποιος ειναι ο δρομος για	Pios eene o thromos ghia
Where are we now	Που ειμαστε τωρα	Poo eemaste tora
What is the name of this place	Πως ονομαζεται αυτο το μερος	Pos onomazete afto dho meros
Where is...	Που ειναι	Poo eene...

Road Signs

ΑΛΤ	STOP
ΑΠΑΓΟΡΕΥΕΤΑΙ Η ΕΙΣΟΔΟΣ	NO ENTRY
ΑΔΙΕΞΟΔΟΣ	NO THROUGH ROAD
ΠΑΡΑΚΑΜΠΤΗΡΙΟΣ	DETOUR
ΕΛΑΤΤΩΣΑΤΕ ΤΑΧΥΤΗΤΑΝ	REDUCE SPEED
ΑΠΑΓΟΡΕΥΕΤΑΙ Η ΑΝΑΜΟΝΗ	NO WAITING
ΕΡΓΑ ΕΠΙ ΤΗΣ ΟΔΟΥ	ROAD REPAIRS
ΚΙΝΔΥΝΟΣ	BEWARE (Caution)
ΑΠΑΓΟΡΕΥΕΤΑΙ ΤΟ ΠΡΟΣΠΕΡΑΣΜΑ	NO OVERTAKING
ΑΠΑΓΟΡΕΥΕΤΑΙ Η ΣΤΑΘΜΕΥΣΙΣ	NO PARKING

GROC's Candid Guides
introduce to readers

Suretravel '87

A comprehensive holiday insurance plan that 'gives cover that many other policies do not reach'....

In addition to the more usual cover offered by other policies the **SURETRAVEL HOLIDAY PLAN** includes (where medically necessary):

24 hour World Wide Medical Emergency Service including, where appropriate, repatriation by air ambulance.

Additionally personal accident and medical & emergency expenses EVEN while hiring a bicycle, scooter or car.

An example premium, in 1987, for a 10-17 day holiday in Greece is £13.40 per person.

Note: All offers & terms are subject to the Insurance Certificate Cover

For an application form please complete the cut-out below and send to:

Willowbridge Enterprises, Bridge House,
Southwick Village, Nr Fareham, Hants. PO17 6DZ

Please forward to *(block capitals please)*

Mr/Mrs/Miss .... Age ....

of ....

....

a **SURETRAVEL** application form.

Date of commencement of holiday .... Duration ....

Signature .... Date ....

6 Island Food & Drink

Let us eat and drink for tomorrow we die. Corinthians

It is a pity that many tourists, prior to visiting Greece, have, in sundry restaurants throughout Europe and North America, 'experienced' the offerings masquerading as Greek food. Greek food and drink does not appear to cross its borders very well and I do not think it is possible to recreate the unique quality of Greek cooking in foreign lands. Perhaps this is because they owe much of their taste to, and are in sympathy with, the very air laden with the scent of the flowers and herbs, the very water, clear and chill, the very soil of the plains and scrubclad mountains, the ethereal and uncapturable quality that is Greece. Incidentally many critics would postulate that it was impossible to create Greek food, full stop, but be that as it may....

Salad does not normally send me into ecstasy but, after a few days in Greece, the very thought of a peasant salad, consisting of endive leaves, sliced tomatoes and cucumber, black olives, olive oil and vinegar dressing, all topped off with feta cheese and sprinkled with oregano, parsley or fennel, sends me salivating to the nearest taverna.

Admittedly, unless you are lucky enough to chance across an outstanding taverna, the majority are surprisingly unadventurous and the choice of menu limited. Mind you there are one or two restaurants serving exciting and unusual meals, if the spelling mistakes are anything to go by. For instance I have observed over the years the following no doubt appetising dishes: *omeled, spachetti botonnaise, shrings salad, bowels entrails, lump cutlets, limp liver, mushed pot, shrimps, crambs, kid chops, grilled meat bolls, spar rips, wine vives, fiant oven, sward fish, pork shops, staffed vine leaves, wild greens, string queens, wildi cherry, bater honi, gregg goti (!), mate with olive oil, bruised meat, forced meat balls and Creek salad* – don't they sound interesting.

On a more positive note, whilst the usual dishes will be known to readers, a recommendation, a mention of a dish I haven't seen before and a 'musing' may not go amiss. As to the recommendation, where an eating house serves up a good, creamy tzatziki and a Greek salad it makes a very refreshing dish to combine the two. This year I came across a meal I have not encountered previously, **ΜΠΟΥΡΕΚΑΚΙΑ** or *bourekakia*. These are long, thin tubes of battered ham filled with feta cheese and are very, very tasty. The ruminative, brown study relates to the humble potato. Why, oh why, taking into account the copious plates of patatas available (thus proving the existence in quantity of the aforesaid tuber) are there no variations on the theme? Where are, oh where are mashed, roast or creamed potatoes to, once in a while, usurp the omnipresent, universal chip?

A FEW HINTS & TIPS

Do not insist upon butter, the Greek variant is not very tasty to the European palate, is expensive and in the heat tends to dissolve into greasy pools.

Sample the retsina wine and after a bottle or two a day for a few days there is every chance you will enjoy it. Moreover, retsina is beneficial (well that's what I tell myself), acting as a splendid anti-agent to the comparative oiliness of some of the food.

Bread is automatically served with a meal – and charged for – unless a diner indicates otherwise but it is very useful for mopping up any excessive olive oil and requires no butter to make it more greasy. It has become a noticeable, and regrettable, feature in recent years that the charge for bread has increased to between 10 and 30 drs per head, and I have seen it as high as 40 drs. Naughty! Many of the N.E. Aegean eateries have a nasty little habit of lumping an extra tax calculation in with the bread charge. That is extra to the usual tax inclusive prices listed on the menu.

Greek food tends to be served on the 'cool' side and even if the meal started out hot, and by some mischance is speedily served, it will arrive on a thoroughly chilled plate.

The selection of both food and drink is almost always limited and unenterprising, unless diners elect to frequent the more international restaurants (but why go to Greece?). On the other hand the choice of establishments in which to eat and/or drink is unlimited, in fact the profusion is such that it can prove very confusing. If in doubt about which particular restaurant or taverna to patronise, use the well tried principle of picking one frequented by the locals. It will inevitably serve good quality food at reasonable prices. It is generally a waste of time to ask a Greek for guidance in selecting a good taverna or restaurant as he will be reluctant to give specific advice in case the recommendation proves unsatisfactory.

Especially in the more rural areas, do not be shy, ask to look over the kitchen to see what's cooking. If denied this traditional right, be on your guard as the food may well be precooked, tasteless and plastic, particularly if the various meals available are displayed in a neon-lit showcase. Do not order the whole meal all at once, as would be usual at home. If you do it will be served simultaneously and/or in the wrong sequence. Order course by course and take your time, everyone else does. Diners are not being ignored if the waiter does not approach the table for anything up to 20 minutes, he is just taking his time and is probably overworked. At first the blood pressure does tend to inexorably rise as the waiter appears to continue to studiously disregard your presence. It makes a visitor's stay in Greece very much more enjoyable if all preconceived ideas of service can be forgotten. Lay back and settle into the glorious and indolent timelessness of the locals' way of life. If in a hurry, pay when the order arrives for if under the impression that it took a disproportionate time to be served, just wait until it comes to settling up. It will probably take twice as long to get the bill (*logariasmo*), as it did to receive the food.

Fish, contrary to expectations, is very expensive, even in comparison with European prices, so you can imagine the disparity with the cost of other Greek food. When ordering fish it is normal to select the choice from 'the ice' and, being priced by weight, it will be put on the scales prior to cooking. This is the reason that fish is listed at so many drachmae per kilo, so is not so outrageously costly as may at first appear.

Government price lists are a legal necessity for most drinking and eating places, and should state the establishment's category and the price of every item served. Two prices are shown, the first being net is not really relevant, the second, showing the price actually charged, includes service and taxes.

Food is natural and very rarely are canned or any frozen items used, even if available. When frozen foods are included in the meal the fact must be indicated on the menu by addition of the initials *KAT*. The olive oil used for cooking is excellent, as are the herbs and lemons, but it can take time to become accustomed to the different flavours imparted to food. Before leaving the subject of hints and tips, remember that olive oil can be pressed into service for removing unwanted beach-tar from clothes.

A most enjoyable road, quayside or ferry-boat breakfast is to buy a large yoghurt and a small pot of honey, mix the honey into the yoghurt and then relish the bitter-sweet delight. If locally produced, natural yoghurt (usually stored in cool tubs and spooned into a container) cannot be purchased, the brand name *Total* is an adequate substitute being made from cow's or sheep's milk. I prefer the sheep derived product and, when words fail, break into a charade of 'baa-ing'. It keeps the other shoppers amused if nothing else. The succulent water melon, a common and inexpensive fruit, provides a juicy lunchtime refreshment.

Apart from waving the tablecloth in the air, or for that matter the table, it is usual to call *parakalo* (please). It is also permissible to say *gharson* or simply 'waiter'.

THE DRINKS
Non-alcoholic beverages Being a cafe (and taverna) society, coffee is drunk at all times of the day and night. Greek coffee (*kafe*) is in fact a leftover from the centuries long Turkish influence, being served without milk in small cups and always with a glass of deliciously cool water. Unless specified otherwise, it will be served sickly sweet or *varigliko*. There are many variations but the three most usual are *sketto* (no sugar), *metrio* (medium) or *glyko* (sweet). Beware not to completely drain the cup, the bitter grains will choke you. Except in the most traditional establishments (*kafeneions*), you can ask for *Nes-kafe* or simply *Nes* which, as you would think, is an instant coffee but this Greek produced version has a comparatively muddy taste. If you require milk with your coffee it is necessary to ask for *meh gala*. A most refreshing version is to have Nes chilled or *frappe*. French coffee (*ghaliko kafe*), served in a coffee pot with a separate jug of hot milk, espresso and cappucino are found in the larger, provincial cities, ports and international establishments. However, having made a detailed request, you may well receive any permutation of all the possibilities listed above, however carefully you think you have ordered.

Tea, (*tsai*), perhaps surprisingly, is quite freely available, made of course with the ubiquitous teabag, which is not so outrageous since they have become so universally commonplace. In more out of the way places herbal tea may be served.

Purchasing bottled mineral waters is not always necessary as, generally, island water is superb but should you wish to have some stashed away in the fridge, brand names include *Loutraki, Nigita,* and *Sariza*. *Sprite* is fizzy and *lemonada/lemonatha* a stillish lemonade. Orangeade (*portokaladha*), cherry soft drink (*visinatha*) and fruit juices are all palatable and sold, as often as not, under brand names, as is the universal *Koka-Kola*.

A word of warning comes from a reader who reported that, in the very hot summer months, some youngsters drink nothing but sweet, fizzy beverages. This can result in mouth ulcers caused by fermenting sugar, so drink some water every day. day.

Alcoholic beverages They are generally sold by weight. Beer comes in 330g tins, very occasionally a small bottle or more usually the large 500g bottles – have the 500g, it is a good measure. Wine is sold in 340/430g (half bottle), 680/730g (1.1 pints) and 950g (1¾ pints) sized bottles.

Beer Greek brewed or bottled beer represents very good value except when served in cans, which are the export version and, I regard, a 'swindle'. This European habit should be resisted for no other reason than it means the cost, quantity for quantity, is almost doubled. Now that *Fix Hellas* is rarely if ever obtainable, due to the founder's death, the only other, widely available, bottled beers are *Amstel* and *Henninger*. Draught lager is insidiously creeping in to various resorts and should be avoided, not only for purist reasons, but because it is comparatively expensive, as are the imported, stronger bottled lagers. No names, no pack drill but *Carlsberg* is one that springs to mind. A small bottle of beer is referred to as a *mikri bira* and a large one, *meghali bira*.

Wine Unresinated (*aretsinoto*) wine is European in style, palatable and popular brands include red and white *Demestika* and *Cambas*. More refined palates will approve of the whites (*aspro*) and the reds (*kokino*) of, say, Limnos island. Greek wine is not so much known for its quality but if quantity of brands can make up for this then Greece will not let you down.

Resinated wine is achieved, if that can be considered the expression, by the barrels, in which the wine is fermented, being internally coated with pine tree resin. The resultant liquid is referred to as retsina, most of which are white, with a *kokkineli* or rose version, being available. Some consider the taste to be similar to chewing wet, lead pencils but this is patently obviously a heresy. Retsina is usually bottled, but some tavernas serve 'open' retsina in metal jugs and when purchased for personal consumption it can be found being dispensed from large vats, buried in side-street cellars, into any container a client might like to press into service. The adjective 'open' is used to describe locally brewed retsina available on draught or more correctly from the barrel. Asking for a *Kortaki* ensures being served the traditional, small bottle of retsina rather than a full sized bottle. Rumour has it that the younger retsinas are more easily palatable, but that is very much a matter of taste. A good 'starter' kit is to drink a bottle or two twice a day for three or four days and if the pain goes....

Spirits & others As elsewhere in the world, sticking to the national drinks represents good value.

Ouzo, much maligned and blamed for other excesses, is, in reality, of the aniseed family of drinks (which include Ricard and Pernod) and, taken with water, is a splendid 'medicine'. Ouzo is traditionally served with *mezethes* (or *mezes*) (the Greek equivalent of Spanish tapas) which is a small plate of, for instance, a slice of cheese, tomato, cucumber and possibly smoked eel, octopus and an olive. When served they are charged for, costing some 20 to 30 drs, but the tradition of offering them is disappearing in many tourist locations. If you specifically do not wish to be served mezes then make the request *ouzo sketto*. *Raki* is a stronger alternative to Ouzo, often 'created' in Crete.

Metaxa brandy, available in three, five and seven star quality, is very palatable but with a certain amount of 'body', whilst *Otys* brandy is smoother. Greek aperitifs include *Vermouth*, *Mastika* and *Citro*.

DRINKING PLACES
Prior to launching into the various branches of this subject, I am at a loss to understand why so many cafe-bar and taverna owners select chairs that are designed to cause the maximum discomfort, even suffering. They are usually too small for any but a very small bottom, too low and made up of wickerwork or rafia that painfully impresses its pattern on the sitter's bare (sun-burnt?) thighs.

Kafeneion (ΚΑΦΕΝΙΟΝ) Greek cafe, serving only Turkish coffee. Very Greek, very masculine and in which women are rarely seen. They are similar to a British working man's club, but with backgammon, worry beads and large open windows giving a dim view of the smoke-laden interior.

Ouzeries (OYZEPI) As above, but the house speciality is (well, well) Ouzo.

Cafe-bar (ΚΑΦΕ ΜΠΑΡ) As above, but serving alcoholic beverages as well as coffee and women are to be seen.

Pavement cafes French in style, with outside tables and chairs sprawling over the road as well as the pavement. Open from mid-morning, throughout the day, to one or two o'clock the next morning. Snacks and sweet cakes are usually available.

Inside any of the above, the locals chat to each other in that peculiar Greek fashion which gives the impression that a full-blooded fight is about to break out at any moment. In reality, they are probably just good friends, chatting to each other over the blaring noise of a televised football match, a plastic, sickly American soap opera or a ghastly English 'comic' programme with Greek subtitles.

Drinks can always be obtained at a taverna or restaurant, but you may be expected to eat, so read on.

It is of course possible to drink at hotel cocktail bars, but why leave home!

EATING PLACES

At the cheapest end of the market, and more especially found in Athens, are pavement-mounted stands serving doughnut-shaped bread which make for an inexpensive nibble.

Pistachio nut & ice-cream vendors They respectively push their wheeled trolleys around the streets, selling a wide variety of nuts in paper bags for 20 drs or so and good value ice-cream in a variety of flavours and prices.

Galaktopoleio (ΓΑΛΑΚΤΟΠΩΛΕΙΟ). Shops selling dairy products including milk (*gala*), butter, yoghurt (*yiaorti*), bread, honey and sometimes omelettes and fritters with honey (*loukoumades*). A traditional but more expensive alternative to a restaurant/bar in which to purchase breakfast.

Zacharoplasteion (ΖΑΧΑΡΟΠΛΑΣΤΕΙΟΝ) Shops specialising in pastries, cakes (*glyko*), chocolates (which are comparatively expensive) and soft drinks as well as, sometimes, a small selection of alcoholic drinks.

Galaktozacharoplasteion A combination of the two previously described establishments.

Snackbar (ΣΝΑΚ-ΜΠΑΡ, Souvlatzidika & Tyropitadika) Snackbars are not so numerous in the less touristy areas, and are often restricted to one or two in the main town. They represent marvellous value for a stand-up snack and the most popular offering is *souvlaki* – pita bread (or a roll) filled with grilled meat or kebab, (*doner kebab* – slices off the rotating vertical spit of an upturned cone of meat also called *giro*), a slice of tomato, chopped onion and a dressing. Be careful, as souvlaki is not to be muddled with *souvlakia* which, when served at a snackbar, consists of pieces of lamb, pork or veal meat grilled on a wooden skewer and is indistinguishable from *Shish-kebab*, or (guess what) souvlakia when served at a sit-down meal where the metal skewered meat pieces are interspersed with vegetables. Other goodies include *tiropites* – hot flaky pastry pies filled with cream cheese; *boogatsa* – a custard filled pastry; a wide variety of rolls and sandwiches (*sanduits*) with cheese, tomato, salami and other spiced meat fillings as well as toasted sandwiches (*tost*).

This reminds me to point out to readers that if 'toast' is ordered as part of a breakfast it is odds on that a toasted cheese sandwich will be served.

Pavement cafes Serve snacks and sweets.

Pizzerias Seem to be on the increase and are restaurants specialising in the imported Italian dish which prompts one to ask why not go to Italy? To be fair they usually represent very good value and a large serving often feeds two.

Tavernas (ΤΑΒΕΡΝΑ), Restaurants (ΕΣΤΙΑΤΟΡΙΟΝ), Rotisserie (ΨΗΣΤΑΡΙΑ) & Rural Centres (ΕΞΟΧΙΚΟΝ ΚΕΝΤΡΟΝ) Four variations on a theme. The traditional Greek taverna is a family concern, frequently only open in the evening. More often than not, the major part of the eating area is outside, under a vine trellis covered patio, along the pavement and/or on a roof garden.

Restaurants tend to be more sophisticated, possibly open all day and night, but the definition between the two is rather blurred. The price lists may include a chancy English translation, the waiter might be smarter and the tablecloth and napkins could well be linen, in place of the taverna's paper table covering and serviettes.

As tavernas often have a spit-roasting device tacked on, there is little, discernible difference between a rotisserie and a taverna. A grilled meat restaurant may also be styled ΨΗΣΤΑΡΙΑ.

The Rural Centre is a mix of cafe-bar and taverna in, you've guessed it, a rural or seaside setting.

Fish tavernas (ΨΑΡΟΤΑΒΕΡΝΑ) Tavernas specialising in fish dishes.

Hotels (ΞΕΝΟΔΟΧΕΙΟΝ). ΞΕΝΟΔΟΧΕΙΟΝ ΥΠΝΟΥ is a hotel that does not serve food, ΠΑΝΔΟΧΕΙΟΝ, a lower category hotel and XENIA, a Government-owned hotel. Xenias are usually well run, the food and drink international, the menu written in French and the prices reflect all these 'attributes'.

An extremely unpleasant manifestation, to old fogeys like me, is illustrated by one or two menus spotted in the more popular holiday resorts, namely Greek bills of fare set out Chinese restaurant style. You know, set 'Meal A' for two, 'Meal B' for three and 'C' for four and more.....!

THE FOOD
Some of the following represents a selection of the wide variety of menu dishes available.

Sample menu

Ψωμί (Psomi)	Bread
ΠΡΩΙΝΟ	BREAKFAST
Αυγά τηγανιτα με μπέικον και τομάτα	Fried egg, bacon & tomato
Τοστ βούτυρο μαρμελάδα	Buttered toast & marmalade
Το πρόγευμα (to pro-ye-vma)	English (or American on some islands) breakfast
ΑΥΓΑ	EGGS
Μελάτα	soft boiled
Σφικτά	hard boiled
Τηγανιτά	fried
Ποσσέ	poached
ΤΟΣΤ ΣΑΝΤΟΥΙΤΣ	TOASTED SANDWICHES
Τοστ με τυρί	toasted cheese
Τοστ (με) ζαμπόν και τυρί	toasted ham & cheese
Μπούρκερ	burger
Χαμπουρκερ	hamburger
Τσίσμπουρκερ	cheeseburger
Σάντουιτς λουκάνικο	hot dog
ΟΡΕΚΤΙΚΑ	APPETIZERS/HORS D'OEUVRES
Αντσούγιες	anchovies
Ελιές	olives
Σαρδέλλες	sardines
Σκορδαλιά	garlic dip
Τζατζίκι	tzatziki (diced cucumber & garlic in yoghurt)
Ταραμοσαλάτα	taramasalata (a fish roe pate)

ΣΟΥΠΕΣ	SOUPS
Σούπα φασόλια	bean
Αυγολέμονο	egg & lemon
Ψαρόσουπα	fish
Κοτόσουπα	chicken
Ντοματόσουπα	tomato
Σούπα λαχανικών	vegetable

ΟΜΕΛΕΤΕΣ	OMELETTES
Ομελέτα μπέικον	bacon
Ομελέτα μπέικον τυρί τομάτα	bacon, cheese & tomato
Ομελέτα τυρί	cheese
Ομελέτα ζαμπόν	ham
Ομελέτα ουκωτάκια πουλιών	chicken liver

ΣΑΛΑΤΕΣ	SALADS
Ντομάτα Σαλάτα	tomato
Αγγούρι Σαλάτα	cucumber
Αγγουροτομάτα Σαλάτα	tomato & cucumber
Χωριάτικη	Greek peasant village salad

ΛΑΧΑΝΙΚΑ (ΛΑΔΕΡΑ*)	VEGETABLES
Πατάτες	potatoes
Πατάτες Τηγανιτές	chips (french fries)
φρέσκα φασολάκια	green beans
Σπαράγκια	asparagus
Κολοκυθάκια	courgettes
Σπανάκι	spinach

*indicates cooked in oil.

Note various methods of cooking include:

Baked – στο φουρνο; boiled – βραστα; creamed – με αοπρη σαλτοα; fried – τηγανιτα; grilled – οτη σχαρα; roasted – ψητα; spit roasted – σουβλας.

ΚΥΜΑΔΕΣ	MINCED MEATS
Μουσακας	moussaka
Ντοματες Γεμιστες	stuffed tomatoes (with rice or minced meat)
Κεφτεδες	meat balls
Ντολμαδακια	stuffed vine leaves (with rice or minced meat)
Παπουτσακια	stuffed vegetable marrow (rice or meat)
Κανελονια	canelloni
Μακαπονια με κυμα	spaghetti bolognese (more correctly with mince)
Παστιτσιο	macaroni, mince and sauce
Σουβλακι	shish-kebab

PYZI	RICE
Πιλαφι	pilaff
Πιλαφι (με) λιαουπτι	with yoghurt
Πιλαφι συκωτακια	with liver
Σπανακοριζο	with spinach
Πιλαφι κυμα	with minced meat

ΠΟΥΛΕΡΙΚΑ	POULTRY
Κοτοπουλο	chicken, roasted
Ποδι κοτας	leg of chicken
Στηθος κοτας	chicken breast
Κοτοπουλο βραστο	boiled chicken
Ψητο κοτοπουλο οτη σουβλα	spit-roasted chicken

ΚΡΕΑΣ	MEAT
Νεφρα	kidneys
Αρνϊ	lamb†
Αρνισιες Μπριζολες	lamb chops
Παιδακια	lamb cutlets
Συκωτι	liver
Χοιρινδ	pork†
Χοιρινες Μπριζολες	pork chops
Λουκανικα	sausages
Μπιφτεκι	steak (beef)
Μοσχαρισιο	veal
Μοσχαρισιες Μπριζολες	veal chops
Μοσχαρι	grilled veal
Ψητο Μοσχαρακι	roast veal

†often with the prefix/suffix to indicated if roasted or grilled

ΨΑΡΙΑ	FISH
Σκουμπρι	mackerel
Συναγριδα	red snapper
Μαριδες	whitebait
Οκταποδι	octopus
Καλαμαρια	squid
Μπαρμπουνι	red mullet
Κεφαλος	mullet
Αυθρινι	grey mullet

ΤΥΡΙΑ	CHEESE
φετα	feta (goat's-milk based)
Γραβιερα	gruyere-type cheese
Κασερι	cheddar-type (sheep's-milk based)

ΦΠΟΥΤΑ	FRUITS
Καρπουζι	water melon
Πεπονι	melon
Μηλα	apple
Πορτοκαλι	oranges
Σταφυλια	grapes
Κομποστα φρουτων	fruit compote

ΠΑΓΩΤΑ	ICE — CREAM
Σπεσιαλ	special
Παγωτο βανιλλια	vanilla
Παγωτο σοκαλατα	chocolate
Παγωτο λεμονι	lemon
Γρανιτα	water ice

ΓΙΥΚΙΣΜΑΤΑ	DESSERTS
Κεικ	cake
φρουτοσαλατα	fruit salad
Κρεμα	milk pudding
Κρεμ καραμελε	cream caramel
Μπακλαβας	crisp pastry with nuts and syrup or honey
Καταιφι	fine shredded pastry with nuts and syrup or honey
Γαλακτομουρεκο	fine crispy pastry with custard and syrup
Γιαουρτι	yoghurt
Μελι	honey

ΑΝΑΨΥΚΤΙΚΑ	COLD DRINKS/SOFT DRINKS
Πορτοκαλι	orange
Πορτοκαλαδα	orangeade

Λεμονάδα	lemonade made with lemon juice
Γκαζόζα (Gazoza)	fizzy lemonade
Μεταλλικο νερο	mineral water
Κοκα κολα	Coca-cola
Πεψι κολα	Pepsi-cola
Σεβεν-απ	Seven Up
Σοδα	soda
Τονικ	tonic
Νερο (Nero)	water

ΚΑΦΕΔΕΣ — **COFFEES**

Ελληνικος (Καφες)	Greek coffee (sometimes called Turkish coffee ie Τουρκικος Καφε)
σκετο (skehto)	no sugar
μετριο (metrio)	medium sweet
γλυκο (ghliko)	sweet (very)

(Unless stipulated it will turn up 'ghliko'. Do not drink before it has settled.)

Νες καφε	Nescafe
Νες (με γαλα) (Nes me ghala)	Nescafe with milk
Εσπρεσσο	espresso
Καπουτσινο	cappucino
φραπε	chilled coffee is known as 'frappe'
Τσαι	tea
Σοκαλατα γαλα	chocolate milk

ΜΠΥΡΕΣ — **BEERS**

ΦΙΞ (ΕΛΛΑΣ) Μπυρα	Fixed (Hellas) beer
φιαλη	bottle
κουτι	can
ΑΜΣΤΕΛ (Αμστελ)	Amstel
ΧΕΝΝΙΝΓΕΡ (Χεννινγκερ)	Henninger (300g usually a can / 500g usually a bottle)

ΠΟΤΑ — **DRINKS**

Ουζο	Ouzo
Κονιακ	Cognac
Μπραντυ	Brandy
Μεταξα	Metaxa
3 ΑΣΤ	3 star
5 ΑΣΤ	5 star
Ουισκυ	Whisky
Τζιν	Gin
Βοτκα	Vodka
Καμπαρι	Campari
Βερμουτ	Vermouth
Μαρτινι	Martini

ΚΡΑΣΙΑ — **WINES**

Κοκκινο	red
Ασπρο	white
Ποζε Κοκκινελι	rose
Ξερο	dry
Γλυκο	sweet
Ρετσινα	resinated wine
e.g. Θεοκριτος	Theokritos
Αρετσινωτο	unresinated wine
e.g. Δεμεστιχα	Demestica

340g is a ½ bottle 680g is a bottle
950g is a large bottle

Useful Greek

English	Greek	Sounds like
Have you a table for...	Εχετε ενα τραπεζι για	Echete enna trapezee ghia...
I'd like...	Θελω	Thelo...
We would like...	Θελουμε	Thelome...
a beer	μια μπυρα	meah beerah
a glass	ενα ποτηρι	ena poteeree
a carafe	μια καραφα	meea karafa
a small bottle	ενα μικρο μπουκαλι	ena mikro bookalee
a large bottle	ενα μεγαλο	ena meghalo bookalee
bread	ψωμι	psomee
tea with milk	τσαι με γαλα	tsai me ghala
with lemon	τσαι με λεμονι	me lemoni
Turkish coffee (Greek)	Τουρκικος καφε	Tourkikos kafes
sweet	γλυκος	ghleekos
medium	μετριος	metreeo
bitter (no sugar)	πικρο	pikro
Black coffee	Nescafe χωρισ γαλα	Nescafe horis ghala
Coffee with milk	Nescafe με γαλα	Nescafe me ghala
a glass of water	ενα ποτη ρι νερο	enna poteeree nero
a napkin	μια πετσετα	mia petseta
an ashtray	ενα σταχτοδοχειο	enna stachdothocheeo
toothpick	μια οδοντογλυφιδα	mea odontoglifidha
the olive oil	το ελαιολαδο	dho eleolatho
Where is the toilet?	Που ειναι η τουαλεττα	Poo eene i(ee) tooaleta?
What is this?	Τι ειναι αυτο	Ti ine afto
This is...	Αυτο ειναι	Afto eene
cold	κρυο	kreeo
bad	χαλασμενο	chalasmeno
stale	μπαγιατικο	bayhiatiko
undercooked	αψητο	apseeto
overcooked	παραβρασμενο	paravrasmeno
The bill please	Το λογαπιασμο παρακαλω	To loghariasmo parakalo
How much is that?	Ποσο κανει αυτο	Poso kanee afto?
That was an excellent meal	Περιφη μο γευμα	Pereefimo yevma
We shall come again	Θα ξαναρθουμε	Tha xanarthoume

7 Shopping & Public Services

Let your purse be your master Proverb

Purchasing items in Greece is still quite an art form or subject for a degree course. The difficulties have been compounded by the rest of the western world becoming nations of supermarket shoppers, whilst the Greeks have stayed traditionally and firmly with their individual shops, selling a fixed number of items and sometimes only one type of a product.

Shopping for a corkscrew, for instance, might well involve calling at two or three seemingly look-alike ironmongers, but no, they each specialise in certain lines of goods and do not stock any items outside those prescribed, almost as if by holy writ.

Bakers usually have to be diligently searched for and when found are frequently located, tucked away in or behind other shops. A pointer to their presence may well be a pile of blackened, twisted olive wood, stacked up to one side of the entrance, and used to fuel the oven fires.

Cake shops (*Zacharoplasteion*) may sell bottled mineral water (ask for a cold bottle).

The question of good and bad buys is a rather personal matter but the items listed below are highlighted on the basis of value for money and quality. Clothing and accessories that are attractive and represent good value include embroidered peasant dresses, leather sandals, woven bags and furs. Day-to-day items that are inexpensive take in Greek cigarettes, drinks including Ouzo, Metaxa brandy and selected island wines. Suitable gifts for family and friends embraces ceramic plates, sponges, Turkish delight and worry beads (*komboloe*). Disproportionately expensive items include camera film, toiletries, books and playing cards. Do not forget to compare prices and preferably shop in the streets and markets, not in airport and hotel concessionary shops, which are often more expensive.

Try not to run short of change. Everybody else does, including bus conductors, taxi drivers and shops.

Opening Hours

Strict or old fashioned summer shop hours are:
Monday, Wednesday and Saturday: 0830-1400 hrs; Tuesday, Thursday and Friday: 0830-1330 hrs & 1730-2030 hrs.

Generally, during the summer months, shops in tourist areas are open Monday to Saturday from 0800-1300 hours. Then they close until 1700 hours, after which they open again until at least 2030 hours, if not 2200 hours. Sundays and Saints' days are more indeterminate, but there is usually a general shop open, somewhere. In very popular tourist resorts and busy ports, shops often open seven days a week.

Drink

Available either in the markets from delicatessen meat/dairy counters or from 'off-licence' type shops.

Smokers

Imported French, English and American cigarettes are inexpensive, compared with European prices, at between 100 and 120 drs for a packet of 20. Greek cigarettes, which have a distinctive and different taste, are excellent. Try *Karellia*, which cost about 68 drs for a packet of 20 and note that the price is printed around the edge of the packet. Even Greek cigars are almost unheard of on the islands, while in Athens, they cost 10 drs and Dutch cigars work out at about 25 drs each. So, if a cigar-smoker, take along your holiday requirements.

Newspapers & Magazines

The *Athens News* is published daily except Mondays in English and costs 50 drs. Overseas newspapers are available up to 24 hours after the day of publication, but note that all printed matter is comparatively expensive.

Photography (Fotografion – ΦΩΤΟΓΡΑΦΕΙΟΝ)

Photographers should carry all the film possible as, being imported, it is comparatively expensive. To counter the very bright sunlight, when using colour film, blue filters should be fitted to the lens.

Tourist Guides & Maps

Shop around before purchasing, as the difference in price of the island guides can be as much as 150 drs, ie from 200-350 drs. Island maps cost between 80-100 drs.

Some major ports and towns have one authentic, well stocked bookshop, usually positioned a little off the town centre. The proprietor often speaks adequate English and courteously answers most enquiries.

SHOPS
Bakers & Bread Shops (ΑΡΤΟΠΟΙΕΙΟΝ, ΑΡΤΟΠΩΛΕΙΟΝ or ΠΡΑΤΗΡΙΟΝ ΑΡΤΟΥ)

For some obscure reason bakers are nearly always difficult to locate, being hidden away, and bread shops tend to be few and far between. Bakers may also sell cheese and meat pies. They are almost always closed on Sundays and all holidays, despite the ovens often being used by the local community to cook their Sunday dinners.

The method of purchasing bread can prove disconcerting, especially when sold by weight. Sometimes the purchaser selects the loaf and then pays but the most bewildering system is where it is necessary to pay first then collect the goods. Difficult if the shopper's level of Greek is limited to grunts, "thank you" and "please"!

Greek bread also has another parameter of measure, that is a graduation in hours – 1 hour, 4 hours and so on. After the period is up, it is usually completely inedible, having transmogrified into a rock-like substance.

Butcher (ΚΡΕΟΠΩΛΕΙΟΝ)

Similar to those at home but the cuts are quite different (surely the Common Market can legislate against this deviation!).

Galaktopoleio *et al.*

See CHAPTER 6

Markets

The smaller ports and towns may have a market street and the larger municipalities often possess a market building. This is thronged with locals and all the basic necessities can be procured inexpensively. Fruit and vegetable stalls are interspaced by butchers and dairy delicatessen shops. During business hours, the proprietors are brought coffee and a glass of water by waiters carrying the cups and glasses, not on open trays, but in round, aluminium salvers with a deep lid, held under a large ring handle, connected to the tray by three flat arms.

Supermarkets (ΥΠΕΡΑΓΟΡΑ/ΣΟΥΠΕΡΜΑΡΚΕΤ)

Very much on the increase and based on smalltown, self-service stores but not to worry, they inherit all those delightful, native Greek qualities including quiet chaos.

Speciality Shops

Found in some big towns and Athens while pavement browsing. The little basement shops are espied down flights of steps, specialising, for instance, in dried fruit, beans, nuts and grains.

Street Kiosks (Periptero/ΠΕΡΙΠΤΕΡΟ)

These unique, pagoda-like huts stay open remarkably long hours, often from early morning to after midnight.they sell a wide range of goods including newspapers, magazines (surprisingly sometimes pornographic literature), postcards, tourist maps, postage stamps, sweets, chocolates, cigarettes and matches. Additionally they form the outlet for the pay phone system and, at the cost of 5 drs, a local call may be made. It is rather incongruous, to observe a Greek making a possibly important business call, in amongst a rack of papers and magazines, with a foreground of jostling pedestrians and a constant stream of noisy traffic in the background.

Alternate Ways of Shopping

Then there are the other ways of shopping: from handcarts, their street-vendor owners selling respectively nuts, ice-cream, milk and yoghurt; from the back of a donkey with vegetable-laden panniers or from two wheeled trailers drawn by fearsome sounding, agricultural rotovator power units. Often the donkey or powered trailer has an enormous set of scales mounted on the back end, swinging like a hangman's scaffold.

If the vegetable/fruit is being sold by 'gypsy-types' then it is advisable to only purchase from those who have their prices written up, usually on a piece of cardboard. Even Anne admits to being ripped off by a roadside banana seller and advises that they are frequently prosecuted for breaking the law.

Frequently used shops include:
ΒΙΒΛΙΟΠΩΛΕΙΟΝ – Bookshop; ΙΧΘΥΟΠΩΛΕΙΟΝ – Fishmonger; ΟΠΩΡΟΠΩΛΕΙΟΝ – Greengrocer; ΠΑΝΤΟΠΩΛΕΙΟΝ – Grocer; ΚΑΠΝΟΠΩΛΕΙΟΝ – Tobacconist. Readers may observe that the above all have a similar ending and it is worth noting that shop titles that terminate in 'ΠΩΛΕΙΟΝ/Πωλειο' are selling something, if that's any help.

SERVICES
The Banks (ΤΡΑΠΕΖΑ)

The minimum opening hours are 0800 to 1330 hrs, Monday to Thursday and 0800 to 1300 hrs on Friday. Some banks, in the most tourist ravaged spots, open on Saturday and a very few on Sunday. Smaller towns, villages or for that matter islands do not have a bank in which case there may be a local money changer acting as agent for this or that National Bank. Do not forget that a passport is almost always required to change travellers' cheques. In the larger cities, personal cheques may be changed at a selected bank when backed by a Eurocheque (or similar) bank guarantee card. A commission charge of between 50 and 150 drs is made, depending on the size of the transaction. Whereas Eurocheques used to be changed in sums up to £50, English sterling, the arrangement now is that a cheque can be cashed in drachmae, up to 17,000 drs. As the charges for changing cheques are based on a sliding scale weighted against smaller amounts, this new arrangement helps save on fees.

The service is generally discourteous and only one employee, if at all, reluctantly speaks English so make sure the correct bank is selected to carry out a particular transaction (such as changing a personal cheque). Each bank displays a window sticker giving an indication of the tourist services transacted. There is nothing worse, after queuing for half an hour or so, than to be rudely told to go away. I once chose the wrong bank to change a personal cheque, only to receive a loud blast of abuse about some long-departed foreigner's bouncing cheque. Most embarrassing.

The larger hotels transact traveller's cheques, but naturally enough at a disadvantageous rate compared with the banks.

Another interesting source of taking currency abroad, for United Kingdom residents, is to use National Giro Post Office cheques which can be cashed at any Post Office in Greece. This is a very useful wheeze, especially on busy tourist islands where foreign currency desks are usually subject to long queues. Detailed arrangements have to be made with the International branch of Giro.

Whilst discoursing on the subject of Post Offices, they now offer a surprisingly wide variety of banking services, for which see below. This is exceptionally helpful on an island where there are no banking services.

The basis of Greek currency is the drachmae. This is nominally divided into 100 lepta and occasionally price lists show a price of, say 62.60 drs. As prices are rounded up (or down), in practice the lepta is not now encountered. Notes are in denominations of 50, 100, 500, and 1000 drs and coins in denominations of 1 and 2 drs (bronze), 5, 10 and 20 and 50 drs (nickel). Do not run out of change, it is always in demand. Repetitious I know, but well worth remembering.

Museums
The following is a mean average of the information to hand but each museum is likely to have its own peculiarities. In the summer season (1st April – 31st October) they open daily 0845-1500/1900 hrs, Sundays and holidays 0930-1430/1530 hrs and are closed Mondays or Tuesdays. They are closed 1st January, 25th March, Good Friday, Easter holiday and 25th December. Admission costs range from free to 100/150 drs, whilst Sundays and holidays are very occasionally free.
free.

The Post Office (ΤΑΧΥΔΡΟΜΕΙΟΝ/ΕΛΤΑ)
Stamps can be bought from kiosks (at a commission) and shops selling postcards as well as from the Post Offices. Post boxes are scattered around, are usually painted yellow, are rather small in size and often difficult to find, being fixed, high up, on side-street walls. In 1986 postage rates for cards to the United Kingdom were 27 drs for a small card and 35 drs for a large one.

Most major town Post Offices are modern and the service received is only slightly less rude than that handed out by bank staff. When confronted by two letter-box openings, the inland service is marked ΕΣΩΤΕΡΙΚΟΥ/Εσωτερικου and the overseas ΕΞΩΤΕΡΙΚΟΥ/Εξωτερικου. Letters can be sent for poste restante collection, but a passport will be required for them to be handed over.

Post Offices are usually only open Monday to Friday between 0730-2030 hrs for stamps, money orders and registered mail; 0730-2000 hrs for poste restante and 0730-1430 hrs for parcels. Parcels have to be collected.

In recent years the range of Post Office services has been expanded to include cashing Eurocheques and Travellers cheques as well as changing currency. All but the most out of the way island offices now offer these facilities. *See* **Banks.**

Telephone Office (OTE)
A separate organisation from the Post Office and to accomplish an overseas or long-distance call it is necessary to go to the OTE office. Here there are separate booths from which to make calls but busy offices usually suffer from long queues. The

counter clerk indicates which compartment is to be used and, in a bank, alongside him are mounted the instruments to meter the cost. Payment is made after completion of the call at a current rate of 3½ drs per unit so ensure that the meter is zeroed prior to making a connection. Opening days and hours vary enormously. Smaller offices may only open weekdays for say 7 hours between 0830-1530 hrs whilst the larger city offices open 24 hours a day, seven days a week.

Overseas dialling codes		Inland services	
Australia	0061	Directory enquiries	131
Canada & USA	001	Provincial enquiries	132
New Zealand	0064	General Information	134
South Africa	0027	Time	141
United Kingdom & Ireland	0044	Medical care	166
Other overseas countries	161	City police	100
		Gendarmerie	109
		Fire	199
		Tourist police	171
		Roadside assistance	104
		Telegrams/cables	165

To dial England, drop the '0' from all four figure codes. Thus making a call to, say Portsmouth, for which the code is 0705, dial 00 44 705 ....

The internal service is both very good and reasonably priced. Local telephone calls cost 5 drs and can be made from some bars and the pavement kiosks (periptero). The presence of a telephone is often indicated by the sign ΕΔΩ ΤΗΛΕΦΩΝΕΙΤΕ, a blue background denotes a local phone, and an orange one, an inter-city phone. Another sign, Εδω Τηλεφωνειτε (the lower case equivalent), signifies 'telephone from here'. The method of operation is to insert the coin and dial. If a connection cannot be made, place the receiver back on the cradle and the money is returned.

Telegrams may be sent from either the OTE or Post Office.

Useful Greek

English	Greek
Stamps	ΓΡΑΜΜΑΤΟΣΗΜΑ
Parcels	ΔΕΜΑΤΑ

Useful Greek

English	Greek	Sounds like
Where is...	Που ειναι	Poo eenne...
Where is the nearest...	Που ειναι η πλησιεστερη	Poo eene i pleesiesteri
baker	ο φουρναρης/ψωμας/	foornaris/psomas/
bakery	Αρτοποιειον	artopieeon
bank	η τραπεζα	i(ee) trapeza
bookshop	το βιβλιοπωλειο	to vivleeopolieo
butchers shop	το χασαπικο	dho hasapiko
chemist shop	το φαρμακειο	to farmakio
dairy shop	το γαλακτοπωλειο	galaktopolieon
doctor	ο γιατρος	o yiahtros
grocer	το μπακαλης	o bakalis
hospital	το νοσοκομειο	to nosokomio
laundry	το πλυντηριο	to plintirio, (plintireeo), since i = ee
liquor store	το ποτοπωλειο	to potopolio (potopoleeo)
photographic shop	το φωτογραφειο	to fotoghrafeeo
post office	το ταχυδρομειο	to tahkithromio

shoe repairer	το τσαγκαραδικο	to tsangkaradiko
tailor	ο ραπτης	o raptis
Have you any...	Εχετε	Ekheteh...
Do you sell...	Πουλατε	Poulate...
How much is this...	Ποσο κανει αυτο	Posso kanee afto...
I want...	Θελω	Thelo...
half kilo/a kilo	μισο κιλο/ενα κιλο	miso kilo/ena kilo
aspirin	η ασπιρινη	aspirini
apple(s)	το μηλο/μηλα	meelo/meela
banana(s)	η μπανανα/μπανανες	banana/bananes
bread	το ψωμι	psomee
butter	το βουτυρο	vutiro
cheese	το τυρι	tiree
cigarettes (filter tip)	το τσιγαρο (με φιλτρο)	to tsigharo (me filtro)
coffee	καφες	cafes
cotton wool	το βαμβακι	to vambaki
crackers	τα κρακερακια	krackerakia
crisps	τσιπς	tsseeps
cucumbers	το αγγουρι	anguree
disinfectant	το απολυμαντικο	to apolimantiko
guide book	ο τουριστικος οδηγος	o touristikos odhigos
ham	το ζαμπον	zambon
ice cream	το παγωτο	paghoto
lemons	το λεμονια	lemonia
lettuce	το μαρουλι	to marooli
map	το χαρτης	o khartis
a box of matches	ενα κουτι σπιρτα	ena kuti spirta
milk	το γαλα	to ghala
pate	πατε	pate
(ball point) pen	το μπικ	to bik
pencil	το μαλυβι	to molivi
pepper	το πιπερι	to piperi
(safety) pins	μια παραμανα	mia (meea) paramana
potatoes	οι πατατες	patates
salad	η σαλατα	i salatah
salami	το σαλαμι	salahmi
sausages	το λουκανικα	lukahniko
soap	το σαπουνι	to sapooni
spaghetti	σπαγγετο	spayehto
string	ο σπαγκος	o spangos
sugar	η ζαχαρη	i zakhahree
tea	το τσαι	to tsai
tomatoes	η ντοματες	domahdes
toothbrush	η οδοντοβουρτσα	odhondovourtsa
toothpaste	η οδοντοχρεμα	odhondokrema
writing paper	το χαρτι γραψιματος	to kharti grapsimatos

8 Greece: History, Mythology, Religion, Present-day Greece, Greeks & their Holidays

All ancient histories, as one of our fine wits said, are but fables that have been accepted. Voltaire

HISTORY

Excavations have shown the presence of Palaeolithic man up to 100,000 years ago. Greece's history and mythology are, like the Greek language, formidable to say the least, with legend, myth, folk tales, fables and religious lore often inextricably mixed up. Archaeologists are now finding that some mythology is in fact based on historical fact. For instance the great Minoan civilisation centred on Crete, which may well have been the fabled Atlantis of pre-history, was mysteriously and suddenly destroyed. Recent, informed speculation leads to the conclusion that about 1700 BC a vast volcanic eruption, presumed to be centred on the island of Santorini (Thira) in the Cyclades, destroyed this flourishing and far reaching culture.

Historically Greeks fought Greeks, Phoenicians and Persians. Under Alexander the Great they conquered Egypt and vast tracts of Asia Minor. Then they were in turn conquered by the Romans. After the splitting of the Roman Kingdom into Western and Eastern Empires, the Greeks, with Constantinople as their capital, were ruled by the Eastern offshoot, only to fall into the hands of the Franks about AD 1200, followed by the Turks. The Venetians, Genoese and finally the Turks ruled most of the islands.

In 1821 the War of Independence commenced, which eventually led to the setting up of a Parliamentary Republic in 1928. Incidentally, Thessaly, Crete and the Dodecanese islands remained under Turkish rule. By the time the Dodecanese islanders had thrown out the Turks, the Italians had taken over. If you are now confused, give up, because it gets even more difficult to follow.

The Greek monarchy, which had come into being in 1833, and was related to the German Royal family, opted in 1913 to side with the Axis powers. The chief politician Eleftherios Venizelos, disagreed, was dismissed and set up a rival government, after which the King, under Allied pressure, retired to Switzerland. In the years following the end of the First World War, the Turks and Greeks agreed, after some fairly bloody fighting, to exchange a total of one and a half million people.

In 1936 a General Metaxas became dictator. He achieved immortal fame by booting out Mussolini's representative, when in 1940, Mussolini demanded permission for Italy's troops to traverse Greece, and received the famous *Ochi* (No). (This day has become a national festival known as *Ochi Day*, celebrated on 28th October.) The Italians demurred and marched on Greece, the soldiers of whom, to the surprise of everybody including themselves, reinforced the refusal by routing them. The Italians were only saved from total humiliation by the intervention of the Germans, who then occupied Greece for the duration of the Second World War. At the end of hostilities, all the Italian held Greek islands were reunited with mainland Greece.

As German ascendancy declined, the Greek freedom fighters split into royalist and communist factions and proceeded to knock even more stuffing out of each other than they had out of the Germans. Until the British intervention, followed by large injections of American money and weapons, it looked as if Greece would go behind the Iron Curtain. A second civil war broke out between 1947 and 1949 and this internal strife was reputed to have cost more Greek lives than were lost during the whole of the Second World War.

In 1951, Greece and Turkey became full members of NATO, but the issue of the ex-British colony of Cyprus was about to rear its ugly head, with the resultant, renewed estrangement between Greece and Turkey.

The various political manoeuvrings, the involvement of the Greek monarchy in domestic affairs and the worsening situation in Cyprus, led to the *coup d'etat* by the Colonel's Junta in 1967, soon after which King Constantine II and his entourage fled to Italy. The Colonel's extremely repressive dictatorship was, seemingly, actively supported by the Americans and condoned by Britain. Popular countrywide feeling and, in particular, student uprisings between 1973-1974, which were initially put down in Athens by brutal tank attacks, led to the eventual collapse of the regime in 1974. In the death-throes of their rule, the Colonels, using the Cyprus dream to distract the ordinary people's feeling of injustice, meddled and attempted to overthrow the vexatious priest, President Makarios. The net result was that the Turks invaded Cyprus and made an enforced division of that unhappy, troubled island.

In 1974, Greece returned to republican democracy and in 1981 joined the EEC.

RELIGION

The Orthodox Church prevails everywhere but there are small pockets of Roman Catholicism as well as very minor enclaves of Muslims on the Dodecanese islands and mainland western Thrace. The schism within the Holy Roman Empire, in 1054, caused the Catholic Church to be centred on Rome and the Orthodox Church on Constantinople.

The Turkish overlords encouraged the continuation of the indigenous church, probably to keep their bondsmen quiet, but it had the invaluable side effect of keeping alive Greek customs and traditions during the centuries of occupation.

The bewildering profusion of small churches, scattered 'indiscriminately' all over the islands, is not proof of the church's wealth, although the Greek people are not entirely convinced of that fact. It is evidence of the piety of the families or individuals who paid to have them erected, in the name of their selected patron saint, as thanksgiving for God's protection. The style of religious architecture changes between the island groups.

Many churches only have one service a year, on the name day of the particular patron saint, and this ceremony is named *Viorti* or *Panayieri*. It is well worth attending one of these self-indulgent extravaganzas to observe and take part in celebratory village religious life and music. One and all are welcome to the carnival festivities which include eating and dancing in, or adjacent to, the particular churchyard.

The words Byzantine and Byzantium crop up frequently with especial reference to churches and appertain to the period between the forth and fourteenth centuries AD. During this epoch Greece was, at least nominally, under the control of Constantinople (Instanbul), built by the Emperor Constantine on the site of the old city of Byzantium. Religious paintings executed on small wooden panels during this period are called ikons. Very, very few original ikons remain available for purchase, so beware if offered an apparent 'bargain'.

When visiting a church, especially noticeable are the pieces of shining, thin metal, placed haphazardly around or pinned to wooden carvings. These *tamata* or *exvotos* represent limbs or portions of the human body and are purchased by worshippers as an offering, in the hope of an illness being cured and/or limbs healed.

GREEKS

In making assessment o the Greek people and their character, it must be remembered that, perhaps even more so than the Spaniards or the Portuguese, Greece has only recently emerged into the twentieth century. Unlike other countries 'discovered' in the 1960s by the holiday industry they have not, in the main, degraded or debased their principles or character, despite the onrush of tourist wealth. For a people to have had so little and to face so much demand for European 'necessities', would have strained a less hardy and well-balanced people.

Greece's recent emergence into the western world is evidenced by the still patriarchal nature of their society, a view supported, for instance, by the oft-seen spectacle of men lazing in the tavernas whilst their womenfolk work in the fields (and why not?).

Often the smallest village, on the remotest island, has an English-speaking islander who lived abroad at some time in his life, earning a living through seafaring, as a hotel waiter, or as a taxi driver. Thus, while making an escape from the comparative poverty at home, for a period of good earnings in the more lucrative world, a working knowledge of English, American or Australian will have been gained. *Greek strine*, or as usually contracted *grine*, simply has to be heard to be believed.

The greatest hurdle to understanding is undoubtedly the language barrier, especially if it is taken into account that the Greeks appear to have some difficulty with their own language in its various forms. Certainly, they seem, on occasions, not to understand each other and the subject matter has to be repeated a number of times. Perhaps that is the reason for all the shouting!

There can be no doubt that the traditional Greek welcome to the *xenos* or *singrafeus*, now increasingly becoming known as *touristas* has, naturally, become rather lukewarm in the more 'besieged' areas. It is often difficult to reconcile the shrugged shoulders of a seemingly disinterested airline official or bus driver, with being stopped in the street by a gold-toothed, smiling Greek proffering some fruit. But remember the bus driver may realise the difficulty of overcoming the language barrier, it is very hot, he has been working long hours earning his living and he is not on holiday.

Sometimes a drink appears mysteriously at one's taverna table, the donor being indicated by a nod of the waiter's head, but a word of warning here. Simply smile and accept the gift graciously. Any attempt to return the kindness by 'putting one in the stable' for your new found friend only results in a 'who buys last' competition which will surely be lost. I know, I am speaking from battle-weary experience. Greeks are very welcoming and may well invite a tourist to their table. But do not expect more, they are reserved and have probably had previous unhappy experiences of ungrateful, rude, overseas visitors.

To look over churches or monasteries visitors must ensure they are adequately covered, including legs and arms, and should note that many religious establishments strictly apply the rules. It seems a pity for a tourist to have made a special excursion, sometimes involving arduous walking, only to be turned away at the gate. Men must wear a shirt and trousers, not shorts, and women a modest blouse, skirt and take a head scarf, it might be required.

Women tourists can travel quite freely in Greece without fear, except from other tourists. On the other hand females should not wear provocative attire or fail to wear sufficient clothing when in close social contact with Greek men, who might well be inflamed into action, or Greek women, whom it will offend, probably because of the effect on their men! Certainly all the above was the case until very recently but the constant stream of 'available' young tourist ladies on the more popular islands, has resulted in the local lads taking both a 'view' and a chance. It almost reminds one of the Costa Brava in the early 1960s. The disparate moral qualities of the native and tourist females is resulting in a conundrum for young Greek wormen. To compete for their men's affections they have to loosen their principles with an unheard of and steadily increasing number of speedily arranged marriages, if you know what I mean.

Do not miss the *Volta* (Βολτα), the traditional family evening walkabout on city, town and village square. Dressed for the event, an important part of the ritual is for the family to show off their marriageable daughters. Good fun and great watching, but the Greeks are rather protective of their family and all things Greek... you may comment favourably, but keep adverse criticism to yourself.

It is interesting to speculate on the influence of the early Greek immigrants on American culture, especially when considering the American habit of serving water with every meal, the ubiquitous hamburger (which is surely a poorly reproduced and inferior souvlaki) and some of the official uniforms, more particularly the flat peaked hats of American postmen and policemen.

THE GREEK NATIONAL HOLIDAYS

Listed below are the national holidays and on these days many areas and islands hold festivals, but with a particular slant and emphasis.

1st January	New Year's Day/The Feast of Saint Basil
6th January	Epiphany/Blessing of the Waters – a cross is immersed in the sea, lake or river during a religious ceremony
The period 27th Jan to 17th February	The Greek Carnival Season
25th March	The Greek National Anniversary/Independence Day
April – Movable days	Good Friday/Procession of the 'Epitaph'; Holy Week Saturday/Ceremony of the Resurrection; Easter Sunday/open air feasts
1st May	May/Labour Day/Feast of the Flowers
1st to 10th July	Greek Navy Week
15th August	Assumption Day/Festival of the Virgin Mary, especially in the Cycladian island of Tinos (beware travelling at this time, anywhere in the area)
28th October	National Holiday/'Ochi' Day
24th December	Christmas Eve/carols evening
25th December	Christmas Day
26th December	St Stephen's Day
31st December	New Year's Eve carols, festivals

In addition to these national days, each island has its own particular festivals and holidays which are listed individually under each island description. Many island churches only have one service a year.

A word of warning to ferry-boat travellers will not go amiss here – DO NOT travel to an island immediately prior to one of these festivals NOR off the island immediately after the event. It will be almost impossible to do other than stand, that is if one has not already been trampled to death in the various stampedes to and from the ferry-boats.

PART TWO
9 ATHENS CITY (ATHINA, AΘHNAI)

There is no end of it in this city, wherever you set your foot, you encounter some memory of the past. Marcus Cicero

Tel. prefix 01

The capital of Greece and major city of Attica. Previously the springboard for travel to most of the Greek islands, but less so since a number of direct flights have become available to the larger islands. Experienced travellers flying into Athens airport, often try to arrange their arrival for early morning and head straight for either West airport (for a domestic flight), Piraeus port, the railway station or bus terminal, so as to be able to get under way immediately.

ARRIVAL BY AIR
International flights other than Olympic Airways land at the:

East airport
Public transport facilities include:
Bus No. 18:   East airport to Leoforos Amalias. Every 20 mins from 0600-2400 hrs.
                Fare 80 drs. Yellow express bus.
Bus No. 121:   East airport to Leoforos Olgas. 0650-2250 hrs. Fare 80 drs.
Bus No. 19:   East airport to Plateia Karaiskaki/Akti Tselepi, Piraeus.
                Every hour from 0800-2000 hrs. Fare 80 drs. Yellow express bus.
Bus No. 101:   East airport via Leoforos Possidonos (coast road) to Klisovis/Theotoki St, Piraeus.
                Every 20 mins from 0500-2245 hrs. Fare 30 drs.

Domestic and all Olympic flights land at the:

West airport
Public transport facilities include:
Bus No. 133:   West airport to Leoforos Square, Leoforos Amalias, Filellinon & Othonos Streets
                (Syntagma Sq). Every ½ hour from 0530-0030 hrs. Fare 30 drs. Blue bus.
Bus No. 122:   West airport to Leoforos Olgas. Every 20 mins. Fare 30 drs. Blue bus.
Buses No.
107 & 109:   West airport via Leoforos Possidonos (coast road) to Klisovis St, Piraeus.

In addition there are Olympic buses connecting West and East airports as well as Olympic buses from the West airport to the Olympic offices (*Tmr* 12C6) on Leoforos Sygrou and Syntagma Square. Every 20 mins between 0600-2000 hrs. Fare 100 drs.

ARRIVAL BY BUS
Inter-country coaches usually decant passengers at Syntagma Sq (*Tmr* 1D/E4/5), Stathmos Larissis Station (*Tmr* B/C1), or close to one of the major city bus terminals.

ARRIVAL BY FERRY
See **Piraeus**, CHAPTER 10

ARRIVAL BY TRAIN
See **Trains, A to Z.**

GENERAL (Illustrations 4 & 5)
Even if a traveller is a European city dweller, Athens will come as a sociological and

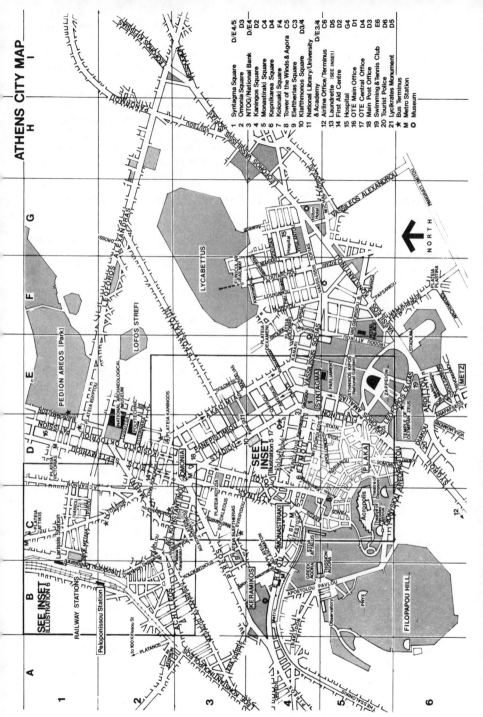

Illustration 4　Athens City

1	Syntagma Square	D/E.4/5
2	Omonia Square	D3
3	NTOG/National Bank	D/E.4
4	Kaningos Square	D2
5	Monastiraki Square	C4
6	Kapnikarea Square	D4
7	Kolonaki Square	F4
8	Tower of the Winds & Agora	C5
9	Eleftherias Square	C3
10	Klafthmonos Square	D3/4
11	National Library/University & Academy	D/E.3/4
12	Airline Office/Terminus	C6
13	Laundrette　(SEE INSET)	D5
14	First Aid Centre	D2
15	Hospital	G4
16	OTE Main Office	D1
17	OTE Central Office	D4
18	Main Post Office	D3
19	Swimming & Tennis Club	E6
20	Tourist Police	D6
21	Lycikrates Monument	D5
★	Museum	
M	Metro Station	
O		

cultural shock to the system. In the summer it is a hot, dusty, dry, crowded, traffic-bound, exhaust polluted bedlam, but always friendly, cosmopolitan and ever on the move.

On arrival in Athens, and planning to stay over, it is best to select the two main squares of Syntagma (*Tmr* 1D/E4/5) and Omonia (*Tmr* 2 D3). These can be used as centres for the initial sally and from which to radiate out to the other squares or plateias.

There is no substitute for a city map which is issued free (yes free) from the Tourist Board desk in the National Bank of Greece on Syntagma Sq (*Tmr* 3, D/E4). *See* **NTOG, A to Z.**

Syntagma Square (Constitution or Parliament Square) (*Tmr* 1D/E4/5). The airport and many other buses stop off here. It is the city centre with the most elite hotels, airline offices, international companies, including the American Express headquarters, smart cafes and the Parliament building all circumscribing the central, sunken square. In the bottom right-hand (or south-east) corner of the plateia, bounded by Odhos Othonos and Leoforos Amalias, are some very clean, attendant minded toilets. There is a charge for the use of the 'squatties'.

To orientate, the Parliament building and Monument to the Unknown Warrior lie to the east of the square. To the north-east, in the middle distance, is one of the twin hills of Athens, Mt Lycabettus (Lykavittos). The other hill is the Acropolis, to the south-west, and not now visible from Syntagma Sq due to high-rise buildings. On the west side of the square are the offices of American Express and a battery of pavement cafes, with Ermou St leading due west to Monastiraki Sq. To the north are the two parallel, main avenues of Stadiou (a one-way street down to Syntagma) and Venizelou or Panepistimiou (a one-way street out of Syntagma) that both run north-west to:

Omonia Square (Concorde or Harmony Square) (*Tmr* 2D3) The 'Piccadilly Circus' or 'Times Square' of Athens but rather tatty really, with a constant stream of traffic bludgeoning its way round the large central island crowned by an impressive fountain. Visitors trying to escape the human bustle on the pavements by stepping off into the kerbside should beware that they are not mown down by a bus, taxi or private car.

Constant activity night and day, with seemingly every nationality cheek by jowl, lends the square a cosmopolitan character all of its own. On every side are hotels, varying from the downright seedy to the better-class tawdry, housed in rather undistinguished, 'neo-city-municipal' style, nineteenth century buildings, almost unique to Athens.

Various Metro train entrance/exits emerge around the square, similar to air raid shelters, spewing out and sucking in travellers. The Omonia underground concourse has a Post Office, telephones, a Bank and, by the Dorou St entrance, a block of 'squatty' toilets for which the attendant charges 10 drs for 2 sheets of paper.

Shops, cafes and booths fill the gaps between the hotels and the eight streets that converge on the Square.

To the north-east side of Omonia, on the corner of Dorou St, is a taxi rank and beyond, on the right, a now rather squalid, covered arcade brimful of reasonably priced snackbars. Through this covered passageway, and turning to the left up 28 Ikosiokto Oktovriou (28th October St)/Patission St, and then right down Veranzerou St, leads to:

Kaningos Square (*Tmr* 4D2) Serves as a Bus terminal for some routes.

To the south of Omonia Sq is Athinas St, the commercial thoroughfare of Athens. Here every conceivable item imaginable, including ironmongery, tools, crockery and clothing, can be purchased, and parallel to which, for half its length, runs Odhos Sokratous, the city street market during the day and the red-light district by night. Athinas St drops due south to:

Monastiraki Square (*Tmr* 5C4) This marks the northernmost edge of the area known as the **Plaka** (*Tmr* D5) bounded by Ermou St to the north, Filellinon St to the east, and to the south by the slopes of the Acropolis.

Many of the alleys in this area follow the course of the old Turkish streets, most of the houses are mid-nineteenth century and represent the 'Old Quarter'.

Climbing the twisting maze of streets and steps of the lower north-east slopes of the Acropolis requires the stamina of a mountain goat. The almost primitive, island-village nature of some of the houses is very noticeable, due, it is said, to a Greek law passed after Independence. This was enacted to alleviate a housing shortage and allowed anyone who could raise the roof of a building, between sunrise and sunset, to finish it off and own the dwelling. Some inhabitants of the Cyclades island of Anafi (Anaphe) were reputed to have been the first to benefit from this new law and others followed to specialise in restoration and rebuilding, thus bringing about a colony of expatriate islanders within the Plaka district.

From the south-west corner of Monastiraki Sq, Ifestou St and its associated byways house the Flea Market, which climaxes on Sunday into stall upon stall of junk, souvenirs, junk, hardware, junk, boots, junk, records, junk, clothes, junk, footwear, junk, pottery and junk. Where Ifestou becomes Odhos Astigos and curves round to join up with Ermou St, there are a couple of extensive secondhand bookshops with reasonably priced (for Greece that is), if battered, paperbacks for sale. From the south-east corner of Monastiraki, Pandrossou St, one of the only enduring reminders of the Turkish Bazaar, contains a better class of antique dealer, sandal and shoe makers, and pottery stores.

Due south of Monastiraki Sq is Odhos Areos, unfortunately the first 100m or so of which is now host to a raggle-taggle band of European and Japanese drop-outs selling junk trinkets from the pavement kerb. They seem to have driven out the original stallholders and shop keepers on this stretch. Climbing Odhos Areos skirts the Roman Agora, from which various streets lead upwards, on ever upwards, containing a plethora of stalls and shops, specialising in leather goods, clothes and souvenirs. The further you climb, the cheaper the goods become. This interestingly enough does not apply to the tavernas and restaurants which seemingly become more expensive as one ascends.

The 'chatty' area known as the **Plaka** is 'littered' with eating places, a few good, some bad, some tourist rip-offs. The liveliest street, Odhos Kidathineon, is jam-packed with cafes, tavernas and restaurants and at night is bestrewn with music-playing layabouts. The class, tone and price of the establishments improves proceeding in a north-eastwards direction. I have to admit to gently knocking the Plaka over the years but it must be acknowledged that the area offers the cheapest accommodation and eating places in Athens and generally appears to have been cleaned up in recent times. In fact, since the 1986 'Libyan' downturn in American tourists, the area has become positively attractive. Early and late in the year the Plaka returns to being a super place to visit. The shopkeepers become human, shopping is inexpensive and the tavernas revert to being 'Greek' and lively. In the last 3 weeks of

February the *Apokria Festival*, a long running 'Halloween' style carnival, is centred on the Plaka. The streets are filled with dozens of revellers dressed in fancy dress, masks and funny hats wandering about, throwing confetti, and creating a marvellous atmosphere. For this event all the tavernas are decorated.

To the east of Monastiraki Sq is Ermou St which is initially lined by clothes and shoe shops. One third of the way towards Syntagma Sq and Odhos Ermou opens out into a small square on which there is the lovely Church of Kapnikarea (*Tmr* 6D4). Continuing eastwards, the shops become smarter with a preponderance of fashion stores whilst parallel to Ermou St is Odhos Ploutonos Kteka, which becomes Odhos Mitropoleos. Facing east, on the right is the city's Greek Orthodox Cathedral, Greek Mitropolis. The Church was built about 1850, from the materials of 70 old churches, to the design of four different architects resulting, not unnaturally, in a building of a rather 'strange' appearance. Alongside and to the south is the diminutive medieval Church, Little Mitropolis or Agios Eleftherios, dating back to at least the twelfth century but which has materials, reliefs and building blocks probably originating from the sixth century AD. A little further on is the intriguing and incongruous site of a small Byzantine church, built over and around by a modern office block, the columns of which tower above and beside the tiny building.

Leaving Syntagma Sq by the north-east corner, along Vassilissis Sofias, and turning left at Odhos Irodou Attikou, runs into:

Kolonaki Square (*Tmr* 7F4) The most fashionable square in the most fashionable area of Athens, around which most of the foreign embassies are located. *The British Council* is located on the square, as are some relatively expensive cafes, restaurants and boutiques.

To the north of Kolonaki, across the pretty orange tree planted Dexameni Sq, is the southernmost edge of **Mt Lycabettus** (*Tmr* F/G3). Access to the summit can be made on foot, by a number of steep paths, the main one of which, a stepped footpath, advances from the north end of Loukianou St, beyond Odhos Kleomenous. A little to the east, at the top of Ploutarchou St, which breaks into a sharply rising flight of steps, is the cable car funicular railway. This runs in a 700ft long tunnel, emerging near to the nineteenth-century chapel, which caps the fir tree-covered mountain, alongside a modern and luxuriously expensive restaurant. There are also some excellent toilets. The railway service runs continuously as follows:
Winter: Wednesday, Saturday, Sunday 0845-0015 hrs; Thursday 1030-0015 hrs; Monday, Tuesday, Friday 0930-0015 hrs.
Summer: As for winter but opening hours extend to 0100 hrs every day. The trip costs 65 drs one-way and 100 drs for a return ticket.

A more relaxed climb, passing the open air theatre, can be made from the north end of Lycabettus.

The topmost part of the mountain, where the funicular emerges, is surprisingly small if not doll-like. The spectacular panorama that spreads out to the horizon, the stupendous views from far above the roar of the Athens traffic, is best seen in the early morning or late afternoon. Naturally the night hours are the time to see the city's lights.

Leaving Plateia Kolonaki from the south corner and turning right at Vassilissis Sofias, sally's forth to the north corner of:-

The National Garden (Ethnikos Kipos) (*Tmr* E5) Here peacocks, waterfowl and songbirds blend with a profusion of shrubbery, subtropical trees, ornamental ponds, various busts and cafe tables through and around which thread neat gravel paths.

To the south of the gardens are the Zappeion Exhibition Halls. To the north-west, the Greek Parliament buildings, the old Royal Palace and the Tomb or Monument to the Unknown Warrior, guarded by the traditionally costumed Evzones, the Greek equivalent of the British Buckingham Palace Guards (*See* **Places of Interest, A to Z**). South-east of the National Gardens is the Olympic Stadium erected in 1896, on the site of the original stadium, built in 330 BC, and situated in a valley of the Arditos Hills. South-west across Leoforos Olgas are the Olympic swimming pool and the Tennis and Athletic Club. To the west of these sporting facilities is the isolated gateway known as the Arch of Hadrian overlooking the busy traffic junction of Leoforos Olgas and Leoforos Amalias. Through the archway, the remains of the Temple of Olympian Zeus are outlined, 15 only of the original 104 Corinthian columns remain standing.

Leaving Hadrian's Arch, westwards along Odhos Dionysiou Areopagitou leads to the south side of:-

The Acropolis (Akropoli) (*Tmr* C5) A 10-acre rock rising 750 ft above the surrounding city and surmounted by the Parthenon Temple, built in approximately 450 BC, the Propylaia Gateway, the Temple to Athena Nike and the triple Temple of Erechtheion. Additionally, there has been added the modern Acropolis Museum, discreetly tucked away, almost out of sight.

At the bottom of the southern slope are the Theatre of Dionysos, originally said to seat up to 30,000 but more probably 17,000, and the smaller, second century AD, Odeion of Herodes Atticus, which has been restored and is used for plays and concerts during the summer festival. It is thought provoking to consider that the Dionysos Odeion is the original theatre where western world drama, as we know it, originated.

The west slope leads to the Hill of Areopagos (Areios Pagos) where, in times of yore, a council of noblemen dispensed supreme judgements. Across Apostolou Pavlou St lie the other tree covered hills of Filopapou (Philopappos/Mouseion), or Hill of Muses, from whence the views are far-reaching and outstanding; Pnyx (Pnyka), where The Assembly once met and a *son et lumiere* is now held, and the Asteroskopeion (Observatory), or the Hill of Nymphs, whereon stands, surprise, surprise, an observatory.

Descending from the Asteroskopeion towards and across Apostolou Pavlou St is:-

The (Greek) Agora (*Tmr* B/C4) The gathering place from whence the Athenians would have approached the Acropolis. This marketplace cum civic centre is now little more than rubble, but the glory that once was is recreated by a model.

Nearby the Temple of Hephaistos or Thission (Theseion) sits on a small hill overlooking the Agora and to one side is the reconstructed marketplace, Stoa Attalus, the cost of which was met from private donations raised by American citizens.

A short distance to the east of the Greek Agora is the site of:-

The Roman Forum (or Agora) (*Tmr* C5) Close by is the Tower of the Winds (*Tmr* 8C5) a remarkable octagonal tower, probably built in the first century BC and which served as a combination water clock, sundial and weather vane. Early descriptions say the building was topped off with a bronze weather vane represented by the mythological Triton complete with a pronged trident. The carved eight gods of wind can be seen, as can traces of the corresponding sundials, but no interior mechanism remains and the building is now used as a store for various stone antiquities.

A short distance to the north-west is an area known as **The Keramikos** (*Tmr* B4), a cemetery or graveyard, containing the Street of the Tombs, a funeral avenue laid out about 400 BC.

In a north-easterly direction from Keramikos along Pireos St, via Eleftherias Sq Bus terminal (*Tmr* 9C3), turning right down Evripidou St, across Athinas and Eolou Streets, leads to:-

Klafthmonos Square (Klathmonos) (*Tmr* 10D3/4)

Supposedly the most attractive Byzantine Church in Athens, Aghii Theodori, is positioned in the west corner of the square.

Looking north-east across Stadiou St, up Korai St and across Panepistimiou Ave, reveals an imposing range of neo-classical buildings (*Tmr* 11D/E3/4), fronted by formal gardens. These comprise the University flanked by, to the left (facing), the National Library, and to the right, the Academy. Behind and running parallel to Stadiou and Panepistimiou, is Akadimias St, on which is another Bus terminal. Just off Akadimias St, in Massalias St, is the Hellenic-American Union, many of whose facilities are open to the general public. These include an English and music library, as well as a cafeteria.

North-west of Klafthmonos Sq, to the left of Eolou St, is:-

Kotzia Square (*Tmr* D3)

A very large plateia around which, on Sunday at least, a profusion of flower sellers' stalls circle the square.

The once paved area has now been dug up by archaeologists who have unearthed a veritable treasure trove of ancient Athens city walls. At the time of writing the fate of the site is in the hands of the opposing and seemingly irreconcilable tugs of the modernists, who have a vision of a vast underground car park, and the traditionalists, who, quite rightly, wish to see the dig preserved for posterity.

Fokionos Negri

Actually a street, if not an avenue, rather than a square but somewhat distant from the city centre almost in the suburbs to the north, and usually just off the street plans of Athens. To reach Fokionos Negri from Omonia Sq, proceed up 28 (Ikosiokto) Oktovriou, which runs into Patission St, on past the National Archaeological Museum and Green Park (Pedion Areos), both on the right, to where Agiou Meletiou St runs across Patission St. Fokionos Negri starts as a fairly narrow sidestreet to the right, but widens out into a tree lined, short, squat avenue with a wide, spacious, centre pedestrian way once gravelled but now subject to extensive resurfacing. Supposedly the *Dolce Vita* or *Via Veneto* of Athens but not out of the ordinary, if quiet wealth is normal. Extremely expensive cafes edge the square halfway up on the right and it certainly becomes extremely lively after nightfall.

Numbers 5, 11, 12 or 13 trolley-bus, going north, trundle past the turning.

THE ACCOMMODATION & EATING OUT

The Accommodation On the islands the haul of accommodation includes even 'E' Class hotels but in Athens I have erred on the side of caution and stuck with 'B', 'C' and some better 'D' class hotels and pensions. No doubt there are some acceptable Class 'E' hotels but....

On Adrianou St (*Tmr* D5) (Plaka district) are a few very cheap dormitories and students' hostels, where a certain amount of rooftop sleeping is allowed, costing upwards of 350 drs per night. Unless set well back from the main road, a set of earmuffs or plugs is almost obligatory to ensure a good night's sleep.

On a cautionary note, since the end of 1981 the Greek authorities have been closing a number of the more 'undesirable', unlicensed hotels, so a particular favourite overnight stop from years gone by may no longer be in business.

Most of the hotel charges listed in this book are priced at the 1986 rates but these

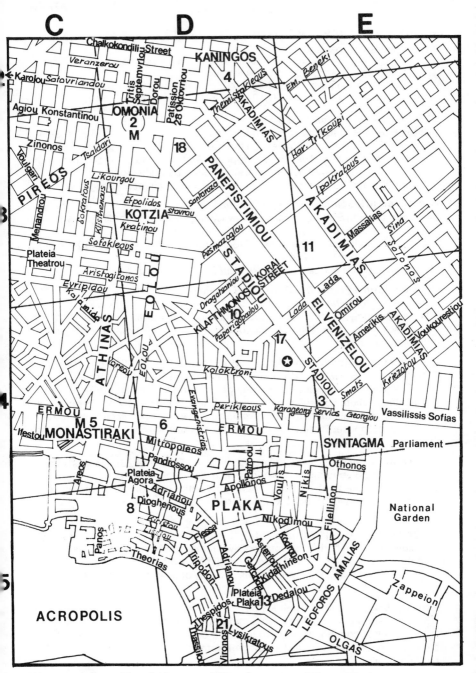

Illustration 5   Athens City Inset – The Plaka

will average out for 1987 as follows:

Class	Single	Double	
A	5200-7200	7500-9500	{ en suite bathroom
B	3300-6700	4600-8700	{ & breakfast included
C	2200-4300	3500-5650	{ sharing bathroom and
D	900-1300	1400-2000	{ room rate only

SYNTAGMA AREA (Tmr 1D/E4/5)
Festos Guest House (Tmr D/E5) 18 Filellinon St   Tel. 323-2455
Directions: From Syntagma Sq, walk up the rise of Odhos Filellinon past a number of cut-price ticket joints and very nearly opposite Ag Nikodimos Church, on the right.

Ethnic guest house with dormitories, triples and quadruplet rooms working out at between 350 and 500 drs per person. For the indiscriminately young at heart!

Hotel Cleo (Cleopatra)(Tmr D4) 3 Patroou St   Tel 322-9053
Directions: Leaving Syntagma Sq, walk down Mitropoleos St, towards Monastiraki Sq and take the fourth turning left.

Well recommended if threadbare. Ground floor dormitory, free baggage store. Double rooms from 1600-2500 drs.

NB. The owners also have a guest house nearby in 18 Apollonos St.

Pension John's Place (Tmr D4) (Class C) 5 Patroou St   Tel 322-9719
Directions: As for *Hotel Cleo* above.

Not surprisingly, the affable old Papa is named John. Well looked after accommotion with singles from 900 drs and doubles from 1300 drs, naturally sharing bathroom facilities.

George's Guest House (Tmr D4) (Class B) 46 Nikis St.   Tel 322-6474 *Directions*:
From Syntagma Sq, walk west along Mitropoleos St and turn down the first left-hand turning and the Guest House is on the right, beyond the first sidestreet.

Calls itself a *Youth Hostel with student prices*. Recommended by four Texas college girls, met on the train to Patras some years ago now and whose first stop in Greece was this guest house. Shared bathroom and hot water in the evening, if you are quick. Doubles from 1200 drs.

Hotel Kimon (Tmr D5) (Class D) 27 Appollonos   Tel 323-5223 *Directions*: Midway
on Appollonos St, one block down from Mitropoleos St.

Old but renovated with all rooms sharing the bathrooms. Single rooms start off at 800 drs increasing to 1000 drs whilst double rooms start at 1000 drs rising to 1200 drs.

YMCA (XAN) (Tmr E4) 28 Omirou St   Tel 362-6970
Directions: From the north-east corner of Syntagma Sq proceed up Panepistimiou St, take the third turning right and across Akadimias Avenue, on the right.

Closed for some years for renovations and may open in 1987..... then again it may not.

YWCA (XEN) (Tmr E4) 11 Amerikis St   Tel 362-4291
Directions: All as above but second turning off Panepistimiou St and on the left.

Apart from accommodation there is a cafe serving sandwiches, a hairdressing salon, library and laundry facilities. Singles from 780 drs and shared rooms 700 drs per head.

OMONIA AREA (Tmr 2D3)
Any hotel or pension rooms facing Omonia Square must be regarded as very noisy.

Hotel Omonia (*Tmr* D3) (Class C) 4 Omonia Sq   Tel 523-7210
Directions: Just stand on Omonia Sq, swivel on your heels and on the north side of the Square.

The reception is on the first floor, as is a cafe-bar and terrace, overlooking the square and its action. Modern but 'worn international' look to the place. Clients may well have to take demi-pension terms. A double room en suite costs from 1500 drs, breakfast 200 drs and a meal from 900 drs.

Hotel Banghion (*Tmr* D3) (Class C) 18b Omonia Sq.   Tel 324-2259
Directions: As for *Hotel Omonia*, but south side of the square.

Elegant and ageing. From 1950 drs for a double room sharing a bathroom, increasing to 2400 drs (16th July - 30th Sept), with breakfast available at 230 drs.

Hotel Carlton (*Tmr* D3) (Class C) 7 Omonia Sq.   Tel 522-3201
Directions: As for *Hotel Omonia*.

Very Greek provincial and old fashioned. Single rooms cost 900 drs and double rooms 1100 drs, both sharing a bathroom.

Hotel Europa (*Tmr* D2) (Class C) 7 Satovriandou St.   Tel 522-3081
Directions: North of Omonia Sq and the second main street up, lying east/west. This if often listed as Chateaubriandou St but the local authorities either have, or have not, been notified of the change. Whatever, the street is now a pedestrian precinct.

Another 'Greek provincial' hotel, the remarkably ancient lift of which creaks its way up and down to the various floors. The rooms are adequate, there is even a wardrobe and the floors are covered with brown linoleum. To use the shower the concierge must be asked for the relevant key, in mime if a guest's Greek is sketchy as the staff's knowledge of English is very limited. When produced, the key might well be adjudged large enough to open the doors of the Bastille. Weighed down by this instrument, the moment of truth is about to dawn, for when the door is opened, sheer disbelief may well be the first reaction, especially if it is the first ever stopover in Athens, as it was mine years ago. A cavernous and be-cobwebbed room reveals plumbing that beggars description. Enough to say the shower is most welcome, even if the lack of a point to anchor the shower head, whilst trying to soap oneself down, requires interesting body contortions. The rate for a single room is 900 drs and for a double is 1400 drs with shared bathrooms.

Hotel Alma (*Tmr* D2/3) (Class C) 5 Dorou   Tel 524-0858
Directions: Dorou St runs north from the north-east corner of Omonia Sq.

Modern and the rooms with a balcony are on the seventh and eighth floors. From 2200 drs for a double room with breakfast costing 200 drs.

Hotel Parnon (*Tmr* D2) (Class C) 20 Tritis Septemvriou/21 Chalkokondili
                                                                     Tel. 523-0014
Directions: North of Omonia Sq on the junction of Tritis Septemvriou and Chalkokondili St.

Modern and noisy. A double room with bath and room service costs 2500 drs (April-October) and a breakfast 350 drs.

Hotel Eva (*Tmr* C2) (Class D) 31 Victoros Ougo   Tel. 522-3079
Directions: West of Omonia, parallel to and two blocks back from Ag. Konstantinou.

Well recommended with single rooms from 1000 drs and double rooms 1700 drs, both with en suite bathrooms. Breakfast costs 200 drs.

Hotel Marina (*Tmr* C3) (Class C) 13 Voulgari   Tel. 523-7832/3
Directions: South-west from Omonia along Odhos Pireos and 4th turning to the right.

Single rooms cost from 800 drs, double rooms 1200 drs, both sharing the bathroom, while rooms with en suite bathrooms cost 1100 drs and 1500 drs respectively. Breakfast is charged at 200 drs.

Hotel Vienna (*Tmr* C3) (Class C) 20 Pireos   Tel. 524-9143
Directions: South-west of Omonia Sq.
New, clean and noisy, at about 2800 drs for a double room en suite, in the early summer, and a breakfast costs 200 drs.

Hotel Athinea (*Tmr* C2) (Class C) 9 Vilara   Tel. 523-3884
Directions: Westwards along Ag. Konstantinou and situated on one side of the small square of Agiou Konstantinou.
Old but beautifully positioned although cabaret night life may intrude. A restaurant and cake shop are close by as is a taxi rank. A single room starts off at 1600 drs and a double 2100 drs en suite. Breakfast is priced at 250 drs.

Hotel Pythagorion (*Tmr* C2/3) (Class C) 28 Ag. Konstantinou   Tel. 524-2811
Directions: West of Omonia Sq.
A single room from 1300 drs and a double room from 1800 drs, both with bath. Breakfast costs 200 drs and lunch/dinner from 700 drs.

Hotel Florida (*Tmr* C3) (Class C) 25 Menandrou   Tel. 522-3214
Directions: Third turning left, south-west along Pireos St.
Single rooms from 950 drs and doubles 1500 drs both without a bathroom, whilst en suite cost 1140 drs and 1690 drs respectively. Breakfast 180 drs.

Hotel Alcestis (Alkistis) (*Tmr* C3) (Class C) 18 Plateia Theatrou   Tel. 321-9811
Directions: From Pireos St, south down either Sokratous or Menandrou Streets and across Odhos Sofokleous St.
Only open March to October. Despite its chromium-plated appearance, all glass and marble with a prairie-sized lobby awash with Americans, it is a Class C hotel in a commercial square. Popular, with double rooms from 2750 drs, breakfast 250 drs and lunch/dinner from 1000 drs.

MONASTIRAKI AREA (*Tmr* 5C4)
Hotel Tembi/Tempi (*Tmr* C/D4) (Class D) 29 Eolou (Aiolu/Aeolou)   Tel. 321-3175
Directions: A main street north of Ermou St, opposite the Church of Ag. Irini.
Pleasant rooms with singles sharing the bathroom start at 950 drs rising to 1200 drs (1st June - 30th Sept). Double rooms sharing cost from 1200 drs and en suite 1400 drs advancing to 1400 drs and 1600 drs respectively.

Hotel Ideal (*Tmr* C/D4) (Class D) 39 Eolou/2 Voreou Sts.   Tel. 321-3195
Directions: On the left of Eolou, walking up from Odhos Ermou, and on the corner with Voreou St.
A perfect example of a weather-worn, 19th century, Athens neo-classical building complete with an old fashioned, metal and glass canopy entrance and matchbox sized, wrought iron balconies. The accommodation lives up to all that the exterior promises. The management are helpful, there is a telephone, TV room, a bar and luggage can be stored. Tourist information is freely available as are battered paperbacks for guests. The bathroom facilities are shared but there is 24 hour hot water – promise!

Hotel Hermion (*Tmr* C/D4) (Class C) 66c Ermou St   Tel. 321-2753
Directions: East of Monastiraki, adjacent to Kapnikarea Church and Square (*Tmr* 6D4).
Old but clean with the reception up the stairs. All rooms share bathrooms with the

single room rate starting off at 900 drs and the double rooms 1800 drs.

Hotel Attalos (*Tmr* C3/4) (Class C) 29 Athinas   Tel. 321-2801
Directions: North from Monastiraki Sq.
Recommended to us by a splendidly eccentric English lady artist who should know – she has been visiting Greece for some 20 years. Between 16th March - 30th June singles cost 1485 drs and doubles, with a shower, 1815 drs rising to 1600 drs and 2000 drs (1st July - 30th Sept). Breakfast is charged at 230 drs.

Hotel Cecil (*Tmr* C3/4) (Class D) 39 Athinas   Tel. 321-7079
Directions: North from Monastiraki Sq and two buildings up from the Kalamida St turning on the left-hand side. This is the other side of the road from a very small chapel, incongruously stuck on the pavement. The 'informative' sign outside the hotel is no help.
Clean looking with a single room costing 1100 drs and a double 1600 drs. The bathrooms are shared.

PLAKA/METZ STADIUM AREAS (*Tmr* D5 & D/E6)
The Plaka is rich in accommodation, as it is in most things!
Hotel Phaedra (*Tmr* D5) (Class D) 4 Adrianou/16 Herephontos   Tel. 323-8461
Directions: Situated close by a multi-junction of various streets including Lysikratous, Galanou, Adrianou and Herephontos, opposite the Byzantine Church of Ag. Aikaterini and its small, attractive gardens.
Pretty area by day, noisy by night. Family hotel with a ground floor bar. Double rooms start off at 1400 drs and rise to 3000 drs. Breakfast costs 200 drs.

Students' Inn (*Tmr* D5) 16 Kidathineon St   Tel. 324-4808
Directions: On the left of Kidathineon St, walking up from the Adrianou St junction, and almost opposite the garden of the Japanese eating house.
Hostelish but recommended as good value with hot showers 'on tap' (sorry) and an English-speaking owner. There is a roof-top, a passable courtyard, a snackbar, the use of a washing machine (which does not always work) and a baggage store costing 50 drs per day. The clean but basic rooms are complete with a rickety oil-cloth covered table and mug. Singles cost between 1200 drs and 1300 drs and doubles from 1500 drs to 1600 drs. The doors are locked at 0200 hrs.

Left off Kidathineon Street, climbing towards Syntagma Sq, is Odhos Kodrou on which are two clean pleasant hotels in a very pleasant area, the:
Hotel Adonis (*Tmr* D5) (Class B) 3 Kodrou   Tel. 324-9737
Directions: As above and on the right.
Actually a pension so the rates are not outrageous. All rooms have en suite bathrooms with singles starting off at 1450 drs and doubles 1600 drs. rising respectively to 1750 drs and 2150 drs (1st July - 30th Sept).

Acropolis House (*Tmr* D5) (Class B) 6-8 Kodrou   Tel. 322-2344
Directions: As above and on the left.
Highly recommended and once again officially classified as a pension with a choice of rooms sharing or complete with en suite bathrooms. Single room rates commence at 1520 drs and doubles 1840 drs rising to 2100 drs and 2540 drs (16th June - 30th Sept).

Closer to Kidathineon St, and on the right is the:
Kouros Pension (*Tmr* D5) (Class C) 11 Kodrou   Tel. 322-7431
Directions: As above.
Rather more provincial than the two establishments detailed above, which lack of

sophistication is reflected in the lower prices (and standards). All rooms share the bathrooms and the single room rate starts at 800 drs and a double 1110 drs climbing to the dizzy heights(!) of 1020 drs and 1600 drs (1st May - 30th Sept).

Hotel Solonion *(Tmr* D5) (Class E) 11 Sp Tsangari/Dedalou   Tel. 322-0008/3080
Directions: To the right of Kidathineon St (facing Syntagma Sq) between Dedalou St and Leoforos Amalias. Odhos Tsangari is a continuation of Asteriou St.

Run by a rather stern faced lady who is assisted by a varied collection of part time assistants to run the old, faded but refurbished building. If a guest strikes lucky the night porter will be a delightful old boy who was once a merchant in the Greek community resident in Turkey, and was caught up in the huge population resettlement of 1922/23. The accommodation is 'student provincial', the rooms being high ceilinged and the rather dodgy floorboards are hidden beneath brown linoleum. The bathrooms are distinctly ethnic and Victorian in style but hot water is promised all day. On a fine day......it is possible to espy the Acropolis... well a bit of it. No single rooms are available, a double room sharing the bathroom costs from 1200 drs, including one bath a day, rising to 1400 drs (1st April - 15th Oct).

Close by the *Hotel Solonion* are the:-
Hotel Kekpoy (Cecrops) *(Tmr* D5) (Class D) 13 Tsangari   Tel. 322-3080
Directions: On the same side as and similar to the *Solonion* but a building or two towards Leoforos Amalias.

All rooms share the bathroom with singles costing 950 drs and doubles 1200 drs.

Hotel Phoebus (Fivos) *(Tmr* D5) (Class C) Asteriou/12 Peta   Tel. 322-0142
Directions: Back towards Kidathineon, on the corner of the Asteriou and Peta Streets.

Rather more up-market than the 3 previously listed hotels. A double room en suite costs 2400 drs rising to 2900 drs (1st June - 30th Sept) and breakfast 250 drs.

A few side streets towards the Acropolis is the:-
Hotel Ava *(Tmr* D5) 9 Lysikratous St   Tel. 323-6618
Directions: As above.

I have no personal experience but the establishment has been mentioned as a possibility and is in an excellent, central but quiet situation although it is rather expensive. All rooms have en suite bathrooms, are heated and air conditioned. Single rooms cost from 2000 drs and doubles from 3000 drs. There are family suites complete with kitchen and regrigerator (sic).

New Clare's House *(Tmr* E6) (Class C Pension) 24 Sorvolou St   Tel. 922-2288
Directions: Rather uniquely, the owners have had a large compliments slip printed with a pen and ink drawing on the face, and on the reverse side, directions in Greek saying: *Show this to the taxi driver*. This includes details of the location, south of the Stadium, on Sorvolou St between Charvouri and Voulgareos Streets. The pension is on the right, halfway down the reverse slope with the description *white building with the green shutters*. From Syntagma proceed south down the sweep of Leoforos Amalias, keeping to the main avenues hugging the Temple of Olympian Zeus and along Odhos Diakou. Where Diakou makes a junction with Vouliagmenis and Ardittou Avenues, Odhos Anapafseos leads off in a south-east direction and Sorvolou St 'crescents' off to the left. Trolley buses 2, 4, 11 & 12 drop travellers off by the Stadium. It is quite a steep climb up Sorvolou St, which breaks into steps, to the pretty and highly recommended area of Metz (highly regarded by Athenians that is). Plus points are that the narrow nature of the lanes, which suddenly become steps, keeps the traffic down to a minimum and the height of the hill raises it above the general level of smog and pollution.

The pleasant, flat fronted pension is on the right and has a marble floor entrance hall. Inside, off to the left, is a large reception/lounge/bar/breakfast/common room and to the right, the lift. The self confident English speaking owner presides over matters from a large desk in the reception area and is warily helpful. The lady staff receptionists do not exactly go wild in an orgy of energy sapping activity, tending to indulge in a saturnalia of TV watching. Guests in the meantime can help themselves to bottles of beer (80 drs) and Coke from the bar, paying when convenient to them and the receptionist. Despite the inferred aura of excellence the usual collection of faults crop up from time to time including: cracked loo seats; no hot water, despite being assured that there is 24 hours hot water (and for longer no doubt were there more hours in the day!); missing locking mechanism on the lavatory door; toilets having to be flushed using a piece of string and the television on the blink. I do not mean to infer that these irritating defects occur all at once – just one or two, every so often. Single rooms sharing a bathroom cost 2000 drs and en suite 2500 drs while double rooms sharing cost 2500 drs and en suite 3300 drs. Incidentally where the well appointed bathrooms are shared, the pleasant rooms only have to go fifty-fifty with one other room. The charges, which include breakfast 'with warm bread every day', may at first impression (and for that matter second and third impression) appear on the expensive side. The 'pain' might be eased by the realisation that the 4th floor has a balcony and a self-catering kitchen, complete with cooker and a fridge, and the 5th floor a laundry room with an iron and 2 rooftop clothes lines. These facilities must of course be taken into account when weighing up comparative prices. The management create an atmosphere that will suit the young, very well behaved student and the older traveller but not exuberant rowdies. Hands are smacked if guests lay around eating a snack on the front steps, hang washing out of the windows or make a noise, especially between the hours of 1330 and 1700 and after 2330 hrs. You know, lights out boys and no smoking in the dorms. *Clare's House* was originally recommended by pension owner Alexis on the island of Kos but in recent years has been included in one or two of the smaller tour companies' brochures for the Athens overnight stop. Certainly an old friend of ours, Peter, who 'has to put up with yachting round the Aegean waters during the summer months', almost always spends some of his winter Athens months at Clare's and swears by the place.

Before leaving the area there is an intriguing possibility, accommodation that is, in a very quiet street edging the west side of the Stadium.
Joseph's House Pension *(Tmr* E6) (Class C) 13 Markou Moussourou   Tel. 923-1204
Directions: From the region of Hadrian's Arch/the Temple of the Olympian Zeus *(Tmr* D6) proceed up Avenue Ardittou in a north-easterly direction towards the Stadium. Odhos Markou Moussourou climbs steeply off to the right, immediately prior to the wooded hillside Arditos. The pension is on the left, beyond Meletiou Riga St. On the other hand it is just as easy to follow the directions to *Clare's House* and proceed east along Charvouri St until it bumps into Markou Moussourou.
    The bathrooms are shared with single rooms charged at 700 drs and doubles at 950 drs.

THISSION AREA (THESION) *(Tmr* B/C4/5)
First south-bound Metro stop after Monastiraki and a much quieter area.
Hotel Phedias *(Tmr* B4) (Class C) 39 Apostolou Pavlou   Tel. 345-9511
Directions: South of the Metro station.
    Modern and friendly with double rooms from 2200 drs and breakfast 250 drs per head.

OLYMPIC OFFICE AREA (*Tmr* C6)
Hotel Karayannis (*Tmr* C6) (Class C) 94 Leoforos Sygrou   Tel. 921-5903
Directions: On the corner of Odhos Byzantiou and Leoforos Sygrou, opposite the
side exit of the Olympic terminal office.

   'Interesting', tatty and noisy, but very necessary for travellers arriving really late at
the terminal. Rooms facing the main road should be avoided. The Athenian traffic,
which appears to roar up and down non-stop round the clock, gives every
appearance of making the journey along Leoforos Sygrou via the hotel balconies,
even three or four storeys up. There are picturesque views of the Acropolis from the
breakfast and bar rooftop terrace, even if they are through a maze of television
aerials. Single rooms with en suite bathroom cost 1310 drs, a double room sharing
1650 drs, and a double room en suite 1780 drs. Breakfast for one costs 220 drs. Best
to splash out for the en suite rooms as the hotel's shared lavatories are of a 'thought
provoking' nature with a number of the unique features detailed under the general
description of bathrooms in CHAPTER 4.

Whilst in this area it would be inappropriate not to mention the:-
Super-Bar Restaurant Odhos Faliron
Directions: As for the *Hotel Karayannis* but behind the Olympic office.

   Now not inexpensive but very conveniently situated, even if it is closed on
Sundays. Snackbar food with 2 Nes meh gala, a toasted cheese and ham sandwich
and boiled egg costing 280 drs. On this occasion I actually wanted toast....

Youth Hostel 57 Kypselis St and Agiou Meletiou 1   Tel. 822-5860
Directions: Located in the Fokionos Negri area of North Athens. Proceed along 28
(Ikosiokto) Oktovriou/Patission Street from Omonia Sq, beyond Pedion Areos Park
to Ag Meletiou St. Turn right and follow until the junction with Kypselis St. Trolley
buses No. 3, 5, 11, 12 & 13 make the journey.

   This is *The Official Youth Hostel* and does fulfil the requirements of those who
require very basic, cheap accommodation, albeit in dormitories. The overnight
charge is 300/500 drs.

Taverna Youth Hostel (*Tmr* G2) 1 Drossi St & 87 Leoforos Alexandra Tel. 646-3669
Directions: East of Pedion Aeros Park along Leoforos Alexandras almost as far as the
junction with Ippokratous St. Odhos Drossi is on the left. It is possible to catch
trolley-bus No. 7 from Panepistimiou Avenue or No. 8 from Kanigos Sq (*Tmr* 4D2) or
Akadimias St.

   Actually a taverna that 'sprouts' an 'unofficial Youth Hostel' for the summer months
only.

If only to receive confirmation regarding the spurious Youth Hostels, it may be worth
visiting the:-
YHA Head Office (*Tmr* D3/4) 4 Dragatsaniou   Tel. 323-4107
Directions: The north side of Plateia Klafthmonos in a street on the left-hand side of
Stadiou St.

   Only open Monday - Friday, 0900 - 1500 hrs. They advise of vacancies in the youth
hostels and issue international youth hostel cards.

LARISSIS STATION AREA (*Tmr* B/C1)
See **Trains, A to Z.**

CAMPING
Sample daily site charges per person vary between 200-300 drs (children half-price)
and the hire of a tent between 150-300 drs.

Sites include the following:-

Distance from Athens	Site name	Amenities
8 km	**Athens Camping.** 198 Athinon Ave. On the road to Dafni (due west of Athens). Tel. 581-4113	Open all year, 25 km from the sea. Bar, shop and showers.
10 km	**Dafni Camping.** Dafni. On the Athens to Corinth National Road. Tel. 581-1562	Open all year. 5 km from the sea. Bar, shop, showers and kitchen facilities.

For the above: Bus 853, Athens - Elefsina, departs Koumoundourou Sq/Deligeorgi St (*Tmr* C2/3) every 20 mins between 0510 - 2215 hrs.

14.5 km	**Patritsia.** Kato Kifissia, N. Athens. Tel. 801-1900. Closed 'temporarily' for 1986, query 1987?	Open June-October. Bar, shop, showers, laundry and kitchen facilities.
16 km	**Nea Kifissia.** Nea Kifissia, N. Athens. Tel. 807-5544	Open April - October. 20 km from the sea. Bar, shop, showers, swimming pool and laundry.
18 km	**Dionyssiotis.** Nea Kifissia, N. Athens. Tel. 807-1494	Open all year.
25 km	**Papa-Camping.** Zorgianni Ag. Stefanos. Tel. 803-3446	Open June-October. 25 km from the sea. Laundry, bar and kitchen facilities.

For the above (sited on or beside the Athens National Road, north to Lamia): Lamia bus from 260 Liossion St (*Tmr* C1/2), every hour from 0615 to 1915 and at 2030 hrs.

35 km	**Marathon Camping.** Kaminia, Marathon. NE of Athens. Tel. 0294-55577	On a sandy beach. Open March to 31st October. Showers, bar, restaurant and kitchen facilities.
35 km	**Nea Makri.** 156 Marathonos Ave, Nea Makri. NE of Athens just south of Marathon. Tel. 0294-92719	Open April - October. 220 m from the sea. Sandy beach, laundry, bar and shop.

For the above: The bus from Odhos Mavrommateon, Plateia Egyptou (*Tmr* D1), every ½ hour from 0530 to 2200 hrs.

26 km	**Cococamp.** Rafina. East of Athens. Tel. 0294-23413	Open all year. On the beach, rocky coast. Laundry, bar, showers, kitchen facilities, shop and restaurant.
29 km	**Kokkino Limanaki Camping.** Kokkino Limanaki, Rafina. Tel. 0294-31602	On the beach. Open April - October.
29 km	**Rafina Camping.** Rafina. East of Athens. Tel. 0294-23118	Open May - October. 4 km from the sandy beach. Showers, bar, laundry, restaurant and shop.

For the above: The Rafina bus from Mavrommateon St, Plateia Egyptou (*Tmr* D1). Twenty-nine departures from 0550 to 2200 hrs.

20 km	**Voula Camping.** 2 Alkyonidon St, Voula. Just below Glyfada and the Airport. Tel. 895-2712	Open all year. On the sandy beach. Showers, laundry, shop and kitchen facilities.
27 km	**Varkiza Beach Camping.** Varkiza. Coastal road Athens-Vouliagmenis-Sounion. Tel. 897-3613	Open all year. By a sandy beach. Bar, shop, supermarket, taverna, laundry and kitchen facilities.
60 km	**Sounion Camping.** Sounion. Tel. 0292-39358	Open all year. By a sandy beach. Bar, shop, laundry, kitchen facilities and a taverna.

76 km   **Vakhos Camping.** Assimaki near   Open June - September. On the beach.
        Sounion. On the Sounion to Lavrion
        road. Tel. 0292-39263

For the above: Buses from Mavrommateon St, Plateia Egyptou (*Tmr* D1) every hour from 0630 to 1730 hrs. Note to get to *Vakhos Camping* catch the Sounion bus via Markopoulo and Lavrion.

The Eating Out
Where to dine out is a very personal choice and in a city the size of Athens there are so many restaurants and tavernas to choose from that only a few recommendations are made. In general, steer clear of Luxury and Class A hotel dining rooms, restaurants offering international cuisine and tavernas with Greek music and/or dancing* which may be very good but are usually on the expensive side.

Note the reference to Greek dancing and music is not derogatory – only an indication that it is often the case that standards of cuisine may not be any better and prices often reflect the 'overheads' attributable to the musicians. But See **Palia & Xynou Tavernas.**

In Athens and the larger, more cosmopolitan, provincial cities, it is usual taverna practice to round off prices, which proves a little disconcerting at first.

In despair it is noted that some restaurants and tavernas climbing the slopes of the Acropolis up Odhos Markou Avrilou, south of Eolou St, are allowing 'Chinese menu' style collective categories (A, B, C etc) to creep into their Greek menu listings.

PLAKA AREA (*Tmr* D5)
A glut of eating houses ranging from the very good and expensive, the very expensive and bad, to some inexpensive and very good.

Taverna Thespis 18 Thespidos St   Tel. 323-8242
Directions: On the right of a lane across the way from Kidathineon St, towards the bottom or south-east end of Adrianou St.

Recommended and noted for its friendly service. The house retsina is served in metal jugs. A two hour slap-up meal of souvlaki, Greek salad, fried zucchini, bread and two carafes of retsina will cost in excess of 1600 drs for two.

Plaka Village 28 Kidathineon
Directions: In the block edged by the streets of Adrianou and Kidathineon.

An excellent souvlaki snackbar but to sit down costs an extra 16 drs per head. Price lists do not make this plain and the annoying habit can cause, at the least, irritation. This practice is also prevalent in the Omonia Square 'souvlaki arcade'. A large bottle of beer costs 80 drs, the home-made tzatziki is good, the service is quick and they even remain open Sunday lunchtimes.

ΟΥΖΕΡΙ Ο ΚΟΥΚΛΗΣ 14 Tripodon St   Tel. 324-7605
Directions: Up the slope from the Thespidos/Kydathineon junction, one to the left of Adrianou (facing Monastiraki Sq), and on the left. Distinguishing the establishment is not difficult as the 1st floor balcony is embellished with a large, stuffed bird and two big, antique record player horns mounted on the wrought iron balustrade.

The taverna, standing on its own, evokes a provincial country atmosphere. It is necessary to arrive early as the ouzerie is well patronised by the locals, which patronage is not surprising considering the inexpensive excellence of one or two of the standard dishes. One of these is the 'flaming sausages' which cook away on stainless steel plates set in front of the diner and are served up with a large bowl full of hors d'oeuvres at a cost of 1000 drs for two. Great value, very filling indeed but watch the napkins don't go up in flames!

Eden Taverna 3 Flessa St
Directions: Off Adrianou St, almost opposite Odhos Nikodimou, and on the left.
Mentioned because their menu includes many offerings that excellently cater (sorry) for vegetarian requirements. Open 1200 hrs to 0100 hrs every day except Tuesdays.

Stamatopoulos Palia Plakiotiki Taverna 26 Lissiou/Flessa Sts   Tel. 322-8722
Directions: Beyond the *Eden Taverna* on the right of the corner of Flessa and Lissiou Streets.
Claims to be one of Athens' oldest tavernas. Anne whose strong recommendation the Palia is, and taking my prejudices to heart, concedes that there is music. But here it is a major attraction in the shape of a huge, spherical man, with a name to match, Stavros Balagouras. He is the resident singer/accordionist/electric pianist and draws tourists and 'real' Greeks alike with his dignified and heartfelt performance. Besides traditional, old national songs there is year-round dancing, if customers feel like it, on the 1 square metre floor space! The taverna is particularly Greek and lively at festival times, added to which the food is good and much cheaper than similar establishments. Cheese and meat dishes with salad and wine for two costs just 1500 drs.

Platanos Taverna 4 Dioghenous St
Directions: Dioghenous St runs parallel to Odhos Adrianou St, at the Monastiraki Square end.
A conventional taverna serving inexpensive lunch and dinner. Closed Sundays.

Michiko Restaurant 27 Kidathineon St   Tel. 324-6851
Directions: On the right, beyond the junction with Asteriou St proceeding in a north-east direction (towards Syntagma Sq), close to a small square and church.
Japanese, if you must, and extremely expensive.

Xynou/Xynos 4 Arghelou Geronda (Angelou Geronta)   Tel. 322-1065
Directions: Left off the lower Plaka Square end of Kidathineon St (facing Syntagma Sq) and on the left, towards the far end of the pedestrian way. The unprepossessing entrance door is tucked away in the corner of a recess and can be missed.
One of the oldest, most highly rated Plaka tavernas and well patronised by Athenians. Evenings only and closed on Saturdays and Sundays. A friend advises me that it is now almost obligatory to book in advance although I have managed to squeeze a table for two early on in the evening.
Mention of its popularity with Athenians prompts me to stress these are well-heeled locals – you know shipowners, ambassadors and ageing playboys. Xynou is definitely on the 'hotel captains' list of recommended eateries and the tourists who eat here tend to look as if they have stepped off the stage-set of Dallas. But it is not surprising that the *cognoscente* gather here. Despite being in the heart of Athens, the single storey, shed like, roof tiled buildings evoke a rural ambience. The buildings edge two sides of the high wall enclosed gravel area, on which the chairs and tables are spread. The food is absolutely excellent and considering the location the prices are not that outrageous. A meal of two dolmades in lemon sauce, a plate of moussaka, a lamb fricassee in lemon sauce, a tomato and cucumber salad, a bottle of kortaki retsina and bread for two costs 1530 drs. It seems a pity that the bread has to be charged at 50 drs but then the ample wine list does include an inexpensive retsina. Three guitarists serenade diners, the napkins are linen, and the service is first class. Readers are recommended to save up and try Xynou's at least once, an experience that will not be easily forgotten.

Plateia Agora is a lovely, elongated, chic Plaka Square formed at the junction of the bottom of Eolou and the top of Adrianou and Kapnikarea Streets. The square spawns a number of cafe-bar restaurants and these include the *Possidion* and *Appollon*, the canopied chairs and tables of which edge the street all the way round the neat, paved plateia. There is a spotless public lavatory at the top (Monastiraki) end. The *Appollon* has a particularly wide range of choice and clients can sit at the comfortable tables for an (expensive) hour or so over a coffee (100 drs), a fried egg breakfast (300 drs) or a full blown meal. Hope your luck is in and the organ grinder wanders through.

From the little square formed by a 'junction of the ways', adjacent to the Lycikrates Monument (*Tmr* 21D5), Odhos Vironos falls down towards the south Acropolis encircling avenue of Dionysiou/Areopagitou.

Snackbar Odhos Vironos
Directions: As above and on the right (Plaka behind one) of the street.
More a small 'doorway' souvlaki pita shop but small is indeed splendid.

Restaurant Olympia 20 Dionysiou Areopagitou
Directions: Proceed along Dionysiou Areopagitou from the junction with Odhos Vironos in a clockwise direction. The restaurant is on the right, close to the junction with Thassilou Lane (that incidentally climbs and bends back up to the top of Odhos Thespidos) hard up against the foot of the Acropolis. Between Thassilou Lane and the sun-blind-shaded lean-to butted on to the side of the restaurant, is a small grassed area and an underground Public toilet.
The prices seem reasonable and the place appears to portend good things but.... I can only report the promise was in reality disappointing. The double Greek salad (185 drs) was in truth only large enough for one, the moussaka (161 drs) was 'inactive', the kalamares were unacceptable and the roast potatoes (yes roast potatoes) were in actuality nothing more than dumpy wedges. Oh dear! They do serve a kortaki retsina for 92 drs.

STADIUM (PANGRATI) AREA (*Tmr* E/F6)
Karavitis Taverna (ΚΑΡΑΒΙΤΗΣ) 4 Pafsaniou (Paysanioy)
Directions: Beyond the Stadium (*Tmr* E/F6) going east (away from the Acropolis) along Vassileos Konstantinou, and Pafsaniou is 3rd turning to the right. The taverna is on the left.
A small, leafy tree shaded gravel square fronts the taverna which is so popular that there is an extension across the street, through a pair of 'field gates'. Our friend Paul will probably berate me (if he was less of a gentleman) for listing this gem. Unknown to visitors but extremely popular with Athenians, more especially those who, when college students, frequented this jewel in the Athens taverna crown. A meal for 4 of a selection of dishes including lamb, beef in clay, giant haricot beans, garlic flavoured meat balls, greens, tzatziki, 2 plates of feta cheese, aubergines, courgettes, bread and 3 jugs of retsina from the barrel for some 2400 drs. Beat that. But some knowledge of Greek is an advantage and the taverna is only open in the evening.

Instead of turning off Vassileos Konstantinou at Odhos Pafsaniou, take the next right proceeding further eastwards.

ΜΑΓΕΜΕΝΟΣ ΑΥΛΟΣ (The Magic Flute) Odhos Aminda (Amynta)
Directions: As above and the restaurant is 20m up on the right.
Swiss dishes including fondue, schnitzels and salads. Despite being rather more expensive than its near neighbours it is well frequented by Athenians including the composer Hadzithakis (so Anne advises me).

Virinis Taverna, Archimedes St.
Directions: Before the side streets to the two restaurant/tavernas detailed above, the 2nd turning to the right off Vassileos Konstantinou, after the Stadium (*Tmr* E/F6) proceeding in an easterly direction, is Odhos Eratosthenous which climbs up to Plateia Plastira. To the right of the square is Archimedes Street. The taverna is about a 100m along on the left. Incidentally, if returning to the centre of Athens it is possible to continue along this street and drop down Odhos Markou Moussourou back to Vassileos Konstantinou.

A good selection of bistro dishes at reasonable prices, including, for instance, beef in wine sauce at a cost of 350 drs. Anne indicated I might find the place rather 'up market' as there were no souvlaki pitas on offer. Cheeky thing! It's only that I have learnt through expensive experience over the years that in Greece gingham tablecloths and French style menus tend to double the prices!

SYNTAGMA AREA (*Tmr* 1D/E4/5)
Corfu Restaurant 6 Kriezotou St   Tel. 361-3011
Directions: North of Syntagma Sq and first turning right off Panepistimiou (El. Venizelou).
   Extensive Greek and European dishes in a modern, friendly restaurant.

Delphi Restaurant 15 Nikis St   Tel. 323-4869
Directions: From the south-west corner of Syntagma Sq, east along Mitropoleos and the first turning left.
   Modern, reasonably priced food and friendly service. Extensive menu.

Sintrivani Restaurant 5 Filellinon St
Directions: South-west corner of Syntagma Sq and due south.
   Garden restaurant serving a traditional menu at reasonable prices.

Vassillis Restaurant 14A Voukourestiou
Directions: North of Syntagma Sq and the second turning off Panepistimiou St to the right along Odhos Smats and across Akadimias St.
   Variety, in traditional surroundings.

Ideal Restaurant 46 Panepistimiou St.
Directions: Proceed up Panepistimiou from the north-east corner of Syntagma Sq and the restaurant is on the right.
   Good food at moderate prices.

YWCA 11 Amerikis St
Directions: North-west up either Stadiou or Panepistimiou St and second or third road to the right, depending which street is used.
   Cafeteria serving inexpensive sandwiches.

There are many cafes in and around Syntagma Square. Recommended, but expensive, is the:
Brazilian Coffee Cafe
Directions: Close by Syntagma Sq in Voukourestiou St.
   Serves coffee, tea, toast, butter and jam, breakfast, ice-creams and pastries.

OMONIA AREA (*Tmr* 2D3)
Elliniki Taverna On the corner of Dorou and Satovriandou Streets.
Directions: North of Omonia Sq, along Dorou St and almost immediately on the left.
   Good value, if a little showy.

Taverna Kostoyannus 37 Zaimi St

Directions: Leave Omonia northwards on 28 (Ikosiokto) Oktovriou, turn right at Odhos Stournara to the near side of the Polytechnic School, and Zaimi St is the second road along. The taverna is to the left approximately behind the National Archaeological Museum.

Good food, acceptable prices and comes well recommended. As in the case of many other Athenian tavernas, it is not open for lunch or on Sundays.

Snackbars

Probably the most compact, reasonably priced 'offerings' but in grubby surroundings, lie in the arcade between Dorou St and 28 (Ikosiokto) Oktovriou, off Omonia Sq. Here are situated cafes and stalls selling almost every variety of Greek convenience fast food. A 'standard'* souvlaki costs 70 drs and a 'spezial'*, or deluxe, 90 drs BUT do not sit down unless you wish to be charged an extra 15-20 drs per head. A beer costs 80 drs.

* Note the 'standard' is a preheated slab of meat whilst the 'spezial' is the traditional, giro meat-sliced offering.

Cafes

Everywhere of course, but on Omonia Sq, alongside Dorou St and adjacent to the *Hotel Carlton*, is a magnificent specimen of the traditional kafeneion.

Greek men sip coffee and tumble their worry beads, as they must have done since the turn of the century.

Bretania Cafe

Directions: On Omonia Square beside the junction with Athinas St.

An excellent, very ethnic, very old fashioned Greek 'sticky' sweet shop which is more a galaktozacharoplasteion than a cafe. Renowned for its range of sweets, yoghurt and honey, cream and honey, rice puddings and so on, all served with sugar sweet bread and drinks until 0200 hrs every day.

Continuing on down Athinas St, beyond Plateia Kotzai, leads past the covered meat market building on the left and the:

'Meat Market' Tavernas

Directions: As above and towards the rear of the building. It has to be admitted it is necessary to pick one's way through piles of bones and general market detritus after dark.

Open 24 hours a day and a find for those who like to slum it in a less expensive establishment of some note.

LYCABETTUS (LYKAVITOS) AREA *(Tmr* F/G4)

As befits an expensive area, these listings are very expensive.

Je Reviens Restaurant 49 Xenokratous St

Directions: North-east from Kolonaki Sq, up Patriachou Ioakim St to the junction with and left on Marasli St, up a flight of steps until it crosses Xenokratous St.

French food. Creditable but expensive. Open midday and evenings.

L'Abreuvoir 51 Xenokratous St

Directions: As for *Je Reviens* as are the comments, but even more expensive.

Al Convento Restaurant *(Tmr* G4) 4 Anapiron   Tel. 723-9163

Directions: North-east from Kolonaki Sq along Patriarchou Ioakim to Marasli St. Turn left and then right along Odhos Souidias and Anapiron St is nearly at the end.

Bonanza Restaurant 14 Voukourestiou
Directions: From the north-west corner of Plateia Kolonaki, take Odhos Skoufa, which crosses Voukourestiou St.
   Once known as the *Stage Coach*. Not only Wild West in decor, air-conditioned and serving American style food but very expensive with steaks as a house speciality. Why not go to the good old US of A? Lunch and evening meals, open 1200 to 1600 hrs and 1900 to 0100 hrs.

THE A TO Z OF USEFUL INFORMATION

AIRLINE OFFICES & TERMINUS *(Tmr* 12C6) Referred to in the introductory paragraphs, as well as under **The Accommodation**, the busy offices are to the left (facing Syntagma Sq), of the frantic Leoforos Sygrou. As with other Olympic facilities the office doubles as a terminus for airport buses arriving from and departing to the East and West Airports. Passengers who land up here should note that the most convenient, combined bus stop to, say Syntagma Square, the centre of Athens, is, (with the building behind one), across the busy thoroughfare and some 50m up the incline of Leoforos Sygrou. This 'hosts' any number of buses and trolley-buses while the stop directly across the road serves only one or two buses and no trolley-buses.

Aircraft Timetables. *See* CHAPTER 3 for general details of the airports described in this guide that are serviced from Athens and the individual chapters for details of the actual timetables.

BANKS (Trapeza – ΤΡΑΠΕΖΑ) Note that if a bank strike is under way (apparently becoming a natural part of the tourist season 'high jinks'), the **National Bank** on Syntagma Sq stays open and in business. However, it becomes more than usually crowded in these circumstances. Banks include the:
National Bank of Greece *(Tmr* 3D/E4) 2 Karageorgi Servias, Syntagma Sq.
   All foreign exchange services: Monday to Thursday 0800 - 1400 hrs; Friday 0800 - 1330 hrs; Saturday, Sunday & holidays 0900 - 1600 hrs. Travellers' cheques & foreign cash exchange services: weekdays 0800 - 2000 hrs; Saturday, Sunday & holidays 0900 - 1600 hrs.
Ionian & Popular Bank *(Tmr* D/E4/5) 1 Mitropoleos St
   Only open normal banking hours.
Commercial Bank of Greece *(Tmr* E4) 11 Panepistimiou (El. Venizelou)
   Only open normal banking hours.
American Express *(Tmr* 1D/E4/5) 2 Ermou St, Syntagma Sq.   Tel. 324-4975/9
   Carries out usual Amex office transactions and is open Monday to Thursday 0830 - 1400 hrs; Friday 0830 - 1330 hrs and Saturday 0830 - 1230 hrs.

BEACHES Athens is not on a river or by the sea, so to enjoy a beach it is necessary to leave the main city and travel to the suburbs by the sea. Very often these beaches are operated under the aegis of the NTOG, or private enterprise in association with a hotel. The NTOG beaches usually have beach huts, cabins, tennis courts, a playground and catering facilities. Entrance charges vary from 25-100 drs.
   There are beaches and/or swimming pools at:

Paleon Faliron/ Faliro	A seaside resort	Bus No. 126: Departs from Odhos Othonos, south side of Syntagma Sq *(Tmr* E5).
Alimos	NTOG beach	Bus No. 133: Departs from Odhos Othonos, south side of Syntagma Sq *(Tmr* E5).
Glyfada (Glifada)	A seaside resort	Bus No. 129: Departs from Leoforos Olgas, south side of the Zappeion Gardens *(Tmr* E5/6).

Voula	NTOG beach Class A	Bus No. 122: Departs from Leoforos Olgas, south side of Zappeion Gardens (*Tmr* E5/6).
Voula	NTOG beach Class B	Bus No. 122: Adults 60 drs, children 40 drs.
Vouliagmeni	A luxury seaside resort and yacht marina. NTOG beach.	Bus No. 118: Departs from Leoforos Olgas, south side of the Zappeion Gardens (*Tmr* E5/6). Adults 70 drs, children 50 drs, cabin 150 drs.
Varkiza	A seaside resort and yacht marina. NTOG beach.	Bus No. 115: Departs from Leoforos Olgas, south side of the Zappeion Gardens (*Tmr* E5/6). Adults 100 drs, children 50 drs.

There are beaches all the way down to Cape Sounion (Sounio) via the coast road. Buses terminus at 14 Mavrommateon St (*Tmr* D/E1) west of Pedion Areos Park and north of Omonia Sq. The Athens/Cape Sounion bus departs every hour from 0630 hrs and leaves Sounion for Athens every hour from 0800-1900 hrs. The one-way fare costs 350 drs and the journey takes 1½ hours.

BOOKSELLERS Apart from the secondhand bookshops in the Plaka Flea Market (*See* **Monastiraki Square, Introduction**), there are three or four on Odhos Nikis (west of Syntagma Sq) and Odhos Amerikis (north-west of Syntagma Sq) as well as one on Lysikratous St, opposite the small church (*Tmr* 21D5). Of all the above it is perhaps invidious to select one but here goes....
The Compendium Bookshop (& Computers) 28 Nikis St.   Tel. 322-6931
Well recommended for a wide range of English language publications. **The Transalpino** travel office is in the basement.

BREAD SHOPS In the more popular shopping areas. Descending along Odhos Adrianou, in the Plaka (*Tmr* D5), from the Odhos Thespidos/Kidathineon end, advances past many shops, general stores and a bread shop (or two). They make way for souvenir and gift shops on the way towards Monastiraki.

BUSES AND TROLLEY-BUSES These run variously between 0500 and 0030 (half an hour past midnight) and are usually crowded, but excellent value with a 'flat rate' charge of 30 drs. Travel between 0500 and 0800 hrs is free, not only on the buses but the Metro as well.

Buses The buses are blue (and green) and bus stops are marked Stasis (ΣΤΑΣΙΣ). Some one-man-operated buses are utilised and a few have an honesty box for fares.

Trolley-Buses Yellow coloured vehicles and bus stops. Entered via a door at the front marked Eisodos (ΕΙΣΟΔΟΣ), with the exit at the rear, marked Exodus (ΕΞΟΔΟΣ). Have the correct money to put into the fare machine as there are no tickets or change disgorged.

Major city terminals & turn-round points (*See* footnote at the end of this section)
Kaningos Sq: (*Tmr* 4D2) North-east of Omonia Sq.
Stadiou/Kolokotroni junction: (*Tmr* D/E4). This has replaced the Korai Sq terminus now that Korai has been pedestrianised.
Liossion St: (*Tmr* C2) North-west of Omonia Sq.
Eleftherias Sq: (*Tmr* 9C3) North-west of Monastiraki Sq.
Leoforos Olgas (*Tmr* D/E5/6) South of the National Garden's Mavvrommateon St:* (*Tmr* D/E1) West of Pedion Areos Park north of Omonia Sq.
* *The tree shaded north-south street is lined with bus departure points.*

85

Egyptou Place (Aigyptou/Egiptou): (*Tmr* D1) Just below the south-west corner of Pedion Areos Park, alongside 28 (Ikosiokto) Oktovriou.

Ag. Asomaton Square: (*Tmr* B/C4) West of Monastiraki Sq.

Koumoundourou St: (*Tmr* C2/3) West of Omonia Sq, third turning right off Ag. Konstantinou.

Trolley-bus timetable
Some major city routes include

No. 1: Plateia Attikis (Metro station) (*Tmr* C1), Stathmos Larissis (railway station) Karaiskaki Place, Ag. Konstantinou, Omonia Sq, Syntagma Sq, Kallithea suburb (SW Athens). Every 10 mins from 0505 - 2350 hrs.

No. 2: Pangrati (*Tmr* G6), Leoforos Amalias (Central), Syntagma Sq, Omonia Sq, 28 Ikosiokto Oktovriou/Patission St, Kipseli (N Athens). From 0630 - 0020 hrs.

No. 10: N. Smirni (S Athens), Leoforos Sygrou, Leoforos Amalias, Syntagma Sq, Panepistimiou St, Stadiou/Kolokotroni junction (*Tmr* D/E4). From 0500 - 2345 hrs.

No. 12: Leoforos Olgas (*Tmr* D/E5/6), Leoforos Amalias, Syntagma Sq, Omonia Sq, 28 Ikosiokto Oktovriou/Patission St (N Athens). From 0630 - 2235 hrs.

Other routes covered by trolley-buses include:

No. 3: Patissia to Erythrea (N to NNE Athens suburbs). From 0625 - 2230 hrs.

No. 4: Odhos Kypselis (*Tmr* E1) (North of Pedion Areos park), Omonia Sq, Syntagma Sq, Leoforos Olgas to Ag Artemios (SSE Athens suburbs). From 0630 - 0020 hrs.

No. 5: Patissia (N. Athens suburb), Omonia Sq, Syntagma Sq, Filellinon St, Koukaki (S Athens suburb). From 0630 - 0015 hrs.

No. 6: Ippokratous St (*Tmr* E3), Panepistimiou St, Omonia Sq to N. Filadelfia (N. Athens suburb). Every 10 mins from 0500 - 2320 hrs.

No. 7: Panepistimiou St (*Tmr* D/E3/4), 28 Ikosiokto Oktovriou/Patission St to Leoforos Alexandras (N. of Lycabettus). From 0630 - 0015 hrs.

No. 8: Plateia Kaningos (*Tmr* 4D2), Odhos Akadimias, Vassilissis Sofias, Leoforos Alexandras, 28 Ikosiokto Oktovriou/Patission St. From 0630 - 0020 hrs.

No. 9: Odhos Kypselis (*Tmr* E1) (North of Pedion Areos park), 28 Ikosiokto Oktovriou/Patission St, Stadiou St, Syntagma Sq, Petralona (W. Athens suburb – far side of Filopapou). Every 10 mins from 0455 - 2345 hrs.

No. 10: Stadiou/Koloktoroni junction (*Tmr* D/E4), Stadiou St, Syntagma Sq, Filellinon St, Leoforos Sygrou, Nea Smirni (S. Athens suburb). Every 10 mins from 0500 - 2345 hrs.

No. 11: Koliatsou (NNE Athens suburb), 28 Ikosiokto Oktovriou/Patission St, Stadiou St, Syntagma Sq, Filellinon St, Plastira Sq, Eftichidou St, N. Pangrati (ESE Athens suburb). Every 5 mins from 0500 - 0010 hrs.

No. 13: 28 Ikosiokto Oktovriou/Patission St, Akadimias St, Vassilissis Sofias, Papadiamantopoulou St, Leoforos Kifissias, Labrini (just beyond Galatsi suburb) (NE Athens suburb). Every 10 mins from 0500 - 2400 hrs.

No. 14: Leoforos Alexandras, 28 Ikosiokto Oktovriou/Patission, Patissia (N. Athens suburb).

Bus timetable
Bus numbers are subject to a certain amount of confusion, but here goes! Some of the routes are as follows:

No. 022: Kaningos Sq (*Tmr* 4D2), Akadimias, Kanari, Patriarchou Ioakim, Marasli, Genadiou St (SE Lycabettus). Every 10 mins from 0520 - 2330 hrs.

No. 024: Leoforos Amalias (*Tmr* D/E5), Syntagma Sq, Panepistimiou St, Omonia Sq, Tritis Septemvriou, Stournara, Sourmeli, Acharnon, Liossion St. Every 20 mins from 0530 - 2400 hrs.
*NB This is the bus that delivers passengers to 260 Liossion St (*Tmr C2), one of the main bus terminals.*

No. 040: Filellinon St (close to Syntagma Sq – *Tmr* D/E4/5), Leoforos Amalias, Leoforos Sygrou to Vassileos Konstantinou, Piraeus. Every 10 mins, 24 hours a day. Green bus.

No. 045: Kaningos Sq (*Tmr* 4D2), Akadimias St, Vassilissis Sofias, Leoforos Kifissias to Kefalari and Politia (NE Athens suburb). Every 15 mins from 0600 - 0100 hrs.

No. 049: Athinas St (*Tmr* C/D3), (S of Omonia Sq), Sofokleous, Pireos, Sotiros, Filonos St, Plateia Themistokleous, Piraeus. Every 10 mins, 24 hours a day. Green bus.

No. 051: Off Ag. Konstantinou (*Tmr* C2/3), W of Omonia Sq, Kolonou St, Platonos St (W. Athens suburb). Every 10 mins from 0500 - 2400 hrs.
*NB This is the bus that connects to the 100 Kifissou St (*Tmr A2), a main bus terminal.*

No. 115: Leoforos Olgas (*Tmr* D/E5/6), Leoforos Sygrou, Leoforos Possidonos (coast road) to Varkiza. Every 20 mins, 24 hours a day.

No. 118: Leoforos Olgas, Leoforos Sygrou, Leoforos Possidonos (coast road) to Vouliagmeni. Every 20 mins from 1245 - 2015 hrs.

No. 122: Leoforos Olgas, Leoforos Sygrou, Leoforos Possidonos (coast road) to Voula. Every 20 mins from 0530 - 2400 hrs.

No. 132: Othonos St (Syntagma Sq, *Tmr* 1D/E4/5), Filellinon St, Leoforos Amalias, Leoforos Sygrou to Edem (SSE Athens suburb). Every 20 mins from 0530 - 1900 hrs.

No. 224: Polygono (N. Athens suburb), 28 Okosiokto Oktovriou/Patission St, Kaningos Sq, Vassilissis Sofias, Democratias St (Kessariani, E. Athens suburb). Every 20 mins from 0500 - 2400 hrs.

No. 230: Ambelokipi (E. Athens suburb), Leoforos Alexandras, Ippokratous St, Akadimias St, Syntagma Sq, Leoforos Amalias, Dionysiou Areopagitou, Apostolou Pavlou, Thission. Every 10 mins from 0500 - 2320 hrs.

No. 510: Kaningos Sq (*Tmr* 4D2), Akadimias St, Ippokratous St, Leoforos Alexandras, Leoforos Kifissias to Dionyssos (NE Athens suburb). Every 20 mins from 0530 - 2250 hrs.

No. 527: Kaningos Sq, (*Tmr* 4D2) Akadimias St, Leoforos Alexandras, Leoforos Kifissias to Amaroussion (NE Athens suburb). Every 15 mins from 0615 - 2215 hrs.

NB The Athens-Attica bus services detailed above cover the city and its environs. The rest of Greece is served by:

1) **KTEL** A pool of bus operators working through one company from two terminals. 260 Liossion St* and 100 Kifissou St**

2) **OSE** (the State Railway Company) Their buses terminus alongside the main railway stations of Stathmos Peloponissou and Larissis. Apart from the domestic services, there is a terminal for other European capitals, including Paris, Instanbul and Munich, at Stathmos Larissis Station.

* **Liossion St** (*Tmr* C2) is to the east of Stathmos Peloponissou Railway Station. The terminus serves Halkida, Edipsos, Kimi, Delphi, Amfissa, Kamena Vourla, Larissa, Thiva, Trikala (Meteora) Livadia, Lamia. **Refer to bus route No. 024 to get to this terminus.**

** **Kifissou St** (*Tmr* A2) is to the west of Omonia Sq, beyond the 'steam railway' lines, across Leoforos Konstantinoupoleos and up Odhos Platonos. The terminus serves Patras, Pirgos (Olympia), Nafplio (Mikines), Adritsena (Vasses), Kalamata, Sparti (Mistras), Githio (Diros), Tripolis, Messolongi, Igoumenitsa, Preveza, Ioanina, Corfu, Zakynthos, Cephalonia, Lefkas, Kozani, Kastoria, Florina, Grevena, Veria, Naoussa, Edessa, Seres, Kilkis, Kavala, Drama, Komotini, Korinthos, Kranidi, Xilokastro. **Refer to bus route No. 051 to get to this terminus.**

For any bus services connecting to the islands detailed in this guide, refer to the relevant Mainland Ports and Island chapters.

CAMPING *See* **The Accommodation.**

CAR HIRE As any other capital city, numerous offices, the majority of which are lined up in the smarter areas and squares, such as Syntagma Sq and Leoforos Amalias. Typical is:

Pappas, 44 Leoforos Amalias   Tel. 322-0087

There are any number of car hire (and travel) firms on the right of Leoforos Sygrou, descending from the 'spaghetti junction' south of the Temple of Olympian Zeus (*Tmr* D6).

CAR REPAIR Help and advice can be obtained by contacting:

The Automobile & Touring Club of Greece (ELPA), 2 Messogion St (*Tmr* I. 3)

Tel. 779-1615

For immediate, emergency attention dial 104.

There are dozens of backstreet car repairers, breakers and spare part shops parallel and to the west of Leoforos Sygrou, in the area between the Olympic office and the Temple of Olympian Zeus.

CHEMIST *See* **Medical Care**

CINEMAS There are a large number of outdoor cinemas. Do not worry about a language barrier as the majority of the films have English (American) dialogue with Greek subtitles.

Aigli in the Zappeion is a must and is situated at the south end of the National Garden. Other cinemas are bunched together on the streets of Stadiou, Panepistimiou and 28 Ikosiokto Oktovriou/Patission.

Anne notes that the cinemas in Athens, of which there are vast numbers, generally show poor quality films with scratches, hisses, jumps, long black gaps and or loss of sound especially between reels. However her recommendation is the:

Radio City 240 Patission St
Large screen, good sound and knowledgeable operators.

CLUBS, BARS & DISCOS Why leave home? But if you must, there are enough to satiate the most voracious desires.

COMMERCIAL SHOPPING AREAS During daylight hours a very large street market ranges up Odhos Athinas (*Tmr* C3/4), Odhos Sokratous and the associated side streets from Ermou St, almost all the way up to Omonia Sq. After dark the shutters are drawn down, the stalls canvassed over and the 'ladies of the night' appear.

Plateia Kotzia (*Tmr* C/D3) spawns a flower market on Sundays whilst the Parliament Building side of Vassilissis Sofias (*Tmr* E4) is lined with smart flower stalls that open daily.

Monastiraki Sq (*Tmr* 5C4) and the various streets that radiate off are abuzz, specialising in widely differing aspects of commercial and tourist trade. Odhos Areos contains a plethora of leather goods shops; the near end of Ifestou lane is edged by stall upon stall of junk and tourist 'omit-abilia' (the forgettable memorabilia); Pandrossou Lane contains a better class of shop and stall selling sandals, pottery and smarter 'memorabilia' while the square itself has a number of handcart hawkers.

The smart department stores are conveniently situated in or around Syntagma Sq, and the main streets that radiate off the square, including Ermou, Stadiou and Panepistimiou.

See **Bread Shops** & **Trains** for details of other markets and shopping areas.

DENTISTS & DOCTORS *See* **Medical Care**

EMBASSIES

Australia: 15 Messogion Av.	Tel. 775-7651
Canada: 4 Ioannou Gennadiou St	Tel. 723-9511
Great Britain: 1 Ploutarchou & Ypsilantou Sts.	Tel. 723-6211
Ireland: 7 Vassileos Konstantinou	Tel. 723-2771
New Zealand: 5-17 Tsoha St.	Tel. 641-0311
South Africa: 124 Kifissias/Iatridou	Tel. 692-2125
USA: 91 Vassilissis Sofias	Tel. 721-2951
Denmark: 15 Philikis Etairias Sq.	Tel. 724-9315
Finland: 1 Eratosthenous & Vas. Konstantinou Streets	Tel. 751-5064
Norway: 7 Vassileos Konstantinou St	Tel. 724-6173
Sweden: 7 Vassileos Konstantinou St	Tel. 722-4504
Belgium: 3 Sekeri St	Tel. 361-7886
France: 7 Vassilissis Sofias	Tel. 361-1663
German Federal Republic: 3 Karaoli/Dimitriou Streets	Tel. 369-4111
Netherlands: 5-7 Vassileos Konstantinou	Tel. 723-9701

HAIRDRESSERS No problems with sufficient in the main shopping areas.

HOSPITALS *See* **Medical Care**

LAUNDRETTES There may be others but a good, central recommendation must be:
Coin-op (*Tmr* 13D5) Angelou Geronda
Directions: From Kidathineon St (proceeding towards Syntagma Sq), at the far end of Plateia Plaka turn right down Angelou Geronda, towards Dedalou, and the laundrette is on the right-hand side.
A machine load costs 200 drs, 9 mins of dryer time 20 drs and a measure of powder 30 drs. In respect of the detergent, why not pop out to Kidathineon St and purchase a small packet of Tide for 38 drs. The staff carry out the wash and dry operation at a cost of 400 drs for customers who are busy and are prepared to leave the laundry behind. Open in the summer daily 0800 - 2100 hrs.
The more usual Athens style is for customers to leave their washing at any one of the countless laundries and collect it next day dry, stiff and bleached (if necessary).
Note that my lavatorial obsession would not be satisfied without mentioning the Public toilet sited on Plateia Plaka.

LOST PROPERTY The main office is situated at: 33 Ag Konstantinou (Tel. 523-0111), the Plateia Omonia end of Ag. Konstantinou. The telephone number is that of the Transport police who are now in charge of lost property (or *Grafio Hamenon Adikimenon*). It is still true to say that you are far more likely to 'lose' personal belongings to other tourists, than to Greeks.

LUGGAGE STORE There is one at No. 26 Nikis St (*Tmr* D5) advertising the service at a cost of 50 drs per day per piece; 250 drs per week and 750 drs per month.

MEDICAL CARE
Chemists/Pharmacies (**Farmakio** – ΦAPMAKEIO) Identified by a green or red cross on a white background. Normal opening hours and a rota operates to give a 'duty' chemist cover.
Dentists & Doctors Ask at the **First Aid Centre** for the address of the School of Dentistry where free treatment is available. Both dentists and doctors advertise widely and there is no shortage of practitioners.
First Aid Centre (KAT) (*Tmr* 14D2) 21 Tritis Septemvriou St, beyond the Chalkokon-dili turning and on the left. Tel. 150
Hospital (*Tmr* 15G4) Do not proceed direct to a hospital but initially attend the **First Aid Centre.** If necessary they direct patients to the correct destination.
Medical Emergency: Tel. 166

METRO/ELEKTRIKOS (HΣAM) The Athens underground or subway system, which operates below ground in the heart of the city and overground for the rest of the journey. It is a simple one track layout from Kifissia (north-east Athens suburb) to Piraeus (south-west of Athens), and represents marvellous value with two rate fares of 30 and 60 drs. Passengers must have the requisite coins to obtain a ticket from the machine, prior to gaining access to the platforms. Everyone is most helpful and will, if the ticket machine 'frightens' a chap, show how it should be operated. Take care, select the ticket value first, then put the coins in the slot and keep the ticket so as to be able to hand it in at the journey's end. The service operates between 0505 and 0015 hrs (the next morning) and travel before 0800 hrs is free. Keep an eye open for the old-fashioned wooden carriages.

Station Stops There are 21 which include Kifissia (NE suburb), Stathmos Attiki (for the main railway stations), Plateia Victorias (N. Athens), Omonia Sq, Monastiraki Sq (Plaka), Plateia Thission (for the Acropolis) and (Piraeus) Port. From the outside, the Piraeus terminus is rather difficult to locate, the entrance being in the left-hand corner of what appears to be an oldish waterfront building. There used to be 20 stations but the new 'Peace Stadium' has acquired a stop called Irene.

MUSIC & DANCING See **Clubs, Bars & Discos & The Eating Out**

NTOG (EOT) The headquarters of the National Tourist Organisation (NTOG) or, in Greek, the EOT (Ellinikos Organismos Tourismou – ΕΛΛΗΝΙΚΟΣ ΟΡΓΑΝΙΣΜΟΣ ΤΟΥΡΙΣΜΟΥ) is on the 5th floor at 2 Amerikis St (*Tmr* E4) close by Syntagma Sq. But this office does not normally handle the usual tourist enquiries although the commissionaires manning the desk do hand out bits and pieces of information.

The information desk, from whence the free Athens map, advice, information folders, bus and boat schedules and hotel facts may be obtained, is situated inside and on the left of the foyer of the:

National Bank of Greece (*Tmr* 3D/E4) 2 Karageorgi Servias, Syntagma Sq

Tel. 322-2545

Directions: As above.

Do not hope to obtain anything other than pamphlets and a snatch of guidance as it would be unrealistic to expect personal attention from staff besieged by wave upon wave of tourists of every creed, race and colour. The hotel information sheets handed out now include a list of Athens Class D & E hotels. Open Monday - Friday, 0800 - 2000 hrs, Saturdays 0900 - 1400 hrs.

There is also an NTOG office conveniently situated at the East Airport.

OPENING HOURS (Summer months) These are only a guideline and apply to Athens (as well as the larger cities). Note that in country and village areas, it is more likely that shops are open from Monday to Saturday inclusive for over 12 hours a day, and on Sundays, holidays and Saints days, for a few hours either side of midday. The afternoon siesta is usually taken between 1300/1400 hrs and 1500/1700 hrs.

Trade Stores & Chemists Monday, Wednesday and Saturday 0800 - 1430 hrs. Tuesday, Thursday and Friday 0900 - 1300 hrs and 1700 - 2000 hrs.

Food Stores Monday, Wednesday and Saturday 0800 - 1500 hrs. Tuesday, Thursday and Friday 0800 - 1400 hrs and 1730 - 2030 hrs.

Art & Gift Shops Weekdays 0800 - 2100 hrs. Sundays (Monastiraki area) 0930 - 1445 hrs.

Restaurants, Pastry Shops, Cafes & Dairy Shops Seven days a week.

Museums See **Museums, Places of Interest.**

Public Services (including Banks) Refer to the relevant **A to Z** heading.

OTE There are offices at: No. 85, 28 Ikosiokto Oktovriou/Patission St (*Tmr* 16D1) (open 24 hrs a day); 15 Stadiou St (*Tmr* 17D4) (open Monday to Friday 0700-2400 hrs, Saturday and Sunday 0800 - 2400 hrs); 53 Solonos (*Tmr* E3) and 7 Kratinou (Plateia Kotzia) (*Tmr* C/D3) (open between 0800 and 2400 hrs). There is also an office at 45 Athinas St (*Tmr* C/D3).

PHARMACIES See **Medical Care**

PLACES OF INTEREST
Parliament Building (*Tmr* E4/5) Syntagma Sq. Here it is possible to watch the Greek

equivalent of the British 'changing the Guard at Buckingham Palace'. The special guards (Evzones) are spectacularly outfitted with tasselled red caps, white shirts (blouses do I hear?), coloured waistcoats, a skirt, white tights, knee-garters and boots topped off with pom-poms. The ceremony officially kicks off at 1100 hrs on Sunday morning but seems to falter into action at about 1045 hrs. Incidentally there is a band thrown in for good measure.

Museums The seasons are split as follows: Winter, 1st November - 31st March; Summer, 1st April - 31st October. Museums are closed on: 1st January, 25th March, Good Friday, Easter Day and Christmas Day. Sunday hours are kept on Epiphany, Ash Monday, Easter Saturday, Easter Monday, 1st May, Whit Sunday, Assumption Day, 28th October and Boxing Day. They are only open in the mornings on Christmas Eve, New Year's Eve, 2nd January, Easter Thursday and Easter Tuesday. Museums are closed on Tuesdays unless otherwise indicated. Students with cards will achieve a reduction in fees.

Acropolis (Tmr C5). The museum exhibits finds made on the site. Of special interest are the sixth century BC statues of Korai women. Entrance charges are included in the admission fee to the Acropolis, which costs 400 drs per head and is open in the Summer: 0730 - 1930 hrs; Sunday and holidays 0800 - 1800 hrs. The museum hours are 0730 - 1930 hrs; Tuesdays 1200 - 1800 hrs; Sundays and holidays 0800 - 1800 hrs.

Benaki (Tmr E/F4) On the corner of Vassilissis Sofias and Koubari (Koumbari) St, close by Plateia Kolonaki. A very interesting variety of exhibitis made up from private collections. Particularly diverting is a display of national costumes. Summer hours: daily 0830 - 1400 hrs, Sundays and holidays 0930 - 1430 hrs. Entrance 100 drs.

Byzantine (Tmr F4/5) 22 Vassilissis Sofias. As one would deduce from the name – Byzantine art. Summer hours: daily 0845 - 1500 hrs; Sunday and holidays, 0930 - 1430 hrs; closed Mondays. Entrance costs 200 drs.

Goulandris 13 Levidou St, Kifissia, N. Athens. Natural History. Summer hours: daily 0900 - 1400 hrs; Sunday and holidays 1000 - 1600 hrs; closed Fridays. Entrance costs 30 drs.

Goulandris (Tmr F4) 4 Neophitou Douka St (off Vassilissis Sofias). The second or 'other' Goulandris Museum. The situation is not helped by the little quirk of some people referring to the Natural History Museum as 'Goulandris'. Help! This Goulandris, that is the Cycladic and Ancient Greek Art Goulandris Museum is open daily in the summer 1000 - 1600 hrs; closed Tuesday, Sunday and holidays. Entrance costs 150 drs.

Kanelloupoulos (Tmr C5) On the corner of Theorias and Panos Sts. (Plaka). A smaller version of the Benaki Museum and located at the foot of the northern slope of the Acropolis, at the Monastiraki end. Summer hours: daily 0845 - 1500 hrs; Sunday and holidays 0930 - 1430 hrs. Entrance costs 100 drs (and is charged Sundays and holidays).

Keramikos (Tmr B4) 148 Ermou St. Finds from Keramikos cemetery. Summer hours: daily 0845 - 1500 hrs; Sunday and holidays 0930 - 1430 hrs. The museum is (apparently) open every day. Entrance to the site and museum costs 100 drs.

National Gallery & Alexandros Soutzos (Tmr G4), 46 Vassileos Konstantinou/Sofias. Mainly 19th and 20th century Greek paintings. Summer hours: 0900 - 1500 hrs; Sunday and holidays 1000 - 1400 hrs; closed on Mondays. Entrance costs 30 drs.

National Historical & Ethnological (*Tmr* D4) Kolokotroni Square, off Stadiou St. Greek history and the War of Independence. Summer hours: 0900 - 1400 hrs; Sunday and holidays 0900 - 1300 hrs; closed Mondays. Entrance costs 100 drs.

National Archaeological (*Tmr* D/E2), 1 Tossitsa St, off 28 Ikosiokto Oktovriou/ Patission St. The largest and possibly the most important Greek museum, covering a wide variety of exhibits. A must if you are a museum buff. Summer hours: 0800 - 1700 hrs; Sunday and holidays 0800 - 1700 hrs; closed on Mondays. Entrance costs 300 drs which includes entrance to the Santorini and Numismatic exhibitions (*See* below).

Numismatic In the same building as the National Archaeological and displaying, as would be imagined, a collection of Greek coins, spanning the ages. Summer hours: 0930 - 1330 hrs; Sunday and holidays 0900 - 1400 hrs; closed on Tuesdays. Admission is free.

Also housed in the same building are the:

Epigraphical Collection: Summer hours: 0830 - 1330 hrs; Sunday and holidays 0900 - 1400 hrs.

Santorini Exhibits: Summer hours: 0930 - 1500 hrs every day, closed on Mondays. and

The Casts and Copies Exhibition: Summer hours: 0900 - 1400 hrs daily; closed Sunday and Mondays.

Popular (Folk) Art (*Tmr* D5) 17 Kidathineon St, The Plaka. Folk art, folklore and popular art. Summer hours: 1000 - 1400 hrs; Sunday and holidays 1000 - 1400 hrs; closed on Mondays. Entrance free.

War (*Tmr* F4/5) 2 Rizari St, off Leoforos Vassilissis Sofias. Warfare exhibits covering a wide variety of subjects. Summer hours: daily 0900 - 1400 hrs; Sunday and holidays 0930 - 1400 hrs; closed on Mondays. Entrance is free.

Theatres & Performances For full, up-to-date details enquire at the NTOG office (*Tmr* 3D/E4). They should be able to hand out a pamphlet giving a precise timetable for the year. As a guide the following are performed year in and year out:

Son et Lumiere. From the Pnyx hillside, a *Son et Lumiere* features the Acropolis. The English performance starts at 2100 hrs every evening, except when the moon is full, and takes 45 minutes. There are French versions at 2215 hrs daily except Tuesdays and Fridays when a German commentary is provided at 2200 hrs. Tickets are available for 300 drs (students 120 drs) at the entrance of the Church, Ag Dimitros Lombardiaris, on the way to the show. Catch a No. 230 bus along Dionysiou Areopagitou St getting off one stop beyond the Odeion (Theatre) of Herodes Atticus and follow the signposted path on the left-hand side.

Athens Festival. This prestigious event takes place in the restored and beautiful Odeion of Herodes Atticus, built in approximately AD 160 as a Roman theatre, seating about 5000 people and situated at the foot of the south-west corner of the Acropolis. The festival lasts from early June to the middle of September, and consists of a series of plays, ballet, concerts and opera. The performances usually commence at 2100 hrs and tickets, which are on sale up to 10 days before the event, are obtainable from the Theatre or from the *Athens Festival booking office* (*Tmr* D/E4), 4 Stadiou St, Tel. 322-1459.

Dora Stratou Theatre. (*Tmr* A6) A short stroll away on Mouseion or Hill of Muses. On the summit stands the Monument of the Filopapou (Philopappos) and nearby the Dora Stratou Theatre, where an internationally renowned troupe of folk dancers, dressed in traditional costumes, perform a series of Greek dances and songs. Performances are timed to coincide with the ending of the *Son et Lumiere,* on the Pnyx. The show, produced from early May up to the end of September, costs between 450-750 drs per head (students 350 drs), starts at about 2215 hrs, lasts approximately one hour, and is well worth a visit. Tickets are available from the Theatre (Tel. 314-4395) between 0900 - 1400 hrs.

Lycabettus Theatre. On the north-east side of Lycabettus Hill (Lykavitos, Likavittos, Lykabettos, etc. etc.). Concerts and theatrical performances take place in the hillside open-air theatre between the middle of June and the first week of September from 2100 hrs. Tickets can be purchased from the theatre box office, one hour before the event, or from the *Athens Festival booking office*, referred to above under *Athens Festival.*

POLICE *See* **Tourist police.**

POST OFFICES (Tachidromio – ΤΑΧΥΔΡΟΜΕΙΟΝ**)** Weekday opening hours, as a guide, are 0800 to 1300 hrs. The Central Post Office at 100 Eolou St *(Tmr* 18D3), close by Omonia Sq, is open Monday - Saturday, 0730 - 1500 hrs. Branch offices are situated on the corner of Othonos and Nikis Streets (Syntagma Sq); at the Omonia Sq underground Metro concourse and on Dionysiou Areopagitou St, at the corner of Tzireon St *(Tmr* D6).

The telephone and telegraph system is run by a separate state organisation. *See* **OTE.**

PHOTOGRAPHY (Fotografion ΦΩΤΟΓΡΑΦΕΙΟΝ**)** Visitors requiring photographs for various membership cards can use the instant photo booth in the Metro underground concourse, Omonia Sq *(Tmr* 2D3).

SHOPPING HOURS *See* **Opening Hours.**

SPORTS FACILITIES
Golf. There is an 18 hole course, the Glifida Golf Club close by the East(ern) Airport. Changing rooms, restaurant and refreshment bar.
Swimming. There is a Swimming (and Tennis) Club on Leoforos Olgas *(Tmr* 19E6), across the way from the Zappeion, National Gardens. The Hilton Hotel *(Tmr* G4) has a swimming pool but, if you are not staying there, use of it costs the price of an (expensive) meal. *See* **Beaches.**
Tennis. There are courts at most of the NTOG beaches *(See* **Beaches**) as well as at the Ag. Kosmas athletics centre, close by the West airport.

TAXIS (ΤΑΞΙ**).** Used extensively and, although they seem to me to be expensive, they are 'officially' the cheapest in Europe. The Athens drivers are, now, generally without scruples. Fares are metered and costed at about 23 drs per kilometre. But they are subject to various surcharges including 15 drs for each piece of baggage, 240 drs per hour of waiting time and 30 drs for picking up at, or delivering to, public transport facilities. There is also an extra charge for the hours between midnight and daylight. When standing at a taxi rank drivers must pick up a fare, but are not obliged to do so when cruising, for which there is an extra 'flag falling' charge of 25 drs. The sign ΕΛΕΥΘΕΡΟΝ indicates a cab is free for hire. The minimum fare is 110 drs and approximate sample fares include: Syntagma/Omonia Squares to the East airport 500 drs and to the West airport 400 drs; the East airport to Piraeus 500 drs and the West airport to Piraeus 350 drs.

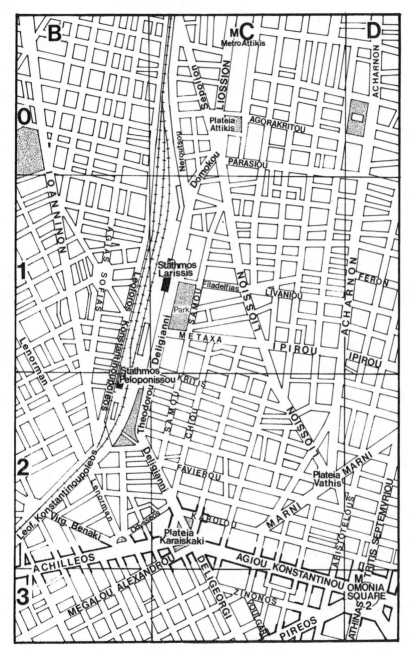

**Illustration 6   Athens City Inset –
The Railway Stations**

TELEPHONE *See* **OTE.**

TOURIST OFFICE/AGENCIES *See* **NTOG** & **Travel Agents.**

TOURIST POLICE (*Tmr* 20D6) I understand, despite the reorganisation of the service, that the Athens headquarters is to remain in operation. This is situated at 7 Leoforos Sygrou (Sygrou/Syngrou/Singrou Av). Open daily 0800 - 2200 hrs. Tel. 923-9224. Tourist information in English is available from the Tourist police on the telephone number 171.

There are also Tourist police offices close by and just to the north of Larissis Railway station (open 0700 - 2400 hrs, tel. 821-3574) and the East airport (open 0730 - 2300 hrs, tel. 981-4093).

TOILETS Apart from the various bus termini and the railway stations, there is a super Public toilet on the south-east corner of Syntagma Sq, as there is a pretty grim 'squatty' in the Omonia Sq Metro concourse. The Plaka is well 'endowed' with one at Plateia Plaka, (on Odhos Kidathineon) and another on the Plateia Agora at the other end of Odhos Adrianou. Visitors to Mt Lycabettus will not be 'caught short' and the toilets there are spotless.

TRAINS (Illustration 6) They arrive at (or depart from) either (a) Larissis Station (Stathmos No. 1) or (b) Peloponissou Station (Stathmos No. 2).

(A) LARISSIS STATION (STATHMOS No. 1) (*Tmr* B/C1)   Tel. 821-3882
The main, more modern station of the two. Connections to the Western European services and the northern provinces of Central Greece, Thessaly, Macedonia and Thrace. The bus stop to the centre of Athens is to the right of the station, with the building behind one. Refer to Buses below.

Services in and around the building include:

The National Bank of Greece. A branch opens Monday to Thursday 0830 - 1400 hrs and Friday 0830 - 1330 hrs.

Post Office. Open Monday to Saturday 0700 - 2000 hrs and Sunday 0900 - 1400 hrs. They transact money exchange and cash travellers' cheques.

Tourist police. There is an office just to the north of the station building. *See* **Tourist police.**

To the front of the station is a pavement cafe-bar (a coffee 56 drs) and an elongated square, well more a widening of the road.

The Accommodation
Even early and late in the summer a number of the hardier stretch out on the pavements around and about the stations (and at the *Hotel Oscar's* rates I'm not surprised). Arrivals, even whilst on the train, are bombarded with offers of accommodation, so much so that the touts are a nuisance.

With the station behind one, to the right, across the concourse and on the corner, is the:

Hotel Lefkos Pirgos (*Tmr* C1) (Class E) 27 Leof. Metaxa/Deligianni   Tel. 821-3765
Directions: as above.

Seedy looking with double rooms sharing bathroom starting at 1100 drs, rising to 1300 drs.

Hotel Nana (*Tmr* C1) (Class C), 29 Leof. Metaxa   Tel. 884-2211
Directions: Alongside the *Hotel Lefkos Pirgos*
Smarter (well it is C class) with the charges reflecting this eminence. A double room

en suite starts off at 2600 drs rising to 3300 drs (16th March - 31st Oct).

Directly opposite the main station entrance is the:

Hotel Oscar (*Tmr* C1) (Class B), 25 Samou/Filadelfias　　　　Tel. 883-4215
Directions: As above.

I hardly dare detail the room rates which for a double room kicks off at 3860 drs rising to 4000 drs, en suite naturally. Breakfast costs 280 drs. I must own up to staying at the *Oscar*. But it was at the end of a long stint on the Greek islands added to which there were a couple of other (good) reasons. Firstly they accept payment by American Express which, as I have written before, may be of great assistance in eking out dwindling funds and secondly the hotel is conveniently close to the railway and the inter-country coach station. Thus the comforts of this hotel, or similar, can be put to good use in order to build up the bodily reserves prior to a planned long distance bus or railway journey! That is not to say that even this luxurious establishment does not escape some of the common faults oft experienced as a 'norm' when staying at its lower classified 'cousins'. The en suite bathroom of our room had a loose lavatory seat, the bath plug had no chain attached (there was a chain but it was not attached), and the small bathroom window was tied up with string. The bedroom sliding balcony window would not completely shut – there was no locking mechanism and the air conditioning didn't. Mind you I must admit to making a reservation without Rosemary, who guarded our backpacks whilst I sorted out the formalities. It may have been the sight of the two towering, afore-mentioned packs backing through the swing doors into reception that resulted in our being allocated this particular 'downtown' room, at the rear of the hotel, overlooking and overlooked by towering blocks of flats.

Hotel Elena (Helena) (*Tmr* B/C1) (Class C) 2 Psiloriti/Samou　　　Tel. 881-3211
Directions: Along Samou St, south from Leof. Metaxa St, and on the right.

Single rooms sharing the bathroom cost 850 drs and en suite 1250 drs; double rooms sharing 1400 drs and en suite 1700 drs.

Hotel Louvre (*Tmr* C2) (Class D) 9 Chiou/Favierou Sts　　　Tel. 522-9891
Directions: Next street back from and parallel to Samou St, towards the south end of Chiou St.

Greek provincial in outward appearance despite the grand and evocative name. Single rooms sharing cost 850 drs; double rooms sharing 1220 drs and en suite 1550 drs.

Joy's Hotel (*Tmr* D1) 38 Feron St　　　　Tel. 823-1012
Directions: Proceed up Odhos Filadelfias, almost directly opposite the main station, across Odhos Liossion continuing along Livaniou St as far as Odhos Acharnon. Turn left and then first right on to Feron St.

Reputedly a good value 'Youth Hostel' style establishment offering accommodation ranging from the roof (300 drs) to quadruples. A single bed starts off at 900 drs and a double 1400 drs.

Street Market Whilst in this area it is worth noting that Odhos Chiou, between Kritis and Favierou Sts, is host to an extensive street market where almost everything is sold from fish to meat and hardware to clothing.

Bread Shop & Supermarket (*Tmr* B/C1/2) On the corner of Samou St and Eratyras St. A bit disorganised but very useful.

Snackbar (*Tmr* B/C1) Odhos Samou
Directions: Across the street from the Park on the stretch of Odhos Samou between Filadelfias and Leof. Metaxa Sts.

A small, convenient souvlaki pita snackbar, run by a very friendly chap, with a souvlaki and bottle of beer costing 125 drs.

Buses: Trolley-bus No. 1 pulls up to the right of the station as do the Nos 2 and 4. The fare to Syntagma Sq is 30 drs.

(B) PELOPONISSOU STATION (STATHMOS NO 2) (*TMR* B1/2)   Tel. 513-1601
The station for trains to the Peloponnese, the ferry connections for some of the Ionian islands and international ferries to Italy from Patras.

TRAINS (General)
Tickets: The concept behind the acquisition of a ticket is similar to that of a lottery. On buying a ticket, a compartment seat is also allocated. In theory this is a splendid scheme, but in practice the idea breaks down in a welter of bad tempered argument over who is occupying whose seat. Manners and quaint old-fashioned habits of giving up one's seat to older people and ladies are best avoided. I write this from the bitter experience of offering my seat to elderly Greek ladies only for their husbands to immediately fill the vacant position. Not what one had in mind! Find your seat and stick to it like glue and if you have made a mistake feign madness, admit to being a foreigner, but do not budge.

At Peloponissou Station the mechanics of buying a ticket take place in organised bedlam. The ticket office 'traps' open half an hour prior to the train's departure. Scenes reminiscent of a Cup Final crowd develop, with prospective travellers pitching about within the barriers of the ticket hatch, and all this in the space of about 10m by 10m. To add to the difficulty, there are two hatch 'slots' and it is anybody's guess which one to select. It really is best to try and steal a march on this 'extra-curricula' activity, diving for a hatch whenever one opens up.

Travellers booking a return journey train ticket to Europe, and routing via Italy, must ensure the ticket is from Patras, not Athens. (Yes, Patras.) Then purchase a separate Athens to Patras ticket thus ensuring a seat. A voyager boarding the train with an open ticket will almost surely have to stand for almost the whole of the 4 hour journey. Most Athens - Patras journeys seem to attract an 'Express' surcharge of between 100-150 drs which is charged by the ticket collector.

Incidentally, the general architecture of the Peloponissou building is delightful, especially the ceiling of the booking office hall, centrally located, under the main clock face. To the left, on entering the building, is a glass-fronted information box with all the train times listed on the window. The staff manning this desk are extremely helpful and speak sufficient English to pose no problems in communication (the very opposite of the disinterest shown at the NTOG desk in the National Bank of Greece, on Syntagma Sq).

Advance Booking Office. Information and advance booking for both stations is now handled at:
No. 6, Sina (*Tmr* E3) off Akadimias St (Tel. 363 4402/4406); No. 1, Karolou (Satovriandou) (*Tmr* C2) west of Omonia Sq. (Tel. 524 0647/8) and No. 17, Filellinon (*Tmr* D/E5) (Tel. 323 6747/6273).

Toilets The station toilets usually, well always, lack toilet paper.

Sustenance (on the train) An attendant brings inexpensive drinks and snacks around from time to time and hot snacks are available from platform trolleys at the major railway stations.

Railway Head Office (*Tmr* C2) Hellenic Railways Organisation (OSE) 1-3 Karolou St.
Tel. 522-2491
Directions: One back from the far end of Ag. Konstantinou west from Omonia Sq.

Provisions Shopping in the area of the railway stations is made easy by the presence of the Street Market on Odhos Chiou (*See* **Larissis Station, Trains**).

Access to the stations
Bus/Trolley-bus. From the Airport, travel on the Olympic bus to the terminal at 96-100 Leoforos Sygrou (which at a cost of 45 drs is extremely good value). Then catch a bus (Nos. 133, 040, 132, 155, 903 and 161 amongst others) across the street from the terminus to Syntagma Sq and then a No. 1 trolley-bus via Omonia Sq to the station. Instead of making a change of bus at Syntagma Sq it is also possible to walk west from the terminal on Leoforos Sygrou across Falirou and Odisseos Androutsou Streets to the parallel street of Odhos Dimitrakopoulou and catch a No. 1 trolley-bus all the way to the stations. From Piraeus Port catch the No. 40 (green) bus on Leoforos Vassileos Konstantinou (parallel to the quay) to Syntagma Sq, or the No. 049 from Plateia Themistokleous to Athinas St, close by Omonia Sq. *See* **Arrival by Air, Introduction; Airline offices & terminus** & **Buses & Trolley-Buses, A to Z.**

Metro The metro station for both railway stations is Attiki, close to Plateia Attikis. From the platform, assuming a traveller has come from the south, dismount and turn right down into the underpass to come out the far or west side of the station on Odhos Liossion. Turn left and walk to the large irregular Plateia Attikis (with the *Hotel Lydia* on the right). Proceed down Domokou St, (the road that exits half-right on the far side of the square), which spills into Plateia Deligianni edged by Stathmos Larissis. A more long-winded alternative is to get off the Metro at Omonia Sq, walk west along Ag. Konstantinou to Karaiskaki Sq and then up Odhos Deligianni, or why not catch a No. 1 trolley-bus.

Taxi A reasonable indulgence, if in a hurry, although it must be noted that in the crowded traffic conditions of Athens it is often quicker to walk than catch a cab. *See* **Taxis.**

Station to Station To get from one to the other, say Stathmos Larissis to Peloponissou, it is necessary to turn right out of the station and climb the steps over the railway line turning left at the bottom of the far side of the steps and walk some 100m to the forecourt in front of Stathmos Peloponissou. Almost, but not quite, adjacent, as some guides put it, if 150m on a very hot day, laden down with cases seems contiguous.

TRAIN TIMETABLES
Peloponissou Station It is easy to read the Peloponissou timetable and come to the conclusion that a large number of trains are leaving the station at the same time. On seeing the single-line track, a newcomer cannot be blamed for feeling apprehensive that it may prove difficult to select the correct carriages. The mystification arises from the fact that the trains are detailed separately from Athens to say Corinthos, Mikines, Argos, Tripolis, Pirgos and etc, etc. There is no mention that the railway line is a circular layout, with single trains circumscribing the route and that each place name is simply a stop on the journey.

Making changes for branch lines can be 'exciting'! Stations are labelled in demotic script and there is no comprehensible announcement from the guard, thus it is easy to fail to make an exit on cue!

Athens to Patras:
Depart   0640, 0826, 1020, 1305, 1542, 1820, 2139 hrs.
Arrive   1055, 1206, 1430, 1653, 2005, 2153, 0149 hrs.

Patras to Athens:
Depart   0630, 0811, 1105, 1350, 1705, 1842, 2013, 0210 hrs.
Arrive   1002, 1257, 1457, 1832, 2118, 2239, 0010, 0636 hrs.
One way fare: Athens to Patras : B class 540 drs, A class 811 drs.

Larissis Station
Athens to Thessaloniki & on to Alexandroupoli:
Depart: 0700, 0800, 1100, 1425, 1900, 2110, 2310 hrs.
Thessaloniki
Arrive: 1448, 1550, 1806, 2217, 0336, 0553, 0750 hrs.
Depart: 1532,   –   1832, 2316,   –   0617, 0924 hrs.
Drama
(for Kavala)
Arrive: 1854,   –   –   0302,   –   1023, 1338 hrs.
Alexandroupoli
Arrive: 2216,   –   –   0655,   –   1412, 1738 hrs.

One-way fare: Athens to Thessaloniki   : B Class 1271 drs, A Class 1909 drs.
    Athens to Drama   : B Class 1656 drs, A Class 2484 drs.
    Athens to Alexandroupoli : B Class 1961 drs, A Class 2944 drs.
Surcharge on Express trains from 170 - 300 drs.

TRAVEL AGENTS There are offices selling tickets for almost anything to almost anywhere which include:
ABC 58 Stadiou St. Tel. 321-1381
CHAT 4 Stadiou St. Tel. 322-2886
Key Tours 5th Floor, 2 Ermou St. Tel. 323-3756
Viking* 3 Filellinon St. Tel. 322-9383
* *Probably the agency most highly regarded by students for prices and variety.*
International Student & Youth Travel Service (SYTS) 11 Nikis St. Tel. 323-3767
For FIYTO membership. Second floor, open Monday - Friday 0900 - 1900 hrs. and Saturday from 0900 - 1200 hrs.

Filellinon and the parallel street of Odhos Nikis, to the west of Syntagma Sq, are jam packed with tourist agencies and student organisations including one or two express coach and train fare companies. A sample, going up the rise from Syntagma Square, includes:
Budget Student Travel On the right opposite a church.
Stafford Travel On the corner of Filellinon and Kidathineon Sts.

YOUTH HOSTEL ASSOCIATION *See* **The Accommodation**

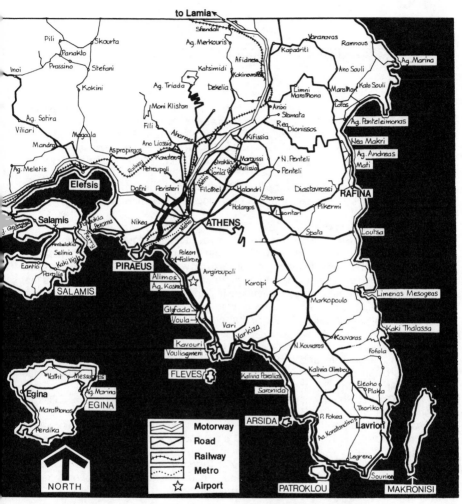

**Illustration 7   Athens Environs, Suburbs,
Bus & Metro Routes**

10 PIREAUS (Pireas, Pireefs)

Fortune and hope farewell! I've found the port you've done with me; go now with others sport From a Greek epigram

Tel. prefix 01

Piraeus is the port of Athens (Illustrations 8, 9 & 10) and the usual ferry-boat departure point for the N.E. Aegean islands as well as most other Aegean islands. A confusing town on first acquaintance, but very unlike the old Piraeus portrayed in the film *Never on Sunday*. The bawdy seaport cafes, tavernas and seedy waterfront have been replaced by smart shipping offices, respectable banks and tree planted thoroughfares, squares and parks.

Arrival at Piraeus will usually be by Metro or bus if coming from inland, or by ferry-boat if arriving by sea. (Well, it would be a long tiring swim, wouldn't it?).

ARRIVAL BY BUS

From Syntagma Sq (Athens), Bus No. 40 arrives at Plateia Korai (*Tmr* C3) but in truth that is rather an over simplification. For a start the bus is absolutely crammed early morning and it is very difficult to know one's exact whereabouts which is germane as the bus hurtles on down to the end of the Piraeus peninsula. The first indicator that the end of the ¾ hour journey is imminent is when the bus runs parallel to the Metro lines. The second is crossing a wide avenue at right-angles (Leoforos Vassileos Georgiou) after which signs for the Archaeological Museum indicate that it is time to bale out.

From Plateia Korai, north-west along Leoforos Vassileos Georgiou (Yeoryiou) leads to the Main (Grand or Central) Harbour (*Tmr* D2); south-east progresses towards Limin Zeas (Pasalimani) (*Tmr* C/D4) and east towards Limin Mounikhias (Tourkolimano) (*Tmr* B5), the latter two being the marina harbours.

From Omonia Sq (Athens) Bus No. 49 arrives at Ethniki Antistaseos (*Tmr* C2); from the East airport, (a yellow) Bus No. 19 (but often numberless), arrives at Karaiskaki Sq (*Tmr* C/D2). Karaiskaki or Akti Tzelepi Square is a main bus terminal. The brackets note regarding the No. 19 bus should be expanded to point out that all the other buses are blue.

Another service (Bus No. 101) arrives at Theotoki St (*Tmr* E/F3/4) from whence head north-east towards Sakhtouri St and turn left in a northerly direction to reach the southern end of the Main Harbour quay front.

ARRIVAL BY METRO

Piraeus Metro station (*Tmr* 1C1/2), the end of the line, is hidden away in the corner of a large but rather inconspicuous building, flanked by Plateia Roosevelt. It could well be a warehouse, an empty shell of an office block, in fact almost anything but a Metro terminus. Passengers emerge opposite the quayside, at the north end of the waterfront.

If catching a ferry almost immediately, it is probably best to make a temporary headquarters by turning right out of the entrance, following the quay round to the left and 'falling' into one of the three or so cafe-bars set in the harbour facing side of a sizeable quayside block of buildings. The importance of establishing a shorebase, or bridgehead, becomes increasingly apparent whilst attempts are made to locate the particular ferry-boat departure point.

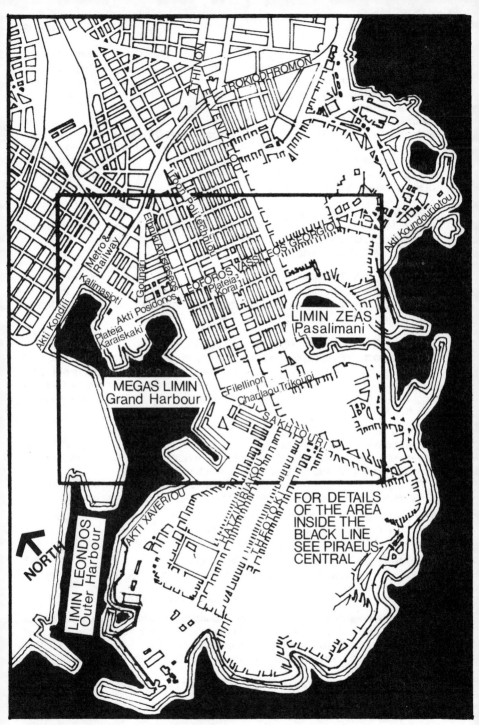

Illustration 8   Piraeus

To obtain tickets turn to the left (*Fsw*) out of the Metro station and follow the quayside round. First major landmark is Karaiskaki (or Akti Tzelepi) Sq (*Tmr* C/D2), fronted by large shipping office buildings which are surmounted by a number of neon lit signs. These advertising slogans change from year to year but the point is that they are a noticeable landmark. Proceed along the quay road (Akti Posidonos), between the Streets of Gounari and Ethniki Antistaseos, (*Tmr* C2), keeping the waterfront to the right. Reference to **Ferry-Boat Ticket Offices, A to Z** gives details of various ticket offices. The port police are located in a quayside shed and must be regarded as favourites to dispense fairly accurate information about ferry-boats. Any information received though is best tucked away for future comparison with the rest of the advice acquired.

ARRIVAL BY FERRY
Reorientate using the above information, but bearing in mind that ferries dock all the way round the Grand Harbour, from the area of the Metro station (*Tmr* 1C1/2) as far down as the Olympic office (*Tmr* 8D3).

ARRIVAL BY TRAIN
If passengers have not alighted at Athens, Peloponnese trains pull up at the same terminus building as the Metro (*Tmr* 1C1/2) and the Northern Greece trains on the far (north-west) side of the Grand Harbour (*Tmr* 19D/E1/2).

THE ACCOMMODATION & EATING OUT
The Accommodation General remarks for Athens also apply here. Although I have never had to doss (or camp) out in Piraeus, I am advised that it is not to be recommended. There are just too many disparate (desperate?) characters wandering about. Anne acidly pointed out that it was not entirely safe for lone females walking round revising a guide book – and requested danger money!

Close by the Metro Station are the:
Hotel Ionion (*Tmr* 4C2) (Class C) 10 Kapodistrion   Tel. 417-0992
Directions: Turn left from the Metro station and/or Roosevelt Sq (*Fsw*) down the quay road, Kalimasioti St, and left again at the first turning.
The hotel, halfway up on the right, is noticeable by the prominent sign promising *Family Hotel and from now on Economical Prices*. But is it with doubles from 2000 drs?

The Delfini (*Tmr* 5C2) (Class C) 7 Leoharous St   Tel. 412-3512
Directions: As above, but the second turning left.
Doubles with shower from 2200 drs.

Hotel Helektra (*Tmr* 6C2) (Class E) 12 Navarinou   Tel. 417-7057
Directions: At the top of Leoharous St, turn right on to Navarinou St and the hotel is at the end of the block.
During the season doubles sharing the bathroom cost 1100 drs.

Following the quay road of Akti Posidonos round to the right along the waterfront of Akti Miaouli towards the Custom's office (*Tmr* 14D/E3), and close by the Church of Ag Nikolaos, advances to the bottom of Leoforos Charilaou Trikoupi (*Tmr* D3). This street runs south-east and is amply furnished with cheaper hotels including the following:
Capitol Hotel (*Tmr* 7D3) (Class C) Ch. Trikoupi/147 Filonos Sts   Tel. 452-4911
Directions: As above
A double en suite costs 1650 drs.

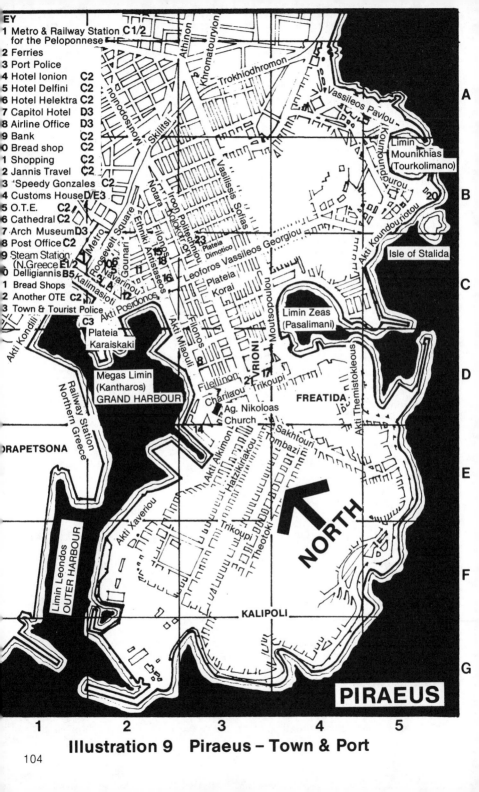

KEY

1 Metro & Railway Station **C1/2**
  for the Peloponnese
2 Ferries
3 Port Police
4 Hotel Ionion **C2**
5 Hotel Delfini **C2**
6 Hotel Helektra **C2**
7 Capitol Hotel **D3**
8 Airline Office **D3**
9 Bank **C2**
10 Bread shop **C2**
11 Shopping **C2**
12 Jannis Travel **C2**
13 'Speedy Gonzales' **C2**
14 Customs House **D/E3**
15 O.T.E. **C2**
16 Cathedral **C2**
17 Arch Museum **D3**
18 Post Office **C2**
19 Steam Station **E1/2**
  (N.Greece)
20 Delligiannis **B5**
21 Bread Shops
22 Another OTE **C2**
23 Town & Tourist Police

Illustration 9   Piraeus – Town & Port

104

Glaros Hotel (Class C) 4 Ch. Trikoupi   Tel. 452-7887
Double rooms start at 1400 drs sharing and 1650 drs en suite. Breakfast costs 180 drs.

Serifos Hotel (Class C) 5 Ch. Trikoupi.   Tel. 452-4967
A double room en suite from 1650 drs.

Santorini Hotel (Class C) 6 Ch. Trikoupi.   Tel. 452-2147
Prices as for the *Serifos Hotel*.

Homeridion Hotel (Class B) 32 Ch. Trikoupi.   Tel. 451-9811
Rather expensive with a double room starting off at 1710 rising during the season to 2250 drs.

Forming a junction with Leoforos Charilaou Trikoupi is Notara St up which turn left. On this street is sited the:
Faros Hotel (Class D) 140 Notara St   Tel. 452-6317
Directions: As above.
    More down-to-earth with a double room en suite from 1465 drs.

Again at right angles to Leoforos Charilaou Trikoupi, is Kolokotroni St on which are situated the following hotels:
Park House (Class B) 103 Kolokotroni St   Tel. 452-4611
Directions: As above.
    Double rooms en suite from 3790 drs including a shower and breakfast.

Aris Hotel (Class D) 117 Kolokotroni St   Tel. 452-0487
A double room sharing from 1250 drs and en suite 1400 drs.

Also leading off to the left is Iroon Politechniou (once Vassileos Konstantinou) whereon:
Noufara Hotel (Class B) 45 Iroon Politechniou   Tel. 411-5541
Directions: As above.
    Doubles start at 3200 drs complete with shower. (Phew!)

Savoy Hotel (Class B) 93 Iroon Politechniou   Tel. 413-1102
Guests will have to be flush with a double room en suite costing 4905 drs including breakfast.

Up Iroon Politechniou, turning right, or south-east, at Plateia Korai along Leoforos Vassileos Georgiou (Vassileos Yeoryiou) proceeds, on the left, to:
Diogenis Hotel (Class B) 27 Leoforos Vassileos Georgiou   Tel. 412-5471
Directions: As above.
    A few hundred drachmae less than the *Savoy* at 4020 drs. The prices include breakfast.

The Eating Out For eating out read the Athens comments as a general guide. Piraeus is not noted for outstanding rendezvous around the Grand Harbour and its encircling terrain, despite the numerous restaurants, tavernas and cafes along the quayside roads. On the other hand there are some excellent eating places in the area bordering the eastern coastline of the Piraeus peninsula, bounded by Akti Moutsopoulou (*Tmr* C/D3/4) and Akti Koumoundourou (*Tmr* B5) encircling (respectively) the Zeas and Mounikhias harbours.

Especially recommended by Anne is the classy:
Delligiannis (*Tmr* 20B5) 1 Akti Koundouriotou   Tel. 413-2013
Directions: A very pleasant setting of the 'pretty' part of Piraeus up on the hill to the

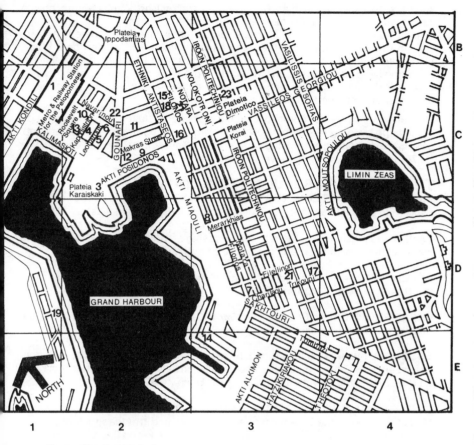

Tmr = Town map reference
Fsw = Facing seawards
Sbo = Sea behind one

Illustration 10   Piraeus Inset

south-west of Limin Mounikhias. This overlooks a few million pounds worth of private yachts lying to anchor in the most attractive harbour.

Apart from the position, the selection of food is excellent and there is outside seating while the inside resembles a high-class saloon bar. The service is quick, friendly and honest. For instance, enquirers will be advised that the 'souvlaki flambe' is nothing more than souvlaki on fire! 'Inside information' advises that the 'birds liver in wine' is delicious, despite being listed as a starter. Costing 450 drs, the portions are larger than most main courses at other tavernas.

On Plateia Karaiskaki, a number of cafe-bar/restaurants stretch along the quayside of the large building that dominates the square. A white van sometimes parks up, early in the day, on the edge of the square, selling small pizzas and feta cheese pies for 70 drs from the back of the vehicle.

THE A TO Z OF USEFUL INFORMATION

AIRLINE OFFICE & TERMINUS (*Tmr* 8D3) The Olympic office is halfway down the Esplanade of Akti Miaouli, at the junction with Odhos II Merarkhias.

BANKS The most impressive is a vast, imposing emporium situated opposite the corner of the Esplanade roads of Posidonos and Miaouli (*Tmr* 9C2).

BEACHES Between Zeas and Mounikhias harbours, opposite Stalida island. Also *See* **Beaches, A to Z, Athens.**

BREAD SHOPS One on Roosevelt Sq (*Tmr* 10C2) and others on Odhos Kolokotroni (*Tmr* 21C2/3) and Charilaou Trikoupi (*Tmr* 21D3).

BUSES Two buses circulate around the peninsula of Piraeus. One proceeds from Roosevelt Sq to Limin Mounikhias, and on to Neon Faliron, and the other from Korai Sq (*Tmr* C3) via the Naval Cadets College to Limin Zeas.

COMMERCIAL SHOPPING AREA (*Tmr* 11C2) There is a flourishing and busy Market area behind the Bank mentioned above, hemmed in by the streets of Gounari and Ethniki Antistaseos. There is an excellent supermarket on the corner of Odhos Makras Stoas, if a shopper cannot be bothered to visit the various shops and stalls of the market. Prices in Piraeus are generally higher than elsewhere in Greece and shop hours are as for Athens.

FERRY-BOATS Most island ferry-boats leave from the area encompassed by Akti Kondili, to the north of the main harbour, Karaiskaki Sq, Akti Posidonos and Akti Miaouli, to the west of the main harbour. As a general rule the Aegean ferries, including those heading for the N.E. Aegean islands, depart from the area of Karaiskaki Square. International ferries leave from the south or far end of the Akti Miaouli quay road.

See CHAPTER 3 for general details in respect of the ferry-boats (Illustration 3), CHAPTER 11 for a synopsis of the islands and ports and the individual islands for details of the timetables.

FERRY-BOAT TICKET OFFICES Yes well, at least they lie extremely thick on the waterfront. It is probably best to make enquiries about the exact location of the particular ferry's departure point when purchasing the tickets. Ticket sellers 'lie in wait' all the way down the quayside streets of Kalimasioti and Akti Posidonos, that is, from the Metro Station, past the Gounari St turning to the bottom of Ethniki

Antistaseos. They tend to refer to a ship's point of departure with an airy wave of the hand.

My two favourite offices lie at opposite ends of the spectrum, as it were, and are: **Jannis Stoulis Travel** (*Tmr* 12C2) 2 Gounari St.   Tel. 417-9491 *Directions:* Situated on the right at Gounari St (*Sbo*).
The owner, who wears a rather disinterested air, is extremely efficient and speaks three languages, including English.

His fast talking, 'speedy Gonzales', counterpart occupies a wall-to-wall stairway on Kalimasioti St (*Tmr* 13C2). My regard for the latter operator may be coloured by the fact that he was the man who sold me my first ever Greek island ferry-boat ticket.

There are two ticket offices on the harbour side of the large building on Plateia Karaiskaki, beyond the cafes, two of almost dozens of ticket offices spaced around this edifice. An enterprising vendor of tickets lurks, from early morning, amongst the ferry-boat stalls on Akti Posidonos.
When searching the quayside for the correct ferry-boat, do not go beyond the Port offices and Custom house (*Tmr* 14D/E3), towards the south end of the harbour, as these berths are for cruise ships only.

NTOG Somewhat inconveniently situated on Zeas Harbour (*Tmr* C/D4) and only open weekdays between 0700 - 1500 hrs.

OTE The main office (*Tmr* 15C2) is north of the Post Office and another is on Odhos Navarinou (*Tmr* 22C2).

PLACES OF INTEREST
Archaeological Museum (*Tmr* 17D3) Situated between Filellinon and Leoforos Charilaou Trikoupi Sts and reopened in the last few years. Reportedly well laid out, with easy to identify exhibits. Opening hours Monday to Saturday, 0845 - 1500 hrs, Sunday 0930 - 1430 hrs and closed Tuesdays. Only Greeks are allowed free admission here, as elsewhere in Greece, foreigners having to pay 100 drs.

Ag Triada (*Tmr* 16C2) The Cathedral was rebuilt in the early 1960s, having been destroyed in 1944. Distinctive, mosaic tile finish.

Zea Theatre Adjacent to the Archaeological Museum, the remains date from about the second century BC.

Limin Zeas (Pasalimani) (*Tmr* C/D4) This semicircular harbour is of great antiquity. Now it shelters fishing boats and caiques, provides a yacht basin for larger, modern yachts, is the location for the Naval Museum of Greece, contains a Flying Dolphin (hydrofoil) terminal as well as a base for yacht charterers. Excavations have shown that, in ancient times, several hundred boat sheds radiated out around the edge of the harbour housing the Triremes, the great, three-banked warships of antiquity.

The Naval Museum of Greece Adjacent to Zeas Harbour with a varied and interesting series of exhibits down through the ages.

Limin Mounikhias (Tourkolimano or Mikrolimano) (*Tmr* B5) Continuing on round the coast cliff road from Limin Zeas, past the bathing beach (facing the tiny island of Stalida) and the Royal Yacht Club of Greece, leads to the renowned, 'chatty', picturesque and again semicircular harbour of Mounikhias. From here racing yachts are believed to have departed for regattas in Saroniko Bay as far back as the 4th century BC, as they do now. The quayside is ringed with tavernas, cafes and restaurants forming a backcloth to the multi-coloured sails of the assembled yachts crowded into the harbour.

The Hill of Kastela overlooks the harbour and has a modern, open-air, marble amphitheatre, wherein theatre and dance displays are staged, more especially during the Athens Festival (*See* **Places of Interest, A to Z, Athens**).

Filonos Street (*Tmr* B/C/D2/3) The 'Soho' of Piraeus, espousing what's left of the old *Never on Sunday* atmosphere of the town.

POLICE
Port On the quay bounded by Akti Posidonos.
Tourist & Town (*Tmr* 23C3) Dimotico Square.

POST OFFICE (*Tmr* 18C2) On Filonos St, north-west of the Cathedral.

RAILWAY STATIONS
Metro (Underground) (*Tmr* 1C1/2). *See* **Arrival by Metro.**
'Steam' Station (*Tmr* 1C1/2) The Peloponnese terminus is alongside and the far side of the Metro Station.
'Steam' Station (*Tmr* 19D/E1/2) The terminus for Northern Greece is situated on the far, north-west side of the Grand Harbour.

SWIMMING POOL Adjacent to Limin Zeas Harbour.

TELEPHONE NUMBERS & ADDRESSES
NTOG (*Tmr* C/D4) Zeas Marina   Tel. 413-5716
Port authorities   Tel. 451-1311

OTHER MAINLAND PORTS
N.E. Aegean. For details of Kavala *See* **Thassos** (CHAPTER 17) and Alexandroupoli *See* **Samothraki** (CHAPTER 18).

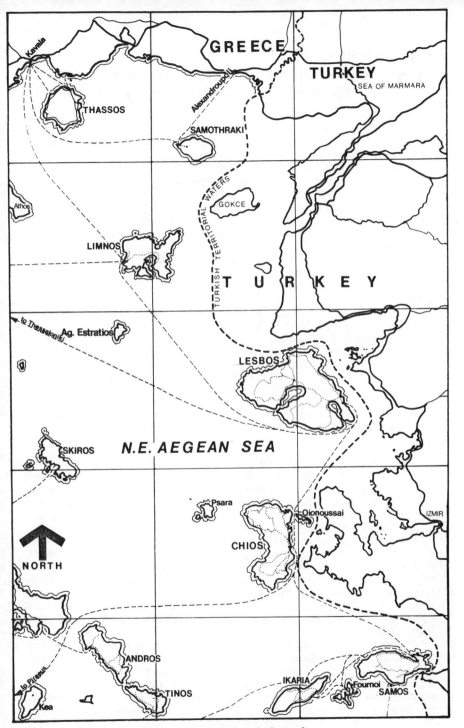

Illustration 11 N.E. Aegean islands

PART THREE
11 Introduction to the N.E. Aegean Islands (Eastern Sporades, Northern Sporades)

The islands that make up the group that I have designated the N.E. Aegean are rather less well-known than most Greek islands, with perhaps the notable exceptions of Samos and Thassos. They are geographically amongst the furthest from the mainland Athens, hugging the west Turkish coastline. For many years, the decision makers of the two largest islands, Chios and Lesbos, actively discouraged tourism. As a result of this comparative insularity, the ferry-boat connections up and down the N.E. Aegean chain are both fragmentary and disjointed.

Oddly enough Samos and Thassos, the two islands that have openly courted holiday-makers, are not only at opposite ends of the group but have developed in totally different ways.

Samos has encouraged and 'massaged' package tourism which the sheer size of this lovely, verdant island has, to date, been well able to contain. Additionally the airport and excellent ferry-boat service from Piraeus have helped to encourage the growth.

On the other hand beautiful Thassos, close by the north-eastern mainland of Greece, has been 'discovered' by Greek and German 'Independents'*. Both groups take advantage of the short sea crossing from the mainland Greece on the well serviced ferry-boat route. The Germans, who find the island particularly attractive motor down through Europe in large numbers to camp or reside in the plenteous accommodation. Almost unbelievably, Thassos is not directly linked by ferry with the other islands of the chain.

'Independents' are vacationers who make their own travel and accommodation arrangements, spurning the siren calls of the organised holiday industry.

Ikaria, which appears to be almost vertically mountainous, lies to the west of Samos. Despite this the island does not enjoy particularly frequent ferry-boat connections and must be a nightmare to anyone who suffers from vertigo. Ag. Kirikos, the main port, is rather dank and the inhabitants are not particularly welcoming; the northern port, Efdilos, is scrubbly and the only worthwhile, sandy beach resort, Armenistis, is reached by a frightening bus journey.

Chios, whose rich ship masters, it is said, rigorously opposed tourism, has finally decided to grasp the uncompromising problem of holiday-makers 'to its fertile soil'. Problematically the loveliness of the countryside and the inland villages, some of which are unique, is more than offset by the almost total lack of sandy beaches. Additionally Chios Town, the capital and main port is most unattractive. Grey, precast concrete, high-rise buildings dominate the seemingly never-ending, treeless, and thus shadeless, harbour quay. Incidentally this facade conceals an intriguing, old market area.

Lesbos is massive, the third largest of all the Greek islands. Mitilini, the main town and port might initially appear almost as unappealing as Chios Town but is saved total undesirability by the harbour's circular nature, the presence of a number of 'stately' buildings and the amply tree planted parks. Furthermore the island is more than fortunate in possessing four most attractive seaside resorts, only Molivos not having a very sandy beach. To atone for this deficiency Molivos boasts a 'film set' port and very attractive hill-hugging Chora.

Limnos is blessed by being the only large N.E. Aegean island to have not one, but three sandy beaches all of which are adjacent to the captivating port and town of Mirina. The countryside is extensively farmed but the downside is that the inland villages and other seaside settlements are, at the best, unattractive...

The N.E Aegean chain is well sprinkled with those 'off the beaten track', small islands which true Grecophiles aspire to visit.

Fournoi, close by Ikaria, more than repays a travellers efforts to 'splashdown'. Addmittedly there is only one settlement of any consequence, the bustling, agreeable fishing boat port, but there are a number of attractive beach walks and the people are excaptionally friendly.

Psara, a four hour, small ferry voyage from Chios, is not a wildly appealing port, being somewhat bedraggled, and the inhabitants are very reserved. However there are two good beaches and few tourists bother to make the journey.

Ag. Estratios, administratively linked with Limnos, is the least winsome of this trio because an earthquake devastated the old port in comparatively recent times. The shattered buildings and homes were replaced by ugly, concrete 'prefabs', during the erection of which the once sandy beach was all but destroyed. Even fewer tourists 'chance' the vagaries of the ferry-boats on this run. None of these islands has a road system to write home about and thus there are very few vehicles.

Last, and least, of the N.E. Aegean group must be Samothraki. The relegation of this alluringly named island to the bottom of the class may well be questioned. To misquote – 'All that sounds appealing does not necessarily engage'. If for no other reason, and there are plenty of reasons, the general difficulty of making a ferry-boat connection might well justify this decision. The island is quite large with lovely countryside, an interesting Chora and a few pretty inland villages. Unfortunately these plus points cannot overcome the lack of any but a large pebble shoreline, that completely encircles the island, and the liabilty of the dusty, dirty, unattractive port of Kamariotisa, the inhabitants of which are noticeably disinterested, if not hostile.

At the end of this chapter there is an alphabetical list of the N.E. Aegean islands, their major town and port(s) as well as a quick reference resume of ferry-boat connections.

The island chapters follow a format which has been devised and developed over the years to make the layout as simple to follow as is possible, without losing the informative nature of the text. Each island is treated in a similar manner, allowing the traveller easy identification of his (or her) immediate requirements. The text is faced by the relevent island, port and town maps with descriptions tied into the various island routes.

Symbols, Keys & Definitions

Below are some notes in respect of the few initials and symbols used in the text as well as an explanation of the possibly idiosyncratic nouns, adjectives and phrases that are to be found scattered throughout the book.

Where and when inserted, a star system of rating indicates my judgement of an island and possibly it's accommodation and restaurant standards by the inclusion of one to five stars. One star signifies bad, two basic, three good, four very good and five excellent. I must admit the ratings are carried out on whimsical grounds and are based purely on personal observation. For instance where a place, establishment or island receives a detailed critique I may consider that sufficient unto the day.... The absence of a star or any mention at all has no detrimental significance and might, for instance, indicate that I did not personally inspect the establishment.

Keys

The key *Tmr* is used as a map reference to aid easy location on port and town maps.

Other keys used include *Sbo* – 'Sea behind one'; *Fsw* – 'Facing seawards'; *Fbqbo* – 'Ferry-boat quay behind one' and OTT – 'Over The Top'.

GROC's definitions,'proper' adjectives & nouns: They definitely require some elucidation as follows:

Backshore: the furthest strip of beach from the sea's edge. The marginal rim edging the shore from the surrounds. *See* **Scrubbly**

Benzina: a small fishing boat.

Chatty: with pretensions to grandeur or sophistication.

Dead: an establishment that appears to be 'terminally' closed and is not about to open for business.

Donkey-droppings: as in 'two donkey-droppings' indicating a very small,'one-eyed' hamlet.

Doo-hickey: an Irish based colloquialism suggesting an extreme lack of sophistication and or rather 'daffy' (despite contrary indications in the authorative *Patridges Dictionary of Slang!*).

Downtown: a rundown/derelict area of a settlement – the wrong side of the railway tracks.

Ethnic: very unsophisticated, Greek indigenous and as a rule applied to hotels and pensions. *See* **Provincial.**

Greasy spoon: a dirty, unwholesome taverna or restaurant.

Great unwashed: the less attractive, modern day mutation of the 1960s hippy. Western European, 'by choice', inactive loafers, layabouts, and or unemployed drop-outs. Once having located a desirable location, often a splendid beach, they camp out usually under plastic and in shabby tents, thus ensuring the spot is made totally unattractive to anyone else. The 'men of the tribe' tend to trail a mangy dog on a piece of string. The women, more often than not with a grubby child or two in train, pester cafe-bar clients to purchase items of jewelry.

Note the above genre appears to be incurably penniless (but then who isn't?).

Hillbilly: another adjective or noun, similar to 'ethnic', often applied to describe countryside or a settlement, as in 'backwoods'.

Hippy: those who live outside the predictable, boring (!) mainstream of life and are frequently genuine if sometimes impecunious travellers. The category may include students or young professionals taking a sabbatical and who are 'negligent' of their sartorial appearance.

Icons: naturally, a religious painting of a holy person or personages, usually executed on a board. During the Middle Ages the Mediterranean would appear to have been almost awash with unmanned rowing boats and caiques ferrying icons hither and thither.

Independents: vacationers who prefer to step off the package holiday carousel and make their own way.

Krifo Scholio: illegal, undercover schools operated during the Turkish occupation, generally run by the inmates of religious orders to educate Greek children in the intricacies of the Orthodox religion and the traditional ways of life.

Mr Big: a local trader or pension owner, an aspiring tycoon, a small fish trying to be a big one in a smaller pool. Flashy with shady overtones.

One-eyed: small

Poom: a descriptive noun borrowed after sighting on Crete, some years ago, a crudely written sign advertising accommodation that simply stated POOMS! The accommodation on offer was crude, low-ceilinged, raftered, earth-floored, window-less rooms simply equipped with a truckle bed and rickety oil-cloth covered washstand – very reminiscent of typical Cycladean cubicles of the 1950/60s period.

Provincial: usually applied to accommodation and is an improvement on *Ethnic*. Not meant to indicate, say, dirty but should conjure up images of faded, rather gloomy establishments with a mausoleum atmosphere; high ceilinged Victorian rooms with worn, brown linoleum; dusty, tired aspidistras; bathrooms of unbelievable antiquity.

Richter scale: borrowed from earthquake seismology and employed to indicate the (appalling) state of toilets, on an 'eye-watering' scale.

Rustic: unsophisticated, unrefined.

Schlepper: vigorous touting for customers by restaurant staff. It is said of a good schlepper, in a market, that he can 'retrieve' a passer-by from up to 30 or 40 metres.

Scrubbly: often applied to a beach and indicating a rather messy, shabby area – often the 'backshore'.

Squatty: A Turkish (French) style ablution arrangement. None of the old familiar lavatory bowl and seat. Oh no, just two moulded footprints edging a dirty looking hole set in a porcelain surround. Apart from the unaccustomed nature of the exercise, the Lord simply did not give us enough limbs to keep one's skirt up and control wayward trousers that constantly attempt to flap down onto the floor, which is awash with goodness knows what! All this has to be enacted whilst gripping the toilet roll in one hand and wiping one's 'botty' with the other hand. Impossible! Incidentally the ladies should perhaps substitute blouse for shirt and skirt for trousers, but then it is easier (I am told) to tuck a skirt into the waistband!

Way-station: mainly used to refer to an office or terminus stuck out in the sticks and cloaked with an abandoned, unwanted air.

N.E. Aegean islands described include:

Island name(s)	Capital	Ports (at which inter island ferry-boats dock)	Ferry connections (M = mainland)
Ag. Estratios (Evstratios, Aistrates, Efstratios)	Ag. Estratios	Ag. Estratios	Mirina (Limnos), Skopelos, Kimi (Evia), Kavala (M).
Chios (Xios, Khios, Hios)	Chios	Chios	Mitilini (Lesbos), Samos, Piraeus (M) Thessaloniki (M), Psara, Oinoussai, Tsesme (Turkey). The **C.F. Kyklades**– when sailing links the following: Mitilini (Lesbos), Mirina (Limnos), Kavala (M), Samos, Ikaria, Leros, Kalimnos, Kos, Rhodes, Chalki, Diafni (Karpathos), Karpathos, Kasos, Sitia (Crete), Ag. Nikolaos (Crete), Anafi, Santorini, Folegandros, Milos, Piraeus (M).
Fournoi (Fournoi, Furni, Phournoi)	Fournoi	Fournoi	Ag. Kirikos (Ikaria), Karlovasion (Samos).
Ikaria	Ag Kirikos (Ag Kirykos)	Ag Kirikos	Samos, Karlovasion (Samos), Fournoi, Piraeus (M). The **C.F. Kyklades** – when sailing links the following:

		Efdilos (Evdilos, Evdhilos)	Samos, Chios, Mitilini (Lesbos), Mirina (Limnos), Kavala (M), Leros, Kalimnos, Kos, Rhodes, Chalki, Diafni (Karpathos), Kasos, Sitia (Crete), Ag. Nikolaos (Crete), Anafi, Santorini, Folegandros, Milos, Piraeus (M). Karlovasion (Samos), Samos, Piraeus (M).
Lesbos (Lesvos, Mitilini, Mytilini)	Mitilini	Mitilini	Chios, Mirina (Limnos), Ag. Estratios, Kavala (M), Piraeus (M), Thessaloniki (M).
			The **C.F. Kyklades**–when sailing links the following: Mirina (Limnos), Kavala (M), Chios, Samos, Ikaria, Leros, Kalimnos, Kos, Rhodes, Chalki, Diafni (Karpathos), Karpathos, Kasos, Sitia (Crete), Ag. Nikolaos (Crete), Anafi, Santorini, Folegandros, Milos, Piraeus (M).
Limnos (Lemnos)	Mirina (Myrina, Kastron)	Mirina	Ag. Estratios, Mitilini (Lesbos), Skopelos, Kavala (M). The **C.F. Kyklades** – when sailing links the following: Kavala (M), Mitilini (Lesbos), Chios, Samos, Ikaria, Leros, Kalimnos, Kos, Rhodes, Chalki, Diafni (Karpathos), Karpathos, Kasos, Sitia (Crete), Ag. Nikolaos (Crete), Anafi, Santorini, Folegandros, Milos, Piraeus (M).
Oinoussai (Oinousses, Oinousai, Oenoussae, Oinousa, Inousses)	Oinoussai (Mandraki)	Oinoussai	Chios
Psara	Psara	Psara	Chios
Samos (ΣΑΜΟΣ)	Samos (Vathy)	Samos (Vathy)	Ag. Kirikos (Ikaria), Paros, Fournoi, Mitilini (Lesbos), Piraeus (M). The **C.F. Kyklades**– when sailing links the following: Chios, Mitilini (Lesbos), Mirina (Lesbos), Ikaria, Leros, Kalimnos, Kos, Rhodes, Chalki, Diafni (Karpathos), Karpathos, Kasos, Sitia (Crete), Ag. Nikolaos (Crete), Anafi, Santorini, Folegandros, Milos, Piraeus (M).
		Karlovasion (Karlovassi)	*See* Samos but not all craft that dock at Samos call at Karlovasion.
		Pythagorian (Tigani)	Angathonisi, Arki, Lipsos, Leros, Kalimnos, Kos, Nisiros, Tilos, Simi, Rhodes.
Samothraki (Samothrace)	Kamariotisa	Kamariotisa	Alexandroupoli (M), Kavala (M).
Thassos (Thasos)	Thassos (Limenas)	Skala Prinos (Ormos Prinos)	Thassos, Kavala (M).
		Thassos	Keramoti (M), Skala Prinos (Thassos), Kavala (M).

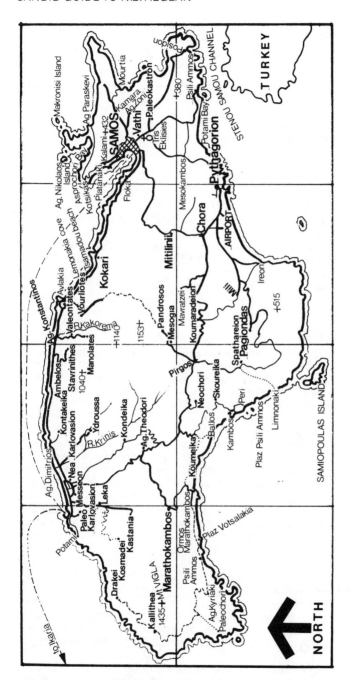

Illustration 12 Samos island

12 SAMOS (ΣΑΜΟΣ)   ★★★★
N.E. Aegean Islands

FIRST IMPRESSIONS
Flowers; yellow broom; birds; beauty of the landscape

SPECIALITIES
Wines, brandy.

RELIGIOUS HOLIDAYS & FESTIVALS
include: Pentecost (Whit Sunday) – Festival of Ag. Triada, Marathokambos; 20th July – Festivals of Profitis (Prophitis) Ilias, Karlovasion & Marathokambos; 6th August – Festivals of Metamorphosis, Pythagorion & Karlovasion; 15th August – Festivals of Panagia, Vourliotes, Karlovasion & Pirgos; 8th September – Festival of Panagia Vrondiani, Vourliotes; 14th September – Festival, Monastery Timiou Stavriou, Mavratzei; 21st November – Festival Eisodia tis Theotokou, Pythagorion; 6th December – Festival of Ag. Nikolaos, Pythagorion & Samos Town; 12th December – Festival of Ag. Spiridon, Samos Town.

VITAL STATISTICS
Tel. prefix 0273. Samos is the administrative centre for the islands of Ikaria, Fournoi and its adjacent islets. The island is some 48 km from east to west, 20 km in depth with an area of 475 sq km. Estimates for the population vary between 31,000 & 42,000, about a quarter of which are split between Samos Town and Karlovasion. The highest mountain (Mt Kerkis) measures 1435m.

HISTORY
Despite a Homeric mention, the history becomes interesting only after a period of overseas expansion, which included the establishment of colonies on Samothraki (7th century BC) and the mainland. The conquering heroes, on their return, installed one Sylosontas, the first of a family dynasty of famous Samos Tyrants during which period the island reached a pinnacle of religious, artistic, philosophical and mathematical achievement. It was Sylosontas's grandson, Polykrates, who took over the mantle of power in 532 BC and raised the island to the heights of accomplishment, gaining historical fame, or notoriety – depending on one's viewpoint. Certainly the world renowned Pythagoras could not live under the regime and joined other Samain exiles on the Italian mainland. But all good (or bad) things must come to an end. The Persians, who Polykrates had given the equivalent of a military bloody nose when they attempted to take Samos, tricked him into a meeting on their ground and then crucified him. From thereon the influence of the island declined, despite which the citizens managed to keep a certain amount of autonomy under various rulers. The Romans made the place popular as a holiday resort, so what's new? Visitors included Anthony and Cleopatra. Did they sign themselves in as Mr. & Mrs. Smith at the Heraion Hotel?

In the Middle Ages, in order of occupation, the Genoese, Venetians and Turks were followed, for a short period, by the Russians who then lost the island again to the Turks. During the War of Independence, Samos ejected the Turks in 1821 and

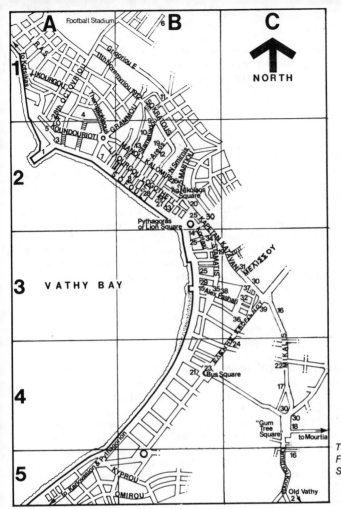

Tmr

1 Ferry-boat quay A2
2 Hotel Ariadni C5
3 Samos Travel & International Tours A2
4 Pension Cactus A1/2
5 Customs & Port police A1/2
6 Pension Dimitra B1
7 'Old' Catholic Church A2
8 Hotel Aeolis B2
9 Pension Mary's House B1/2
10 Hotel Marianna B1/2
11 Pension Athina B1
12 Pension Avli B2
13 Hotel Parthenon B2
14 Hotel Artemis B3
15 Xenia Hotel B3
16 Rooms
17 Pension El Greco C4
18 'Gum Tree' Taverna C4
19 Snackbars

20 Samos Grill House B2
21 Restaurant O Tasos B4
22 Gregori's C4
23 Bus Square B4
24 Olympic Airways C3/4
25 Banks
26 Graceland No 2 Scooter hire B2
27 Marin Cocktail Cafe-bar B2
28 The Market B2
29 Rooms Lito/Rent-A-Bike B3
30 Bread shops
31 Cinema C3
32 Post Office/Plateia ΗΡΩΩΝ C3
33 Drink shops
34 Foto-Faros B/C2/3
35 'Public Garden' Square B/C3
36 OTE office C3
37 Archaeological Museum C3
38 Public Gardens B/C3
39 Town police C3

Illustration 13 Samos (Vathy) Town & Port

kept them out until 1830, when the European Great Powers ruled that Samos should become an autonomous state under the overall care of the Turkish Sultan. This state of affairs was finally transformed in 1912 when Samos was integrated with the Greek nation.

GENERAL

A wonderfully verdant and, in places, lush island with a varied range of scenery to suit most tastes. Sandy beaches; agricultural plains; hillsides thick with a wide variety of trees and pierced by running streams; terraced vineyards; majestic mountains; colourful ports and attractive seaside locations. What more could a traveller require? Mark you with the building of the airport, and, some 5 or 6 years ago, the possibility of extensive package holiday involvement by British firms, I feared for the worst. Imagine my delight on revisiting Samos, to carry out the final research for this guide, to find my misgivings to be, in the main, groundless. Perhaps the island's size and spirit has helped. Certainly the lack of easily accessible, sandy beaches must have assisted but Samos has changed little, so far absorbing the worst vices of organised, mass travel. Naturally there are more tour offices, an almost infinite number of vehicle rental firms and an increased number of package holiday hotels but none of these developments has yet intruded upon or ruined the environment. And, as before, there are delightful mountain villages where life has remained largely unaltered for years and one or two still relatively undiscovered beaches. In fact Samos has maintained its ranking as one of the most attractive of all the Greek islands. Need one say more.

SAMOS (Vathy): capital town & main port (Illustration 13). Also

listed, especially on ferry-boat schedules, as Vathy, which is in reality the old town, to one side and above Samos. The port and town are situated to the left (*Sbo*) of the deeply indented Vathy Bay, with the main development ascending the steep hill, a few streets back from the Esplanade that encircles half the 'U' of the bay. Despite the demands of package holiday-makers and a formidable military presence, even the waterfront has retained a dignified appearance, with many of the large 19th century buildings remaining intact. In fact some are in the process of being restored! (Compare this state of affairs with the modern high-rise, faceless concrete constructions edging Chios Town Esplanade).

Behind and parallel to the Esplanade (Akti Sofouli), between the Ferry-boat quay (*Tmr* 1A2) and Plateia Pythagoras (*Tmr* B2/3), are two narrow streets, Likourgou Logotheti and Manoli Kalomiri. From the furthest, Manoli Kalomiri, lanes and alleys branch off rising steeply up the hillside, a number giving way to steps in the scramble. Further round, on the far side of the Lion statue dominated Main Square (Pythagoras), Odhos Kapetan Katavani makes off towards 'Gum Tree' Square (*Tmr* C4), from which branches a road to Mourtia as well as the winding street connecting Old Vathy with the Port.

ARRIVAL BY AIR

The airport has been built on a plain very close to the south coast, between Pythagorion and Ireon, some 15 km from Samos Town. The aircrafts approach, between low hills, may well prove to be an interesting experience with an impression, only an impression, that the wings are actually touching the vines as the aircraft is forced to bank steeply to line up with the runway. The airport buildings and services are rather basic.

The usual airport bus connects with Samos Town at the universal cost of 45 drs. Surely this fare will rise soon as it must now represent the very best transport bargain available anywhere on the Greek islands.

ARRIVAL BY FERRY

The island of Samos, even if 'far flung', acts as a pivotal point for north-south ferry-boat travel up and down the islands skirting the western Turkish coastline. Readers will note the word island and not Samos Town, where the Piraeus ferries dock as do the comparatively small ferries that connect with Chios island. The ferries that link up with the Dodecanese islands dock at Pythagorion, that is apart from the 'maverick' **CF Kyklades**. The wandering, much maligned **Kyklades**, despite possibly sustaining a fire early in 1986, is reputed to still be threading its almost circular, multi-island voyage round the Aegean sea, a passage that takes in Crete, some of the Dodecanese and a number of the N.E. Aegean islands.

The Ferry-boat quay (*Tmr* 1A2) is, for all intents and purposes, at the far left-hand end of Samos (*Sbo*). Thus, from the bottom of the pier, it is only necessary to turn right for the town. There are a number of buildings on the quay itself including a sleazy cafe, an office, once the abode of the Tourist police, but now occupied by the Port police and an information office, which is usually locked.

Only one or two owners of accommodation meet the ferries including the persistent proprietors of the *Hotel Ariadni* (*Tmr* 2C5). On te other hand two or more of the prominent tour offices stay open for incoming Piraeus craft (*See* **The Accommodation**).

THE ACCOMMODATION & EATING OUT

The Accommodation Pensions, if not **Rooms**, are plentiful but, as elsewhere in the N.E. Aegean, the owners do not go wild advertising their existence, so they have to be diligently searched for in the maze of side streets. A number of the hotels are now booked by package holiday firms.

The uncertain can make directly for **Samos Travel** (*Tmr* 3A2), which shares an imposing building with **International Tours**. The young Greek manager of Samos Travel, Simos Alexis, has a remarkable command of a number of European languages. The staff will locate accommodation, but for those travellers who like to search out their own... From the bottom of the Ferry-boat quay, turning right along the wide dual carriageway Esplanade leads past the:

Hotel Samos (*Tmr* A2) (Class C) 6 Sofouli St   Tel.28377
Directions: As above in the third block of buildings along the Esplanade.

Very smart with an 'en suite' restaurant on the ground floor. Mainly occupied by package tourists but, either side of the height of summer onslaught, has rooms with en suite bathrooms available for those who require home comforts in a West European style hotel. From 1st May – 30th September a single room costs 1720 drs and a double room 2150 drs. Continental breakfast may be obligatory at 200 drs.

Pension Cactus (*Tmr* 4A1/2) Odhos Sidari Zis   Tel. 28754/28248
Directions: On the far side of the *Hotel Samos*, a narrow lane edges the building breaking into ascending steps and spills on the Odhos Koundourioti. To the right, across the road, more steps lead to another street (Odhos Sidari Zis), parallel to the waterfront. The pension is to the left and a cactus is, not unnaturally, prominent.

The accommodation is grouped in two buildings. The far, smart, modern block houses en suite double rooms from 1700 drs and is used by at least one package tour firm. The older building, set behind a garden, has double rooms sharing the bathroom facilities from 1400 drs.

Pension Dimitra, (*Tmr* 6B1) ΑΡΧΙΕΡΕΩΣ ΑΛΕΞΑΝΔΡΟΥ   Tel. 27324
Directions: To the left at the bottom of the Ferry-boat quay, is an imposing building in

which are located the offices of the Customs and Port police (*Tmr* 5A1/2). Behind this block and leading steeply uphill, off Odhos Koundourioti, is Odhos 28 Oktovriou which climbs up to the Football Stadium. Almost opposite the stadium gates is a lateral street to the right. The third turning off to the left is a cul-de-sac and the pension is on the right at the far end.

Once a very smart, spotless house but Papa and Mama Dimitra, who have been the owners for quite a few years, have allowed standards to slip a little, Each agreeable room opens out on to a pleasant, if rather narrow balcony that encircles the building. The ground floor, shared bathroom is not kept as clean as it should be, and once was. Incidentally there is another bathroom on the next floor up which is useful to know when the other facility is 'booked up'. The awful beds are boxed and the edges, which stand proud, dig in to the anatomy whilst the loose mattress buttons seem to march across the bed all night. Papa is 'something' in the Market. A double room costs 1000 drs.

Hotel Aeolis (*Tmr* 8B2) (Class B) 33 Sofouli/Stamatiadou St   Tel. 28904
Directions: On the Esplanade, five side streets beyond the old Catholic Church (*Tmr* 7A2).

As one would expect of a B class hotel, in this position, expensive. A single room en suite costs 2100 drs and a double 3000 drs apart from the height of the season period (16th June – 30th Sept) when rates rise to 2650 drs and 3800 drs respectively.

The richest vein of pensions to be mined is in three parallel streets at right angles to the waterfront and two blocks back. The key turning off the Esplanade is Odhos Stamatiadou, wedged between a **Budget Rent A Car** office and the *Hotel Aeolis* (*Tmr* 8B2). This lane crosses the market street of Odhos Likourgou Logotheti (ΛΥΚΟΡΓΟΥ ΛΟΓΟΘΕΤΗ), then followed by Odhos Manoli Kalomiri, and goes on to junction with Odhos Sokratous.

Proceeding along Odhos Stamatiadou, at Manoli Kalomiri St turn left and on the left is the:
Pension Ionia (*Tmr* B2) 5 Manoli Kalomiri   Tel. 28782
Directions: As above
The owner is a very pleasant, helpful man who speaks English. A double room sharing the bathroom costs 1000 drs in mid season. The proprietor also has another house (or two) where a double room, with en suite bathroom, costs 1400 drs mid-season.

Other accommodation hereabouts includes the:
Pension Vassou (*Tmr* B2)   Tel. 28846
Directions: Continue on across Odhos Manoli Kalomiri from the Odhos Stamatiadou junction up the steep steps and the pension is on the left.

Pension Mary's House (*Tmr* 9B1/2) 4 Sokratous/Stamatiadou Streets   Tel. 23054
Directions: Continue up the steps of Odhos Stamatiadou beyond *Pension Vassou* and at the junction with Sokratous St, turn left and the pension is on the left.

Marko and his wife Maria open up this 300 year old house, which they rent, for the summer months. There is one very decorative ceiling. Burly Marko, who irresistibly reminds one of an Irish tarmacadam layer, speaks a little English. The accommodation is 'rustic provincial' (if there is such a thing) with a double room and shared bathroom costing 1200 drs. The hot water is always hot (so Marko assures me) and there is a communal fridge.

Hotel Marianna (*Tmr* 10B1/2) (Class D) 22 Manoli Kalomiri   Tel. 27369
Directions: Back at the junction of Odhos Stamatiadou and Manoli Kalomiri turn left (*Sbo*) past *Pension Ionia* and follow the road round to the right (not proceeding straight

on). The hotel is on the right-hand side. No single rooms with double rooms sharing the bathroom, costing 1300 drs and en suite 1600 drs.

Pension Trova
Directions: Just beyond the *Hotel Marianna* (*Tmr* 10B1/2) and on the same side of the street.

Pension Athina (*Tmr* 11B1)
Directions: Continue on along Odhos Manoli Kalomiri, past *Hotel Marianna* (*Tmr* 10B1/2) and *Pension Trova*. The street bends around to the left into Odhos 11th Novemvriou 1912. (At the junction, at right angles, steps climb back up to Odhos Sokratous). The first turning to the right off 11th Novemriou 1912 curves around to the right and the pension is on the right, on the next corner.

Back at the junction of Odhos Stamatiadou and Manoli Kalomiri St, turn right (*Sbo*) on Kalamiri St and then left up the steep steps of Areos Lane. This leads, on the right, to one of the most dramatically unexpected and unusual pensions I have ever stayed in, the:

Pension Avli (Αυλη) (*Tmr* 12B2) Areos St   Tel. 22939
Directions: As above. The doorway is let into the high, enclosing wall.

The Greek word Avli means courtyard and the amazing feature of this establishment is, not unnaturally, a large courtyard. A raised area to the left is shaded by an overhanging, colonnade supported, first floor. The 150 year old building was a Roman Catholic convent. The first floor rooms to the left of the courtyard have been converted to include an en suite bathroom by the incorporation of a fibreglass module, and are let out to package holiday-makers. The wags rather disparagingly refer to the pastel coloured bathroom units as the *Tardis* (with acknowledgements to *Dr Who*). The first floor rooms to the right have been left almost as they were. The spacious and high ceilinged bedrooms were originally nuns' quarters. The 'batched' and numbered cubicle toilets have been kept, the number corresponding to the individual room numbers, thus ensuring each room has its own private bathroom. They sometimes become a little smelly (where wouldn't some ten Greek toilets gathered together) but they are kept spotlessly clean, on a daily basis. The rather rudimentary showers are situated in the old basement boiler washroom but it is necessary to request the heating to be switched on to enjoy hot water. If the accommodation is a superb find, then Spiros Karatzimas, the owner and an Athenian lawyer, who takes up his pension duties for the summer months, must be considered a delight. He is a quiet, scholarly man with subtle sense of humour and satisfactory English who will do all in his power to make guests more than welcome. Spiros is usually to be found around the premises and in the evenings joins his 'flock' at the tables which are pleasantly spread about the courtyard. Guests are encouraged to purchase any drink they may require to while away the night hours before and/or after returning from their evening meal. The steady flow of relaxed chatter and background music murmurs on with the large, paved courtyard illuminated by gentle splashes of light which keeps at bay the enveloping darkness. The mid-season rate for a double room and separate bathroom is 1000 drs whilst a room in the en suite package holiday side costs 1200 drs. A very good 'help-yourself' breakfast of bread, butter, jam and large cups of Nescafe is available at a cost of 150 drs. Guests gather up the constituents from the bar counter, tucked into the corner of the courtyard beneath the first floor overhang. The nuns' private chapel is still extant in the basement and can be viewed on request. Spiros plans to sort out the small garden area to the front of the building for 1987 or 1988 or... Taken all-round the Pension Avli and 'mine host' must rate as one of the best combinations I have ever encountered.

Further on up the steps from the *Pension Avli*, on the left, is the:
Pension Dreams (*Tmr* B2) 9 Areos St   Tel. 23037
Directions: As above.

Back on the waterfront is the:
Hotel Parthenon (*Tmr* 13B2) (Class E) Sofouli   Tel. 27234
Directions: On the Esplanade but above the smart, rock music *Alexis Bar*, so it is noisy
late into the early morning hours.
 'Antique Provincial', as one would expect of an E class hotel, with single rooms
costing 700 drs and a double room 900 drs, both sharing the bathrooms.

Hotel Artemis (*Tmr* 14B3) (Class D) 4 Kontaxi   Tel. 27792
Directions: The entrance is in narrow Odhos Kontaxi which leads off the far, south-
east side of Plateia Pythagoras. The hotel is built over the top of a Tour office and
cafe-bar restaurant that faces on to the Esplanade.
 Room rates are 600 drs/900 drs for a single room and 900 drs/1120 drs for a
double room, respectively sharing and with en suite bathrooms. The height of
season rates (16th June – 30th Sept) rise to 720/1100 drs and 1120/1350 drs.

Continuing on round the waterfront leads to the:
Xenia Hotel (*Tmr* 15B3) (Class B) 23 Sofouli   Tel. 27463
Directions: South along the Esplanade, opposite a small fishing boat quay.
Expensive, but not outrageously so, with en suite rooms for one costing 1850 drs and
for two 2450 drs rising to 2050 drs and 2850 drs (May to Sept).

In the block prior to the *Xenia Hotel* (*Tmr* 15B3) is the:
Rooms Lito (*Tmr* 29B3) Sofouli Esplanade   Tel. 28749
Directions: As above and over a two wheeled rental office, 'Rent A Honda, Vespa,
Bicycle'.

Note that the seafront south from the *Hotel Xenia* (*Tmr* 15B3), to beyond the turning
up to the Bus Square (*Tmr* 23B4), is rather smelly and the seashore from about the
'Bus Square' turnoff to the far end of the bay is rocky and rather dirty. People
considering staying in accommodation hereabouts should bear this in mind.

Odhos Mikalis continues on from Odhos Kapetan Katavani, leading to 'Gum Tree'
Square (*Tmr* C4) and the Vathy road. There are **Rooms** (*Tmr* 16C3) at No 21 Mikalis
(Tel. 28237/22822), just after the meeting of the ways of Kapetan Katavani, Mikalis
and ΕΛΕΝΗΣ ΣΒΟΡΩΝΟΥ; the tour operator booked *Pension El Greco* (*Tmr* 17C4);
Rooms (*Tmr* 16C4/5) in the narrow lane of Soula A Papagou
and the:
Hotel Ariadni (*Tmr* 2C5) 2 Dimitriou Karida   Tel. 27147
Directions: From the 'Gum Tree' Sq (*Tmr* C4) proceed up along the Vathy road. The
pension (not a hotel) is around a kink in the street, on the left.
 Whereas in days of old it was the neat, bearded owner who met the ferries, it is now
his son Gregory who persistently scoops up ferry-boat arrivals. The rooms are small,
the en suite bathrooms diminutive and the pension is rather far out of town, even if it is
conveniently close to the superb '*Gum Tree' Taverna* (*Tmr* 18C4). A double room, mid-
season costs 1000 drs.

The Eating Out There are a number of establishments serving food as well as an
inordinate quantity of cafe and cocktail bars but only a few out of the ordinary places
at which to eat.

Restaurant Dionysos (*Tmr* A2). Sofouli Esplanade
Directions: Butting up to the Esplanade pavement, to the Ferry-boat quay side of the

old Catholic Church (*Tmr* 7A2). This Church has had a boutique and ferry-boat ticket office let into the front of the building, a conversion that leaves one somewhat disconcerted.

Back to the restaurant, or more correctly the 'sanitised taverna' which sports clean ashtrays, clean wicker trellis work and clean crunching gravel under foot, all lit by discreet spotlights at night. The tables are numbered, the waiters attentive and command sufficient English, French and German to keep the clients happy. Many of the customers are 'escapees' from the smart, Esplanade package tour hotels who have 'got over the wire' in order to sample the 'real Greece' (and why not?). Certainly the Dionysos is a most acceptable compromise as they would probably find the *'Gum Tree' Taverna* rather rustic. The young man who runs the outfit keeps a tight control, the food is hot and well prepared at acceptable prices and small bottles of retsina are available. On the other hand the menu choice on offer diminishes rapidly as the evening progresses. A meal for two of mince and rice (220 drs), two Greek salads (190 drs each), meatballs and pasta (220 drs), two bottles of retsina (85 drs each), a plate of cherries (50 drs), bread and cover charge (20 drs), costs 1060 drs.

Ouzerie No.1 (*Tmr* A/B2) Sofouli Esplanade
Directions: A metre or three beyond the old Catholic Church (*Tmr* 7A2), next door to a tourist gift shop.

A narrow fronted snackbar with an awning stretching out on to the wide Esplanade pavement. Well patronised by Greeks, and no wonder, with an excellent and fair plateful of kalamares (232 drs), an unusual dish of Giro sliced meat (299 drs) and a Greek salad (148 drs). Amstel beer is available (70 drs), as is a rather pricey bottle of retsina (88/92 drs).

Snackbar (*Tmr* 19B2) Likourgou Logotheti
Directions: Towards the Plateia Pythagoras end of the Market Street
More a counter facing the street and, of its kind, the best value in town. They sell a number of 'scrummy' pies including spinach ('spanakopita', 55 drs), feta (50 drs), meat (60 drs) and tiropites (40 drs).

Mind you there are three of five other passable snackbars including a counter service, stick souvlaki establishment on the south-east side of Plateia Ag. Nikolaos (*Tmr* B2). A small plate of patatas costs 50 drs, a stick of souvlaki 45 drs, and a bottle of Henninger 85 drs. There is a *Snackbar* in the narrow side street connecting the Squares of Ag. Nikolaos and Pythagoras, in the area of the old Bus office (which is now a pin-ball machine hall) as well as a popular *Snackbar* (*Tmr* 19B/C3) on the left of Odhos Kapetan Stamatis.

Taverna Chris (*Tmr* B2)
Directions: In the narrow lane off the west corner of Plateia Ag. Nikolaos with tables and chairs spread about which almost fill the alleyway. A fairly extensive menu at average prices.

Samos Grill House (*Tmr* 20B2) Plateia Pythagoras
Directions: To the left of the far back edge of Plateia Pythagoras (*Sbo*), next door to a 'chatty' cafe-bar.

The grill-house proclaims it is a family taverna. The proprietor, George Elias Chrisakis, certainly runs a popular establishment with a varied menu at prices that are competitive, if only competitive with the other Esplanade eating houses.

Restaurant O Tasos (*Tmr* 21B4)
Directions: Proceed southwards right round the Esplanade as far as the street that branches up to the 'Bus Sq'. Turn up this and the restaurant is on the right, beyond

the small, 'way station', 'shed-like' office of Rhenia Tours.

'Greek Food'. The main meals are nicely cooked, plenteous and the menu lists some vegetables, even out of season, which may include giant beans, greens (I've dreamt of greens) and fried aubergines. A meal for two of stuffed zucchini (209 drs), moussaka in a pot (250 drs), a Greek salad (172 drs), a bottle of retsina (82 drs) and very reasonably priced bread (7 drs), all for 726 drs.

Some way along Odhos Mikalis, on the road to Vathy, and to the right, on a corner is:
Gregori's (*Tmr* 22C4)
Directions: As above.

It may well be that I am biased (hush my mouth) but in the past I was never able to take to this taverna and now less so. Gregori's ample frame seems, over the last six or seven years, to have been exhausted of the old *bonhomie* and his largish daughter, who used to be smiling and cuddly, appears to have developed a harder nature. I think they prefer to cater for the tour parties 'evening out in a real taverna in the old quarter'. My disquiet is not because much of the limited menu is costly, since generally the prices are as reasonable as most of their competitors. Competitive they may be but the food is often not up to the mark, is served up cold and, to complement the general feeling of dissatisfaction, the service is offhand. Only grilled meals as well as chicken and chicken livers (if requested) are available. A meal of veal chop (actually beef cutlet, 340 drs), chicken livers (200 drs), a definitely substandard Greek salad (plentiful feta and tomatoes, a few tired olives and 'rock-all-else', 120 drs), a plate of tired, cold, uncooked chips (31 drs), a bottle of retsina (61 drs) and bread costs a total of 770 drs.

But not all is lost because 'a metre or 100' further along the road, on the left of Plateia 'Gum Tree' is the:
'Gum Tree' Taverna (*Tmr* 18C4)
Directions: As above.

Actually the correct name is 'Ta Kotopoula' or 'The Chickens', but we have always known it as 'Gum Tree' ever since our first visit because the small, unnamed, irregular square boasts a large tree smack in the middle of the road. Stelios, the unflappable owner, can still work at a pretty fast pace but does now have some help in the shape of Adonis, a son in-law, for further details of whom *See* **Commercial Shopping Area, A to Z**. A truly, rural taverna on the outskirts of the town. At lunch time the bar only opens up to serve the few locals with coffee and bottles of beer. It has to be admitted that the setting is not exactly rural and the menu is limited. But I can assure readers that what is on offer is extremely well cooked and very good value, a fact confirmed by the fact that the terrace tables are very rarely empty. The inside is more or less the province of locals watching the television and enjoying the usual Greek shouting match, quaintly referred to as conversation. The freshly spit cooked souvlakis (350 drs) are almost unequalled, in my experience, anywhere on the Greek islands; the half portion, spit roasted chicken (180 drs) is very tasty; the kalamares (160 drs) may be imported, but there is always a good plateful; meatballs, chicken livers and omelettes are more than acceptable. Incidentally, the tzatziki (50 drs) is excellent so why not try some with a Greek salad? A couple requiring an inexpensive meal could do no better than plump for 2 omelettes, a plate of chicken livers with a few chips, a bottle of retsina and bread at an all in cost of 350 drs. To put this in perspective, an Esplanade cafe-bar restaurant charges some 250 drs for three milky coffees and two ouzos!

A minor entertainment is provided by the friendly periptero owner from across the square who stays open late into the night but wanders across to order an evening plate of this and that. Unfortunately as soon as he sits down, Murphy decrees a customer turns up so he legs it back to the store. This sets the pattern for the evening and I have rarely seen him eat a meal undisturbed or without one or other of his companions finishing off the helping.

THE A TO Z OF USEFUL INFORMATION

AIRLINE OFFICE AND TERMINUS (*Tmr* 24C3/4). Between Plateia HPΩΩN (surrounding Ag. Spiridon Church) and the 'Bus' Square, on Odhos ΕΛΕΝΗΣ ΣΒΟΡΩΝΟΥ. The office opens Monday to Saturday between 0600 – 2030 hrs but is closed on Sundays.

Aircraft timetables
30th March to 27th September
Samos to Athens (& vice versa)
A minimum of two flights a day, every day, with three on Mondays and Fridays.
Between the 15th June and 20th September there is one extra flight a day.
One-way fare 2870 drs; duration ¾ hrs.

Samos to Chios
Up to 14th June
Sunday   1140 hrs.
After 15th June
Thursday & Sunday   1705 hrs.
Return
Up to 14th June
Sunday   1235 hrs.
After 15th June
Thursday & Sunday   1800 hrs.
One-way fare 2480 drs; duration 35 mins.

Samos to Lesbos (Mitilini)
Up to 14th June
Wednesday   1140 hrs.
After 15th June
Wednesday & Saturday   1705 hrs.
Return
Up to 14th June
Wednesday   1255 hrs.
After 15th June
Wednesday & Saturday   1820 hrs.
One-way fare 2870 drs; duration 55 mins.

Samos to Mykonos
Up to 14th June
Wednesday   1410 hrs.
Sunday   1330 hrs.
After 15th June
Wednesday & Saturday   1935 hrs.
Thursday & Sunday   1855 hrs.
Return
Up to 14th June
Wednesday & Sunday   1040 hrs.
After 15th June
Wednesday, Thursday,
Saturday & Sunday   1605 hrs.
One-way fare 2730 drs; duration 40 mins.

BANKS Two prominent and one 'disguised'.

The Bank of Greece (*Tmr* 25B3). Sofouli Esplanade. An imposing building facing out over Vathy Bay, beyond the **National Bank** (*Tmr* 25B3) from Plateia Pythagoras. Changes Eurocheques. The staff attitude is very helpful but the service is slow, very slow and at the height of the season it may be necessary to allow several hours to effect a transaction.

Commercial Bank (*Tmr* 25B2). Almost hidden away and entered from the narrow lane, Odhos Kapetan Katavani, behind Plateia Pythagoras.

BEACHES Although the island has some splendid beaches, Samos Town is ill served with only Gangou Beach, fifteen minutes walk north of the Ferry-boat quay (*Tmr* 1A2). After four minutes the route passes the *Hotel Acropolis* (Tel. 27604), opposite which is a tiny, angular, pebbly piece of foreshore at the foot of a low cliff with a small mole to the left (*Fsw*). The road winds past the (modern) Hospital on the right, the *Hotel Pythagoras* (Tel. 28422), with an international pay telephone, and the *Surf-Side Hotel*, both on the left. At a fork in the road is the *Hotel Myrini* and the road to the left leads down to:

Gangou Beach. A small cove with a narrow, pebble and sand beach which is tree and bamboo edged. On the far side of the cove, on a hill, is a building housing the *Samos Beach Bouziki* and, on the distant corner, a taverna. The problem is that this beach must cater for a lot of Samos Town and even in mid May gets fairly packed...

BICYCLE, SCOOTER & CAR HIRE Fairly well organised but scooter hire from the larger organisations is comparatively expensive at 1300/1500 drs per day. Car hire is simply expensive at about 5100/6000 drs a day, which works out at three times the listed figures, due to the necessary and unavoidable extras.

Graceland No.2 (*Tmr* 26B2). Situated on the far, north side of Plateia Ag. Nikolaos. The owner, Mr. Vagelis, is a pleasant man and, although his scooters may not always be in tip-top condition, they are certainly less expensive at 800 drs per day than the larger firms that 'litter' the Esplanade.

Centaur Rent-A-Vespa (*Tmr* B2). On the left of the alley alongside the smart, cocktail *Cafe-bar Marin* (*Tmr* 27B2). Louie, the engaging young proprietor, speaks excellent English but is kept fairly busy working part-time in the *Marin* which his partner Stefano, the original proprietor of Centaur, now owns.

Other Esplanade firms include **Budget Rent-A-Car** (*Tmr* A/B2), alongside Odhos Stamatiadou; **Rent-A-Vespa** (*Tmr* B2), alongside Odhos Areos; **Rent-A-Bike** close by the Market (*Tmr* 28B2), **Budget** (again), and, beyond Pythagoras Sq, the premises of **Rent-A-Honda, Vespa, Bicycle,** in the ground floor of *Rooms Lito* (*Tmr* 29B3). Note that scooter hire is significantly cheaper in Pythagorion port (*See* ROUTE FIVE).

BOOKSELLERS There is an international paper shop on the far side (*Sbo*) of Plateia Pythagoras (*Tmr* B2). Another fascinating bookshop (*Tmr* B/C2/3) is situated on the left of Odhos Kapetan Katavani, just beyond the fork with Kapetan Stamatis, where it climbs a slight rise. The inside of the shop is piled high with stacks of books presided over by a courteous gentleman. There are a few foreign language books, some very cheap, somewhat out of date postcards and, stuck up in the shop windows, details of any island music concerts. The owner is a fund of information dispensed in quiet, correct English but has become fascinated by the delights of mainland Mt. Athos and may well close up shop every so often to indulge in the odd sabbatical.

BREAD SHOPS There are two in Odhos Likourgou Logotheti, the 'Market' St, between Areos St and Plateia Pythagoras. They both sell cakes and the one closest to Odhos Areos also sells ice-creams. A number are spread out along the length of Odhos Kapetan Katavani (including *Tmr* 30B2 & 30C3) and two on Odhos Mikalis (*Tmr* 30C4), close by 'Gum Tree' Square.

BUSES They now 'terminus' on a dusty square (*Tmr* 23B4) towards the south end of the town, on the edge of which is the Bus office. Until a few years ago they used to park up on Plateia Ag. Nikolaos and exit via the narrow alley that connects to Plateia Pythagoras. This squeeze made for a number of 'interesting', close shaves between buses and the shop fronts.

To decipher the bus timetables it is probably favourite to wander along to friendly **Samos Travel Tours** (*Tmr* 3A2), who post the current details on a board, rather than attempt to translate the Bus office hieroglyphics.

Bus timetable
Samos Town to Chora, Pirgos, Karlovasion
Monday to Friday   0730, 1400 hrs.
Saturday   1300 hrs.
Return journey
Monday to Friday   0615, 1400 hrs.
Saturday   0800 hrs.
Samos Town to Karlovasion, Marathokambos
Monday to Friday   1115 hrs.
Samos Town to Karlovasion, Drakei
Monday to Friday only 1115 hrs.
Samos Town to Mavratzei
Monday to Friday only 0600, 1230 hrs.
Samos Town to Pagiondas
Monday to Friday   0600, 1400 hrs.
Saturday   0600, 1300 hrs.
Samos Town to Mitilinii
Monday to Saturday   0800, 0945, 1300 hrs.
Samos Town to Pythagorion
Monday to Friday   0600, 0730, 1115, 1245, 1600 hrs.
Saturday   3 a day but I'm not sure of the times.
Return journey
Monday to Friday   0715, 0800, 1015, 1130, 1305, 1510, 1615 hrs.
Saturday via Mitilinii   0945, 1115, 1615 hrs.
Samos Town to Kokari, Tsamadou
Monday to Friday   0830, 1100, 1245, 1600 hrs.
Return journey (from Kokari)
Monday to Friday   0710, 0900, 0930, 1305, 1715 hrs.
Samos Town to Kokari, Avlakia, Platanakia, Ag. Konstantinos, Karlovasion
Monday to Friday   0830, 1115, 1245, 1400, 1600 hrs.
Saturday   0830, 1130, 1400 hrs.
Sunday   0830 hrs.
Return journey
Monday to Friday   0630, 0815, 0845, 1230, 1645 hrs.
Saturday   0830, 1115, 1515 hrs.
Sunday   0715, 1130 hrs.
Sample one-way fares: Samos Town to Pythagorion 75 drs.
        Samos Town to Mitilinii 105 drs.

CINEMAS One (*Tmr* 31C3) on the left of Odhos Kapetan Katavani.

COMMERCIAL SHOPPING AREA Samos not only has a 'Market' Street, Likourgou Logotheti, but a Market building (*Tmr* 28B2) wherein fish and vegetables are sold. The exterior is unprepossessing and the cruciform interior very gloomy and dark with up against the rear wall of the building, a cafe-bar that serves bowls of soup to the traders. In the narrow street alongside and to the right of the Market building (*Sbo*) are a butcher and a supermarket. It is probably no coincidence that the butcher is married to one of Stelios's daughters (he of the *'Gum Tree' Taverna*) which may well account for the high quality meat dished up there. Incidentally young Adonis, who also works in the butcher's shop, is married to another of Stelios's daughters and has to rush off when the shop closes to double up as a waiter at the taverna.

There is a 'bit of a morning market' with fruit and vegetables on sale in front of the Post Office (*Tmr* 32C3) on Plateia ΗΡΩΩΝ. Two drink shops spring to mind, both close to Plateia Pythagoras. The one (*Tmr* 33B2) to the north of the square is in the narrow lane that runs down from Plateia Ag. Nikɔlaos to the Esplanade and the other, that dispenses a number of wines, as well as brandy and retsina from the barrel, is on the right of Odhos ΜΕΛΑΧΡΟΙΝΟΥ, a street that runs up the south side of the National Bank between the Esplanade Odhos Kapetan Stamatis. A vegetable shop is hidden away in the basement of the building that houses Samos Travel and International Tours (*Tmr* 3A2).

One or two other shops deserve a mention, although they are not provenders. One **Foto-Faros** (*Tmr* 34B/C2/3) on the fork of Odhos Kapetan Katavani and Stamatis displays and sells a fascinating series of three photo albums depicting Samos scenes and personalities of yesteryear labelled *The Passing Generations*. I would dearly have liked to buy one or more, preferably all three, but they cost 1500 drs each. They would make a lovely present. The other is **Stavrinos Since 1870** (*Tmr* B/C2/3), on Odhos Kontaxi. They sell some interesting jewellery but is worth the mention because of the display of reasonably priced, secondhand items.

FERRY-BOATS An excellent service from Piraeus with stop-offs at, amongst other islands in the N.E. Aegean group, Ikaria and Fournoi. But if it were not for our good friend, **the CF Kyklades**, there most surprisingly would be no ferry making a run along the length of the N.E. Aegean group of islands. In fact, apart from the **Kyklades**, there is only a small interisland ferry, the **Kapetan Stamatis** (ΚΑΜΕΤΑΝ ΣΤΑΜΑΤΗΣ), which connects with Chios, the next island in the chain but which does not proceed any further.

See **Karlovasion** for a once or twice a week interisland caique to **Fournoi** and **Pythagorion** for (other) connections to the **Dodecanese** islands.

Ferry-boat timetable (Mid-season)

Day	Departure time	Ferry-boat	Ports/Islands of Call
Monday	0930 hrs	Aegeon	Ag. Kirikos (Ikaria), Paros, Piraeus (M) (2130 hrs).
	1300 hrs	Kapetan Stamatis	Chios
	1350 hrs	Kyklades	Chios, Mitilini (Lesbos), Limnos, Kavala (M)
Tuesday	0615 hrs	Ikaros	Karlovasion (Samos), Ag. Kirikos (Ikaria), Syros, Piraeus (M),
Wednesday	0620 hrs	Aegeon	Ag. Kirikos (Ikaria), Paros, Piraeus (M) (1830 hrs).
	0700 hrs	Samaina	Karlovasion (Samos), Ag. Kirikos (Ikaria), Piraeus (M).
	1430 hrs	Kyklades	Ag. Kirikos (Ikaria), Leros, Kalimnos, Kos, Rhodes, Chalki, Diafni (Karpathos), Karpathos, Kasos, Sitia (Crete), Ag. Nikolaos (Crete), Anafi, Thira (Santorini), Folegandros, Milos, Piraeus (M).

Thursday	0615 hrs	Ikaros	Karlovasion (Samos), Efdilos (Ikaria), Syros, Piraeus (M).
Friday	0500 hrs	Samaina	Karlovasion (Samos), Ag. Kirikos (Ikaria), Piraeus (M).
	0620 hrs	Aegeon	Ag. Kirikos (Ikaria), Paros, Piraeus (M) (1830 hrs).
	1300 hrs	Kapetan Stamatis	Chios
Saturday	0615 hrs	Ikaros	Karlovasion (Samos), Efdilos (Ikaria), Piraeus (M).
Sunday	0500 hrs	Samaina	Karlovasion (Samos), Ag. Kirikos (Ikaria), Piraeus (M).
	0620 hrs	Aegeon	Ag. Kirikos (Ikaria), Paros, Piraeus (M) (1830 hrs).

N.B. I think it is the CF Aegeon ferry that 'pulls up' off Fournoi island but....
One-way fares: Samos to Chios   775 drs; duration 4¾ hrs.
Ikaria   670 drs; duration 2½ hrs.
Piraeus 1645 drs; duration 12 hrs.

FERRY-BOAT TICKET OFFICES
Dovelos Travel (*Tmr* A2) 12 Sofouli   Tel. 28295
Directions: On the Esplanade, in the same stretch but to the south of the old Catholic Church (*Tmr* 7A2).
Ferry-boat tickets for the Chios island connection on the **FB Kapetan Stamatis**
Pythagoras Tours (*Tmr* 7A2) Sofouli Esplanade   Tel. 27240
Directions: The office is let into the front of the old Catholic Church, close to **Dovelos Tours**.
They sell tickets for Piraeus bound ferry-boats but the owner is rather surly.
There is another ticket office (*Tmr* B2), on the Esplanade, south of the side street Odhos Areos, which also sells ferry-boat tickets to Piraeus but who sells tickets for the **CF Kyklades?**

HAIRDRESSERS Two on Odhos Kapetan Katavani

LUGGAGE STORE *See,* **International Tours, Travel Agents.**

MEDICAL CARE
Chemists & Pharmacies. Surprisingly, for a town of this size, not a great many. There is one on the right and at the end of Odhos Kapetan Stamatis, where it spills on to the 'Public Garden' Square (*Tmr* 35B/C3) at the rear of the *Hotel Xenia* (*Tmr* 15B3). There is another on Plateia Pythagoras.
Clinic (*Tmr* C3) on Plateia ΗΡΩΩΝ, alongside the OTE office (*Tmr* 36C3).
Dentist Three with telephone numbers 22700/28344 & 27159.
Doctors Three with telephone numbers 22633/27269 & 28290.
Hospital A large, modern facility on the right of the road to Gangou Beach. (*See* **Beaches.**

NTOG None

OTE (*Tmr* 36C3) Open 24 hrs a day, seven days a week.

PETROL A number of stations around the town including one on Plateia Pythagoras, one on the road connecting Plateia ΗΡΩΩΝ (*Tmr* 32C3) and the 'Bus' Sq (*Tmr* 23B4) and yet another just before the turning up to the 'Bus' Sq, alongside the Esplanade.

But note that N.E. Aegean petrol stations generally close at 1930 hrs and on Sundays, in Samos Town, only one opens, on a rota basis.

PLACES OF INTEREST
Museums
Archaeological (*Tmr* 37C3) The building designated as the museum is empty at the moment, so what's new! Close by is a once magnificent structure, now a roofless ruin.
Byzantine On Odhos 28 Octovriou, which stretches up the hillside from behind the Customs & Port police building (*Tmr* 5A1/2). On the right is the Cathedral of Ag. Theodori and in the next block, the Museum.

Public Gardens (*Tmr* 38B/C3) A pleasant municipal feature with a very sad aviary and one or two caged animals at the Post Office end. The gardens are kept in a nice state of presentation by one gardener who once lived in England and deservedly appreciates any laudations.

Turkey. Samos Town excursion boats sailing to Turkey land at Kusadasi (Ephesus) and between mid April and mid October they depart twice a day for the two hour trip. The round journey, including landing taxes, costs about 5000 drs per head. From Kusadasi bus connections can be made every hour to Izmir from whence there are buses to Istanbul and Ankara. A specimen schedule is as follows:
Samos Town to Kusadasi
Daily   0800, 1700 hrs
Return journey
Daily   0830, 1730 hrs.

Holiday-makers at the beginning and end of the summer season must bear in mind that the weather and sea conditions affect sailing schedules and that in the months of April, May & October cancellations may spread over several days. One other important point is that it is not possible to simply hop on the boat at will, as the Greek authorities require a minimum of 24 hours notice. This delay is necessary so as to be difficult! No, it is in order to complete the necessary documentary formalities.

POLICE
Port (*Tmr* 5A1/2). In the large building to the left (*Sbo*) across the Esplanade from the bottom of the Ferry-boat quay.
Town (*Tmr* 39C3) on Odhos ΕΛΕΝΗΣ ΕΒΟΡΩΝΟΥ, behind Ag Spyridon Church.

POST OFFICE (*Tmr* 32C3) On Plateia ΗΡΩΩΝ in an imposing building, the upper floor of which houses the Assembly Hall. There are a number of large portrait paintings of island heroes of yesteryear spaced around the first floor gallery.

TAXIS Rank up on Plateia Pythagoras.

TELEPHONE NUMBERS
British Consulate, c/o Rhenia Tours, 15 Sofouli St.	Tel. 27314
German Consulate, 36 Sofouli St.	Tel. 27257
Hospital	Tel. 27407/27250
Police, town (*Tmr* 39C3)	Tel. 22100
Port office (*Tmr* 32C3)	Tel. 27318
Taxi rank	Tel. 28404

TOILETS Several including a block a few metres on beyond and to the west of the 'Bus' Sq (*Tmr* 23B4). Note the nearside door is the gentleman's which has clean 'squatties'. It is necessary to pinpoint the unlabelled entrances to save ladies and or chaps the embarrassing few moments I had to endure when I entered the incorrect portal..... The ladies is usually in an awful state and there is rarely water or toilet paper in either.

There is another public toilet at the Municipal Gardens (*Tmr* 38B/C3) end of Odhos Kapetan Stamatis but they register 10 on the 'Richter scale'.

TRAVEL AGENTS Apart from the two or three offices selling ferry-boat tickets, the vast majority appear to be mainly engaged in peddling tickets for the Turkish connection, as well as 'TOURS' and 'PICK NICKS' (sic). In years gone by Pythagorion was the sole embarkation point for boat trips to the Turkish mainland but it would appear that once the trade became substantial, Samos Town had to cash in.

I have drawn attention to the excellent **Samos Travel** (*Tmr* 3A2) under **The Accommodation** as I have **Dovelos Travel** under **Ferry-Boat Ticket Offices**. Another office worthy of a mention is:
International Tours (*Tmr* 3A2) 5 Sofouli St. Tel. 28601
Directions: In the same building and to the left (*Sbo*) of **Samos Travel**, opposite the bottom of the Ferry-boat quay.

The proprietor, George Michalakis, is a great self publicist and a rather larger than life character. A sign advises *Safe Your Luggage Here To Be Free* (sic).

EXCURSION TO SAMOS TOWN SURROUNDS
Excursion to Vathi: old capital (about 2 km) This attractive, small town
built on a steeply sloping hillside can be approached from Samos Town via 'Gum Tree' Square or from the Mitilinii-Pythagorion main road that loops up around the back of Samos Town.

Technically speaking Vathi is impassable to motor driven traffic but the locals seem to be able to get cars in and out of the most unlikely places. From top to bottom, the upper Main Square, if a 45° angled convergence of alleys can be called a square, is marked by the *Cafe-bar* FREIZEIT and the Kafenion ΑΤΖΑΜΟΥΔΑΚΗΣ – where the donkey rubbish man holes out. Vathi was the location from which I chose the definition of the unspoilt, typical Greek town (*See* CHAPTER 3).

There are three bakers and, at No. 862, a taverna/cafe-bar opposite a wood-working shop on the edge of (another) irregular square. The lower Main Square is almost abuzz with commercial activity and is edged by a zacharoplasteion, an ouzerie, a butcher indicated by a painted sign, a galaktopoleion, a taverna and, just up an incline, a 'front room' ladies' hairdresser. This latter is not exactly a Mayfair establishment and the anteroom is definitely 'doo hickey' as evidenced by the sloped, oiled hardboard floor covering.

ROUTE ONE
To Ag Paraskevi (8 km). This country lane follows the road past the Gangou
Beach turning and initially spaced out holiday villas. The asphalted road surface deteriorates becoming unsurfaced after about four kilometres.

KOTSIKAS (5 km from Samos Town) A few dwellings and the Panagia Monastery, set in hedgerowed, green countryside.

The route now breaks out into open countryside with to the left, a headland promontory forming the pretty Bay of Asprochori, off which are a number of small islets. It is unfortunate that the small cove at the end of this bay, down below the hillside routed track, is grossly polluted with kelp and sea driven debris.

At the far side of the base of the headland, the track peters out at the very small fishing hamlet of:

AG. PARASKEVI. The scattering of dwellings is set on a lovely, small circular bay with, to the left, the:

Pension Glaros Tel. 27351

Beautifully situated on a broom covered hillside, overlooking the tranquil bay.

The owner, Fotis Vettas, is a taciturn, rather disdainful, moustachioed gentleman of Cretan appearance. The rooms are reasonably sized cabins and in mid-season a double room en suite costs 1300 drs. The pension hires out a few scooters and, at the height of the season, groups of tourists from Samos Town are accommodated. One of the very pleasant features is the spacious patio which looks out over the bay.

To the right is the narrow, fishing harbour foreshore, edged by a rocky breakwater and closed off by a horn of land. The only deprecatory note must be that there is no sandy beach.

ROUTE TWO

To Mourtia (6 km) (as well as Ag Zoni Monastery (3 km) & Zoodochos Pighi Monastery (6 km) The road makes off up the mountainside from the 'Gum Tree' Square and is paralleled, on the hillside, by the original, old paved thoroughfare. Where the road levels out on to an agricultural plain, the Ag Zoni Monastery turning off to the right is proceeded by a 'dead' Landrover and is overlooked by the *Samos By Night Disco*.

Monastery of Ag Zoni (3 km from Samos Town) Built in 1695 on the site of an earlier church.

After four kilometres the main road passes through the hamlet of **Kamara**. The dirt track to the seaside fishing hamlet of Mourtia turns down the steep mountainside whilst the surfaced road winds on up through the pine tree clad mountain to the:

Monastery of Zoodochos Pighi (6 km from Samos Town) The Monastery is based on a 17th century church and is noticeable for a column supported dome, and the carved wooden screen.

MOURTIA (6 km from Samos Town) A pretty but 'doo-hickey' fishing boat cove with fishermen's shanty shacks scattered about the shore. The irregular water's edge is pebbly and the weedy seabed, rocky. There are a few oldish caravans littering the backshore and a palm tree shaded taverna to the right (*Fsw*).

ROUTE THREE

To Psili Ammos (8 km) & Posidon (9 km) The road from the far end of Vathy Bay forks right, along the north coast, and left up and behind Samos Town to another junction, alongside which is the **Church of tris Eklisies**. Right makes off for Pythagorion, whilst a little further on a left turning branches off for Posidon and right for:

PSILI AMMOS (8 km from Samos Town) The approach road loops along a big pebble shoreline to the right. The inland side is marshy, low-lying and swampy and some of this area is wired off due to the presence of minefields, which are signed. The road then circles around a small headland, occupied by the Army, and curves down to the right-hand side of a fine sand beach, backed by spindly arethemusa trees and dunes self-planted with low vegetation. A two kilometre wide sea channel separates Samos from the mountain backed shores of Turkey.

The seabed is made up of lovely, gently sloping sand, on which are 'planted' some beach umbrellas, and there are two beach tavernas, the *El Greco* and the *Psili Ammos*, to the right of the bay (*Fsw*). This very pleasant spot gets crowded with holiday makers, even in May.....!

POSIDON (9 km from Samos Town) Back at the **Church of tris Eklisies**, almost immediately after the left-hand fork the road winds round the pleasant, 'standard' Greek village of **Paleokastron**. Watch out for the very sharp left angled bend in the middle of the village where it is all too easy to hurtle straight on into a cul-de-sac.

The drive downhill to Posidon is spectacular, the road finally levelling out over an olive tree planted, shallow, saucer shaped plain backing the small bay on the edge of which the road runs out. The foreshore is not really suitable for bathing apart from a very thin sliver of pebbly beach beyond and to the right of the very attractively situated:

Taverna Posidonio.

The patio of the taverna juts out into the sea and makes an extremely pleasant watering hole.

The various menu offerings include baby squid (300 drs), Greek salad (120 drs), pork souvlaki (360 drs) but the house specialities are fish including red mullet (2000 drs), crayfish (1500 drs) and lobster (3000 drs), all priced per kilo. A bottle of retsina costs 80 drs, a bottle of Henninger beer 70 drs and Demestica wine 170 drs. Oh, by the way, the lavatories are clean, the old outside toilets having been abandoned some years ago.

A third of the way down to Posidon a track wanders down towards **Kerveli Cove,** the left-hand hillside of which, now occupied by the Army, looks over a very narrow band of shingle beach, backed by a fertile plain.

Immediately prior to the plain of Posidon, a short, dirt forest track descends to the left through tree clad slopes to a clearing edging a small cove with a seashore made up of large pebbles. To the left is a stone built fisherman's hut and, on the right, just before the clearing and set in the trees, is evidence of an organised, rustic B-B-Q bounded by ranch fencing. Do I detect an 'Excursion' location?

ROUTE FOUR
To Karlovasion (36 kms) via Kokari, Ag Konstantinos & Inland
Excursions. From the west end of Vathy Bay the northern road, for most of it's route, edges the coastline. The lush, tree clad interior mountains dominate the inland vista.

It is a pity that the winery on the west side of Vathy Bay has effectively despoiled the **Malagari** portion of the shoreline. After some 2½ km there is a small cove north of a headland complete with a church but the shale and pebble shore is dirty and kelpy. At a distance of 7½ km from Samos Town the flattish coastline has a narrow, pebbly shingle, foreshore.

KOKARI (Kokkarion) (10 km from Samos Town) The original headland village and port has been swamped and enlarged by the development necessary to support a package holiday industry but still remains picturesque.

The main road (Odhos Ag NIKOΛAOΥ) skirts the village leaving it to the right and passes, on the left, a large, prominent church. In front of the church is a bus stop. A little further on (in a westerly direction), across the road from the church, is ΜΥΘΑΓΟΡΑΣ, a souvenir shop, down the far side of which is a lane leading past a baker towards the jumbled waterfront and the prominent headland. This promontory divides up the long sweep of pebble beach to the left (*Fsw*) and the shorter, curved, almost enclosed cove to the right which is stopped off by a blob of sea stranded rock. Beyond this operates a windsurfing school. In the region of the waterfront, in the centre of the village, a number of small, sea edging squares are hemmed in by a jumble of houses. In amongst them is the:

Australia House Rooms.
Directions: As above, alongside the rather smelly, concrete lined river-bed.
Opposite is *Rooms Sophia.*
From the vantage point of the river-bed (*Fsw*), there is a pharmacy to the right and to the left, in the direction of the left-hand headland, the Police station as well as a store, pizzeria and **Rooms**.

Other pensions and hotels include the:
Hotel Vicky (Class D)   Tel. 92231
Rates for a single room en suite are 900 drs and for a double room 1200 drs respectively, rising to 1000 drs and 1400 drs (July - Sept).

Pension Blue Sky Rooms & Manolis Rooms (Tel. 92283).
Both are Class E establishments with similar rates. A single en suite costs 850 drs per night and a double room 1200 drs.

On the main road is the:
Hotel Galini (Class B)   Tel. 92331
Actually classified as a pension. The rooms, with en suite bathrooms, cost 1400 drs for a single and 1920 drs for a double rising to 1600 drs and 2000 drs (5th June - 17th Sept).
Scooter hire is available in the village.

To the west or left of Kokari (*Fsw*) the sea-shore stretches away around the shallow curve of the bay. A certain amount of boat building takes place on the backshore. This is edged by the road to Ag. Konstantinos, passing a doctor, a rustic Post Office, a number of hotels and a goodly number of **Rooms**. Opposite the *Kokkari Beach Hotel* (Class C, tel. 92263), at the far end of the beach, are beach showers.
One word of warning to drivers will not go amiss. When swooping along the road from the Ag. Konstantinos direction towards Kokari, beware because the main road turns sharply to the right on the outskirts the seaside village but the beach road makes it appear as if the main road goes straight on. In fact this is an accident blackspot!

From Kokari the road climbs up to a headland on the top of which is an unsurfaced layby overlooking:
TSAMADOU BEACH (11 km from Samos Town) A lovely, crescent shaped cove reached down a path to the left of the enclosed, small, single storey building bearing *No Camping* signs. The rather overrated pebble beach is backed by agricultural holdings.
From the headland there is a view to the right over another cove with a pebble foreshore and a windsurfing school in action.

Further westward, around the next bluff, is the 'Tsamadou look-alike' cove of **Lemonakia**. The road 'corniches' alongside the coastline to:
AVLAKIA (16 km from Samos Town)
A once dying, small fishing port clinging to a bluff but now being gently massaged back to life by tourism. The small beach is made up of pebbles.
There is a hotel, the:
Avlakia Hotel (Class C)   Tel. 94230
No single rooms, but reasonably priced en suite doubles are charged at 1250 drs per day rising to 1600 drs (July & Aug).

INLAND EXCURSIONS TO VOURLIOTES
Beyond Avlakia (at 16½ km) is a turning to the left from whence the old road winds up

the verdant, cypress, olive tree and bush covered mountainside to the lovely, hill-hugging:

VOURLIOTES (21 km from Samos Town) In the heart of the village is an old world plateia with almost more kafenions per Greek square than.... Each side has at least one cafe-bar with another on each corner, and inexpensive at that. Two large Nes meh ghala (carnation milk), mezes and an ouzo costs 135 drs. The village has a store but perhaps more importantly some two kilometres on up the mountain track is:

Vrontianni Monastery Reputed to be one of the oldest monasteries on Samos.

The main coastal road, now on the side of the mountain, skirts a lovely cove with clean foreshore of small and large pebbles. This is backed by a pleasant green-sward on which are dotted about an old well, the remains of house foundations and field enclosures. Almost reminiscent of a Minoan site but not sufficiently forbidding.

PLATANAKIA (19½ km from Samos Town) Almost on the outskirts of Ag. Konstantinos, and set in amongst high, shady, plane trees at the mouth of the Kakorema river. Prominent is the *'Night Out' Taverna*!

INLAND EXCURSION TO MANOLATES

At the outset of this lovely drive, a rather tasteless *'Forest Lodge' Restaurant* is accessed over a timber bridge fording the rocky river-bed (I bet they serve Black Forest gateau). The road winds up alongside a summer dry river for about two-thirds of its distance, rather evocative of a hot North Wales river gorge, on the way up to:

MANOLATES (24 km from Samos Town) Despite the positioning on some maps, the rather pinched village, with a small main square, is high on the mountainside. There are a number of stores as well as the usual kafenions and cafe-bars.

Back on the coastal route is:

AG. KONSTANTINOS (20 km from Samos Town) A rather narrow, dusty, large village of red tiled roofs which is trapped between the sea and the now refurbished main road. The waterfront is backed by an 'Esplanade' if that is not too grand a description for the rubbly swathe that edges the wave tossed backshore of the large pebble foreshore, now being lined by a concrete sea protection wall. This sea facade of the village is rather deserted and lifeless whilst that facing the main road is much livelier.

It was at Ag. Konstantinos years ago that I first observed, through the open window, a taverna owner cum barber in operation. One of his clients had left his walking hay-stack (a donkey obscured by mounds of straw) tethered to the door jamb. After a drink or three we wandered back to the hire car only to find a local fisherman had stealthily left us a handful of small fish on one of the seats. Nice that.

On the side of the main road are the:

Hotel Ariadne (Class E)   Tel. 94205
Only double rooms en suite at a cost of 1200 drs rising to 1500 drs (July & Aug).
and the
Pension Atlantis (Class E)   Tel. 94257
Doubles en suite cost 1400 drs
as well as the *Pension Four Seasons*.

The flat bay on which Ag. Konstantinos stands stretches away to the right (*Fsw*) but despite indications on some maps of a beach, don't hope for sand as the foreshore is made up of big pebbles on to which the sea pounds in windy conditions.

INLAND EXCURSION TO STRAVRINITHES

Beyond Ag. Konstantinos is a branch road off to the left, past a pine tree shaded

Pinknic Area (sic) and up a stream water washed road to a wasteland area on the edge of the spread out:

AMBELOS (24 km from Samos Town) The village streets and lanes wander up and down along the hillside, all dominated by a rather garish and oversized church. There are a number of shops but only a kafenion or two and no tavernas.

The mountain road to Stravrinithes makes off prior to Ambelos village and is 'deformed' in a number of places more especially where winter torrents pour across the road.

STRAVRINITHES (26 km from Samos Town) The (only) street of this pretty, agricultural village runs out on a small square edged by a friendly kafenion and church.

Returning to the coast, stretches of the route between Ag. Konstantinos and Ag. Dimitrios are under reconstruction. Beyond **Ag. Dimitrios** (28 km) the plain is afflicted by some intensive plastic greenhouses and single storey factory buildings.

INLAND EXCURSION TO YDROUSSA

At 29½ km a side road branches off alongside an initially ugly, wide river-bed but which progresses through very pleasant, rolling countryside, planted with vines and trees. Quite a contrast to the previous mountainous nature of the land.

YDROUSSA (33 km from Samos Town) A 'standard' village with plenty of water.

KARLOVASION (Karlovassi): (33/36 km from Samos Town) (Illustration 14).

The second town and port of Samos island. Considering that a number of the Piraeus ferries stop off here it is a great pity Karlovasion is such an uninviting place. An extract from the catalogue of drawbacks perhaps makes my point. The three centres that make up the whole of Karlovasion are very spread out, being up to some 4 km apart; the town and port, once a well-to-do industrial centre with a preponderance of tanneries, has suffered a serious decline, so much so that the originally grand, four-square buildings spaced out along the very long waterfront now resembles some run-down, inner city dockland area added to which, and to cap it all, Karlovasion is simply not attractive!

ARRIVAL BY FERRY

If the above thumbnail sketch has not put off any prospective visitor from making a voluntary stopover, then here goes.

The ferries dock (*Tmr* 1A1) in the large harbour at Paleo (Limani) Karlovasion which marks the westernmost part of the town. The other side of the harbour wall is a boatbuilding and repair yard. The port is dominated by the incongruous, pinnacle topping Chapel of Ag. Triada. Disembarking passengers must make off past the quayside buildings and turn left (*Sbo*) along the Esplanade road.

Ferry-boat timetables

Day	Departure time	Ferry-boat	Ports/Islands of Call
Monday	1800 or 2230 hrs	Ikaros	Samos Town
Tuesday	0715 hrs	Ikaros	Ag. Kirikos (Ikaria), Syros, Piraeus (M)
	1800 hrs	Samaina	Samos Town

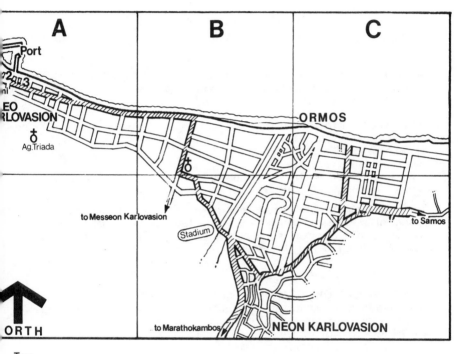

Tmr

1 Ferry-boat quay A1
2 Port police A1
3 Hotel Aktaeon A1

Tmr = Town map reference
Fsw = Facing seawards
Sbo = Sea behind one

Illustration 14 Karlovasion Port

Wednesday	0800 hrs	Samaina	Ag. Kirikos (Ikaria), Piraeus (M)
	1815 hrs	Ikaros	Samos Town
Thursday	0715 hrs	Ikaros	Efdilos (Ikaria), Syros, Piraeus (M)
	1800 hrs	Samaina	Samos Town
Friday	0600 hrs	Samaina	Ag. Kirikos (Ikaria), Piraeus (M)
	1730 hrs	Ikaros	Samos Town
Saturday	0715 hrs	Ikaros	Efdilos (Ikaria), Piraeus (M)
	1800 hrs	Samaina	Samos Town
Sunday	0600 hrs	Samaina	Ag. Kirikos (Ikaria), Piraeus (M)

See **Ferry-boat timetables, A to Z, Samos Town & Ikaria island** (CHAPTER 13)

A most interesting caique connection is the twice weekly scheduled trip to Fournoi Island. For more details *See* **Ferry-boats, A to Z, Fournoi** and or make enquiries of the Port police (*Tmr* 2A1).

The Accommodation Fifty metres to the east from the harbour along the waterfront 'Esplanade' is the:
Hotel Aktaeon (*Tmr* 3A1) (Class D)   Tel. 32356
Directions: As above, on the left.
   In the light of its classification, the hotel is not cheap. The rooms share a bathroom with a single costing 900 drs and a double room 1600 drs.

A few paces further on from the *Hotel Aktaeon*, on the right, are neat **Rooms**.
   Another two hundred metres of industrial factories and isolated buildings in various states of disrepair as well as a working winery, and a right-hand turning, signposted *Post*, proceeds up to Messeon Karlovasion. The waterfront continues on to become Ormos Karlovasion and is lined with cut stone buildings, many of which are simply roofless shells.

MESSEON KARLOVASION The street spills on to a small, irregular square off which are **Rooms**. On the way towards Messeon and alongside a large, almost disproportionately large, and colourful church, a street to the left leads to:
NEON KARLOVASION. Neon is the modern town part of Karlovasion accommodating the OTE, Post Office and Police station as well as the Bus Square, banks and a petrol station. The main street around which Neon is spread describes a large loop from the turning off the Messeon road up into Neon dropping back to the waterfront at Ormos Karlovasion.
   Neon Karlovasion sprawls along the coast almost as far as the River Krinis.

EXCURSIONS TO KARLOVASION SURROUNDS
Excursion to Potami (1½ km) and beyond. On the far, west side of the harbour wall of the port, a road climbs up through blasted rock past a rather surprisingly avant-garde church built out on a bluff and down to the large, curving, pebbly **Potami Bay**, hemmed in by the tree covered hillsides. There is some tar on the beach and at the nearside is a disco and restaurant. A rough dirt track from the far side of the beach sallies forth to:
   Mikro Seitani – a distance of some 1½ km and a small, dark sand cove set in rugged rocks –
and
Megalo Seitani – about 3 km and a large cove with a pebble/sand beach, encircled by tree covered slopes.

Excursion to Kastanea (6 km) From Messeon Karlovasion the road climbs to **Leka** village (2½ km from Messeon Karlovasion). Continuing on the road and after about 1 km a right-hand track scrambles off to:
NIKOLOUDES (6 km from Messeon Karlovasion) Noted for an enormous plane tree, reputedly the oldest and largest on Samos. The track continues on for anc er 1½ km to the mountain village of **Kosmadei**.

Back on the road and the trail ends at:
KASTANIA (6 km from Messeon Karlovasion) A large, wooded village famed for chestnut trees and the Second World War massacre of its civilians in 1943, an event remembered by a pilgrimage on 30th August.

From Neon Karlovasion a road proceeds from north to south to connect up with the south coast road at **Ag Theodoroi** (*See* ROUTE SIX).

ROUTE FIVE
To Pythagorion (10 km) and Ireon (19 km) The most pleasant, quickest road route to Pythagorion from Samos Town is to climb to the road junction close by the **Church of tris Eklisies** (*See* ROUTE THREE) and take the right-hand turning (*See* ROUTE SIX for the other road to Pythagorion). This climbs on upwards and then, once over the crest, swoops down on a well engineered road past the hamlet of **Mesokambos** (5 km) where there is a petrol station on the left. A glance backwards over the left shoulder reveals a wonderful view of the sweep of the plain of Mesokambos, Potami Bay, the Steno Samou Channel and the Turkish mainland.

PYTHAGORION (Pithagorion, Tigani): (10 km from Samos Town): port (Illustration 15).
A most picturesque location and understandably popular with yachtsman, package holiday-makers and backpackers alike. The port and Ferry-boat quay (*Tmr* 1B3) are most usefully situated due to the central location of the harbour and the compact nature of the village, which is conveniently laid out on a grid system. Naturally, those who can remember their schooldays and more especially the mathmatics lessons will have no difficulty in recalling the person after whom the port is named and his famous theorem. Hands up all those who cannot.

Pythagorion was the ancient capital of Samos island. The present harbour is supposed to overlay part of the port, built by the tyrant Polykrates, and which was double the size of its modern counterpart.

ARRIVAL BY FERRY
Pythagorion, more a yacht than a commercial harbour, is the third most important port of the island and the only departure point for scheduled and Express ferry connections to the Dodecanese. That is if it were not for the eccentric **C.F. Kyklades** (*See* **Ferry-boats, A to Z, Samos Town**). Pythagorion is also an embarkation point for trip boats to Turkey and once, before Samos Town got in on the act, was the only island connection.

THE ACCOMMODATION & EATING OUT
The Accommodation. Most of the hotels are tour operator booked but out of the height of the season there is 'room at most of the inns'. The harbour and wide Esplanade is laid out in a semicircle, with the High St, Odhos Logotheti, angling up the hillside from the centre of the curve.
To the left of the waterfront (*Sbo*) are the:

Hotel Acropole (*Tmr* 2B3) (Class E)   Tel. 61261
Directions: As above and at the far end of the block containing the Port police (*Tmr* 3B3).
   A tour operator pension with single rooms costing 1800 drs and charging 2500 drs for a double room.

Hotel Polyxeni (*Tmr* B3) (Class C)   Tel. 61359
Directions: Next door to the *Hotel Acropole.*
Even more expensive than the *Acropole* with a single room at 2060 drs and a double 2637 drs.

Hotel Damo (*Tmr* 4B3) (Class C)   Tel. 61303
Directions: In the next block along, over the OTE office.
   Double rooms only, with en suite bathrooms, starting at 2300 drs and rising to 2550 drs (16th May – 30th Sept).

Hotel Tarsanas (*Tmr* 5B3) (Class B)   Tel. 61162
Directions: Continue on around the Esplanade quay side from the Ferry-boat quay and cross over the narrow neck of land to the seafront on the west side of Pythagorion.
   The hotel, an old building of square, cut stone construction, is very pleasantly situated on the edge of a small beach. This is unfortunately made up of large pebbles in which are mixed up some very rounded brick rubble. Double rooms only at a cost of 200 drs.

Hotel Paris Sea (*Tmr* 6B3)   Tel. 61513
Directions: Up Odhos Pipinou from behind the *Hotel Tarsanas* and in the second lane to the right.

Rooms (*Tmr* 7A/B3) Odhos Aristarhou
Directions: In the next side street up from the lane in which is located the *Hotel Paris Sea*, next door to and over a small store.

To the right of the waterfront (*Sbo*) are the:
Pension ΜΑΡΚΟΥ ΝΑΥΤΙΛΙΑΚΑ (*Tmr* 8B2/3)   Tel. 61480
Directions: In the first block to the right of the High Street (*Sbo*) overlooking the waterfront. The entrance is almost smothered by restaurants.
the:
Hotel Delphini (Dolfini) (*Tmr* 9C2) (Class C), Paralia   Tel. 61205
Directions: Third block to the right along the harbour quayside (*Sbo*), prior to the Customs office.
   A single room en suite costs 1200 drs, a double room sharing the bathroom 1420 drs and en suite 1560 drs.
and the:
Rooms (*Tmr* 10C2/3)
Directions: Towards the far right-hand end of the Harbour Esplanade (*Sbo*). At the end of the row, in which is situated the Customs office (*Tmr* 11C2), turn left and the accommodation is in the second block on the right, edged by Odhos Polikratous.

Captains House Hotel (*Tmr* 12B2) (Class C)   Tel. 61266
Directions: Up the High St and just beyond the small Public Gardens on the opposite side of the street.
   All rooms and with en suite bathroom, singles costing 1400 drs and doubles 2000 drs.

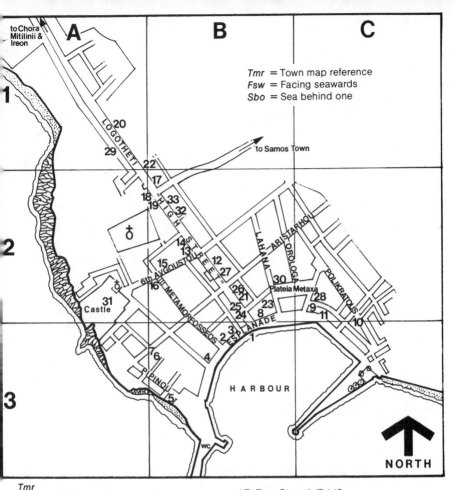

Illustration 15 Pythagorion Port

142

Central Rooms Pension (*Tmr* 13B2)
Directions: On the left of the High St, at the junction with Odhos 6th Augustou.

Hotel Fillis (*Tmr* 14B2) (Class B)   Tel. 61296
Directions: Next door to the *Central Rooms*.
Tour operator booked and smart, very smart. The en suite rooms cost 1800 drs for a single and 2160 drs for a double.

Pension Anna (*Tmr* 15B2)
Directions: Proceed up the gently rising Odhos 6th Augustou and the pension is on the right.
   Very friendly with a double room sharing bathroom costing 1200 drs.

Hotel Alexandra (*Tmr* 16A/B2) (Class D) 11 Metamorfosseos   Tel. 61429
Directions: Further along Odhos 6th Augustou from the *Pension Anna* and across the steps to the left which drop down to Odhos Metamorfosseos. The hotel is in the angle of the street and the steps, on the left.
   More a pension and rather soulless but well established with doubles sharing the bathroom rising from 1300 drs to 1500 drs. One word of warning is that the water heating is solar and first served may get hot water but last definitely not...

The Eating Out The harbour waterfront is awash with restaurants stretching away to either side of the bottom of the High Street but I cannot put my hand on my digestive juices and rave about any particular establishment.
   Alongside the Bus park up (*Tmr* 17A/B 1/2) on the High Street there is a small, 'doo-hickey' kafenion serving reasonably priced coffee and brandy (two Nes meh ghala and 2 brandies for 200 drs). Very convenient when waiting for a bus. Next door is a souvlaki pita snackbar.

Across the High St and down past the Petrol station (*Tmr* 18 A/B2) is:
Robinson Fast Food (*Tmr* 19A/B2)
Directions: As above but where do they get these names from?
Serves souvlaki pita from 1700 hrs on.

THE A TO Z OF USEFUL INFORMATION
AIRLINE OFFICE & TERMINUS (*Tmr* 20A1). At the far, top end of the High St, on the right

Aircraft timetables
See **Aircraft timetables, A to Z, Samos Town.**

BANKS
Commercial Bank (*Tmr* 21B2). Not far up the High St from the harbour and on the right. Accepts Eurocheques.
National Bank (*Tmr* 22 A/B 1/2). On the right of the High St but at the top end, beyond the Samos turning and only open Monday, Wednesday and Friday 0900 – 1230 hrs.

BEACHES One in front of the *Hotel Tarsanas* (*Tmr* 5B3). Small and clean but composed of large pebbles, stones and broken bricks. Yes house-bricks which are admittedly rounded off and worn down by the action of the sea. The other small beach is beyond the harbour breakwater at the far right of the harbour (*Sbo*).

BICYCLE, SCOOTER & CAR HIRE There are almost more scooter and car hire offices in the High St than tour offices, and there are a lot of tour offices. At least scooter hire can be considerably cheaper in Pythagorion than Samos Town. For example a daily scooter rate of 700 drs per day drops to 650 drs for 2/3 days. Also on hire are some old fashioned sit-up-and-beg bicycles costing 100 drs a day. A bicycle is a possible option as the plain between Pythagorion and Ireon, some seven kilometres distant, is comparatively flat.

BREAD SHOPS A baker (*Tmr* 23B2) is located on the left of Odhos Lahana, which branches off the Harbour Esplanade, prior to Plateia Metaxa. He also sells pies but is closed on Sundays. Across the street is a barber.

BUSES The bus stop (*Tmr* 17A/B 1/2) is situated by the junction of the High St and the Samos Town road.
Bus timetable. *See* **Bus timetable, A to Z, Samos Town.**

COMMERCIAL SHOPPING AREA None but a fair scattering of shops on the High Street includes a butcher (*Tmr* 24B2/3), a fish shop (*Tmr* 25B2/3), a 'supermarket' (really a shop) (*Tmr* 26B2) and a greengrocer (*Tmr* 27B2). The general store (*Tmr* 28C2) is to be recommended.
Before leaving the subject, but hardly because of its excellence, attention should be drawn to the **Photography Shop** on the left of the High St (*Sbo*). The point is that this establishment, run by a woman, now rather a harridan but who may well have been, once upon a year, an 'exciting lass', is typical of how many shopkeepers used to live yesteryear. She and her children subsist in a tiny space behind a blanketed off area to the back of the shop. Some years ago there was a similar fruit and vegetable shop, on the other side of the road and closer to the waterfront, run by a very old lady. The produce was awful but we always bought something so she could keep body and soul together but maybe this ancient bundle of black clothes and knee stockings owned most of the High St!

FERRY-BOATS An important port for connections to the Dodecanese islands, a Patmos Express Service and of course the Turkey link. Mark you do not bother to make any enquiries about Pythagorion scheduled ferries in Samos Town. They feign deafness and or ignorance!

Ferry-boat timetables

Day	Departure time	Ferry-boat	Ports/Islands of Call
Tuesday	1000 hrs	Panormitis	Angathonisi, Arki, Patmos, Lipsos, Leros, Kalimnos, Kos, Nisiros, Tilos, Simi, Rhodes.

Pythagorion to Patmos (passenger trip)
Monday, Wednesday & Friday. For details contact **Samos Travel, Travel Agents, A to Z, Samos Town.**

For details of day trips to Samiopoulas island, *See* **Places of Interest.**

FERRY-BOAT TICKET OFFICES
K (anakis) Travel (*Tmr* 29A1) Odhos Logotheti   Tel. 61335
Directions: Rather inconveniently situated at the far top end of the High St, on the left (*Sbo*).
   Very helpful and English is spoken. The office acts for the **FB Panormitis**, **Samaina** and **Ikaros**.

HAIRDRESSERS A ladies hairdresser is sited on the left of the High St, towards the Samos Town road junction.

MEDICAL CARE
Chemists & Pharmacies: Two in the High St.

OTE (*Tmr* 4B3). On the harbour waterfront in the ground floor of the *Hotel Damo*. Open weekdays only 0730 – 1510 hrs.

PETROL (*Tmr* 18A/B2) On the High St, opposite the Samos Town road junction.

PLACES OF INTEREST
Archaeological Museum (*Tmr* 30B2). On the pretty tree shaded Plateia Metaxa, opposite the junction with Odhos Lahana. Apart from the exhibits inside there are many humps of ancient stonework scattered about the Square.

Castle of Logothetis (*Tmr* 31A2). Occupies a 'low rise' hillock on the west shore of Pythagorion. The present remains, built on the walls of a Venetian Castle, achieved fame due to the exploits of one Lykourgos Logothetis and his men who valiantly fought off the Turks in 1824, after the Declaration of Independence.

Church of Transfiguration Next door to the Castle. It is here on the 6th August that the 1824 victory is celebrated.

Ancient Wall. This enclosed ancient Samos City, had a length of some 5,500m with 35 towers, 12 gates and its construction is attributed to Polykrates (550-522 BC). The fortification not only encompassed the town and port but the hills of Spilianis and Kastri as well as other (now) archaeological sites. The track to them is off to the left of the main road from Pythagorion to Samos Town, some 200/300m from the junction with the High St and is signposted *To the Tunnel distance 2 km*. The sites include the:
Ancient Theatre: Not a lot left but sited below the:
Monastery of Panagia Spiliani: From the track to the Theatre proceed up to the right. The monastery is built on the slopes of Kastri Hill and inside is a cave into which is built a small church.

Eupalinus Tunnel: Further on from the Theatre. It was really an aquaduct, built at the instigation of Polykrates, to carry water to the city from the north of the mountain, in the direction of Mitilinii. The tunnel, named after the chief engineer and about 1100/1200m long, was dug from both ends at once and the engineers very nearly made a perfect job of the coupling, there being only a small difference in levels and alignment. It was hacked out of rock with a height of 1¾m and a width of 2⅓m with a conduit duct in the floor. The southern end is fronted by an ornamental stone gate but only about 700m is now walkable due to a rock fall. Open every Monday to Thursday and Saturday between 1000 and 1240 hrs.

Samiopoulas Island (Son of Samos) Three rumbustious brothers still run their daily caique trip to the island south of Samos at a cost of 650 drs per head, weather permitting. Departure from the harbour wall is at approximately 0915 hrs, returning at 1715 hrs but they now have competition, for which ask at the waterfront travel offices.

Sanctuary of Heraion. *See* ROUTE SIX

POLICE
Port (*Tmr* 3B3). On the harbour waterfront, to the left of the High St (*Sbo*).
Town (*Tmr* 32B2). Halfway up the High St, on the right.

POST OFFICE (*Tmr* 33B2). On the right of the High St, almost as far up as the Samos Town turning.

TAXIS Rank on the junction of the High St and Samos Town road.

TELEPHONE NUMBERS & ADDRESSES

Police (*Tmr* 32B2)	Tel. 61333
Taxi rank	Tel. 61450

TOILETS A public lavatory is situated on the far left breakwater (*Sbo*) of the harbour.

TRAVEL AGENTS Quite a few on the harbour waterfront and ranged up the High St.

ROUTE SIX
To Ormos Marathokambos (50 km) and on to Drakei (75 km) via Mitilinii, Chora, Ireon, Pirgos and Marathokambos.
Back at Samos Town, the Mitilinii road is signposted from the far, west end of Vathy Bay, first curving left away from the north coast route and then climbing off to the right at the fork where the road to the south coast branches left. The road rises steeply to a crest, marked by a small chapel, above:

MITILINII (8 km from Samos Town) A boring 'High St' of a village with two petrol stations (which close on Sundays). Boring it may be but the Palaeontological Museum is located here. Mitilinii is the site of an ancient city which it is believed was once ruled by a matriarchy.

Another four kilometres on is the village of:

CHORA (12 km from Samos Town). Hardly a Chora in the usual sense of the word but certainly an important junction, straddled by a couple of 'local' kafenions.

The road to the left proceeds towards Pythagorion, passing two petrol stations and the Airport/Ireon turning, beyond which the land is low-lying and rather marshy. In this area there are a number of expensive hotels to the right of the road, close by the sea's edge. An acute, right angled turning back towards the south-west encompasses a plain between the road, the coastline and the:

Airport (15 km from Samos Town) Off to the left. For more details *See* **Arrival by Air, Samos Town.**

Beyond the airport, three kilometres from the Pythagorion fork, is another junction, the right-hand of which heads towards **Mili** and the left towards the seaside village of Ireon. Off this latter road a lane branches to the left to the archaeological remains of:
SANCTUARY OF HERAION (18 km from Samos Town) Also known as *Kolonna* due to the single column left standing on the site, once a supporting column of the (Polykrates) **Temple of Hera.** The temple measured some 105m by 54m and was 23m in height. The original building constructed in the 8th century BC, was rebuilt on a number of different occasions over the next 500 or 600 years. There is a school of thought that the first temple was built of wood as early as the 13th century BC. A shrine revered a sacred tree, the **Lygos or Osier Tree.** Excavations in 1963 revealed roots, possibly 'The Roots', enclosed by the **Roikos Altar**, reconstructed by the Romans in their time. Apart from the **Sanctuary**, which included temples, porticos and an altar, there was also a town. This was first desolated in AD 270, subsequently rebuilt with a Christian basilica but all to nought as almost everything was destroyed again, leaving the whole area to become arable. When the 1855 excavations commenced the site was actually a vineyard.

The Sanctuary was connected to the Ancient City of Samos by a Sacred Road, some 5000m in length. On either side of this Via Sacra were statues, temples and tombs.

IREON (19 km from Samos Town) After the 'Lord Mayor's Show'.... Despite being the namesake of the Sanctuary there the similarity ends.

Ireon is now a dusty, incomplete sprawl of picturesque squalor which has spread along the seafront from the few original dwellings. These are at the far right end of the settlement (*Fsw*) and once formed the nucleus of a fishing village. Unmade dirt roads enclose some out-of-place, smart hotels which jostle with waste plots, cafe-bars, restaurants, lesser hotels and pensions. The beach of varying size pebbles and fine shingle is broken up by a scattering of tavernas and their patios that jut out on to the backshore.

Accommodation includes the *Hotel/Restaurant Hera* (Class D, tel 61180), the *Marialena Pansion* (sic) and a scattering of **Rooms**.

There are bikes and scooters for hire.

If the intention is to proceed on to Marathokambos and beyond, it is shorter and quicker to return to Chora village and to take the Koumaradeion road (For details of which read on) but......
From Ireon it is possible, instead of returning to the Mili fork, to take a track which cuts off the corner, connecting with the surfaced road beyond the turning off to Mili. The advantage of this trek is that it leads past:-
Sarakini's Tower A defensive tower still complete with the stone bowls once used to ladle boiling water or tar over undesirables and generally discourage 'naughty chappies' bent on ousting the residents.

From the tower, the Ireon road connects with the more direct route at Pirgos. After a winding climb to **Pagiondas**, a wide track proceeds all the way to Spathareion which must be one of the loveliest drives on the island. It progresses high up on the steeply sloping mountainside, set in amongst pine trees which only allow tantalising, almost aerial glimpses of **Samiopoulas island**. Note, if approaching this route from Pirgos, in **Spathareion** take the right-hand, lower road and then keep to the left – where indicated by the hand painted sign.

On the other hand, back at Chora village the right-hand turning, to which previous reference has been made, crosses the lower part of the island in an east/west direction.

INLAND EXCURSION TO MAVRATZIE
After 2½ km, a turning to the right winds steeply up the once pine tree covered mountainside. I write once because a devastating fire has swept through the area leaving blackened, dead tree trunks starkly bearing mute testament to the holocaust.

Monastery Timiou Stavrou (Holy Cross) (15½ km from Samos Town). Fortunately these rather lovely religious buildings escaped the forest fire which appears to have raged all around them. Holy intervention? There are two, welcoming freshwater wells, one on the outside wall and the other in the courtyard. The original church was built in the 1580s and the present complex completed in the 1830s. The usual strictures in respect of clothing are adhered to strictly, that is ladies must wear skirts and gentlemen trousers (not shorts), accompanied by, respectively, blouses and shirts. Women should also have a headscarf.

Another 1½ km beyond the Monastery and the steep climb ends on the small irregular square of:-
MAVRATZEI (17 km from Samos Town) An attractive mountain village with several kafenions edging the Main Square. On the left of the approach to the village is a higgledy-piggledy general store that stays open late into the night. Service can be slow if there is anything, yes anything, being transmitted on the television. A large

set dominates the dark room and the owners and friends sit amongst the piled up goods in the dark, illuminated solely by the light of the screen.

Fresh yoghurt is available from a pampered, barn-closeted cow. The mountain streams source a communal washing area and continually flush the Public toilet which is built out over one of the torrents.

Back on the main road, at **Koumaradeion**, a track to the left connects with Mili village.

PIRGOS (24 km from Samos Town) The road is bridged by an aqueduct arch. Close to the old waterway, across the way from where the buses park up, is a restaurant. The service is attentive, but not inexpensive considering the locality, and the owner speaks some English. Two sausage omelettes (300 drs), a plate of patatas (40 drs), a Greek salad (150 drs), bread (20 drs) and two beers (134 drs) all for 649 drs.

The alternative southern loop from Ireon, via Spathareion, rejoins the main road at Pirgos. From this village the route progresses through pleasant mountain country, towards Ag Theodori. There are various branch roads and unmade tracks off to the left to **Neochori; Koumeika,** with further tracks down to the seaside fishing hamlets of **Ballos, Skoureika, Kambos** and **Peri,** (beyond which is confusingly another **Plaz Psili Ammos**); as well as north to Platanos and Neon Karlovasion.

AG. THEODORI (41 km from Samos Town) A fork ½ km beyond the village of Ag. Theodori branches right (and north) to Karlovasion and left to Marathokambos. This latter road is unsurfaced for some half of it's length and throughout is badly potholed all the way to:-
MARATHOKAMBOS (46 km from Samos Town). Almost a small town draped over the hillside and worth wandering through the streets and lanes, even if one's eyes are irresistibly drawn towards the bay down below.

The delights of the three kilometre, very scenic drive down to the coast may well be rudely interrupted by unexpected, unmade sections dotted about the tarmacadam surface.

ORMOS MARATHOKAMBOS (49 km from Samos Town) The road to the waterfront of this small, truly delightful, attractively native, dusty, stony, fishing and boat building port, advances down to the far right-hand (*Fsw*) end of the bay. The foreshore of small pebble and shale stretches away to the left beyond a tiny stretch of sand snuggled in the angle of a large quay that juts out from the waterfront. On the approach road to the 'Esplanade' (if that is not too grand a word for the unmade track that edges the backshore), there are **Rooms** to the left. On the left-hand corner of the last street, parallel and one back from the waterfront, is a baker.

At the junction with the 'Esplanade', steps to the right up the hillside ascend to *Rooms for Rent* (painted on the wall of the house in red). Directly ahead is an irregular, unsurfaced expanse, formed by the large sea protection/harbour wall to the right, on which are scattered fishing craft. Immediately to the right is a cafe-bar shop. Advancing along the backshore 'Esplanade' to the left, beyond the first few houses, is a small store in the ground floor of an old house set back from the 'building line' and conspicuous by it's external staircase. Beyond the store are the *Restaurant Costas*, the ('dead'?) *Pizza Cave* and the very large smart *Hotel/Restaurant Kerkis Bay* which stretches right back to the street behind. When I saw the foundations going down some seven years ago I feared for Ormos Marathokambos but I need not have worried for in the intervening period the tour operators withdrew from this section of the island. In fact it would be fair to say that to date all attempts to 'modernise' Ormos have totally failed, for which let us be truly thankful.

Beyond the *Hotel Kerkis Bay* is a garage but which does not possess any petrol pumps (although fuel might be obtained) and an incongruous, balconied house in the ground floor of which a 'dead self service' store has been built, the sightless windows covered with breeze flapping plastic. A street to the left has **Rooms**. Hereabouts the boat littered seashore angles back towards the 'Esplanade', resulting in a narrow band of stony beach edging the road. Almost opposite a backshore periptero is the rustic *Cafe-bar Ta Kymata*, where a couple of coffees and local Samos brandies cost 200 drs. Further on, another street to the left marks the end of the fishing village's development and on the right there is an open air boatyard with one very large trading craft under construction. I am fairly certain I observed the frame of this craft being laid down some years ago. Halfway up the street, on the left, is a surprisingly modern souvenir shop with an impressive display of tasteful 'touristabilia'. I cannot think where all the customers spring from to make the venture worthwhile but there you go.....

Most of the boats have bow mounted hooks to which hawsers can be attached in order to beach them and lining the backshore are the traditional post winches with which to haul them out.

From Ormos the coast road is signposted and over the headland is:-

PLAZ VOTSALAKIA (52½ km from Samos Town) An unexpected, spread out ribbon development, scattered along the long, sand and pebble beach edging the coastal plain. There are plenty of **Rooms** dotted about. At the outset of this rather Greek resort is a very small, pleasant, sandy cove, snuggled in by a rocky headland.

Samos Town buses terminate at Plaz Votsalakia so, unless in possession of transport, it is a dusty 1½ km walk along the unsurfaced road to:-

PSILI AMMOS (of Marathokambos) (54 km from Samos Town) Beyond a steep, narrow track off to the right, leading to **Rooms**, the road rounds a bluff quite high up the mountainside. The *Kalamaki Taverna* is built round the sharp bend in the road, on the right, and almost straight ahead, sheltered in the curving contour of the land, lies the stunning, white shingle and sand expanse of Psili Ammos beach, edging the turquoise Caribbean coloured sea. Closer examination, achieved by clambering down the zig-zag path halfway round the bay, reveals that the sandy portions of the beach are large areas, set in amongst fine shingle. The excellence of the beach is mirrored in the number of people who manage to reach this far-flung outpost. Don't misunderstand the inference of a crush as on a mid-May afternoon they can amount to all of twenty people! Oh yes, nude bathing is permitted.

It is best to take drinking water and any snack requirements to the beach for it is quite a walk back to the:-

Taverna Kalamaki
Gloriously situated overlooking the whole expanse of the beach and owned by the delightful couple, Manolis and his fair, English wife Sarah. Classical music accompanies some excellent, imaginative cuisine. Even in the out of season months, Sarah offers a dish of the day. A sample meal for two of Greek salad with lettuce (yes lettuce – 140 drs), splendid casseroled lamb chops (several) with new potatoes and carrots (280 drs), bread (20 drs), and a bottle of beer (70 drs), costs about 860 drs. It is a great pity that energy and money has not yet allowed them to construct some accommodation but I hope they soon manage the task, for this is a truly lovely situation.

Not all is lost on the accommodation front because up the previously referred to track, prior to the taverna, is a chalet with four self contained double rooms which cost 1000 drs a day each in mid-season. Sarah, she of the *Taverna Kalamaki* and originally from Kent and who not unnaturally speaks English, said that one of the guests who stayed at the chalet, an ornithologist, had been delighted with a head count of 140 different varieties of birds. No chaps, the feathered species! Maybe the authorities have confiscated all the shot guns, for on most Greek islands any wildlife that dares to make its presence known is quickly dispatched. Unfortunately the telephone company has not yet discovered this end of Samos. As pointed out it is possible to bus to Plaz Votsalakia and walk the rest of the route although hitchhikers invariably get a lift from locals or more fortunate, car hiring fellow tourists. One last rejoinder is to remember to address any correspondence to 'Psili Ammos, Marathokambos' so as to distinguish this delightful spot from the (two) other Samos island Psili Ammos.

At the far, western end of Psili Ammos beach, and around the headland, is **Ormos Limionas**, another expanse of beach with a scattering of houses set on the plain backing the bay.

If visitors can drag themselves away from the captivations of this western Psili then the balance of the journey round to Drakei is really only for purists. The route edges around **Mt Kerkis** and there are only two large villages (Kallithea and Drakei) on the rest of this unsurfaced road that treks through the granite landscape at this end of the island. Some two kilometres after the hamlet of **Ag Kyriaki** (59 km from Samos Town), there are a couple of branch tracks. One tumbles down to **Paleochori**, beyond which is St Johns Church and another kilometre further on is a track branching off to **Plaka** and a stony, pebble foreshore. At **Kallithea** (65 km from Samos Town) keep to the left or lower road to reach:-

DRAKEI (70 km from Samos Town) Do not drive into the village but park up on the outskirts as there is no through road. Disbelieving locals silently watch intrusive tourists as they thunder into the village only to watch them as they ignominiously back out some minutes later. There are a kafenion or three and this typical mountain village is only of note because it marks the end of the road, despite the occasional map sketching in a 'phantom' encircling coastal track on to Karlovasion.

Between Kallithea and Drakei the road, which is very high up on the mountainside, overlooks a track that winds down to a very small harbour and shipyard set on a rocky promontory which juts into Ormos Ag Isidorou.

Before closing this Chapter it will not go amiss to address a paragraph to:-
Mt Kerkis (1435m) This mountain dominates the western end of Samos island and is riddled with caves and dotted with chapels as well as the Evagelistria Convent. I am reticent to try to pinpoint the caves as my descriptive powers would not hold up to the task. More importantly, in the interests of life and limb, it is a 'must' to employ the service of a knowledgeable guide if you wish to explore. It will require at least a week, if not a lifetime, to enjoy to the full the hidden delights of this mountain vastness. Best wishes.

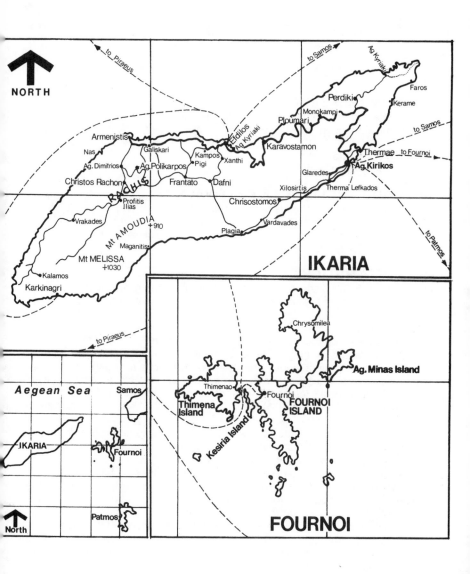

Illustration 16 Ikaria & Fournoi islands

13 IKARIA
& Fournoi (Fourni, Furni) ***** *
N.E. Aegean Islands

FIRST IMPRESSIONS
The mountain range; unfriendly islanders; sleazy kafenions; smell of friar's balsam; goat skins; thermal baths; (only) Greek spoken; indented coastline.

SPECIALITIES
Thermal baths; goat skins.

RELIGIOUS HOLIDAYS & FESTIVALS
include: 17th July – Festival to celebrate defeat of the Turks, Ag Kirikos; 26th July – Festival at Ag. Paraskevi, Xilosirtis; 27th July – Festival at Ag. Panteleimon; 6th August – Festival at Christos Rachon; 15th August – Festival at Chrisostomos; 8th September – Festival at Maganitis.

VITAL STATISTICS
Tel. prefix 0275. The island is 40 km in overall length (north-east to south-west), up to 9 km in width with an area of 270 sq kms and a population of about 8,000.

HISTORY
Little notable although mythology has assured the island's place in the legends of the world. Daedalus and Icarus, father and son, chose to flee from King Minos of Crete by fashioning giant wings in the style of birds in order to fly away to safety. But Icarus, delirious at the delights of airborne travel, flew too close to the sun which melted the wax fixing the feathers. The wings disintegrated causing him to plunge to is death (supposedly off Xilosirtis) to the south of the island which then adopted his name.

Perhaps the most noticeable feature is that over the centuries the island has been used as a place of exile, which may well be a pointer to the islanders character! This practice dates back as long ago as the Byzantine Empire.

Venetian overlords were followed by Chios based Genoese nobility and the Turks, who were booted out by the islanders in July 1912. The Ikarians then set up an independent state issuing their own money and stamps but this gesture of 'UDI' only lasted until October of the same year when a Greek fleet knocked on the door! The islanders grumble that since they were clasped to the bosom of the Greek nation they have been forgotten by the mainlanders. That is until central government wanted somewhere to unload up to 15,000 communists. Then Ikaria was remembered – no wonder the locals are rather 'bolshie'.

GENERAL
I am of the opinion that Ikarians do not want those visitors that do drop in – that is apart from the villagers of seaside Armenistis. The majority of ferries dock at the southern port of Ag. Kirikos. If the stop-off is late afternoon, after the sun has left the port in the shade, the closeness of the dark and steep mountainside gives the port and its surrounds a sombre, dark, if not forbidding atmosphere. This mood is heightened if the mountain top is shrouded by cloud.

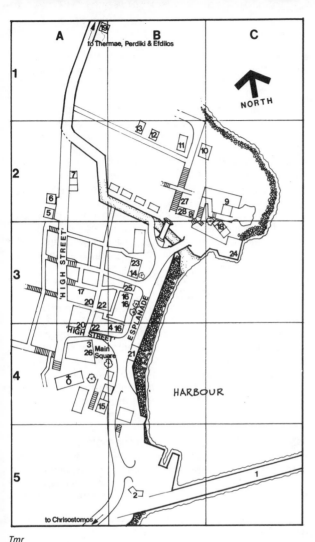

Tmr = Town map reference
Fsw = Facing seawards
Sbo = Sea behind one

Tmr

1 Ferry-boat quay C2
2 Best Snackbar B5
3 Hotel Isabella's & Bank A4
4 Hotel Adam's & chemist A/B3/4
5 Post Office A2
6 OTE A2
7 Pension A2
8 Hotel ΟΚΑΡΡΑΣ/Bank B2
9 Hotel Akti C2
10 Police station B/C2
11 Thermal baths B2
12 Pension B2
13 Rooms B1/2
14 Restaurant Samos B3

15 Restaurant A/B4
16 Kafenions B3 & B3/4
17 Restaurant ΚΛΗΜΑΤΑΡΙΑ A3
18 Bank B/C2/3 See TMR 3 & 8
19 Garage A/B1
20 Bread Shops
21 Bus/Taxi lay-by B4
22 General stores
23 Fish shop B3
24 Local boat quay C3
25 Ferry-boat ticket office/Port police B3
26 Ferry-boat ticket office A4
27 Chemist B2
28 Dolichi Tours B2

Illustration 17 Ag Kirikos Capital & Main Port

154

The mountains range the length and fill out the middle of the elongated island sloping steeply to the sea on both north and south coasts. The flanks of the towering terrain are remarkably well vegetated with plenty of trees but they do not appear to be so at first sight.

Early and late summer travellers to the island will not be impressed as the residents deem that the tourist season does not commence until June and that it ends with the close of September. Outside these months the buses run a skeletal service added to which many businesses and most tavernas are closed. So there! Even during the summer onslaught only Armenistis really welcomes the holiday-maker, the inhabitants of the two ports of Ag. Kirikos and Efdilos tolerating them with a lack of grace. Many visitors stop off only to get straight back on the very next ferry!

The mountainous countryside does not lend itself to walking so the unreliable bus service, with its incomprehensible journey schedules, and the not inexpensive taxis are the only methods of medium distance travel. Discovering any information is similar to locating 'dragons teeth' as most enquiries are met with graceless disinterest or disinformation. Greek is almost an essential prerequisite, that is until the same man has the 'tiring' task of chatting up a 'likely looking' female tourist! Notwithstanding, it becomes apparent that quite a number of locals speak English but are generally very reluctant to come forward.

Efdilos, as an alternative port, is rather derelict but, despite being a mere 'way station' between Ag. Kirikos and Armenistis, does possess a fair beach.

The residents of Armenistis are friendly and there are two large, magnificent beaches. Unfortunately the 'great unwashed' of Western Europe have also heard of this amenity and up to a thousand of them hit the spot at the height of the season, many camping out on the backshore of the until then, lovely beaches.

The renowned thermal baths dotted about the island ensure that, in the busy summer months, overseas intruders must compete with the Greeks for accommodation, eating out and the haphazard services. Up to you.

AG. KIRIKOS (Ag. Kirykos): capital & main port (Illustration 17).

Outwardly rather similar to Astipalaia (Cyclades) with a languid air of disrepair and ennui, which makes it all the more of a pity that the Ikarians do not have the same pleasant nature as their 'look-alikes'! Possibly the overlay of communist exiles has had some effect on the locals, if not by interbreeding then by propaganda and association.

ARRIVAL BY FERRY

A very large harbour breakwater still does not make it easy for ferry-boat skippers to dock and the Ikarian sea is renowned for its bad weather. However compared to the days when the port was open to the elements, as portrayed on one or two of the 'days of yore' postcards, it must be a doddle.

It is a fair walk round from the disembarkation point (*Tmr* 1C2) to the centre of the town. At the end of the quay it is necessary to turn right across the 'dead ground' at the bottom of the harbour wall, leaving *The Best Snackbar* (*Tmr* 2B5) on the left, and then right again (*Sbo*) along the Esplanade. The Esplanade edges the harbour wall and runs the length of the town, which is conveniently closed in by the Ferry-boat quay on the left-hand and the hillside to the right (*Sbo*).

THE ACCOMMODATION & EATING OUT

The Accommodation At the end of the quay turn to the left for about 100m on the Chrisostomos road for the:

Pension Fleves
Directions: As above and signposted along a short track off to the right. En suite double rooms at average prices.

For most of the accommodation turn right along the Esplanade at the end of the harbour quay.

Hotel Isabella's *(Tmr* 3A4) (Class E)   Tel. 22839
Directions: On the corner of a parade of shops edging the 'Main', large, irregular plateia, above a bank. The entrance is round the back.

A single room, en suite, costs 750 drs and an en suite double room 1000 drs, rising to 950 drs and 1480 drs respectively (1st May - 30th Sept).

Hotel Adam's *(Tmr* 4A/B3/4) (Class B)   Tel. 22418
Directions: Diagonally across the street from the *Hotel Isabella*, over and above a chemist's shop, with the entrance in the alleyway at the back.

Classified as a pension, all rooms are en suite, with a single room costing 850 drs and a double room 1250 drs. For the height of season (1st May - 30th Sept) these rates rise to 950 drs and 1480 drs. This establishment fills up quickly.

Following the 'High' Street, that the *Hotels Isabella* and *Adam* straddle, up the short, steep incline, round the sharp right-hand bend in the road, along the still rising straight stretch of road, past the Post Office *(Tmr* 5A2) and the OTE *(Tmr* 6A2), and across the road is the:
Pension *(Tmr* 7A2).
Directions: As above, on the right, in the two side by side houses. The painter who has executed the signs has been around a bit as his style is noticeable elsewhere.
Inexpensive.

Back on the waterfront, the Esplanade runs out on the hillside to the right of the town *(Sbo)*, the road curving left on to a river-bed converted to street use. Straight ahead a concrete footbridge spans the summer dry watercourse and a wide flight of stone steps ascends the steep incline.

Hotel Ο ΚΑΡΡΑΣ *(Tmr* 8B2) (Class C)   Tel. 22494
Directions: Proceed as above across the footbridge and the hotel is over the Bank, to the right of the foot of the flight of stone steps.

Actually a pension with single rooms sharing the bathroom costing 680 drs, en suite 930 drs; double rooms sharing 1000 drs and en suite 1200 drs.

Hotel Akti *(Tmr* 9C2) (Class C)   Tel. 22064
Directions: Classified as a pension. It lies draped over the headland, peeking out over the terrace of buildings (including another Bank) built into the side of the bluff. It is easy enough to see the *Hotel Akti* but rather difficult to find the actual entrance, but here goes. Climb the small steps at the far side of the Bank *(Tmr* 8B2), beneath the *Hotel Ο ΚΑΡΡΑΣ*, up another flight of steps, right at the top, right again and then left up a few more steps. Okay? Best to follow the plan.

Probably one of the better value for money, provincial pensions I have stayed in, weighing price against the facilities and situation. The elderly, beret wearing Papa, Dimitrios lurks, no other word will describe it, lurks on the Esplanade. He looks over disembarking travellers with a beady eye, sizing up potential clients and making up his mind whether or not to offer his accommodation. His lovely, smiley, younger wife, Theologia, seems to do all the work (so what's new) and hails from the island of Patmos. The clean rooms are pleasantly furnished, spacious and the en suite bathrooms are nicely appointed. Each corridor has a communal fridge. Travellers should carefully note their date of arrival to save any errors when it comes to settling up the bill. Papa, who handles the purse strings, can become confused, usually a miscalculation that errs in his favour! By the way, I am convinced this misjudgement is entirely without malice. Single rooms en suite are priced at 1000 drs and doubles, sharing the bathroom, 1100 drs whilst en suite rooms cost 1400 drs. Lack of clients may well allow prices to soften. For instance a double room en suite, out of the height of season, drops to 800 drs.

From the Esplanade the large, wide flight of steps across from the footbridge climbs steeply towards, on the right, the Police station (*Tmr* 10B/C2) and, on the left, some Thermal Baths (*Tmr* 11B2). A lane branches off prior to the baths and, on the right, overlooking the port and town is a:

Pension (*Tmr* 12B2)   Tel. 22808
Directions: As above.

The pension is in a very large building signed *Rooms for Rent* – well it would be.

Further on, in the next building, is **Rooms** (*Tmr* 13B1/2).

The Eating Out
Yes, well. There may be reasonably plentiful accommodation but eating out, that's a different plate of moussaka.

Restaurant Samos (*Tmr* 14B3)
Directions: Towards the eastern or right-hand end of the Esplanade (*Sbo*), to the left, on the corner of an alley. The narrow restaurant front is almost hidden by one of the pollarded mulberry trees that line the Esplanade.

More a very small taverna than a restaurant with an interesting if restricted selection of meals on offer. The food is usually good but often served up cold. A meal for two of (hot and substantial) chicken soup (150 drs), pistachio (very, very large but cold, 250 drs), a (very cold) plate of patatas (50 drs), bread (15 drs), and a bottle of retsina (65 drs) all for 780 drs; (meaty) lamb chops (350 drs), chips (50 drs), bread (15 drs) and a bottle of retsina (65 drs) costs 830 drs.

There are a few other establishments scattered about, the largest and most prominent of which is the:

Restaurant (*Tmr* 15A/B4)
Directions: Beneath the Town Hall, and almost the first building on the way round from the Ferry-boat quay.

Average fare at to be expected prices but remains closed apart from the height of season summer months.

Across the road from the restaurant building is a large, bamboo trellis covered patio extension beneath which is the 'chatty' Ouzerie Τα ΚΑΡΑΦΑΚΙΑ.

Perhaps the most remarkable feature are the three truly traditional:

Kafenions (*Tmr* 16B3 & B3/4)
Directions: They edge the broad, mulberry tree lined pavement bordering the Esplanade.

'Hillbilly', narrow fronted kafenions with their long, soulless interiors cluttered by 'forgettabilia', crates and stack pipe stoves. They are usually crowded out by locals playing backgammon or glued to the ever present, ever switched on television sets, seated at the jumble of tables and chairs. Outsiders are sure to experience that 'western-movie, stranger in town feeling' – you know the 'honky-tonk' stops on entering the swing doors. Well here it's the background babble and clack of backgammon pieces that dies down.

The best service, if up to a ½ hr wait can be bracketed with any adjective indicating excellence, is obtained at the right-hand kafenion (*Sbo*) where a Nes meh ghala (white coffee) costs 50 drs.

Restaurant H ΚΛΗΜΑΤΑΡΙΑ (*Tmr* 17A3)
Directions: In the shambles or maze of alleys between the Esplanade buildings and the High Street. A dentist's surgery is located on the first floor.

THE A TO Z OF USEFUL INFORMATION

BANKS Three would you believe? (*Tmr* 18B/C2/3, 3A4 & 8B2). Also *See* **Post Office.**

BEACHES None, it being necessary to go to Thermae (4 km) or walk south-west on the Chrisostomos road along which, in the first quarter of an hour, are three coves of pebble and small boulder beaches (as well as three discos and the island's Generating Station).

BICYCLE, SCOOTER & CAR HIRE 'Cum the season' – not before or after. The town's garage and petrol station (*Tmr* 19A/B1) hires out scooters. It is situated 50m along the main road, north-east out of town and on the right. The owner speaks English.

There are two faded signs reading *Apollo Rent-A-Car, Scooter at Port Tel. 31366* but if the number is telephoned non-comprehension is the order of the day.

BREAD SHOPS One (*Tmr* 20A3/4) is on the right of the High St (*Sbo*), to the right of the 'Main' Square and the other (*Tmr* 20A3), an old fashioned one, is in the 'shambles'.

BUSES As with many other things on Ikaria, the buses are an unsatisfactory, mystical happening and note that I eschew the word service. They park up on the Esplanade, either on a lay-by with the taxis (*Tmr* 21B4), opposite the 'Main' Square, or alongside the pavement, almost in front of the row of kafenions (*Tmr* 16B3).

Bus journeys are definitely not for the faint-hearted as the mountain route to Efdilos can prove a terrifying experience to those of a nervous disposition.

Bus timetable
I am reluctant to list a timetable although the following is almost indisputable:
Ag. Kirikos to Efdilos
Daily   1200 hrs (ish).
One-way fare 150 drs; duration 1 ½ hrs.

Note this bus does not return until the next day(!), well certainly not either side of the height of season months.

From here on nothing is a certainty! The bus may well proceed on to Armenistis but, if there is a connection, a change of bus is probably necessary. During term times there is a school bus from Efdilos to Armenistis that can be caught but only if there is room. To reiterate, do not rely on a same day return service.

A separate bus journeys to Perdiki but that appears to be mainly for the convenience of the personnel based at the large Army camp in the vicinity. Two or three times a week a bus ventures forth to the south-western villages of Xilosirtis and Chrisostomos and western Christos Rachon.

COMMERCIAL SHOPPING AREA None but a scattering of shops including a general store (*Tmr* 22A3/4) selling cold meats; a general store also selling fruit and vegetables (*Tmr* 22A/B3) and a fish shop (*Tmr* 23B3). Shops close for a late, strictly observed siesta not re-opening before 1800 hrs.

DISCOS Three within ¼ hr walk, south-west of Ag. Kirikos on the Chrisostomos road.

FERRY-BOATS It would be out of character if Ikaria's ferry-boat connections were anything but complicated and mystifying. At least once a week a boat stops at Efdilos and not Ag. Kirikos and as Ikaria is not the end of the line, the next port(s) of call may well be of definite interest. Confusingly the occasional ferry anchors off Fournoi island before going on to Samos where some craft stop at Karlovasion before ending their voyage at Samos Town (Vathy). Just to keep everyone on their toes the Ferry-boat companies often list ports' names without mentioning the island, so it may be necessary to refer to CHAPTER 11. A closing note is that the **CF Ikaros** disappeared off the schedules in 1986, or did it?

Ferry-boat timetables

Day	Departure time	Ferry-boat	Ports/Islands of Call
Monday	0500 hrs	Aegeon	Samos Town
	1030 hrs	Kyklades	Samos (Vathy), Chios, Mitilini (Lesbos), Limnos, Kavala (M).
	1130 hrs	Aegeon	Paros, Piraeus (M) (2130 hrs)
	1700 or 2130 hrs!	Ikaros	Syros, Piraeus (M)
Tuesday	0945 hrs	Ikaros	Syros, Piraeus (M)
	1700 hrs	Samaina	Karlovasion (Samos), Samos Town
	1800 hrs	Aegeon	Samos Town
Wednesday	0900 hrs	Aegeon	Paros, Piraeus (M) (1830 hrs)
	0915 hrs	Samaina	Piraeus (M)
	1715 hrs	Ikaros	Efdilos † (Ikaria), Karlovasion (Samos), Samos Town
	1730 hrs	Kyklades	Leros, Kalimnos, Kos, Rhodes, Chalki, Diafni (Karpathos), Karpathos, Kasos, Sitia (Crete), Ag. Nikolaos (Crete), Anafi, Thira (Santorini), Folegandros, Milos, Piraeus (M)
Thursday	0930 hrs	Ikaros	Efdilos † (Ikaria), Syros, Piraeus (M)
	1700 hrs	Samaina	Karlovasion (Samos), Samos Town
	1800 hrs	Aegeon	Samos Town
Friday	0915 hrs	Samaina	Piraeus (M)
	0900 hrs	Aegeon	Paros, Piraeus (M) (1830 hrs)
	1630 hrs	Ikaros	Efdilos † (Ikaria), Karlovasion (Samos), Samos Town
Saturday	0930 hrs	Ikaros	Efdilos † (Ikaria), Piraeus (M)
	1700 hrs	Samaina	Karlovasion (Samos), Samos Town
	1800 hrs	Aegeon	Samos Town
Sunday	0915 hrs	Samaina	Piraeus (M)
	0900 hrs	Aegeon	Paros, Piraeus (M) (1830 hrs)

† Possibly calls at Efdilos, possibly not. If not it stops at Ag. Kirikos (!). Note that no ferry stops at both ports.
One-way fare: Ikaria to Piraeus 1230 drs; duration 8 hrs.
Ikaria to Samos (Vathy) 670 drs; duration 2½ hrs.

Note these are mid-season schedules. Early and late in the year they are severely restricted.

To Fournoi Island
Local services connect daily with Fournoi island. The caique **Maria Express** departs from the local boat quay (*Tmr* 24C3) in the lee of the north-eastern harbour

headland, almost beneath the *Hotel Akti.* This service is scheduled to depart at 1300 hrs but....

On other occasions another caique (ΕΥΑΓΓΕΛΙΣΤΡΙΑ) motors across from Fournoi island at about 1600/1630 hrs. This craft moors up on the main quay wall in order to pick up passengers that disembark from the Piraeus ferry-boats that dock late afternoon. So take your choice.

The one-way fare costs from 150 drs per head and the crossing takes up to 1½ hrs but the service is at the mercy of weather and sea conditions. During inclement weather, when the craft can still sail, they motor to the west of Thimena island coming round from the south. Normally they slot down between the islands of Thimena and Fournoi, calling at Thimenao port first and then completing the voyage across to Fournoi. For further details *See* **Fournoi island**. For local boat trips *See* **Places of Interest.**

FERRY-BOAT TICKET OFFICES Two. The one (*Tmr* 25B3) sells tickets for the **FB Aegeon** and is also a gift shop. The owner really couldn't care less and 'won't' understand English. The owner of the other office (*Tmr* 26A4) is very polite and to facilitate a dialogue with tourists calls in a friend to translate. This office handles the **FB Samaina, Ikaros** and **Delos**. (Transactions with either office underlines the desirability of speaking some Greek.) The 'gift shop' ticket office (*Tmr* 25B3) opens morning and evening whilst the 'Main Sq' office (*Tmr* 26A4) opens when appropriate.

MEDICAL CARE
Chemists & Pharmacies: One (*Tmr* 27B2) up the wide flight of steps at the north-eastern end of the Esplanade.
Dentist: Over the *Restaurant* ΚΛΙΜΑΤΑΡΙΑ (*Tmr* 17A3).
Hospital: *See* **Telephone Numbers & Addresses.**

OTE: (*Tmr* 6A2) Open weekdays only between 0730 - 1510 hrs.

PETROL: Available from the garage (*Tmr* 19A/B1) 50m along the main road to Thermae.

PLACES OF INTEREST: At the height of the season there are water taxis round to Thermae (*See* EXCURSIONS TO AG. KIRIKOS TOWN SURROUNDS). Local boats also run daily to **Faros** & **Kerame** on the north-east coast. Both have beaches and Faros is the site of a 3rd century BC tower.

Weekly caique connections run to:
Maganitis & Karkinagri: Both are very isolated fishing boat hamlets built on steep hillsides on the south-west coast and inaccessible to road traffic.

Ag. Kirikos sights of interest must include the multi-coloured car which slowly shudders and jerks its way along the Esplanade. The frequency of the appearances indicates that the owner is afraid that if the vehicle is not kept in continual use it may well never get up and go again.

POLICE
Port (*Tmr* 25B3). Above an Esplanade Ferry-boat ticket office.
Town (*Tmr* 10B/C2). The office is in a large building reached up the wide steps at the right-hand end of the Esplanade (*Sbo*), opposite the Thermal Baths.

POST OFFICE (*Tmr* 5A2). Exchanges Eurocheques, 'travellers' cheques and currency.

TAXIS (*Tmr* 21B4) Rank up adjacent to the buses. Due to the vagaries of the bus service, it may well be necessary to use the taxis. Fare examples include to Efdilos 1600 drs and Armenistis 2300/2500 drs.

TELEPHONE NUMBERS & ADDRESSES
Hospital   Tel. 22330
Police, town   Tel. 22222
Surgery   Tel. 22236

TRAVEL AGENTS Dolichi Tours (*Tmr* 28B2). More a Tour office but sells local excursion tickets.

EXCURSIONS TO AG. KIRIKOS TOWN SURROUNDS
Excursion to Thermae (4 km) A pleasant walk which will take ¾ hr. The road climbs out of the port from the top, north-east end. At the first (unsigned) turning, branch right. Even on the lowlands of the road to Thermae it is possible, on a cloudless day, to see clearly Patmos island in the distance, which the white, hilltopping Monastery of St John causes to look like a capped tooth. The road serpentines down the long, narrow, summer dry, profusely flowered river valley all the way to:
THERMAE (Therma): thermal seaside resort.
The settlement was known to the Romans. The higgledy-piggledy buildings of the village, quite a number of which are modern, are jammed into the available space between the steep, constricting hillsides.

On the way down the valley the first hotel on the right is the *Hotel Anna* (Class C, tel. 22905). Further on, again to the right-hand side of the road, and over the OTE and a Ferry-boat office (tickets for the boats **Samaina** and **Ikaros**), are **Rooms**. Beyond a taverna on the right, is a turning, off to the right, on the corner of which is *Rooms Kratsas* and:
Hotel George (Class B)   Tel. 22517
Directions: Beyond *Rooms Kratsas*, in the side street.
Double rooms, en suite cost 1650 drs.

Across the side street from the *Hotel George* are **Rooms**.

Returning to the High Street, and on the right is a grocery shop. Close to where the main street joins the right-hand side of the waterfront, the road is almost filled by an 'end-on' building housing the thermal baths.

A clean beach of fine pebble edges the rather short waterfront of the 'U' shaped cove. The backshore to left and right is edged by rather refined (as in 'nice') bars and tavernas. The seabed quickly becomes large pebble either side of the small jetty which is to the left of the High Street's junction with the waterfront. Distant Fournoi islands seem to be framed in the mouth of the bay.

At the far, left-hand end of the beach backshore is the *Hotel Apollon* (Class C, tel. 22477). To the right, just beyond the thermal baths is the:
Hotel Ikarion (Class D)   Tel. 22481 *Directions:* As above.
Single rooms sharing the bathroom cost 690 drs; double rooms sharing cost 900 drs and en suite 1345 drs. These charges rise (1st July - 31st Aug) to 790 drs, 1070 drs and 1495 drs respectively.

On the far right-hand cliffside is the *Hotel Marina*. Close by the steps that lead past the *Hotel Marina* are some simple **Rooms**.

Thermae certainly makes a very pleasant alternative to Ag. Kirikos in which to stay. However out of the height of season (before 1st June and after September) very little is open and during the height of summer the Greek tourists compete for each and every facility.

There is chatter about a cliff-walk path between Thermae and Ag. Kirikos but this is only for the stout heeled and hearted.

Excursion to Chrisostomos (12 km) The first 1½ km (or ¼ hr walk) of the sea edging route to the south-west is rather unattractive, taking in three coves with pebble and boulder beaches, three discos and the island's electricity Generating Station.

Close by **Glaredes** the road becomes unsurfaced and about one kilometre further on is a very large hotel, standing well back on the right, which is also the site of the thermal spa, **Therma Lefkados**.

After yet another kilometre the road (now relatively high up on the lower flanks of the mountainside) loops around a small, attractive, seemingly deserted bay which unfortunately is not very suitable for swimming. The foreshore is narrow and boulderous, as is the seabed. At the far end is a small jetty to which are moored a few benzinas. In the area of **Evagelistrias**, the location of a religious house, the wide track passes through a very green, lush spot with running water. But note that signs declare that the stream is not fit for humans to drink. On the left of the road is a patch of ground that must once have been the purlieus of habitations. Not another Minoan site, surely?

A gently descending incline, walled on the sea side of the track approaches:
XILOSIRTIS (10 kms from Ag. Kirikos). This is a very pretty, green, profusely tree planted, stream-running village and small port balanced on and around a headland bluff. The 'High Road' that keeps straight on leaving Xilosirtis to the left, passes, on the right, a municipal or thermal bath building followed by a long, low shack which houses a combined kafenion and baker. Rather than walk on why not fritter away an hour, a day or a week at friendly Xilosirtis, which is famed for its apricots. Surely a far better bet than the stiff walk on to:
CHRISOSTOMOS (15 kms from Ag. Kirikos) The last kilometre or so of this almost entirely uphill climb is on the steep side of a relatively bare, sloping mountainside. It is an arduous, 'last gasp' to the large, spread out village straddling a summer dry riverbed.

The natives are not particularly friendly and the couple of cafe-bars only tolerate tourists in the height of season.

Beyond Chrisostomos the road trickles on into the interior making forays to the far south-west, inland and across to Efdilos (*See* ROUTE ONE).

ROUTE ONE
To Efdilos (41 kms) & on to Armenistis (57 kms). From Ag. Kirikos port all the way to beyond the Perdiki turning (at about 12 km) is a very steep, winding climb up the face of the mountain on to which cling the villages of **Koudoumas** and **Mavrikato**. At the branch road to **Perdiki** is a large Army camp.

Round the corner, as it were, from the Perdiki junction, and now travelling parallel to the north coast in a south-west direction, the slopes are still well covered with waist-high shrubs that include a lot of thyme. As the road begins the winding descent to the coastline, the tree cover increases. The northern coastline is ruggedly indented where the winter rain filled crevices meet the sea.

MONOKAMPI (20 kms from Ag. Kirikos) A mountain hugging village in a precipitous, fertile and green ravine with extensive agricultural terracing. There is evidence of quarrying in the area as the road from hereabouts commences to serpentine steeply down to:

KARAVOSTAMON (31 kms from Ag. Kirikos). A quite large fishing port with most of the village to the right of the road.

Between Karavostamon and Efdilos are three or more small, grey sand/shingle beaches with some kelp. The largest of these is close to the **Finikas** turning. There is a petrol station at Ag. Kyriaki, adjacent to:

EFDILOS (Evdilos, Evdhilos) (41 kms from Ag. Kirikos). Port (Illustration 18).

Could be a pretty fishing port but somehow misses the boat (Sorry!). I cannot pretend that I find Efdilos simpatico which lack of rapport is probably related to the inhabitants' attitude, as it is in Ag. Kirikos. That is a personal opinion, as is most of the rhetoric in the Candid Guides, and I must report that some authorities recommend the spot.

ARRIVAL BY BUS

The bus impossibly squeezes through the narrow lanes to the Main Square edging the seawall that encloses the curve of the small harbour. See below for further snippets in respect of the schedules.

ARRIVAL BY FERRY

One (or two?) ferry-boats a week dock at the quay (*Tmr* 1B/C1). For details of the timetables *See* **Ferry-boat timetables, A to Z, Ag. Kirikos** (& **Samos Town**, CHAPTER 12).

THE ACCOMMODATION & EATING OUT

The Accommodation There is certainly sufficient accommodation out of season including the:

Hotel Provincial (*Tmr* 2A3)
Directions: Just off the centre of the Main Sq, up the steps and across to the left (*Fsw*) in a narrow, open alley.

'Provincial' – need one say more?

Pension Evdoxia (Class B)   Tel. 31502
Directions: Modernish and set high up on the left-hand hillside (*Fsw*) overlooking the centre of the village.

Very expensive, with singles en suite 3000 drs and double rooms, sharing a bathroom, 4000 drs.

Rooms are available.

The Eating Out Apart from the to-be-expected scattering of cafe-bars and kafe-nions there is a:

Bar/Restaurant (*Tmr* 3A3)
Directions: To the left of the Main Square (*Fsw*).

The good meals available must be weighed against the almost total disinterest in serving a customer. A big bowl of pea soup, a good Greek salad, 2 small omlettes, bread and 2 beers cost 560 drs.

The small harbour's narrow beach is piled high with kelp and littered with rubbish.

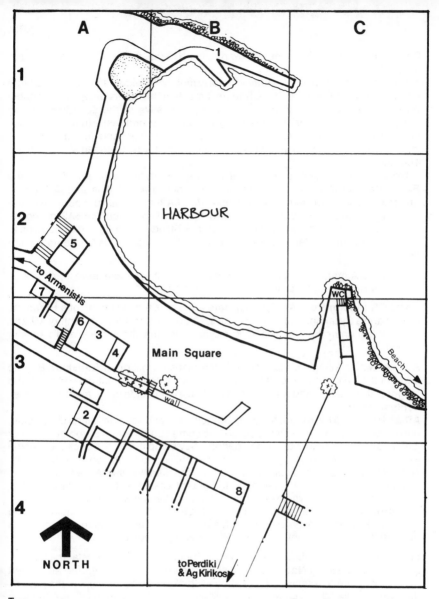

Illustration 18 Efdilos Port

164

On the other hand, around the narrow headland to the right (*Fsw*), is a large beach cove.

The local school children gather in a noisy mob on weekday afternoons at a large bar (*Tmr* 4A3) on the edge of the Square. I mention the pupils because the school buses are an 'off-the-record', if unreliable, alternative to the scheduled island transport to and from Armenistis (and Ag. Kirikos?). The problem is that the daily bus from Ag. Kirikos does not return the same day. On the other hand during the season the bus from Ag. Kirikos, or another bus, should continue on to Armenistis at a cost of 100 drs.

Taxis informally rank to the left of the Main Harbour Square, in front of the Bar/Restaurant (*Tmr* 3A3), and charge 1600 drs to Ag. Kirikos and 700 drs to Armenistis. There is a baker, a supermarket (*Tmr* 6A3), ice-cream parlour/drink shop (*Tmr* 7A2/3) and a doctor but no scooters for hire. The Post Office (*Tmr* 5A2) overlooks the harbour and a Ferry-boat ticket office (*Tmr* 8B4) edges the Ag. Kirikos road on to the south side of the Main Square. The office sells tickets for the **CF Samaina** and **Ikaros**.

The route to Armenistis passes through pine forests that tumble down from the area known as Rachis, high up on the mountain range.

KAMPOS (44 km from Ag Kirikos) Here are a museum, the ruins of a Byzantine palace and a Byzantine Church, Ag Irene's. This dates from the 11th century AD, and is the oldest church on the island. Kampos is also the site of the island's ancient capital.

Another twelve kilometres further on is the pleasant village of **Galiskari**. But the jewel in the beach crown of Ikaria, very popular with the 'great unwashed' at the height of the season (and with those in the know either side of the months of June - September) is:

ARMENISTIS (57 km from Kirikos) This jetty port and seaside village is very quiet out of season but suffers an invasion of up to some 1000 Western European summer loafers during the height of season period. They camp out on the backshore of the extensive, golden, coarse grained sand beach, divided into two by a headland. Naturally some debris results and the Plaz Messachtis, the far beach from the village, is edged by rather swampy, tufted grass backshore. The two beaches lie to the east of Armenistis which is spread over a bluff at the west end.

Rooms, which are plentiful, start off at about 700 drs for a double room rising to 1000 drs. Five or six tavernas cope with the inner man and a couple of discos help out with the entertainment. The Post Office changes money.

From Armenistis it is about a seven kilometre hike along the coastal track to the archaeological site of **Nas**. A local priest is rumoured to have ordered an ancient Kouros or statue of Artemis to be destroyed, thinking it was the work of the devil as the eyes followed the onlooker! Well at least it didn't finish up in either Athens or, worse still, the British Museum! There is a taverna and small beach.

An inland track ascends to the mountain hamlets of the **Rachis** and the village of:
CHRISTOS RACHON (Hristos) (11 km from Armenistis). The paved Main Square dominates the village which is set in pine covered mountains, with excellent views over the island, the surrounding seas and neighbouring islands. For the traveller who is prepared to walk and is self-sufficient many of the south-western villages are unbelievably isolated but a passing knowledge of Greek would be a prerequisite.

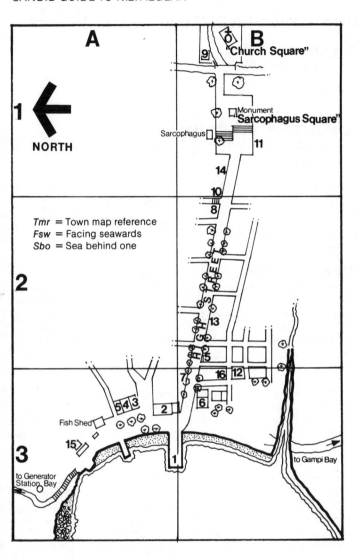

Tmr

1 Ferry-boat quay A/B3
2 Pension/Restaurant Maounis A3
3 Pension/Restaurant O Miltos A3
4 Rooms & Kafenion A3
5 Rooms
6 Kafenion B3
7 Snackbar A/B3
8 Ouzerie B1/2

9 Kafenion B1
10 Store/Money exchange B1/2
11 Bread Shop B1
12 Unisex Haircutting B2/3
13 Port police B2
14 Post Office B1
15 Toilet block A3
16 Ferry-boat ticket office B2/3

Illustration 19 Fournoi Port

EXCURSION TO FOURNOI (Fourni, Furni, Phournoi) ISLANDS

FIRST IMPRESSIONS
Friendly, 'smiley' people; bustle; fishing boats; the unusual High Street.

SPECIALITIES
Fish

RELIGIOUS HOLIDAYS & FESTIVALS
include: 23rd April – Festival Ag. Georgios; 6th December – Festival Ag. Nikolaos.

VITAL STATISTICS
Tel. prefix 0275

GENERAL
The Fournoi group comprises a collection of some twelve islands, only two of which have settlements of any size (one each) and only one of which, Fournoi island, encourages visitors.

FOURNOI: main village & port (Illustration 19)
The extensive fishing fleet, which varies from small to medium sized caiques, ensures that the life of the port carries on regardless of outsiders. Added to this, the lack of a sizeable Ferry-boat quay ensures that the tourists that do land are dedicated island hoppers. Visitors who make the effort will not be disappointed as many of the fast disappearing, traditional island human qualities are not found to be lacking here. These include welcoming, candid curiosity, a wish to be friendly and to show appreciation that a *xenos* (a guest) has paid them the compliment of 'dropping in'.

Naturally enough, as there are (as yet) no roads, the normal method of travel is by water. At the last count, apart from the occasional wheeled rotovator, there were only two trucks on the island. These are used to move essential supplies about the port and immediate environs. Mark you the comparative isolation means that 'the arriving' requires an effort, 'the departing' a lot of effort and some Greek is almost obligatory.

THIMENA. The other large island in the group has one village, **Thimenao**. The dwellings steeply climb up the hillside, almost like a flight of steps from the small quay, on the edge of the medium sized bay. The inhabitants actively discourage visitors so it is best to resist the temptation to get off the interisland caique, as there are no facilities whatsoever. This is a pity because there are one or two fine beaches especially one at a bay south of Thimenao. Here a large, middle distance Egyptian fishing fleet anchors up and on the edge of the backshore is a tiny hamlet above the pleasant beach, with an accommodation block for the fishermen. *See* **Beaches, A to Z.**

Thimenao may shun tourists but the inhabitants of Fournoi, this remarkable, bustling, friendly and surprisingly large fishing port, more than compensate. So much so that it is one of the small exclusive clutch of islands that have achieved the distinction of being included in the *GROC's Almost Impossible To Leave Club*. Thankfully few holiday-makers are prepared to undergo the minor difficulties necessary to make a landing.

The paved High Street which climbs steadily to the upper part of the village is lined with carefully pollarded plane trees, the trunks of which are painted white with an unusual blue streak. Most of the trees are planted in the actual street and many have litter bins clamped to them. Parallel to the High St. and to the right (*Sbo*), is another street lined with lovely oleanders.

ARRIVAL BY FERRY

At least one scheduled Ferry-boat a week pulls up in the bay in order to effect the caique transfer of people, chattels and animals. Probably the most reliable route (and reliable is a comparative word) is to catch either the daily caique from Ikaria island or the large caique that connects twice a week with Karlovasion (Samos). The planned timetables are subject to a certain amount of uncertainty and, in the nervous, might induce a state of hysteria, added to which inclement weather can play havoc with the schedules because the craft are small.

THE ACCOMMODATION & EATING OUT

The Accommodation Whatever other guides indicate, apart from **Rooms** there are two pensions, the:

Pension (& Restaurant) Maounis (*Tmr* 2A3)   Tel. 51367
Directions: Almost on the shore end of the Ferry-boat quay (*Tmr* 1A/B3).

Mrs. Maounis is very welcoming and the rooms are better appointed than the islands isolation would lead one to believe. Mark you this insularity has not kept prices down and an adequate double room with an en suite bathroom costs 1000 drs in mid-season. At least the beds are comfortable and the shower water hot. For more details *See* **The Eating Out.**

Pension (& Restaurant) O Miltos (*Tmr* 3A3)
Directions: To the left (*Sbo*) of the bottom end of the Ferry-boat quay (*Tmr* 1A/B3) and across a side street from the *Pension Maounis*. For more details *See* **The Eating Out**.

Rooms (& Kafenion) (*Tmr* 4A3)
Directions: Next door to the *Pension & Restaurant O Miltos*.

Comes highly recommended by Gisella, a regular *xenos*. A very tidy kafenion run by a very neat couple. Inside the building, on the left, is a carefully partitioned barbers parlour. There is a lovely garden and a Nes meh ghala is charged at a very reasonable 52 drs. A double room sharing the bathroom costs between 600 and 800 drs per night.

Other accommodation includes:
Rooms (*Tmr* 5A3)
Directions: Next door to the *Kafenion Rooms* above.
Rooms (*Tmr* 5B2/3)
Directions: On the right of the High St, over a china shop.

The Eating Out

Restaurant (& Pension) Maounis (*Tmr* 2A3)
On the ground floor of the pension but the restaurant is let out to a third party so it is difficult to enthuse, especially when there is the:
Restaurant O Miltos (*Tmr* 3A3)

Run by round faced Miltos, a native of Fournoi, and his attractive, and I suspect independent spirited wife, Dina, born on Lipsos. I mention their birth places because it appears to be tradition that a Fournoi man takes a Lipsos woman (or, if talking to the lady, she will maintain that she captured a Fournoi man!) Dina has her hands full with two spirited youngsters and the taverna to run. On the other hand Miltos, once a merchant seaman who docked in various ports around the British Isles, and thus has a smattering of English, is not always an 'active fisherman'. This results in his having an hour or three in which to sit around discussing matters of grave importance with a few of his cronies. Almost a recipe for the occasional marital disagreement! Nod, nod, wink, wink. Two matters about which there can be no doubt are the excellence of the food and the friendliness of the company. Naturally it would be surprising if fish were not a major constituent of the menu. When Miltos can be persuaded that a tourist is poor he might offer very reasonably priced fish, in addition to the usual, more expensive alternatives and lobsters. Another tasty dish is the fish steaks with garlic sauce – last encountered on Astipalaia island. A meal for three of kalamares (250 drs), a Greek salad (140 drs), a green salad (yes a salad of greens – 60 drs), patatas (50 drs) and bread (10 drs) costs 1080 drs. The kalamares are very good, fresh and not swamped with the ubiquitous batter – despite all of which Miltos apologises if they are more than one day old! Added to this the Greek salads are excellent – and I've dreamt of greens. Incidentally the retsina is dispensed by the litre from rather 'off putting' plastic containers but is a soft, Sparta retsina of which Miltos is justifiably proud. I cannot quote a price because I have never managed to buy any, a bottle always turning up from one or another patron! This engaging habit can lead to bacchanalian evenings trying to return the generosity. A meal for two of babouni fish (540 drs), Greek salad (140 drs), beers (70 drs), and bread (10 drs) cost 840 drs. A Nes meh ghala costs 55 drs and a brandy 65 drs. Follow that! A great watering hole.

The Kafenion (*Tmr* 6B3)
On the waterfront and serves a splendid octopus mezes with an ouzo, all for 40 drs.

The Kafenion (*Tmr* 4A3) referred to under **The Accommodation** must not be forgotten; there is a Snackbar (*Tmr* 7A/B3) on the left of the High St and an Ouzerie (*Tmr* 8B1/2), further up on the left.

On the edge of the second plateia, 'Church' Square, the one beyond 'Sarcophagus' Square, is:
Kafenion (*Tmr* 9B1)
Directions: as above.

A typical island kafenion, of a bygone age, with the tables and chairs squashed in around a pot belly stove in a 'sort of' front room. Normally an appealing spot in which to slum it but a sheer delight if you are 'unfortunate' enough to be introduced to 'the Goatherd' when he comes to town. His father being Cretan, as a young man he fought the Turks. Now 80'ish he complains of some rheumatism in his wrists but admits that one hand suffered from a bullet wound received in his youth. Age has encouraged him to allow his herd to dwindle to a mere 100, from the original 400, but he still rises at 4am to milk and tend his flock. Back to the point, if you are introduced he will not consider the evening has received justice until the morning hours. The kafenion owner's family 'give in' and sit around watching the endless retsinas cross the narrow counter of the bar. As there are no toilets it's outside for all and sundry!

THE A TO Z OF USEFUL INFORMATION

BANKS Bearing in mind the usual paucity of any facilities on the smaller, out of the way islands it is pleasant to record that there is a Store (*Tmr* 10B1/2) at which transactions can take place. The proprietor may well change travellers' cheques (and Eurocheques if you are more than a transient visitor) but has to telephone Ikaria for up to date details and rates of exchange. Despite their admonishments to be careful and 'ware the tourist', he is friendly and helpful.

BEACHES The port foreshore is sandy, if a bit messy but probably polluted and so is only suitable for a quick dip. To the right (*Fsw*) a path leads over a headland, past a tower to:

'Generator Station' Cove There is no background noise as the station, once housed in the large shed beyond the backshore, is silent, the supply now being received from Samos. The sand and pebble beach is not very clean with occasional clumps of sea and wind blown debris dotted about as well as the odd bits and pieces of fishermen's gear. There is a small jetty and some low sheds at the far side. It is approximately offshore from this cove that the large ferries pull up while transferring passengers and goods to and from the shore boat. There is another sandy beach beyond this bay, on around the coast a metre or so!

The best beach is:

Gampi Located south or to the left (*Fsw*) of Fournoi port. It is necessary to walk past the far sand and pebble portion of the harbour (very scrubbly and dirty with sea-blown rubbish), climb the zig-zagging dirt road past the church, campanile and terraced cemetery, up to the saddle of the hillside. A number of 'dead' windmills stand silent sentinel on this ridge, beyond which is a view down to the fishing boat bay and sandy beach, set in a deeply indented bay. At the height of the season there are simple **Rooms** and a taverna. Take the tracks down the steep hillside.

The best beaches though are on Thimena island and, bearing in mind the cavats in respect of the islanders' reluctance to host visitors, it is possible to take the early morning boat that calls in at Thimenao (and then proceeds on to Ikaria) and catch the afternoon boat back. But check the planned sailing times for that day as this proposal is fraught with difficulties. *See* **Ferry-boats, A to Z, Ag. Kirikos, Ikaria** and **Fournoi.**

BREAD SHOP (*Tmr* 11B1)

COMMERCIAL SHOPPING AREA There must be more general stores in the High St than anywhere else in Greece, so I have not pinpointed them. Perhaps mention should be made of the **Unisex Haircutting**.... (*Tmr* 12B2/3). All shops observe the usual siesta.

FERRY-BOATS & TIMETABLES. Yes well.
For details of scheduled Ferry-boats *See* **Ferry-boat timetables, A to Z, Ikaria** and **Samos** (CHAPTER 12).

Local services include:
Fournoi to Ikaria
The official theory is that the caique **Maria-Express** departs daily from Fournoi quay (*Tmr* 1A/B3) at 0800 hrs (note that 0700 & 0730 hrs are also quoted) for Ikaria island, calling at Thimenao *en route* and docking some 1½ hrs later in the lee of *The Hotel Akti* headland in Ag. Kirikos harbour. The same boat departs from Ag. Kirikos and retraces its steps at about 1300 hrs. The skipper, who is in his middle 30s, speaks good English. The one-way fare costs a very reasonable 150 drs.

If the 0800 hrs boat does not run, another, the ΕΥΑΓΓΕΛΙΣΤΡΙΑ, may well cast off from Fournoi at 1500 hrs (beware it may be 1430 hrs), to moor up at the usual point in Ag. Kirikos harbour, wandering across, close to the main Ferry-boat quay to pick up late afternoon Piraeus ferry-boat arrivals. Knowing this may well save a fruitless wait at the wrong location! The fare on this boat is a few drachmae more expensive.

Fournoi to Karlovasion, Samos
A large purposeful caique, with white hull, blue stripe and narrow, yellow rubbing band, the ΚΟΤΤΑΡΑΣΓ, departs on Mondays and Thursdays at 0700 hrs for Karlovasion (Samos) returning the same day.

FERRY-BOAT TICKET OFFICE
There is an office (*Tmr* 16B2/3) located on the corner of the street parallel to the High Street. They sell tickets for the **CF Samaina** and **Ikaros**.

POLICE
Port (*Tmr* 13B2) An office on the High St.

POST OFFICE (*Tmr* 14B1)

TOILETS (*Tmr* 15A3) There is, or more correctly was, a public toilet block, beyond the fish refrigerator shed. What is left is in an awful condition. The ladies is semi-demolished with only a crater where the 'squatty' used to be and the men's is in a disgusting state.

CHRISOMILEA
A track is slowly being blasted through to connect Fournoi port with the northern, fishing boat hamlet of Chrisomilea. Why I am not sure as there is only a very small jetty, three or four dwellings, a kafenion and some six hundred odd steps to the upper village and not a lot else. Added to this the swimming is not very good.

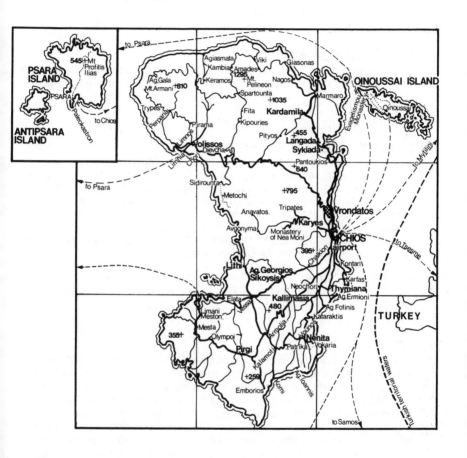

Illustration 20 Chios island

14 CHIOS (Xios, Khios, Hios), Psara & Oinoussai (Oinousses, Oinousai, Oenoussae, Oinousa, Inousses)

Chios Port ★★
The island ★★★★

N.E. Aegean Islands

FIRST IMPRESSIONS

Comparative lack of tourists; young men; army; motorbikes; traffic; friendliness; very few cats; Pirgi village; large lizards; mobile banks; donkey agriculture in the south.

SPECIALITIES

Mastic (lentisk trees).

RELIGIOUS HOLIDAYS & FESTIVALS

include: 23rd April - Festival of Ag. Georgios, Vrondatos; Easter Monday - Festival of old traditions, Mesta; 14th May - Festival of Ag. Isidoros, Chios Town; 1st July - Festival Ag. Anargyri, Thymiana; 22nd July - Festival Ag. Markella, Volissos; 27th July - Festival Ag. Panteleimon, Volissos; 6th August - Festival of Metamorphosi, Kardamila & Volissos; 15th August - Festival of Panagia, Vrondatos, Pirgi, Mesta, Kardamila, Volissos; 4th September - Festival Ag. Ermioni, Thymiana; 8th November - Festival of Taxiarches, Mesta; 11th November - Festival of Ag. Minas, Chios Town; 21st November - Festival of the Monastery of Mersinidiou, Vrondatos.

VITAL STATISTICS

Tel prefix 0271. The population of about 50,000 live on an island up to 50 km from top to bottom and 28 km from side to side with a land mass of 841 sq km. Half the islanders live in the capital, Chios Town.

HISTORY

A long recorded history dating back beyond the 10th century BC when the Ionian culture settled on Chios. The island also claims (together with some seven other islands) to be the birthplace of Homer (8th century BC) at either Kardamila or Volissos. The golden age, both commercially and artistically, was the 7/6th century BC. The Persians ruled for a short time, circa 500 BC, but after their overthrow the inhabitants swayed between allegiance to the Athenian Confederancy and the Spartans. Chios declared independence in the 350s BC, was taken over about 330 BC by Alexander the Great who was followed by the Romans, only to suffer destruction by Mithridates in the 80s BC. The Romans reasserted their suzerainty but after their decline the island experienced the ravages of pirates and 'barbarians' for the first ten centuries AD.

During the 11th century the island's prosperity began to recover causing the Venetians and Genoese to show a great deal of interest in Chios, despite the continued presence of the ailing Byzantine Empire. The prize was mastic (a resin from the lentisk tree). The Genoese won the deal in 1261, with the permission of the Byzantine Emperor, and 'took over the freehold' in 1346, remaining as rulers until 1566 when they lost out to the Turks. The Genoese, during their two hundred or so years of supremacy, formed a semi-autonomous society and made the island very prosperous, exploiting the mastic trade for all it was worth.

The Samiots persuaded the islanders to join them in the 1822 Independence uprising but the Turks recaptured the island and spent a very thorough five months or so exacting a terrible revenge, slaughtering a large number of the natives. The quoted figures for those butchered in this blood bath varies between 25,000 and 70,000 out of a total population of 100,000. These Turkish atrocities were brought to the world's attention by prominent Europeans and reaction produced a painting by Delacroix and a Victor Hugo poem. Admiral Kanaris, a Greek born on the adjacent island of Psara, managed to exact some retribution by firing the Turkish flagship in Chios harbour. It took until 1912 for the island to be united with Greece, despite an earlier campaign by the French Army officer Fabvier.

In the meantime the cataclysmic earthquake of 1881 destroyed most of those gracious and magnificent Genoese mansions and buildings that the Turks had left standing, as well as further decimating the population that the Turks had left living.

GENERAL

The massive, uninviting port and town of Chios is unfortunately often a visitor's first (and only?) sight of the island. The mess of high-rise prefabricated concrete is reminiscent of Iraklion (Crete), or even Piraeus, with the few stately mansions and houses left jostled by the appalling, modern day edifices. This initially unattractive appearance, combined with a massive traffic of high powered motorbikes and cars, similar to the Athens density, persuades many travellers to seek fresh pastures, quickly. It does not help that the distant, dry stone covered mountainsides, apparently indicating a lifeless and arid interior, appear to reinforce the first impressions. These intitial impulses should be resisted at all costs, for the ugly facade of Chios Town hides a fabric and lifestyle in many ways almost more Greek than Greece. The immeasurable variety of everyday life throbs away with the mishmash of traditional kafenions, snackbars, cafe-bars, zacharoplasteion, galaktopoleio, cobblers, stores, grocers, bakers, tailors, hardware, dress shops and peripteros, by the score, all vying with fast-food and burger joints. The shambling lanes and alleys of the widespread market area simply should not be missed.

I have not detailed tavernas because strangely, with one or two noticeable exceptions, they are substandard but then the splendid soulvaki pita bars and galaktozacharoplasteions more than compensate.

There is no doubt that the very large number of islanders who have spent a period of their life in the USA, only to return comparatively wealthy and with seemingly large families of young men, have made a singular impact on Chios Town. Manifestations include probably the greatest number of powerful motorbikes I have ever seen on any one Greek island waterfront Esplanade, as well as a scattering of car and motorbike showrooms. The large number of young men with disposable income, probably gifted by indulgent parents, and the massive Army presence has spawned an Esplanade crammed with smart, sprawling cafe-bars patronised by an almost inexhaustable supply of youth.

The countryside presents an amazing variety and incorporates almost every known feature and possible facet of Greek island topography including dry, unyielding mountains, soft lush valleys, water rich plains, rivers, quiet fishing hamlets, traditional agricultural pursuits and some magnificent, if somewhat far-flung, beaches. Added to this there are not just one, or even two, but half a dozen medieval, inland villages each one of which, on any other tourist orientated island, would be subjected to endless coach trips. This conveniently brings one to the hub of the matter in respect of Chios, the fact that the island has been almost entirely unexploited. This is rumoured to be because the wealthy island shipowners and industrialists, wishing to preserve their island, discouraged the growth of tourism. It would appear democracy and the voice of the 'not-so-well-heeled' has, in recent years, begun to overcome these prejudices. Despite this, early or late in the year it is not unusual to be able to recognise most of the ferry-boat tourists on the island. If these hints are not enough for the true Grecophile, then the balance might be tipped by the ever present and startling contrasts of the old and new ways; of simple, rural peasants, astride their donkeys leading goats, sheep and or more donkeys, and the brash, chromium plated cars of their wealthy fellow compatriots.

Chiots are great travellers and it seems that almost everybody has been to North America and made his 'stack', but do not be fooled - the basic Greek character never mutates. Even citizens with fifteen to twenty years overseas very soon remember little English but appear to have re-imported one trait that has been submerged elsewhere in recent years - an overwhelming friendliness and kindness to *xenos*.

CHIOS (Xios, Khios, Hios): capital town & main port
(Illustration 21).

The first reaction to the port Esplanade must be one of some dismay and disbelief that any 'town council' could have allowed even one, let alone scores of high-rise concrete blocks to be erected along the very long waterfront. A reminder that the earthquake of 1881 'rubbled' most of the fine old buildings tends to mollify initial reactions but a sneaking feeling remains that the 'city fathers' have a lot to answer for in the future. On the other hand readers should not get the impression that there are not some pleasant areas of the city. Indeed there are still a number of once lovely old buildings, now often decrepit and crumbling, a state accentuated by their being left empty or used for unsuitable uses. It is a pity that Chios could not take an example from some of the other islands where restoration is now becoming the order of the day.

ARRIVAL BY AIR
The airport is conveniently close and to the south of the town, on the plain of Kambos (Kampos), (*See* ROUTE THREE).

ARRIVAL BY FERRY
The interisland ferries moor up (*Tmr* 1B2) in the right-hand corner of the harbour (*Sbo*) while the local ferries and Samos island boats moor up at the other end (*Tmr* 2B3 & 3C3). The great length of the Esplanade makes it imperative to make immediate decisions in respect of accommodation for it is far too long a trudge to walk from one end to the other, and possibly all the way back again. Room owners generally do not meet the ferries and whilst there are exceptions, about which more later, the police actually discourage the habit of passengers being propositioned.

THE ACCOMMODATION & EATING OUT
The Accommodation There is much more than at first appears to be the case but it is widely spaced out. Where rates are not listed the average mid-season pension charges of 800/900 drs for a single room and 1200/1300 drs for a double room should be used as a guide.

Assuming the reader has docked at the main Ferry-boat quay (*Tmr* 1B2) in that area are:-

Hatzelenis Tours (*Tmr* 4B2) Akti Prokymaias   Tel. 26743
Directions: At the north end of the Esplanade, across the road from where the ferry ties up.

I know it is 'out of norm' to list a tour office in this section but young Tassos is so very helpful that, unless travellers are absolutely certain where they wish to stay, it is well worth popping in to see him. *See* **Ferry-boat Ticket Offices, A to Z**. It may also

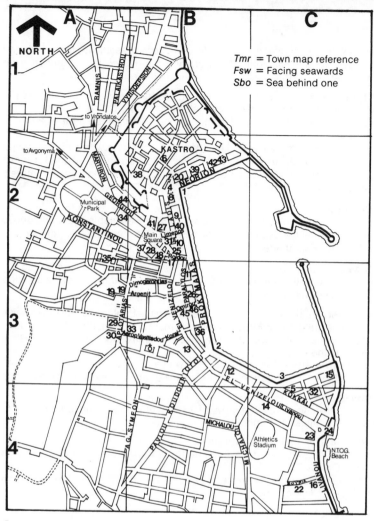

1 Main International Ferry-boat quay B2
2 Local ferries B3
3 Samos ferries C3
4 Hatzelinis Tours B2
5 Hatzelinis Tourist office Rooms C3/4
6 Rooms/Hotel Rodon B2
7 Rent-A-Motorbike B2
8 Rooms/Restaurant ΜΟΥΡΑΓΙΟ (Mouragio) B2
9 Customs Building B2
10 Acropolis Inn B2
11 Stella's Rooms B3
12 Rooms B3
13 Hotel Diana B3
14 Pansion Giannis C4
15 Hotel Chandris C3
16 Hotel Xenia C4
17 Hotel Palladiou B2/3
18 Hotel Filoxenia B2/3
19 Pension Roussos
20 Taverna B2
21 Souvlaki snackbar A/B2
22 Taverna ΧΡΥΣΟΒΑΡΕΛΙ C4
23 Tassos Restaurant C4

24 Nautical Club C4
25 Houlis Pastry Shop B2/3
26 Airline office B3
27 National Bank B2
28 General & Hellenic B2/3
29 National Bank A3
30 Bank of Crete A3
31 Chios Tourist office B2
32 A parade containing Mr. Georgoulis scooter hire, Rent-A-Car & newspaper shop C3/4
33 Bookshop A/B3
34 Town Bus terminus A/b2
35 Country Bus terminus A2/3
36 Astir Gnema B3
37 Old Mosque B2
38 Turkish Cemetry Square A/B2
39 Miniotis Lines B2
40 Ferry-boat ticket office B2
41 OTE B2
42 Port police B2
43 Town police B2
44 (Another) Town police office A/B2
45 Post Office B3
46 Travel shop B3

Illustration 21 Chios Town & Port

be worth mentioning at this stage that his wife runs a very pleasant, well recommended pension - *Tourist Office Rooms* (*Tmr* 5C3/4), of which there are details further on in the text. (I am not related to the family!).

Rooms/Hotel Rodon (*Tmr* 6B2) 17 Zachariou Frourion   Tel. 24335
Directions: Along the narrow street from Hatzelenis Tours Office, leaving Rent-A-Motorbike (*Tmr* 7B2) on the left, and in the second block on the right, in a part of downtown Chios.

Owned by Dimitrios Psaltakis. Rooms share the bathroom with singles costing 600 drs and doubles 1000 drs rising respectively to 800 drs and 1200 drs (1st June - 30th Sept). Note that the height of the season rate tends to be charged prematurely or rather earlier than they should!

Rooms (*Tmr* 8B2)
Directions: In the next block south or to the left (*Sbo*) of Hatzelenis Tours and above the ground floor, rather sleazy *Restaurant* MOYPAΓIO. The entrance is in Odhos Ladis one back from the Esplanade.

Rooms Sideratos (*Tmr* B2) 2 Odhos Ladis   Tel. 24770/25780
Directions: Next door to the **Rooms** (*Tmr* 8B2) above. The ground floor of the building is occupied by the *Cafe-bar Manikas*.

Continuing in a southerly direction, or left (*Sbo*), along the Esplanade Akti Prokymaias past the Customs building (*Tmr* 9B2), across the main street of Odhos Limenos and, in the next block, the *Grand Hotel Aktaion,* above the *Kafenion Aktaion,* is closed. But a few metres on is the:-
Acropolis Inn (*Tmr* 10B2) (Class A) Akti Prokymaias   Tel. 24842
Directions: As above. The entrance is in the small square at the rear of the building.

Rooms (*Tmr* B2)
Directions: South of the *Acropolis Inn* (*Tmr* 10B2), over a ticket tours office.
Charges as for similar accommodation.

Stella's Rooms (*Tmr* 11B3) Akti Prokymaias   Tel. 20364
Directions: About midway along the Esplanade, over a Toyota car showroom. The entrance is in Odhos Paralylos.

Stella's husband Don is a New Zealander and it is reported that the couple can't do enough for clients. Average rates.

Rooms (*Tmr* 12B3)
Directions: Continuing southwards on the Esplanade and just beyond the abrupt turn in the quay wall, where the Psara ferry moors (*Tmr* 2B3).

Hotel Diana (*Tmr* 13B3) (Class C) 92 El. Venizelou   Tel. 25993
Directions: Where the harbour wall kinks, at about the point that the Psara ferry-boat moors up, Odhos Pavlou Koudouriotou branches off. The second street parallel to the Esplanade, on the right-hand is El. Venizelou. The very smart hotel on the left of the street is flanked by a cinema and *Taverna John*.

All rooms are en suite, which they should be at these prices, with a single room costing 1800 drs and a double room 2850 drs. These rates rise to 2800 drs and 3750 drs respectively (1st July - 30th Sept).

Where the harbour wall makes another angle, close by the point at which the Samos-Chios ferry docks (*Tmr* 3C3), a side street leads off the Esplanade to make a junction with Odhos El. Venizelou. Across the road is the:-
Pansion (sic) Giannis (with Garden) (*Tmr* 14C4) 48-50 El. Venizelou (Livanou)
Tel. 27433
Directions: as above.

A rather 'down at the heel', rustic pension which is the only one in town that employs a *schlepper* to meet ferry-boat arrivals - the long, curly-haired, not so young Vangelis. Mind you he has to exercise caution as the police rigorously discourage this activity. The owner of the pension is a lean, short man who speaks excellent American, having lived in the USA for eleven years, and offers a cup of coffee to new arrivals. As he is so helpful, it is a pity that his wife is rather sour and uncommunicative. Guests staying here should take an en suite room. Despite the extra cost, and the unsatisfactory nature of the conversion necessary to squeeze in the toilet and shower, it saves having to use the garden toilets and showers which are definitely ethnic. Ground floor rooms are adjacent to the guests' kitchen as well as the garden patio and have to put up with the noisy revelries of other guests whiling away the late hours. The 24 hour hot water is not (!), the garden encourages mosquitoes and watch out for the last step on the first floor stairs. A double room en suite, in mid-season, costs 1300 drs.

Rooms Hatzelenis (Tourist Office Rooms) (*Tmr* 5C3/4)   Tel.27295
Directions: On the Esplanade around the angle of the quay from the Chios-Samos ferry-boat berth (*Tmr* 3C3).
   The building is an old style, 'Victorian' town house which Tassos (yes he of Hatzelenis Tours) and his French wife Margaret saved from destruction and are patiently restoring. The couple, who met in England while studying, both speak excellent English and could not be more helpful. The stairs are wood panelled, as is the huge first floor hallway, the rooms are of magnificent proportions, with high, wood panelled ceilings, and most rooms have a small balcony. A very thoughtful 'extra' to the rooms accoutrements is the supply of a mosquito 'frying pan' (*See* CHAPTER ONE). The shared toilets/showers are adequate and the water, despite being solar heated, is very hot and seems to stay so rather longer than is usually the case. It is a pity that the bathrooms are not always clean and the toilet paper bins are allowed to fill up for somewhat longer than seems necessary. Margaret is present most of the day, apart from baby duties and siesta, as they have opened up a tasteful tourist shop in the ground floor of the building. Mid-season rates for a double room, sharing a bathroom, are 1200 drs while the en suite room rate is 1500 drs. Tassos, true to the spirit of his scathing comments regarding the 'city fathers' wholesale butchery of trees, has insisted on keeping a lovely, mature plane tree that grows close to the house.

Two other waterfront hotels worthy of a mention, even if they are costly, are the:-
Hotel Chandris (*Tmr* 15C3) (Class B) Akti Prokymaias   Tel. 25761
Directions: On the far, south corner of the harbour.
   Expensive with chandeliers in the dining room. Very few of the pensions I stay in have chandeliers! All rooms are en suite with singles 2267 drs and doubles 3467 drs, rising to 3422 drs and 4356 drs (1st July - 30th Sept).

Hotel Xenia (*Tmr* 16C4) (Class B) Akti Livanou/Odhos ΣΟΥΡΙΑ   Tel. 23507
Directions: On the southern waterfront, across the road from the town beach, but rather run down in outward appearance.
   Both singles and double rooms can be booked sharing a bathroom or en suite. Single room rates start off at 760/1600 drs rising to 850/2500 drs and double 1300/2500 drs and 2000/3500 drs.

Back to reality, and off the Esplanade at about the centre of the port is the:-
Hotel Palladion (*Tmr* 17B2/3) (Class D) El. Venizelou/1 Roidou   Tel.22555
Directions: Odhos Roidou branches off the Esplanade in between the buildings in which are situated *Stella's Rooms* (*Tmr* 11B3) (above the Toyota showroom) on the

south side and the *Acropolis Inn* (*Tmr* 10B2) on the north side. Set in the ground floor are a Dry Cleaner's and a Video Shop.

All rooms share the bathrooms with single room rates starting off at 600 drs and double rooms 1000 drs, rising to respectively 800 drs and 1200 drs (1st June - 30th Sept).

Hotel Filoxenia (*Tmr* 18B2/3) (Class D) Voupalou/Roidou Sts.   Tel.22813
Directions: Further up Odhos Roidou from the *Hotel Palladion* (*Tmr* 17B2/3), towards the south-east end of the Main Square Municipal Gardens. There is a Barber installed in the ground floor.

Single rooms sharing the bathroom cost between 700 and 900 drs with en suite at 1200 drs all rising to 1000/1250 drs and 1650 drs (1st June - 30th Sept). Double rooms start off at 1000/1400 drs sharing and 1800 drs en suite increasing to 1700/2350 drs and 2750 drs respectively.

Pension Roussos (*Tmr* 19A3) Odhos Aplotarias/2Vassilikari.   Tel.24572/29702
Directions: Probably best reached from the south-eastern corner of the Main Square Municipal Gardens from whence it is easy to walk along Odhos Aplotarias. The side street, Odhos Vassilikari, is on the right and the pension is in one of the buildings immediately on the right, in a rather run-down area.

The seedy entrance hall resembles a 1930s apartment block. The rather shabby 'Mr. Big', Dimitris Roussos, owns two properties and can ring the changes. A number of guests are long term, for which the rates obviously tumble but mid-season double rooms with en suite bathrooms work out at about 1300 drs a night. The other house, which I am assured is much smarter, has doubles costing 1500 drs a night.

The Eating Out
Perhaps this facet of the town best mirrors the brash Greek-Americanism of Chios. On one stretch of the Esplanade the wildly dissimilar old-world kafenions, with their barrackroom, soulless interiors, and new style coffee shops, with pool tables and pinball machines, rub shoulders with inordinately expensive and smart, almost sumptuous, cafe-bar restaurants.

Throughout the town there are numerous souvlaki snackbars but very few tavernas so it may be invidious to select one or two establishments, but here goes.

Taverna (*Tmr* 20B2) Akti Neorion
Directions: Across the Esplanade road, almost on the corner of the right-angled turn at the northern end of the harbour, across the way from the main Piraeus Ferry-boat quay (*Tmr* 1B2).

Once an all night taverna, it now simply stays open very late.

Cafe Manikas (*Tmr* B2) Akti Prokymaias
Directions: Across the Esplanade from the main Piraeus Ferry-boat quay (*Tmr* 1B2) and next door to the *Restaurant* ΜΟΥΡΑΓΙΟ (*Mouragio*) (*Tmr* 8B2). Incidentally the Mouragio is a 'greasy spoon'.

The very hot coffee and hot milk are served separately, the measure being the equivalent of 1½ cups, at a cost of 70 drs; ouzo with nuts 40 drs and a bottle of beer 70 drs.

Souvlaki Snackbar (*Tmr* 21A/B2)
Directions: Towards the bottom right-hand of the Main Square Municipal Gardens, between the Town Hall and the Fire Station.

Reputedly the best in town. This impression was confirmed by the French speaking mother of the chief administrator of the Archaeological Museum, who we once met in the queue that rapidly forms. A good 'pita-ful' for 70 drs.

Taverna ΧΡΥΣΟΒΑΡΕΛΙ *(Tmr* 22C4) Odhos ΣΟΥΡΙΑ (Souria)
Directions: Along the southern waterfront, around the corner from the *Chandris Hotel* *(Tmr* 15C3), up the side street to the nearside of the *Hotel Xenia (Tmr* 16C4) and on the left.

A rather barn-like building, down the side of which is a small, outside patio, situated in an area of high-rise flats. The owner Michael Lagoudis is rather taciturn and rarely breaks into a smile. Maybe he is troubled by the thought that he runs, without doubt, the best eating house in the town, a fact of which few seem to be aware. The kitchens are spotless, the food is well cooked but the menu is relatively limited and most of the vegetables are cooked in batter. Offerings include a plate of giro carved meat (300 drs), a pizza (200 drs), liver (190 drs), spaghetti milanaise in pots (140 drs), patatas (55 drs), tomato & cucumber salad (73 drs), tzatziki (85 drs), spaghetti special (130 drs), zucchini in batter (55 drs), courgettes in batter (55 drs), 'open' (draught) retsina (50 drs) and bread (10 drs).

Tassos Restaurant *(Tmr* 23C4) 6 Livanou St
Directions: On the south waterfront Esplanade, almost directly opposite the Nautical Club *(Tmr* 24C4).

Popular with a pleasantly shaded garden but......the prices are average Chios (i.e. a shade expensive) and all the food is precooked, most of it simmering away in bains-marie.

Houlis Pastry Shop *(Tmr* 25B2/3) Roidou St
Directions: Almost opposite the *Hotel Palladion (Tmr* 17B2/3), just up from the Esplanade.

Scrumptious loukamades, advertised as a *kind of fritter*, cost 80 drs. They also serve coffee as well as milk, butter, honey, yoghurt and cheese.

THE A TO Z OF USEFUL INFORMATION
AIRLINE OFFICE & TERMINUS *(Tmr* 26B3). Situated on the Esplanade and open daily between 0600-2000 hrs.
Aircraft timetable

Chios to Athens

Daily	1030, 1705 hrs.
Up to 14th June additionally	
Monday, Thursday, Sunday	1805 hrs.
Wednesday, Thursday, Saturday & Sunday	0810 hrs.
From 15th June additionally	
Monday, Thursday, Saturday & Sunday	1805 hrs.
Wednesday, Thursday, Sunday	0810 hrs.
Return	
Daily	0910, 1545 hrs.
Up to 14th June additionally	
Monday, Thursday, Sunday	1645 hrs.
Wednesday, Thursday, Saturday & Sunday	0650 hrs.
From 15th June additionally	
Monday, Thursday, Saturday & Sunday	1645 hrs.
Wednesday, Thursday, Sunday	0650 hrs.

One-way fare 2480 drs; nonstop flights duration 40 mins.

Chios to Lesbos

Monday	1155 hrs.
After 15th June	
Monday & Friday	1720 hrs.

Return

Up to 14th June	
Monday	1255 hrs.
From 15th June	
Monday, Friday	1820 hrs.

One-way fare 2500 drs; nonstop flights duration 40 mins..

Chios to Mykonos

Up to 14th June	
Monday	1355 hrs.
After 15th June	
Monday, Friday	1920 hrs.

Return

Up to 14th June	
Monday	1040 hrs.
After 15th June	
Monday, Friday	1605 hrs.

One-way fare 4100 drs; nonstop flights duration 55 mins.

Chios to Samos

Up to 14th June	
Sunday	1235 hrs.
After 14th June	
Thursday, Sunday	1800 hrs.

Return

Up to 14th June	
Sunday	1140 hrs.
After 15th June	
Thursday, Sunday	1705 hrs.

One-way fare 2300 drs; nonstop flights duration 35 mins.

BANKS Three banks are scattered about Plateia Vounakiou at the eastern end of the Main Park Municipal Gardens, the:-
National Bank (*Tmr* 27B2), the **Ionian & Popular**, diagonally across Odhos Limenos and the **General & Hellenic** (*Tmr* 28B2/3), which changes Eurocheques.

There are two other banks (at least) at the south end of Odhos Aplotarias the **National Bank** (*Tmr* 29A3) and the **Bank of Crete** (*Tmr* 30A3) as well as the **Commercial Bank** on the Esplanade, Akti Prokymaias, north of the *Acropolis Inn* (*Tmr* 10B2).

One other banking service that is rather unusual, but not unique as Lesbos has them, are the mobile banks used to service the outlying areas. The closest contact that a visitor may make is the necessity to take to the ditch as one of the large 'bus banks' looms into view on a narrow country lane bend.

BEACHES The only town beach is a man-made facility alongside the south Esplanade, Akti Livanou. When complete the complex will be very nice but in 1986 the project was unfinished. This is not so surprising when it is realised that it was the intention of the NTOG, who pioneered the project, to charge an entrance fee. The worthy citizens of Chios objected vigorously - that is to paying and the plan was postponed. Do not be put off by the impression that the beach is fenced off as entrance can be made alongside the Nautical Club (*Tmr* 24C4). This club incidentally sports a sea filled swimming pool so why not buy a drink or snack and make use of this facility? Back to the beach. It is made up of 'imported' sand, pebble and irritatingly tiny gravel and is rather dirty with the odd dollop of tar. The sea has formed a miniature cliff of the foreshore to the left (*Fsw*) and the sea bottom is made up of pebbles.

BICYCLE, SCOOTER & CAR HIRE Probably a little more costly than some of the other N.E. Aegean islands, but vehicle hire in the whole chain is expensive compared to say the Cyclades. The average scooter costs 1500 drs a day and cars the 'national' average of 5000/6000 drs a day (once the cost of comprehensive insurance and other mandatory extras are added in). There are no agencies accepting payment by American Express. Outfits include:-

Bolakis (*Tmr* B2) 1D Polychronopoulou   Tel. 29083

Directions: In a narrow lane left off Odhos Limenos (*Sbo*) alongside the Chios Tourist Office (*Tmr* 31 B2)

Costas, an engaging ex-merchant seaman, hires out mopeds and scooters from an alley behind the Tourist office. He reduces the rate for say 3 days to 4000 drs but requests clients who receive this 'concession' not to advise his competitors.

Other firms include **Rent-A-Motorbike** (*Tmr* 7B2), situated in a low shed beyond Hatzelenis Tours; **Rent-A-Car** (*Tmr* A2), located about the middle of Vas. Konstantinou, that edges the south side of the Main Square Municipal Gardens; **M. Georgoulis Bike, Moped and Scooter Hire** (*Tmr* 32C3/4), one block back from the harbour close by the *Chandris Hotel* (*Tmr* 15C3), and **Rent-A-Car**, a few doors along the same arcade, beneath a block of flats.

BOOKSELLERS There is an excellent bookshop (*Tmr* 33A/B3) selling Greek and English language books, as well as foreign newspapers, on the right of Odhos Aerop Vasiliadou on up from the Cathedral. In the parade (*Tmr* 32C3/4), behind and to the right (*Sbo*) of the *Chandris Hotel* (*Tmr* 15C3) is a foreign newspaper shop also selling some English language paperbacks. On the Esplanade, south of the *Acropolis Inn* (*Tmr* 10B2) and next door to the *Cafe Bistro*, is a well organised gift shop selling English language paperbacks, magazines and papers.

BREAD SHOPS *See* **Commercial Shopping Area.**

BUSES As on some other larger islands, such as Rhodes (Dodecanese), there are two bus termini.

Town Bus (blue) Terminus (*Tmr* 34A/B2). Odhos Vassileos Georgiou. On the right (*Sbo*) of the Main Square Municipal Park, almost opposite the Fire Station. Only a Greek timetable is available and it is necessary to enquire about each specific destination. The town buses cover a radius up to about seven kilometres distance from Chios Town, including Vrondatos, Karfas (for Thymiana) & Karyes.

Country Bus (green) Terminus (*Tmr* 35A2/3) 22 Vlattarias St, off Vassileos Konstantinou. On the left of the Main Square Municipal Park, behind the imposing Municipal offices, on an untidy, small square. In the window of the Bus office building is a timetable in English. Note schedules are open to much alteration, and even the English language version is almost impossible to comprehend, but here goes.

Bus (Country) timetable
Chios Town to Kardamila, Kambia (North island)

Weekdays	0510, 0645, 1140, 1240 hrs.
Saturday, Sunday/holidays	
(Kardamila only)	0645, 1100, 1340 hrs.

Return journey
Weekdays   1140, 1610 hrs.
(Kambia to Kardamila)
(Kardamila to
Chios Town)   0645, 0800, 1310, 1430, 1710 hrs.
Saturday, Sunday/holidays
(Kardamila to Chios Town)   0800, 1215, 1450 hrs.
Chios Town to Kalamoti, Komi (South island)
Weekdays   0645, 1110, 1240, 1340, 1510, 1630, 1910 hrs.
Saturday, Sunday/holidays   0645, 1110, 1340, 1510 hrs.
Return journey
Weekdays
(Kalamoti to Chios Town)   0700, 0815, 1330, 1500, 1710 hrs.
Saturdays, Sunday/holidays
(Kalamoti to Chios Town)   0800, 1230, 1300, 1645 hrs.
NB Obviously buses return from Komi but....!
Chios Town to Armolia, Pirgi, Olympoi, Mesta (South-west island)
Weekdays   0645, 1110, 1310, 1510 hrs.
Saturdays, Sunday/holidays   1110, 1310, 1510 hrs.
Return journey
Weekdays   0700, 1220, 1430, 1645 hrs.
Saturday, Sunday/holidays   1220, 1430, 1645 hrs.
Chios Town to Ag. Georgios, Sikoysis, Lithi (West-south-west island)
Weekdays   0610, 0810, 1220, 1340 hrs.
Saturday, Sunday/holidays   0610, 0800, 1400 hrs.
Return journey
Weekdays   0730, 0840, 1500 hrs.
Saturday, Sunday/holidays   0715, 0830, 1500 hrs.
Chios Town to Avgonyma, Anavatos (West island)
Thursday   0815, 1430 hrs.
Return journey
Thursday   0915, 1530 hrs.
Chios Town to Lithi, Elata (South-west island)
Daily   0610, 1340 hrs.
Return journey
Daily   0715, 1445 hrs.
Chios Town to Volissos (West-north-west island)
Monday, Wednesday, Friday   0300, 1310 hrs.
Return journey
Monday, Wednesday, Friday   1930 hrs.

Note the timetables are subject to constant variation and despite the listings there are often additional buses operating.

CINEMAS At least three, **The Rex**, on the northern edge of the harbour alongside the *Taverna* (*Tmr* 20B2), one alongside the *Hotel Diana* (*Tmr* 13B3) and **The Astir** (*Tmr* 36B3), on the main Esplanade.

COMMERCIAL SHOPPING AREA Almost a bazaar comprising an amazing maze of lanes crammed with shops of all shapes and sizes bounded by Odhos El. Venizelou, Dimogerontias, Argenti and Aplotarias (*Tmr* B3). The butchers and fish stalls are grouped around the south and east side of the Old Mosque (*Tmr* 37B2). There is a baker on the west side of the Mosque.

Odhos Ladis, parallel to the Esplanade, and to the rear of the Customs building (*Tmr* 9B2), is lined with old fashioned shops including a cobbler, and a snackbar which is often frequented by Turkish gypsy lorry drivers and their tribes of wives and children. Further back from Odhos Ladis, inside the Old Kastro walls, is a square (*Tmr*

38A/B2) around the edge of which is a defunct hotel, now used as a furniture repair shop, a bread shop and the remains of a Turkish cemetery complete with a number of the distinctive carved headstones (*See* **Places of Interest**). There is a 'bulk-drink' shop in the small street across Odhos Roidou from the *Hotel Filoxenia* (*Tmr* 18B2/3). Generally opening hours are subject to a strict siesta except, naturally enough, for the Esplanade cafes.

FERRY-BOATS The N.E. Aegean does not have pivotal or junction ports in the manner of the Cyclades islands of Paros, Santorini or Naxos. Chios is the closest to an axial ferry-boat island (not forgetting perhaps Lesbos) with, connections, albeit spasmodic, to the islands of Lesbos, Psara, Oinoussai, Samos as well as Piraeus (M) and Thessaloniki (M). The Piraeus based ferry-boats **Sappho** and **Nissos Chios** are large modern craft, the **Nissos Chios** being a particularly nicely appointed, well-looked after ship with showers, trailing plants and a good snackbar.

The Psara, Oinoussai and Samos island craft are small interisland boats with room for a few cars. There is also a Turkish connection to Tsesme.

Ferry-boat timetables

Day	Departure time	Ferry-boat	Ports/Islands of Call
Daily (from Piraeus 1800 hrs)	0530 hrs*	Sappho/Nissos Chios	Mitilini (Lesbos)
	1400 hrs	Oinousses	Oinoussai
	2030 hrs*	Sappho/Nissos Chios	Piraeus (M)

This service early mid-season and late in the year decreases to once every other day i.e. Tuesday, Thursday and Saturday.

Monday	0700 hrs	Capetan Stamatis	Samos
	1800 hrs	Kyklades	Mitilini (Lesbos), Limnos, Kavala (M)

Tuesday	0700 hrs	Capetan Psara	Psara

Note: This craft returns the same day at 1230 hrs.

Wednesday	0800 hrs	Capetan Stamatis	Tsesme (Turkey)

Note: This craft returns the same day at 1800 hrs.

	1000 hrs	Kyklades	Samos (Vathy), Ag. Kirikos (Ikaria), Leros, Kalimnos, Kos, Rhodes, Chalki, Diafni (Karpathos), Karpathos, Kasos, Sitia (Crete), Ag. Nikolaos (Crete), Anafi, Thira (Santorini), Folegandros, Milos, Piraeus (M).

Thursday	0700 hrs	Capetan Psara	Psara

Note: This craft returns the same day at 1230 hrs

Friday	0700 hrs	Capetan Stamatis	Samos

Note: This craft returns the same day at 1300 hrs

Saturday	0700 hrs	Capetan Psara	Psara

Note: This craft returns the same day at 1230 hrs

	0800 hrs	Capetan Stamatis	Tsesme (Turkey)

Note: This craft returns the same day at 1800 hrs

	1330 hrs	Sappho	Thessaloniki (M)

Note: This craft returns the same day at 2300 hrs

Sunday †   0800 hrs   Capetan Stamatis   Tsesme (Turkey)
Note: This craft returns the same day at 1800 hrs
† *Early mid-season this boat does not run.*

One-way fare: to Psara   722 drs; duration 3¾ hrs. (*Note passengers travel free during the months of April, May, September and October.*)
One-way fare: to Samos   775 drs; duration 4¾ hrs.
One-way fare: to Lesbos   1013 drs; duration 4 hrs.
One-way fare: to Piraeus   1369 drs; duration 10 hrs.

FERRY-BOAT TICKET OFFICES: A rather antediluvian number of offices spread out along the north end of the harbour.
Miniotis Lines (*Tmr* 39B2) This office handles Psara and Samos island and Tsesme (Turkey) bookings.

The **FB Homerus, Alcaeos, Sappho** and **Arion** are dealt with by the office (*Tmr* 40B2) to the south side of the Customs building (*Tmr* 9B2).

The **FB Nissos Chios** tickets are sold from the office in the same block of buildings as the *Restaurant* ΜΟΥΡΑΓΙΟ (*Tmr* 8B2), and by **Hatzelenis Tours** (*Tmr* 4B2).

HAIRDRESSERS (LADIES) At least one on Akti Livanou, just beyond the Nautical Club (*Tmr* 24C4).

LAUNDRY There are any number of dry-cleaners (and tailor shops).

LUGGAGE STORE Tassos may allow friendly clients to store a rucksack in his tourist and travel office (*Tmr* 4B2).

MEDICAL CARE
Chemists & Pharmacies Enough, with one on the Esplanade next door to *Pension Stella* (*Tmr* 11B3) and three on Odhos Aplotarias (the commercial street).

Dentist & Doctors As one would expect of an island with so many returned expatriate American Greeks, not only dentists and doctors but opticians, pathologists, a dermatologist and cardiologists. (Also listed are two veterinarians!)

Hospital A large modern facility some two kilometres north of Chios Town on the Vrondatos road. Sited on the right of the road, on a bluff beyond the windmills (on the right) and a caique boat building yard (on the left).

NTOG Apart from the Hatzelenis Tours office (*Tmr* 4B2), which acts as an unofficial tourist centre, the worthy citizens of Chios operate the:-
Chios Tourist Office (*Tmr* 31B2) Odhos Limenos (Kanari). Well appointed and able to provide aircraft, bus and ferry-boat timetables, brochures and wall prints as well as 'guarded' information. Unfortunately the office hours are rather restricted, only opening mid-morning and early evening.

OTE (*Tmr* 41B2) A large, modern building which confusingly is not entered from one of its sides but from an unprepossessing entrance off Odhos Ladis, alongside a large store. The office is open 0600-2400 hrs daily between mid April and mid October.

PETROL Any number of fuel stations with three or four spotted around the large Main Square. There is a BP petrol station on Vassileos Georgiou beyond the Fire Station, opposite the Town 'Blue' Bus terminus (*Tmr* 34A/B2).

PLACES OF INTEREST The most interesting sites and buildings are outside the city. That is apart from the Market Bazaar (*See* **Commercial Shopping Area**); the occasional areas in which are still standing old buildings; the remains of the **Genoese Fort** (*Tmr* B1/2); the **Museum of Byzantine and Post Byzantine Art** housed in the Old Mosque (*Tmr* 37B2) (and closed in 1986 for the inevitable 'repair'), and the **Archaeological Museum** (*Tmr* B4). This later museum is not where usually indicated on town maps, to the south-east of the Main Square (Plateia Vounakiou), but is on 10 Michalou St.

Certainly the depredations of the Turks in 1822 and the earthquake of 1881 ensured that very few old buildings remained standing in the city.

Turkish Cemetery (*Tmr* 38A/B2). Within the walls of the old Kastro, on the edge of a small square. The cemetery is very small but does have some of the distinctive, carved headstones. One of the notables buried here is the Turkish Admiral, Kara Ali, who met his death when the Greek Admiral Kanaris fired the Turkish fleet in June 1822.

The Kastro (*Tmr* B1/2) The original structure was Byzantine but the present castle is the result of various reconstructions between 1330 and 1748. As was the normal practice, the fort housed the Turkish Quarter but suffered extensive damage from the Turkish attacks in 1828 and 'natural causes' in 1881. Additionally the south wall was pulled down to allow extensions to the harbour, the moat filled in and other defensive works removed.

Municipal Gardens, Park & Main Square (Plateia Vounakiou) (*Tmr* A/B2) A well laid out garden and paved area which forms an attractive 'lung' for the city centre, and around which the main road circles in a giant one-way system.

POLICE
Port (*Tmr* 42B2) On the north side of the harbour.

Tourist The office is combined with the Town police.

Town(*Tmr* 43B2) Beyond the Port police office. There is another police station (*Tmr* 44A/B2) in Vassileos Georgiou, on the north edge of the Main Square Municipal Park, close to the Fire Station.

POST OFFICE (*Tmr* 45B3) In Odhos Omirou the street that branches off the Esplanade alongside the Travel Shop office (*Tmr* 46B3), across Odhos Paralylos (Rodokanaki) and on the left.

TAXIS The main rank (*Tmr* B2/3) is on Plateia Vounakiou, south-east of the Main Square Municipal Gardens. The friendly drivers bring to mind the popular image of New York taxi drivers as portrayed on the television - probably because many of them have returned from the U.S.A!

TELEPHONE NUMBERS & ADDRESSES

Bus station (town) (*Tmr* 34A/B2) Vas. Georgiou II		Tel. 22079
Bus station (country) (*Tmr* 35A2/3) 22 Vlattarias St.		Tel. 27507
Hospital		Tel. 23495
Olympic Airways (*Tmr* 26B3) Akti Prokymaias		Tel. 22414
Police (*Tmr* 43B2) 37 Neorion St.	Town police	Tel. 22098
	Tourist police	Tel. 26555
Taxis (Radio)		Tel. 21111
Tourist office (*Tmr* 31B2) 11 Limenos (Kanari) St		Tel. 24217

TOILETS Several Public toilets including an underground one on the left (*Sbo*) of the south section of the Municipal Park. This one is in a disgusting condition despite the attendant expecting, no demanding, a minimum of a 20 drs tip. There is another on the right of Odhos Ladis, coming round from Hatzelenis Tours (*Tmr* 4B2), set in a small garden.

TRAVEL AGENTS There is of course the oft mentioned **Hatzelenis Tourist and Travel** (*Tmr* 4B2), which also offers an excellent information service and operates an informal bookswap. In addition to the various Ferry-boat ticket offices there are a number of smart tour and travel firms spread along the Esplanade.

ROUTE ONE
To the Monasteries of Kourma, Ag Markou, Ag Pateron & Nea Moni & on beyond to Anavatos (22km).
The road is signposted from the north-east of the one-way system around the Main Square Park and climbs steeply on a good surface to:-

KARYES (6 km from Chios Town). Looks out over the distant Chios Town Bay. The four faces of the village church clock show four different times.

Beyond Karyes, in the pine tree covered mountainsides, the road passes the uninteresting **Kourma Monastery** and an unmade track leads steeply off to the left to:-

Monastery of Ag Markou (8 km from Chios Town) Excellent views but little else although it has to be admitted that they would have to be remarkable attributes to rival the delights of the:-

Monastery of Nea Moni (12 km from Chios Town) The three kilometre road to this 'premier division' monastery is to the left of the main route. Despite the nomenclature New, this was only true some 940 years ago when the three monks, who discovered a miraculous icon on the existing religious site, were afforded royal patronage by the then Emperor, Constantine Monomachos. It may have helped that the 'worthies' forecast his return as ruler to Chios, he being temporarily exiled at the time but there you go! Despite the destruction of most of the complex, which had been much enlarged over the centuries, by the Turkish reprisals of 1822 and the depredations of the 1881 earthquake, a number of marvellous mosaics have been restored. Much restoration and rebuilding has been carried out to the Church Katholikon (mosaics and an altar cloth), the refectory (marble table), the vaulted cistern, a 1900s bell tower and the charnel house chapel. This latter building was constructed in 1881 and packed with the skulls and bones of islanders slaughtered by the Turks in the great massacre. The monastery became a convent after the Second World War. Do make the trek.

About one kilometre south of Nea Moni is the **Monastery of Ag. Pateron** founded in 1868.

The main road (if that is the correct work for at the best an indifferently surfaced track) steeply climbs to the mountain crest, on which is an Army camp, from whence the now unsurfaced road falls downhill all the way to:-

AVGONYMA (15 km from Chios Town) At first glance the village appears to be a local 'prefab' housing estate bunched up on a hillock. But make the short detour because appearances are deceptive and the settlement is an absolute photographer's delight. The piled up jumble of 'Cycladean like' whitewashed cubes are heaped on each other and spread around an irregular square in a shambles of narrow lanes. There are some lovely doorways as well as many external cooking ovens. The rarely glimpsed, small number of inhabitants are cautiously friendly.

The track proceeds northwards through olive groves to:-

ANAVATOS (19 km from Chios Town). As Avgonyma is bright and light so the deserted, stone built fortified, medieval village of Anavatos, impossibly scaling a very steep mountainside, is dour, dark and lifeless. I write deserted but there is one old lady who lives close by the entrance to the village, beyond the church, who proffers bunches of herbs to visitors, for which, incidentally, she requires a *pourboire*. There is at least one other couple who are domiciled higher up on the angled terraces. The path zig-zags very, very arduously up the various levels past ruined, dressed stone houses; the occasional dilapidated chapel; the Church of Theotokos, which is undergoing restoration, all the way up to the ruined Castle. The fortress topped, rocky fastness is edged, on the west side, by an almost vertical cliff-face that plunges precipitously to a rocky gorge far below. It was over this edge that the inhabitants, numbering some 400, are reported to have thrown themselves when the 1822 siege by the Turkish forces could no longer be repulsed.

ROUTE TWO
To Kardamila via Vrondatos & on to Kambia, Volissos, Limnos, Limnia & back to Vrondatos (circa 122 km).
The northern route out of Chios Town is initially unattractive but does pass the town's Hospital and a pair of much photographed windmills, built on a narrow spit into the sea.

VRONDATOS (5 km from Chios Town) Almost the Greek equivalent of a coastal 'Garden City', the spread out, small town covering a large area. The seafront is a series of narrow, dirty, kelpy, shallow curving coves but beyond the sea water swimming pool, a headland, and a fishing boat harbour, is the only shore which is really suitable for swimming. This beach is made up of large pebbles, as is the seabed. It is edged by fancy landscaped, tree planted gardens and a couple of large, modern restaurant bars. If one must, a beer at one of the restaurants costs 90 drs. Behind rises the hillside on which is **Homer's Stone** or **Teacher's Rock** where Homer is reputed to have lectured. Close by is a rather dank, tree shaded spring.

There are several petrol stations on the Volissos road that angles off around the back of Vrondatos.

The east coast road climbs out of Vrondatos passing the:-
Monastery of Mirtidiotissa (circa 9 km from Chios Town). Built about ninety years ago and recently occupied by a dozen or so monks.

A couple of kilometres further on, the route passes above and to the right of a lovely, sandy cove edging the turquoise sea. The beauty of the setting is rather blighted by an old crane dumped on the foreshore and a large, working quarry across the road.

After two more kilometres the road curves inland leaving the indented coast, where there is a caique repair yard in the first fjord like inlet.

PANTOUKIOS (15 km from Chios Town). The road sweeps by above the attractive sea inlet and a patch of shingle foreshore.

Another three kilometres leads to:-
LANGADA (18 km from Chios Town) A very attractive fishing village set at the end of a bay which forms a natural harbour edged, on the south side, by thickly planted, pine tree clad slopes. Also on the south side of the pretty, quayside waterfront, bestrewn with kafenions and tavernas, is a river inlet and the only smidgin of shingle foreshore that could be considered suitable for swimming. Information regarding *Rooms* is available from the **Mini-Market** (tel 74367), on the short lane down from the main road to the waterfront.

The road heads up and off in a north-west direction towards Kardamila. Some three kilometres beyond Langada an inviting dirt track wanders down towards the sea and a small chapel close to the sea-shore, off which is the islet of Tavros. Resist the temptation to explore as the ride is rough, very rough, and peters out by a shepherd's small holding, on the edge of a large swampy area guarded by an Army post. Perhaps history has prompted the present day defence forces to encamp here, on the ancient site of Delphini, a naval base as long ago as 412 BC when the Athenians occupied the area. There are a few remains of the old fortress building blocks from this era but, if one really must visit the site, it is best achieved by following the track from Langada village.

On the road again, there is an oleander filled river-bed to the right, on the flank of Mt Korifi, after which the unexceptional village of **Kardamila** where petrol is available.

MARMARO (28 km from Chios Town). This unattactive seaport and its large waterfront is set in a big bay. There is a bank, at least one house with accommodation and a disco scattered throughout the development, which spreads up the valley. At the far bottom of the bay is a shingle, kelpy, dirty foreshore.

Advancing to Nagos, the poorly surfaced, potholed road skirts a hamlet edging a medium sized bay backed by a pleasant, green valley. The narrow, shingle foreshore is littered with kelp, piled up like rocks, and seaborne rubbish which is a pity for the enterprising pension/restaurant owner who has set up business here.

NAGOS (31 km from Chios Town). This pleasant hamlet is situated on a deeply inset, large cove with a clean, grey pebble beach. Beyond the bluff at the far left-hand side (*Fsw*), topped by a church and the Army, is a fairly long pebble beach.

The next kilometre or so proceeds close to sea-level through very lush countryside with bowers of trees, summer flowing streams and climbing roses. It is not a bad idea to take advantage of this uncharacteristic phenomena for, beyond the map marked spot of **Giosonas,** the road climbs up on to a steep, comparatively barren mountainside leaving the coastline far below.

AMADES (38 km from Chios Town). Prior to this mountain village a sign indicates the long, stony track that zig-zags all the way down to **Amadon Beach**, close by which is a lighthouse mounted rock. The elongated, pebble/shingle beach is narrowish, with a large pebble backshore and a small huddle of agricultural buildings at the far left (*Fsw*).

Between Amades and Viki the countryside has an abundance of fir trees and broom.

VIKI (40 km from Chios Town). Another mountain clinging village on the approach to which are old and new water wells set in a tree shaded arbour. There is a track down to a small cove and a chapel or two.

Some three kilometres along the route, which is now rounding the northern side of Mt Pelineon (1290m), the road surface finally goes unmetalled. I write finally because the authorities have beavered away to improve this once rough track and managed to asphalt as far as this point. Most maps mark the 'cut off' of road to track at Giosonas. After another three kilometres the route passes through the village of:

KAMBIA (46 km from Chios Town). There are extensive views across the large, rolling valley to Mt Amani, around the shoulders of which are scattered a number of simple, agricultural hamlets. To reach these it is possible to spur off at the next village of Spartounta. The undulating, green covered mountain slopes between Kambia and Spartounta have experienced severe fire damage, as evidenced by outcrops of blackened and dead pine trees.

Beyond **Spartounta** is a very large, active quarry and after passing through **Fita** and **Kipouries,** the traveller arrives at:

DIEVCHA (57 km from Chios Town). 'Ware' here and keep to the high road as the low road angles into the cul-de-sac village, passing the lovely, medieval, once flourishing but now deserted complex of buildings that make up the **Monastery of Moundon.**

After another half kilometre the main Vrondatos - Volissos road is joined. To the left, 1 ½ km from the road junction, a track leads off the other side of the main road to the village of **Sidirounta,** the Genoese defence walls of which are still in evidence. The track runs out beyond the hamlet of **Metochi.**

Back at the junction with the main road and 11 km to the right is:
VOLISSOS (47 km from Chios Town). Yet another claimant to be the birthplace of Homer. The village is overlooked and crowned by a hill topping, ruined medieval Castle, the walls and towers of which are still in fair condition.

From Volissos roads proceed to:
LIMNOS (50 km from Chios Town). A small one-eyed fishing hamlet with a scattering of houses and two 'dead' tavernas edging the pleasant, brown sand and pebble beach on the small bay.

LIMNIA (49 km from Chios Town). Simply a harbour with a splendid, brown sand and pebble beach to both sides. There is accommodation, the:
Taverna/Rooms   Tel. 31400
The owner, Kostas, and his wife lived in America for eleven years and could not be more helpful. Simple meals are available and a double room with a shower en suite, costs a rather expensive (?) 1500 drs in mid-season. I am sure it was here that one of the internal columns supporting the roof span of the barn like interior has been set down rather out of position. So much so that I found it difficult to stop my gaze from continually straying back to the offending, precast concrete pillar.

The Psara island mail boat uses the harbour and weather permitting operates a daily service. Note this is not an official passenger carrying connection. Apart from this caveat the times of departure are indeterminate to say the least, varying between 0900 hrs and 1200 hrs.

Between the hamlets of **Skariotis** and **Chori,** a wide, almost summer dry river-bed cuts a swathe down to the sea-shore south-east of Limnia. The brown sand and shingle beach is very, very long with the pebble backshore fringed by bamboo groves. This idyllic spot is deserted out of the height of season, that is apart from the occasional peasant watering the family cow from one of the river-bed pools or a black clothed crone out walking her donkey and a couple of goats. The beach is accessible from either end or along the river-bed.

Volissos is a convenient jumping off spot from which to complete the circum-navigation of Mt Amani. The track progresses through a number of poor, agricultural hamlets including **Pirama, Perparia, Trypes, Melanios, Ag.Gala, Nenitouria, Kourounia, Egrigoros, Keramos** round to **Chalandra.**

Worthy of note in this 'straggle' is:
AG. GALA (67 km from Chios Town). Notable for a number of interconnecting natural caves beneath the village. In the entrance to the first cave is built a church

with yet another, smaller church constructed further into the cave.

A track branches off from the hamlet of Keramos down to:
AGIASMATA (60 km from Chios Town). An almost deserted, once busy, mining and health spa village. The track enters left of centre of the grey sand/shingle foreshore from which juts a small, high standing pier. To the right of this (*Fsw*) are a number of substantial, but mostly ruined, dressed brown stone buildings with sightless window openings. To the left of the main body of the village are some waterfront buildings, a quay wall and, on the far left, a bluff capping, walled church.

To the side of the main Volissos to Vrondatos road are continual sightings of the old road, especially in the fire wracked hillsides and the bottom of dry river gorges.

A left-hand track at about halfway makes off towards Kardamila passing through:
PITYOS (27km from Chios Town). A medieval settlement with the remains of a fortified wall and dominated by a rock topping, two storey tower.

The road from the Pityos turning to Vrondatos passes over gently undulating, bare granite mountain-moorland scenery.

ROUTE THREE

To Komi via Thymiana & Kataraktis (33 km). This route passes through
the flat agricultural area south of Chios Town known as the **Kambos**. Despite the ravages of the Turks in 1822 and the earthquake of 1881, there are still extant a number of the unique, walled garden, Genoese, two or three storey mansions dating back to the 14th century. It is stated that there were up to two hundred of these mansion estates at one time and examples of the genre are still to be seen along the road to the village of **Neochori**. Probably the most outstanding of the *archontika*, as they were known, is the Philip Argentis estate, partly restored in 1937/39. The feature that I find especially interesting are the large, mosaic surrounded waterwheels.

The sea-level coastal road passes the Airport and the Generating Station in a scrubbly setting.

KARFAS (7 km from Chios Town). The large, clean, fine sand beach edging the bay is the nearest presentable beach to Chios Town. On the left, angled back from the road against the backshore is a large restaurant. Behind this is a pink 'British Army barracks' type of building with a colonnaded first storey, green doors and shutters. Is it an old people's home?

Between Karfas and Ag.Ermioni, in the hillsides to the right, is some strange walling.

AG.ERMIONI (9 km from Chios Town). The original, old fishing port, which possesses two quite large, small boat harbours and several rock coves, is being expanded. There are several waterside tavernas and, at the far end, a small, pebble cove. On the approach from Karfas, close by a 'dead' bus, are *Rooms* (Tel 22979/31718).

The road now passes through aging olive groves to:
THYMIANA (11 km from Chios Town). A large, old town to one side of the main road with a very confusing one-way system and friendly people.

The next village on the Thymiana to Kataraktis road is **Neochori**, beyond which is a turning off to the left to **Ag. Minas Monastery**, originally constructed in the 1590s but which achieved island fame during the Turkish massacres of 1822. Some 300 villagers gathered here for refuge from the marauding Turks, who were hell bent on exacting revenge, and, after a short battle, the Chiots were all slaughtered. The building has been reconstructed twice since the event and the bones of the dead recovered and stored in a charnel-house. I hope readers will not mind if I own up to not being able to swear that this is not the same building as referred to in the description of Ag. Fotinis below.

AG. FOTINIS (12 km from Chios Town). The side road passes through lovely countryside past a pleasantly secluded religious building to the clean, large bay with pebble beach. Gathered round the road end are a few buildings including a taverna with **Rooms** (Tel 31131) to the right (*Fsw*) and a taverna to the left.

The main road passes through:
KALLIMASIA (12 km from Chios Town). During the Middle Ages the then fortified village was of 'first division' status but the 1881 earthquake destroyed the settlement. Only the remains of a tower and the walls still stand.

AG. AIMILIANOS (14 km from Chios Town). Another branch off the main road winds down to this small, pebble cove with a church as the only building.

KATARAKTIS (16 km from Chios Town). Considering the village was relocated from an inland site as late as the 1881 earthquake, it it a very attractive, unspoilt, working fishing boat port with a long sea frontage, dotted with kafenions and tavernas, The waterfront follows the undulating line of the backshore with a large pebble, kelpy, small foreshore in the shelter of the harbour wall. To the right (*Fsw*), close to the summer dry river-bed, is a toilet block and shower head.

NENITA (20 km from Chios Town). An agricultural, tree lined village, four kilometres south of Kataraktis, beyond which is a very confusing network of tracks down to the south-east portion of the coastline. Petrol is available.

Due east is a straightforward road to:
VOKARIA (21 km from Chios Town). No buildings, only a comparatively large, man-made harbour and very small bit of shingle foreshore.

Travellers intending to take on the punishing tracks south of Nenita (instead of the main road to Komi via the hamlets and villages of **Vounos, Patrika** and **Kalamoti**, through one of the most prolific of the old mastic producing areas) should be prepared to ask, as often as necessary, where on earth they are? Start the enquiries in Nenita, as the maps do not help!

The hamlet of **Flatsia** is pivotal to reaching the coast at:
AG. IOANNIS (25 km from Chios Town). A boulderous fishing hamlet, the track from which is a bit of a moonscape ride all the way to :
KOMI (28 km from Chios Town). Situated on a long, large, flat bay with a sand and pebble beach. To the left, on the way over from Ag. Ioannis, is a very sandy cove, part of a rock breakwater enclosed, small benzina harbour. The main beach is subject to kelp at the left-hand end. Towards the far right, where the main road spills on to the waterfront track, are three tavernas, one located on the backshore. The beaches are kept clean.
There is a track that connects Komi with the village of **Emborios**.

ROUTE FOUR
To Limani & back to Chios Town via Pirgi, Olympoi & Mesta (67 km).
The main road to Armolia and beyond passes through the central mastic producing area, once so vital to the well-being of the island.

VAVILOI (8 km from Chios Town). A pretty village, despite being quite modern, from which it is worth taking the right-hand track towards the hamlet of Sklavia. After a kilometre a path (and quarter of an hour walk) to the right advances through fields and olive groves to the rather prettily situated **Church of Panagia Krina**. This is in a comparatively good state of preservation, considering its 700 odd years.

SKLAVIA (10 km from Chios Town). It may well be considered worth continuing on to this hamlet. Apart from being beautifully situated with splendid views and plentiful springs, there are the remains of one of the original Genoese estates complete with the ruined main body of the buildings including the house, a tower, church, chapel and cistern.

Back on the main road and beyond **Tholopotami** leads to:
ARMOLIA (21 km from Chios Town). The restored old village, once famous for its pottery, is on and close to a number of road junctions with routes to Kalamoti (SE), Vessa (NW), and on round to Limani.

Immediately prior to Pirgi there is a turning off to the left to:
EMBORIOS (33 km from Chios Town). The road down to the coast runs alongside a wide, summer dry river-bed, narrowing down to squeeze between the buildings of the village and opening out on the right of the 'U' shaped, narrow bay. A fishing boat port with hills to left and right. In the lee of the left-hand hillside is a meagre, dark sand and pebble cove with kelp. The rest of the foreshore is narrow and pebbly with a number of green litter bins on the road side. As well as small boats, one or two large fishing craft moor up to the central concrete pier. There is a general store, and several tavernas. A number of the buildings exhibit the 'Pirgi' style patterned plasterwork, but the modern day fame of Emborios is due to the spendid, volcanic black pebble and sand beach hemmed in by rock faces. This is reached from the village by proceeding around the right-hand (*Fsw*), conical hillside.

PIRGI (26 km from Chios Town). The main road, which hosts a petrol station, bypasses this truly amazing, medieval village set down on low hills.
    The main street into Pirgi climbs up and opens out on to a small, 'primary' Square on the far side of which is the:
Hotel Koinotikos.
Directions: As above.
    Reported to be 'bit of a doss-house' or, as one friend put it to me, a 'flea-bag' despite which it is conveniently situated. A double room, sharing the bathroom, starts at 800 drs.

The best point of enquiry, conveniently located on the same square, must be the **Women's Agricultural and Tourist Cooperative.** This phenomena, one shared with the island of Lesbos, is an organisation to market the homes of women who have **Rooms**. But remember that, especially away from the main port of any island in the N.E. Aegean, Rooms are not readily available until June, at the earliest.
    This 'primary' square is bordered by a pharmacy, the village Police, a 'Pirgi Art & Tradition' gift shop and a store.
    To reach the centre of the village walk up the long street (in a westerly direction), from the far side of the *Hotel Koinotikos*, turn right at the east aspect of the perimeter

wall (of the main defensive tower), then left and after another right the lane spills on to the Main Square. This is dominated by the Church of Koimisis tis Theotokou, built in 1694 and richly decorated, as is almost everything else in the village, with *xysta* or *sgraffiti*. This is a method of engraving plasterwork with black and white patterns for which the village is rightly famed.

On the east side of the Square, the other side from Koimisis tis Theotokou Church, is a short, narrow, roofed lane. This leads to the Church of Ag. Apostoloi, which dates back to the 14th century. This church is famed as a superb example of Byzantine architecture, more especially the perfect, domed roofs and internal murals, the most renowned of which is the painting of the Pantokrator and the prophets.

The village gives an impression of light and airiness despite the multitudinous maze of lanes and alleys. Every twist and turn reveals an artist's or photographer's dream and around almost every corner the village ladies are to be found in gossiping, black huddles. The house martins, swallows and swifts must 'raise a beak' to the countless balconies which furnish multi-occupation nesting spots. The locals fasten cardboard boxes beneath the massed mud homes to save doorsteps becoming littered with the birds droppings.

Mark you Pirgi is not the only amazing medieval village – no Chios has three in this area which surely would be enough to ensure the eternal happiness of tour operators on any other island.

One kilometre beyond Pirgi, a six kilometre track leads down to the coast where there is a beach. Immediately prior to the village of Olympoi another track branches off via the scattered dwellings of **Fana** to a natural harbour and beach on **Ormos Kato Fana**, the ancient site of the 9th century BC Temple of Apollo Phanaios.

OLYMPOI (33 km from Chios Town). Anywhere else this fortified village would rate as a jewel in some islands crown but it is, figuratively speaking in the shadow of Pirgi and:
MESTA (36 km from Chios Town). Totally different from the exuberant atmosphere of Pirgi, possessing more a cloistered 'museum calm' with most of the lanes being covered in by arched and vaulted stonework. The main road loops around the walled village past an irregular Square with **Rooms**, a plan of the village and directional signboards. The modern entrance to Mesta is down to the right from this Square. The centre of the village and Main Square is dominated by the splendid Church of Meghas Taxiarchis and a kafenion caters for the inner man (or woman). There is also a small store and, rather incongruously, a *Taxi 24 hours service. Tel. 76236*.

On the right of the very narrow alley off the north-west corner of the Main Square (or right-hand far corner with the kafenion behind one) is the:
Medieval Hotel/Hotel Maion, Mary's   Tel. 76217/Athens 9754208
Directions: As above.

An amalgamation and conversion of several village houses and rather smart but in perfect keeping with the surroundings.

The main road now turns northwards and joins the coast at:
LIMANI MESTON (40 km from Chios Town). Some maps fail to mark the port, (or for that matter the road on to Elata) that is scattered around this large, almost circular and enclosed bay. The road enters on the left-hand side of the bay (*Fsw*) with a large tower dominating the headland to the left. The foreshore is narrow, pebbly and rather dirty. The embryonic commercial development is almost dormant but there are two large restaurants spaced around the waters edge or, more correctly, the road edge. There are **Rooms** to the right and, on the far side of the bay, a large quay with a

'dead' ticket office hut. The **FB Nissos Chios** is rumoured to stop off here in the summer months but why? On the way out of the far side of Limani Meston is the very nice looking, modern hillside terrace of *Bungalows to Rent* (Tel. 22573).

Beyond Limani Meston the road climbs up the hillsides passing three small bays before striking inland. The first bay is very pretty and secluded with two, small, shingle coves divided by an islet. The nearest cove suffers from seaborne rubbish. The track down is overlooked by a ruined tower on the far right-hand side (*Fsw*). The next bay along is small and the shoreline a shallow curve. The usually deserted beach is made up of shingle, littered with kelp and rubbish. The last bay is small and 'U' shaped with a chapel, a two storey house and a jetty. The beach is sand and pebble with some kelp.

Beyond the village of Elata is:
VESSA (19 km from Chios Town). It could be a French provincial village, and was once a medieval fortified settlement, few vestiges of which are now visible!

A turning makes off north to **Lithi** village and beyond to the unlikely coastal resort of:
LITHI PAPORI (25 km from Chios Town). The track joins the backshore of this medium sized bay almost at the right-hand end, there only being a small section of rocky foreshore away to the right. To the left-hand stretches the wide sandy foreshore and sand/pebble backshore. In the middle distance a tower dominates a headland away to the right. The maps mark this **Kastella** so it was probably the site of a Genoese Fort. Immediately to the left of the junction is a taverna that offers a solid meal - an unpretentious feta salad, omlettes for two and a bottle of retsina costs 510 drs. The friendly proprietor, with the looks of a particularly tough Mafia boss, speaks excellent American. Originally he and his family had an establishment on a more tourist popular island, working hard to be able to acquire these present premises, his dream.

The taverna is followed by a snackbar and then beach. The backshore is duney and tree planted and the middleshore has some kelp. Surprisingly for such an out-of-the-way place there are more tourists here (well at least twelve) than one might see out of the height of season on any other Chios beach. During the daylight hours the sunbathers are draped in and around the abandoned bits and pieces of derelict fishing boats that litter the shore. At the far left corner of the beach is a cafe-bar and to the left, a restaurant at the back of which are **Rooms**. Behind and above this small complex is the *Hotel* ΑΓΚΙΣΤΡΙ. The bay then curves sharply round past a fishing boat harbour.

From Vessa back to Chios Town the road passes through unattractive countryside with vestiges of the old road dotted about. There is a petrol station at the village of **Chalkion.**

EXCURSION TO PSARA ISLAND

FIRST IMPRESSIONS
Haphazard streets; churches with unusual roofs (and many of them); wind; some cats; a scattering of red fire hydrants.

SPECIALITIES
None that spring to mind.

VITAL STATISTICS
Tel prefix 0272. Approximately 41 sq.km in area with a population of about 400/500.

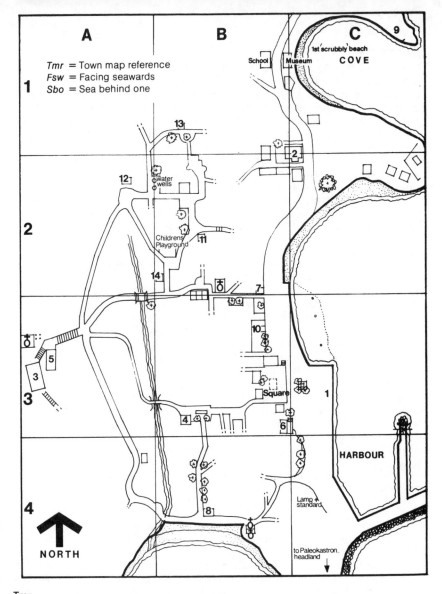

Tmr

1 Ferry-boat quay C3
2 Pension/Restaurant B/C1/2
3 Hotel 'Alcatraz' A3
4 OTE B3
5 Police & Customs office A3
6 Cafe-bar taverna O Kanaris B/C3/4
7 Kafenion B2/3

8 Cafe/ouzeria B2/3
9 Restaurant Epitalia C1
10 Bank B3
11 Baker B2
12 'Retsina' store A2
13 'Cigarettes' store B1
14 General store A/B2

Illustration 22 Psara Village & Port

HISTORY

The birthplace of Admiral Kanaris, the Greek Naval officer who used fire ships to such good effect against the Turkish Navy and merchant shipping during the Wars of Independence. The islanders, then numbering some 6000, had been, in the main, left to their own devices during Turkish suzerainty and had built up a wealthy merchant fleet. Biting the hand, as it were, they joined forces with Admiral Kanaris to such effect that the then Sultan decreed the island was to be laid to waste. Due to adverse weather conditions, the Turkish forces could not embark on this task until the June of 1824 but the delay did not blunt their enthusiasm. Oh no! After the assault only a few, a very few, of the population, swollen to between twenty and thirty thousand by refugees from other islands, survived the annihilation. One story goes that rather than submit to capture, and the inevitable torture, many of the islanders blew themselves up. Those left living, and who escaped, established a settlement at Nea Psara on Evia island, but Psara never recovered from the cataclysm.

GENERAL

Most of the information, or lack of information, regarding Psara is based on rumour and second or third hand impressions. Thus it it not surprising to hear that the islanders are, at the least, unfriendly, and probably eat children! Not really. This is a favourite ploy used by tour offices to dissuade travellers from visiting offshore islands (as exemplified by the Niots of the Cyclades island of Ios when discussing neighbouring Sikinos). It therefore comes as something of a shock to discover that the Chiots are not pulling the 'donkey droppings over one's eyes' – the inhabitants of Psara are unquestionably 'reserved'. No let's not beat about the olive tree, they are disinterested, a characteristic bought sharply into focus after the uninhibited friendliness of the Chiots.

Despite the valiant pioneer work of the NTOG in converting a prison into a hotel and a quarantine station into a restaurant, apart from the height of season, these no doubt excellent facilities remain firmly closed. Furthermore the present manager of the only other accommodation certainly does not go looking for possible clients. When the **FB Psara** docks, he has to be winkled out. The main taverna, the *Taverna O Kanaris* (*Tmr* 6B/C3/4), does not open early enough for early morning refreshment, not serving food until the evening, and the suprisingly numerous shops have to be deliberately tracked down.

Generally speaking the scenery is unlovely, arid and unimpressive and the layout of the sole village port is dusty and disorganised. But for those travellers not over concerned about surroundings and requiring peaceful solitude, Psara may well be ideal. There is one fine, easily attainably beach and the citizens do warm, if slowly, to those who reside for more than a day or two.

Some Greek is essential although there are quite a number of islanders who, having spent their working life in the United States, have returned home to retire and speak more than adequate American. But unlike Chios, and in line with the islanders underlying characteristic of diffidence, they are rather slow to come forward. The necessity for some Greek is best evidenced by the following cautionary tale. After disembarking on our last visit we located the general store and, whilst purchasing 'K' rations, asked a tall, good looking lady for directions to an acceptable taverna in which to eat that night. Or at least I thought I asked the whereabouts of a good taverna! As far as I could make out she indicated it was necessary to go to the Monastery. Now this was a puzzler as the only monastery on the island is on the north coast some eight kilometres trek over Mt Psara. I knew the island was not exactly the height of sophistication but this was ridiculous. It turned out that the lady I was chatting to was Maria, the daughter of the owners of the ports *Taverna O'Kanaris*

(Tmr 6B/C3/4), so perhaps my Greek was not so perfect! Incidentally there is no settlement, let alone taverna, on the north coast. Goodness knows what we were talking about but after that first verbal intercourse Maria tended to eye me rather quizzically.

PSARA: only village & port. (Illustration 22)
Most has been said in the introductory remarks, but note that the islanders do not consider the holiday season opens until the 15th June.

ARRIVAL BY FERRY
The small **FB Psara** is more than adequate and the crew friendly, especially the Captain who is a friend of Tassos Hatzelenis *(See* **Ferry-boat Ticket Offices, A to Z, Chios Town**). Tickets are purchased on board and the craft berths *(Tmr* 1 C3) almost at the centre of the port. The craft's arrival appears to be met by most of the islands inhabitants with the to be expected quayside melee.

Notice Board. Disembarking ferry-boat visitors are faced by a most imposing sign on the edge of the raised Main Square that can only impart a welcoming feeling. I record the same for posterity:

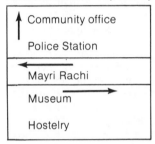

THE ACCOMMODATION & EATING OUT
Yes, well. Naturally not a lot although as the height of season approaches a number of establishments open their doors.

The Accommodation
Pension/Restaurant *(Tmr* 2B/C 1/2)   Tel. 61196
Directions: Along the waterfront road to the right *(Sbo)*, past a large tree (on the right) at which the track gently climbs upwards. The single storey building is on the left. The rooms are approached from the rear.

The present manager, Babis, might not be in charge in future years as the tenancy is only let out from year to year. Nobody goes wild attracting custom and this establishment is no exception. Babis usually has to be searched out amongst the mass of humanity, stores and goods that are being loaded and unloaded during the scenes of frantic activity that persist during the ferry-boats occupancy of the quay. Not outstanding or very clean, the rooms remind one of a sanatorium. A double room sharing the bathroom costs a rather princely 1100 drs. The two rooms fronting on to the road have pleasantly large patios that are sheltered by large, windshields. These are absolutely necessary as the almost always present wind can blow strongly.

There is a hotel high up on the hillside overlooking the port, the:
Hotel Alcatraz *(Tmr* 3 A3)
Directions: Across the left-hand side of the Main Square *(Sbo)* and along the lane to a small rhododendron planted rectangular Square in front of the OTE *(Tmr* 4 B3).

Leave the OTE to the left, walk over a small bridge and follow the lane round to the right and then left which finishes up at the bottom of a long flight of steps. These climb steeply past the Police and Customs office (*Tmr* 5 A3) to the hotel and a church which dominates the hillside backing the port. The rather forbidding appearance of the hotel, which is not helped by the extensive use of brown paint, may well be something to do with the fact that the building was erected as a special prison for 'hard men', an 'Alcatraz'. Definitely not open out of the height of the summer months.

The Eating Out
Cafe-bar/Taverna O Kanaris (*Tmr* 6B/C 3/4)
Directions: Across the way from the harbour, to the left of the Ferry -boat quay (*Tmr* 1 C3). The building is set on the edge of a raised, tree shaded patio. The front room ceiling appears to be in imminent danger of collapse.

Coffee and drink is available during the day (a Nes meh ghala costs 70 drs, spirits 30 drs) but no food is on offer until the evening. The choice is restricted to a set meal of the day, made rather expensive by the costly charge for bread (20 drs), the lack of retsina and the addition of an 11% tax. This tax may well all but disappear when the landlord and his wife ascertain that a customer is a regular. Maria, their tall, good looking daughter is the only one of the family who speaks the odd word or two of English. There is no table service, it being necessary to order at the large, glass cabinet jammed into the narrow down leg of the L shaped room beyond which is the kitchen. A meal of two plates of kalamares (250 drs each), a Greek salad (100 drs), a bottle of Demestica (200 drs), a plate of patatas (50 drs), bread and tax costs a total of 985 drs. Other offerings may include chicken and boiled potatoes for two (500 drs), or meat balls and rice (500 drs). In fact most main dish items seem to cost 250 drs per head. The small range of wines available does not include retsina, which some may consider a distinct advantage! Unfortunately only canned beer is available (80 drs). A number of fishermen, often accompanied by the local priest, take a table or two for apparently appetizing, especially prepared evening meals which include plates of soup and fish.

During our last visit we met and became friendly with a Naval officer serving on a Greek Hydrographical vessel temporarily stationed at Psara. He was a sub aqua devotee and spent most off duty daylight hours in pursuit of his sport. One late afternoon he walked past our pension patio, where we were resting (Okay sleeping off a hectic lunch time), triumphantly holding aloft a massive octopus. During the chatter, and whilst displaying the indentations on his arm made by the creatures suckers in the underwater fight, Georgios promised us a taste when we met in the taverna that night. Forgetting the offer we polished off a hearty meal of casseroled chicken only for Georgios to turn up and wave on the taverna owners proffering a large, steaming bowl of brown boiled octopus swimming in an inky solution. Now boiled octopus is pretty chewy at the best of times, even if most enjoyable, that is unless you have just eaten a meal of casseroled chicken! But... as we were being appreciatively and approvingly scrutinized by not only the donor of the octopus but the taverna's total clientele, we had no choice but to eat every drop. Oh dear! The taverna possesses a metered telephone into which the locals bellow during the evenings.

Kafenion (*Tmr* 7B2/3)
Directions: To the right along the waterfront (*Sbo*).

A very 'local' local, only serving Greek coffee (34 drs), which closes at midday for a siesta. There are some interesting, old shipping company pictures hanging on the inside walls.

Cafe/Ouzerie To ΗΛΙΟΒΑΣΙΛΕΜΑ (*Tmr* 8 B4)
Directions: From the left-hand part of the harbour (*Sbo*), take the track that sets off close by a lamp standard, across the narrow neck of land at the base of the towering Paleokastron headland. Keep over to the left, leaving the twin chapels on the left, to the bay the other side of the mountain outcrop. The cafe-bar/taverna edges the track that runs along the beach backshore.

A rather 'doo-hickey' place with a small veranda patio. The service is rather surly, the table tops are not always clean but they sell bottled beer (80 drs). A Greek salad costs 110 drs, which is rather expensive for a plate of tomatoes and feta cheese.

Pension/Restaurant (*Tmr* 2 B/C 1/2)
Directions: As for the Pension. (*See* **The Accommodation**).
The restaurant only opens in the evening and the menu is mainly restricted to souvlaki sticks and pita. On the other hand Amstel beer and bottles of retsina are available (Oh joy!). Many a convivial evening can be spent in the rather barnlike interior.

Restaurant Epitalia ('Lazaretto') (*Tmr* 9 C1)
Directions: To the right along the waterfront road (*Sbo*), past the Museum and School and round the small semicircular bay with two small beaches to the far side.

The curious restaurant building, with 'Santorini-like' barrel roofs, is set on a low bluff that forms the far horn of the cove. The structure was originally a Lazaretto or quarantine station, possibly once used as a hospital for the prison. The tasteful conversion was an NTOG project.

THE A TO Z OF USEFUL INFORMATION
BANKS There is a hut-like building (*Tmr* 10B3) labelled *Bank of Greece Correspondent Psara,* but the workings of this 'Temple of Mammon' are not known to me.

BEACHES
Beach 1. To the left (*Sbo*) along the waterfront road past the dirty, grey sand and pebble beach edging the bay.
Beaches 2 & 3. Proceed to the right (*Sbo*) along the waterfront road past the *Pension/Restaurant* (*Tmr* 2B/C1/2), the tiniest chapel in the world(!) (in the grass on the right), the large, square, cut stone, two storey Museum on the right, the School on the left, a church and cemetery and round the edge of the small cove, on the far side of which is the *'Lazaretto' Restaurant* (*Tmr* 9C1). The road is now an unsurfaced track and, in a wide swathe, makes off on a left-hand curve. (*See* **Beach 4.)**

Here, by angling to the right, a path leads to:
Beach 2. The 'Generator Station' beach is dirty and smells of diesel, added to which there is the constant throb of the engines of the backshore 'electric maker'.
Beach 3. Across Beach 2 and over a bluff by a chapel, advances to a splendid, wide, sandy beach edging a large cove. The distant backshore is rather littered with scattered rubbish but this does not detract from the clean sweep of the fine beach and the clear sea bottom.
Beach 4. Returning to the wide swathe of track outside the port, as described by Beach 2 & 3, follow the left-hand sweep on round and, by keeping to the right, the way descends on to an agricultural plain set in low hills. The beaten path runs out on a dry, stony river-bed which, to the right, decants on to the majestic, wide sweep of 'Cow' Beach. The nickname relates to the almost complete leather hide of a long dead beast lying stretched out in a sandy hollow. The walk takes about half an hour. The backshore is a little scrubbly and consists of flat pebbles set in sand whilst the foreshore is a sweep of fine sand. The sea's edge from about the centre of the beach

away to the right (*Fsw*), is made up of biscuit rock which, towards the far end, forms a lagoon. Climbers can scale the steep, rocky face that encircles the far right-hand side of the bay and pick their way back to Beach 3.

BICYCLE, SCOOTER & CAR HIRE/CINEMAS/BOOKSELLERS/BUSES/ MEDICAL CARE/NTOG/PETROL/TAXIS/TRAVEL AGENTS. None.

There are very few vehicles, just one or two trucks, which is fair enough as the only road is the unsurfaced track to the north-east of the island and the 18th century **Monastery Kimisis Theotokou.** It is certainly best not to be ill on Psara or want to book a Mediterranean cruise!

BREAD SHOPS Despite the occasional guide book denial there is a baker (*Tmr* 11B2) in the maze of tracks close to a small, children's playground. He serves a very good loaf.

COMMERCIAL SHOPPING AREA Quite a surprising number of small stores scattered about the village including one that sells retsina (*Tmr* 12A2), another that sells cigarettes (*Tmr* 13B1) and a well-stocked general store (*Tmr* 14A/B2) opposite the children's playground. Siesta is adhered to rigidly.

FERRY-BOATS: See Ferry-Boats, A to Z, Chios Town. The boat departs on the same morning as it arrives, after the frantic activity necessary to unload and load all the essential stores, goods and materials. Departure time is between 1230 & 1300 hrs. Tickets are purchased on board.

OTE (*Tmr* 4B3) Next door to the small Town Hall and combines the functions of a Post Office. Open Monday to Friday 0800-1310 hrs.

PLACES OF INTEREST Apart from the prison, now a hotel, the quarantine station, now a restaurant, and the (closed) Museum, it will not go amiss to clamber up the steep hillside on the left (*Sbo*) to the:
Paleokastron. The path up leaves an old windmill to the left. Some maniac has attempted to cut a wide track to the top, probably for defence purposes. At the crest of the outcrop are a few remains of the Castle that once dominated the hill, a pair of chapels and a monument to the Psarian dead, from the base of which two of the four cannon balls are missing. These heights allow clear views out over the uninhabited island of Antipsara which lies four kilometres off in an easterly direction. On the aspect facing Psara is a long sweeping gash of a beach.
Pelican. In common with some other Greek islands, Psara has a resident pelican.

POLICE The combined office (*Tmr* 5A3) of the police and port officials is halfway up the steps to the ridge top *Hotel Alcatraz*.

POST OFFICE *See* **OTE.**

EXCURSION TO OINOUSSAI (Oinousses, Oinousai, Oenoussae, Oinousa, Inousses) ISLAND
Tel prefix 0272.

A group of islets, the largest of which, Oinoussai, is inhabited. A daily ferry-boat departs Chios Town at 1400 hrs, returning the next day at 0800 hrs. Fortunately there are two hotels so an overnight stay is possible.

Initially Oinoussai (Mandraki) port and village appears to be a very prosperous location. But not all that is imposing at first sight is more than a facade as many of the once elegant mansions are no more than shells. The nice village feel is pervaded by the obvious wealth – similar to a Home Counties commuter hamlet?

The island's affluence was based on the seafarers who made good and in gratitude constructed a nautical boarding school, the Navtiko Gymnasio. No wonder Oinoussai is titled *The Ships Owners Island*. To the west of the port is a medieval castle.

THE ACCOMMODATION & EATING OUT
The Accommodation: There are two hotels, the inexpensive *Hotel Prassonissia* (Class D, tel 51313) and the expensive *Hotel Thalassoporos* (Class D, tel. 51475).

The Eating Out. A number of kafenions and tavernas with fish being a strong suit.

There is a Post Office and there are reputed to be one or two satisfactory beaches.

To the north-west of the island is the Monastery Evagelismou, actually a convent and still in business.

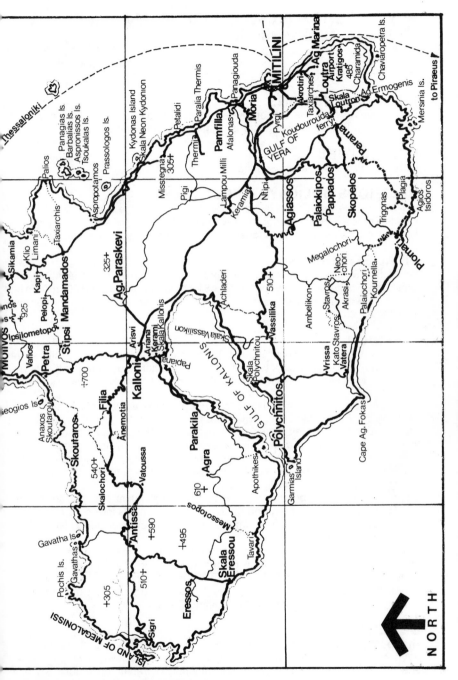

Illustration 23 Lesbos island

15 LESBOS (Lesvos, Mitilini, Mytiline)
N.E. AEGEAN ISLANDS

Straights ★★★★
Lesbians ★★★★★

FIRST IMPRESSIONS
Olive groves as far as the eye can see; snakes; unhobbled animals; wild hollyhocks; verdant countryside; men in headress; goat skins; no water shortage.

SPECIALITIES
Olive oil; ouzo; the poetess Sappho.

RELIGIOUS HOLIDAYS & FESTIVALS
include: Very few really for such a large island outside the Nationally celebrated events. There are the following: 8th May – Festival of Theologos, Antissa; 26th July – Festival, Ag. Paraskevi; 26th August – Festival of St Ermolaou, Palaiokipos.

VITAL STATISTICS
Tel prefix – See individual areas. The third largest island in the Aegean Sea after Crete and Evia (Euboea). Lesbos is up to 68 km from side to side and 50 km from top to bottom with an area of 1625 sq km. Estimates of population vary between 100,000 & 120,000.

HISTORY
British excavations between 1930-1933 revealed the existence of a civilisation based on Thermi dating back to circa 3000 BC, a culture closely tied to that of Troy and invaded by incoming Aeolians in 1000 BC. Homer refers to the island in the *Iliad* and *Odyssey*.

The efflorescence of the island's cultural and intellectual achievements was between the 7th and 6th century BC, more especially under the rule of the dictator Pittakos, one of the Seven Sages of Ancient Greece. Sappho, the poetess, was his contemporary and rightly or wrongly achieved immortal fame (!) throughout the ages, not so much for her poetry but because of her school for females. Her notoriety was such that the island's name has been hijacked to describe female homosexuality – is that a contradiction of terms?

Overall control of Lesbos, never in the hands of the islanders, swapped sovereignty often between the 5th century and 88 BC when the Romans took over. Under their rule the island was put to such disparate uses as a holiday resort and a place of exile. St Paul dropped in.

After the division of the Roman Empire the island experienced a number of plunderings and invasions until a comparative period of peace and prosperity under the Genoese. They ruled between 1355 and 1462 until ousted by the Turks. They in their turn held on until 1912, after which a couple more years passed prior to formal recognition of the union with mainland Greece.

GENERAL
The countryside of Lesbos, the third largest of the Greek islands, is most attractive, if not beautiful. Almost the whole landscape appears to be covered with olive trees and that which is not thus clad, in the more mountainous areas, grows forests of pine trees. Even the moorland tracts of the north-west are well covered and green. The

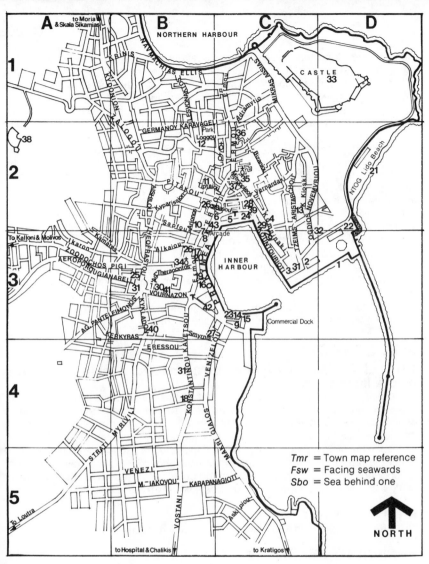

Illustration 24 Mitilini Town & Port

206

various roads lead through marvellous scenery with many wonderful vistas but rather surprisingly, with Chios in mind, the villages are generally unexceptional and first class beaches few and far between. The island is host to a number of well exploited package holiday centres, fortunately very spaced out. These are as diverse as Molivos (the Lindos of Lesbos) in the north; Plomari, still essentially a Greek fishing town with a bustling, provincial Chora, and Skala Eressou. This latter seaside resort, the Kardamena of the island, is set in lovely surroundings and possesses a magnificent beach with a small development, almost entirely the result of tourism. Mind you, the sheer size of Lesbos easily absorbs all the manifestations of the holiday industry still leaving a number of wholly unexposed seaside ports and villages, more than enough to content most island Grecophiles. This size also helps to negate the effects of the large Army and Navy presence.

The islands association with female love for females is only too apparent in the strangely inordinate number of 'paired' ladies who crop up in noticeable numbers at a few of the resorts, a veritable paradise for those of a lesbian bent.

The overall size of Lesbos is such that, for the purposes of this guide book and for the ease of readers, the island has been divided into two almost equal portions. That is south-east and north-west either side of an imaginary north-south line drawn through Argennos to Ag. Paraskevi, with Mitilini and Molivos as the individual centres. The distance involved and the configuration of the coastline make it difficult to explore the island other than from the two locations.

S.E. LESBOS
MITILINI, (Mytilini, Mytiline): capital & main port (of the whole island) (Illustration 24) Tel prefix 0251

The capital and main port appears, on first impression, despite its large size and industrial nature, to have retained an attractive character. This perception is confirmed on second and third sight and is much to do with the circular port layout, the mature parks, attractive old commercial quarter and many impressive mansions.

Despite the almost permanent roar of traffic along the Esplanade thankfully there is not the preponderance of 'mega motorbikes' that infest Chios Town. The inner harbour hosts at least a dozen large fishing boats, a number of purposeful looking Navy patrol craft and a few excursion boats (*See* **Ferry-Boats, A to Z)**.

ARRIVAL BY AIR
The airport is some nine kilometres south of Mitilini, on the Amali peninsula.

ARRIVAL BY FERRY
Ferries moor alongside a long quay wall (*Tmr* 1D3), which extends all the way round the almost circular inner port located inside the main (southern) harbour. To reach the centre of the town from the Ferry-boat quay it is necessary to turn left after disembarking (*Ship behind one*), turn right through the gates at the far end of the quay and follow the Esplanade road round. Most of the ferry-boats servicing this route tie up and 'jettison' passengers from amidships down a long, inclined ladder.

THE ACCOMMODATION & EATING OUT
The Accommodation Considering the extensive amount of accommodation actually available it is rather strange that the worthy owners make little or no effort to procure trade. Apart from relatives and taxi drivers, the only people who meet the ferries are an Army 'reception committee' there to shepherd new recruits and replacements on to transport.

I was once shadowed along the Esplanade by a 'Clouseau like' character who I was under the impression would offer me a 'white woman'! Sadly he turned out to be the owner of a newly acquired accommodation and had, at that time, not learnt to 'hang loose'.

It may well be that the owners take account of Mitilini's almost unique facility, Tourist policemen. As this eminently sensible and still very necessary service is generally fast disappearing, and/or being absorbed by the Town police, it comes as a welcome shock to find the travellers old friend still in occupation here. Thus I will discourse in respect of their noble cause first.

Tourist Police office(*Tmr* 2C3) This is conveniently located close by the Ferry-boat quay and up to three or four officers are present. There is much detailed information, including a plethora of accommodation particulars. During the summer months, the office is open daily between 0730-2100 hrs.

Lest my enthusiasm carries me away let's get down to the business of listing some of the available accommodation options, which include the:-

Hotel Blue Sea (*Tmr* 3C3) (Class B) 91 Prokymea Kountourioti   Tel. 23994/5
Directions: At the Ferry-boat quay end of the inner harbour.
   Convenient it may be, but it is also extremely expensive. A double room en suite sets a client back 3000 drs rising to 3600 drs (16th June – 15th Sept). Breakfast (200/250 drs) may be compulsory. Ouch!
After the Lord Mayor's show ……!

Pension AΓEA (*Tmr* 4C2/3) 33 Komninaki   Tel. 25977
Directions: Follow the harbour road, Odhos P. Kountourioutou, along the east side, turn up one of the two side streets straddled by a number of Ferry-boat ticket offices on to the parallel street of Odhos Komninaki. Turn left on the unsurfaced road and the pension is on the right, in a dubious, downtown stretch of the street.

Rooms (*Tmr* 6B/C2/3)   Tel. 24134
Directions: Along the Esplanade, round past the Park/Town Bus terminal (*Tmr* 5C2) and opposite the next left turn in the harbour wall, above the General Hellenic Bank.
   Very sleazy, in a noisy location with a mid-season double room, sharing the bathroom, costing 900 drs a night.

Hotel Sappho (*Tmr* 7B/C2/3) (Class C) P. Kountourioti   Tel. 28415
Directions: Over the 'Omega' signed Arcade on the Esplanade.
   A single room sharing the bathroom costs 900 drs, rising to 1000 drs (11th July – 4th Sept). A double room sharing is charged at 1450 drs and en suite 1700, rising to 1650 and 2000 drs respectively.

Hotel Lesvion (*Tmr* B/C2/3) (Class B) 27 P. Kountourioti   Tel. 22038
Directions: Next door, to the left (*Sbo*) of the National Bank of Greece (*Tmr* 8B/C2/3), on the Esplanade.
   A single room sharing the bathroom costs 800/900 drs, en suite 1200 drs rising to 870/1100 drs and 1500 drs (1st June – 30th Sept). A double room sharing costs 1350 drs, en suite 1800 drs, increasing to 1680 and 2800 drs.

At the far side of the inner port, the other side of a large building is:-
Rooms (*Tmr* 9C3) Odhos Manou Katraki   Tel. 28708
Directions: In an unprepossessing area close to the Commercial Dock.

Parallel and one back from the sweep of the Esplanade is the main Commercial Street, Odhos Ermou, and in the area of the 'Omega Arcade' is the:-

Pension Fontana (*Tmr* 10B2/3) 10 Arionos St.   Tel. 24333
Directions: As above and one block back from Odhos Ermou, accessed by ascending Sapfous St which branches off opposite the National Bank (*Tmr* 8B/C2/3). Turn first right along Odhos Arionos and the pension is on the right.

There was a discotheque in the basement once upon a year and one can only hope for guests' sake that it is not resurrected. The proprietors (new in 1986) maintained that the pension was A class but I doubt it. It would be unfair to comment on the general condition as the rooms were fundamentally sound with en suite bathrooms, but the usual faults were to hand. We had to request curtains, which were nailed to the wall on the spot (yes, nailed to .....); a tap in the bathroom ran constantly; the shower water did not drain away but lay in a deep puddle where one's feet take root when sitting on the lavatory; the toilet flush pull was a piece of string and the bathroom door would not shut. But I carp. It was only when one of the enthusiastic, very helpful proprietors assured me that they were prospecting for package company clients that I blanched at the thought of the less travel hardened having to put up with eccentricities to which we are inured! A mid-season double room costs 1500 drs a night. I hope Nicos and his partner achieve the standards and quality to which they aspire.

Rooms (*Tmr* 11B2) 6 Tiptaiou St.   Tel. 29203
Directions: Proceed north along Odhos Ermou (the Market St), to the street beyond Odhos Pitakou, the gently curving Odhos Tiptaiou. The nice looking building is the one on the right with ornate, wrought iron gates.

Rooms (*Tmr* 12B/C2) 3 Loggou   Tel. 28949
Directions: Further along the Old Quarter stretch of Ermou St, beyond the backward angled junction with Odhos Mitropoleos, and second turning to the left which leads towards Ag. Apostoli Church. At the junction turn sharp right, leaving Ag. Georgios Church on the left, and turn left on Odhos Loggou. The accommodation is on the left, opposite a park.

Hotel Rex (*Tmr* 13C2) (Class C) 3 Katasakouli Kioski   Tel. 28523
Directions: From the Ferry-boat quay area (*Tmr* 1D3) follow the main road away from the harbour in a northerly direction up Odhos Tzeims Aristarchou (or Ogdois Novemvriou St) and turn up the street to the left. The hotel is in a pleasant, dignified, well-heeled suburban area of the town (Hampstead?).

The rates reflect the attributes of the location with a single room starting off at 1800 drs and a double room 2400 drs, both en suite. Some double rooms are available sharing a bathroom from 2100 drs. The rates rise to 2000 drs and 2500/2800 drs (1st June – 31st Oct).

The Eating Out
The general standard is not very appetising. The west harbour Esplanade establishments that offer meals are generally not worth patronising. The food is on the whole 'tired' and served up cold – 'properties' not reflected by commensurately cheaper charges. The cost of a Nescafe with milk at one of the harbour restaurants is 70 drs but waiter service adds another 10 drs.

The least expensive outfit is a rather down-at-heel cafe-bar situated close to the 'Omega Arcade'. It is run by a 'fullsome barmaid' and her husband, who only appears for the evening session and becomes 'tired'. They charge 65 drs for a Nes meh ghala.

The gourmet is saved by the eateries situated on the south side of the harbour, located on the quay stretching between the Esplanade and the Commercial Dock. Here are a taverna/restaurant, and, in the next block along, a row of two taverna/restaurants and a cafe-bar.

Taverna/Restaurant Katzoinos (*Tmr* 14C3)
Directions: As above and the first on this stretch of harbourside.
A good restaurant, even if the outside of the retsina bottles are left rather dirty. A meal for two of a veal chop (300 drs), meat balls (160 drs), 'Giant' beans (120 drs), chips (45 drs), 4 bourekakia* (240 drs), 2 bottles of retsina (65 drs each), bread and tax (35 drs) totalled 1030 drs.
° *bourekakia* (ΜΠΟΥΡΕΚΑΚΙΑ) - *Long, thin, battered ham (okay, ham in batter) and cheese tubes - a sort of canneloni but filled with feta.*

Beyond this restaurant is a motorcycle repair outfit and an old, two storey clapboard shed in which are stored fish boxes. Across the side lane is the:-
Cafe-bar To ΦΑΝΑΡΙ (*Tmr* 15C3)
Directions: As above.
In actual fact a taverna masquerading as a cafe-bar and serving a fair selection. Kalamares for two (420 drs), a Greek salad (145 drs), a bottle of retsina (70 drs), bread and tax (30 drs) costs 715 drs.

Fish Taverna/Restaurant Katerina (*Tmr* C3)
Directions: As above.
Prices are within 5 drs of the *Cafe-bar To* ΦΑΝΑΡΙ.

Behind the imposing Town Hall (*Tmr* 16B3), and boxed in by an electricity substation, is a Swiss chalet type of wooden building from which operates a:-
'Kafenion in the Park'!
Directions: As above.
In the evenings a large television is propped up for the clientele's delectation. A periptero owner, awkwardly sited to one side, attempts to watch this set but sometimes has to bring along an additional television for his personal viewing. One drawback to the situation is that the tall trees shading the area are utilised by a flock of birds for early evening roosting. This results in bits of leaf, tree or worse showering down from above! I usually lounge in my seat with a hand hovering over the cup or glass!

Towards the south end of the market street, Odhos Ermou, are a number of snackbars including:-
G. Souvlaki (*Tmr* 17B3)
Directions: On Odhos Ermou alongside a fish shop on the corner of the lane, Odhos Alkaiou, that cuts down to the Esplanade and almost directly across the way from a baker's.
A souvlaki pita complete with some yoghurt filling costs 70 drs.

THE A TO Z OF USEFUL INFORMATION
AIRLINE OFFICE & TERMINUS (*Tmr* 18B4) A large facility on Odhos Konstantinou Kavetsou, south of the town in an area of smart, high-rise flats. The office is open daily 0730 – 1700 hrs.

Aircraft timetable: (30th March - 27th Sept)
Lesbos to Athens (& vice versa)
A minimum of four flights a day with a fifth on Monday, Thursday, Friday, Saturday and Sunday. From the 15th June, there is an additional daily flight and a second further flight on Tuesday, Thursday, Friday and Sunday.
One-way fare 2870 drs; duration 45 mins.
Lesbos to Chios
Mondays only   1255 hrs.

From 15th June
Monday & Friday   1820 hrs.
Return
Mondays only   1155 hrs.
From 15th June
Monday & Friday   1720 hrs.
One-way fare 2500 drs; duration 40 mins.

Lesbos to Limnos
Monday, Wednesday,
Friday & Saturday   1200 hrs.
Return
Monday, Wednesday,
Friday & Saturday   1050 hrs.
One-way fare 2600 drs; duration 50 mins.

Lesbos to Rhodes
Monday, Wednesday,
Friday   1700 hrs.
Return
Monday, Wednesday,
Friday   1835 hrs.
One-way fare 7100 drs. duration 1 hr 20 mins.

Lesbos to Samos
Wednesday   1255 hrs.
From 15th June
Wednesday & Saturday 1820 hrs.
Return
Wednesday   1140 hrs.
From 15th June
Wednesday & Saturday 1705 hrs
One-way fare 4400 drs; duration 55 mins.

Lesbos to Thessaloniki (M)
Monday, Wednesday,
Friday   2025 hrs.
Tuesday, Thursday,
Sunday   1235 hrs.
Saturday   1700 hrs.
Return
Monday, Wednesday,
Friday   1515 hrs.
Tuesday, Thursday,
Sunday   1050 hrs.
Saturday   1515 hrs.
One-way fare 4890 drs; duration 1 hr 20 mins.

BANKS A number on the harbour Esplanade including the **General Hellenic** (*Tmr* 6B/C2/3) that changes Eurocheques; the **National Bank** (*Tmr* 8B/C2/3) (next door to which is the *Hotel Lesvion*); the imposing **Bank of Greece** (*Tmr* 19B3) and the **Ionian & Popular** (*Tmr* 20B3). There is another branch of the National Bank close by Odhos Hiou (*See* **Ferry-Boat Ticket Offices**).

Lesbos, in common with Chios, operates a number of mobile 'bus banks' that call at the more remote areas. *En passant*, on the east side of the inner harbour is a most unusual building. An engraved stone plaque still in position proclaims that this was once the *Banque Imperiale Ottomane*, presently inappropriately and sadly housing a disco.

BEACHES There is a NTOG man-made Lido beach (*Tmr* 21D2) in the south-east lee of the large, tree planted bluff, which is dominated by the Castle. The 'beach' is gravel and pebble with a stony sea bed. Plenty of chairs, two jetties but you have to pay 50 drs or so.

The locals cheat a little and, to save money, swim off the concrete harbour wall, over some rocks, in the shadow of the large *Statue of Liberty* (*Tmr* 22D2/3). Not an ideal spot but there are two side by side changing room huts let into the base rock of the statue, even if they have no doors. Do not bother to consider the trek to the northern harbour which one or two of the local guides have managed, with much guile and cunning, to make look attractive. The area backing the filthy, narrow, stony foreshore is decayed 'downtown'.

BICYCLE, SCOOTER & CAR HIRE Credit cards are not accepted in Mitilini at any of the hire firms. Most of the businesses advertising scooters for hire are 'front men' and in any case are only really interested in hiring cars.

Arion Rent-A-Car & Motorcycles (*Tmr* 23C3) Tel. 26113/26762
Directions: On the south side of the harbour.

Enquiries are met by disinterested ignorance. Cars cost from 4500 drs plus 13.6% tax and 20 drs per kilometre over 100 km per day.

Eoliki (Egeon) Rent-A-Car Odhos Hiou (or Samou) . Tel. 20111
Directions: Down the narrow street branching off from behind the temporary Post Office (*Tmr* 24C2), set down on the 'barrack square' Park.

Offers Vespas at 1400 drs a day and cars from 4000 drs per day plus 13.6% tax with 140 km free daily milage.

Just Rent-A-Motorbike 24 Kavetsou St. Tel. 20514
The firm has a Mitilini office in Kavetsou St (the Olympic Office street) and hires Vespas for 1500 drs a day.

But the cheapest firm in town is:-
Giorgos Nanavachis (*Tmr* 25B3) Tel. 21887/21832
Directions: Take the Kalloni/Molivos road out of the city, along Odhos Vournazon, past the Post Office (*Tmr* 41B3) and the OTE (*Tmr* 30B3) to the 'Five Ways' junction. Proceed half-right along Odhos Aeroporou Gianarelli, against the stream of one-way traffic. The business is on the right.

Seemingly a rather suspicious and offhand man, Giorgos warms to those clients who return his charges all in one piece. His attitude or possible disquiet, is quite justified because Lesbos is an enormous island around which to travel. Furthermore apart from the main roads, some of the 'off the beaten tracks' are in a horrendous state. He can be persuaded to reduce the daily rate to 1300 drs a day for three or more days but do not tell everybody.

BOOKSELLERS A periptero to the right (*Sbo*) of the Bank of Greece (*Tmr* 19B3) sells foreign language newspapers. There are a number of bookshops at the south end of Ermou St that sell English language books.

BREAD SHOPS There is a baker (*Tmr* 26B3) at the south, or Ag. Therapon Church end, of Ermou St; one (*Tmr* 26B/C2) towards the middle of Ermou St and another in the lane opposite, Odhos Basou.

BUSES Two termini. The Town Buses park up on a 'barrack square' Park (*Tmr* 5C2), on the north side of the harbour. The Country Buses park up on a tarmacadam square (*Tmr* 27B/C3/4), behind the south-west corner of the harbour. Their respective offices edge the termini. Note tickets for country buses are sold from the office prior to the buses' departure and a seat allocated, so arrive early otherwise there may be no room. AND do check the schedules as quite often buses do not depart according to the official timetables, or for that matter travel at all!

Bus timetable
The Tourist police (*Tmr* 2C3) have up-to-date schedules of bus times and routes but here goes with a sample of that on offer.

Mitilini to Molivos (often signed as Mythimna) via Kalloni, Petra.

Monday to Friday	0900, 1100, 1315, 1800 hrs.
Saturday	0900, 1300, 1800 hrs.
Sunday/holidays	0700, 1200 hrs.

Return journey

Monday to Friday	0630, 1100, 1300, 1600 hrs*
Saturday	0645, 1300, 1600 hrs*
Sunday/holidays	0645, 0930, 1600 hrs*

* Note the 1600 hrs bus is, up to mid-season, denied at Molivos!
One-way fare 320 drs; duration 2 hrs (Kalloni: 200 drs; 1 hr).

Mitilini to Plomari

Monday to Friday	0715, 1000, 1100, 1230, 1500, 1800 hrs.
Saturday, Sunday & holidays	0800, 1200, 1800 hrs.

Return journey

Monday to Friday	0515, 0700, 0745, 1315, 1600 hrs.
Saturday, Sunday & holidays	0615, 1000, 1600 hrs.

One-way fare 210 drs; duration 1½ hrs.

Mitilini to Agiassos & on to Polychnitos

Daily	1100, 1400, 1600 hrs.
Sunday/holidays	0700, 1200 hrs.

Return journey

Daily	0700, 1300 hrs (from Vatera 1630, 1830 hrs; Nyfida 0530 hrs; Polichnitos 0700, 1800 hrs).

One-way fare 240 drs; duration 2 hrs.

Mitilini to Skala Eressou, via Kalloni

Daily	0800, 1100, 1315 hrs.
Sunday/holidays	0730, 1200 hrs.

Return journey

Daily	0615, 0820, 1630 hrs.
Sunday/holidays	1630 hrs.

One-way fare 500 drs; duration 3 hrs.

Mitilini to Sigri via Kalloni

Daily	0800, 1315 hrs.
Sunday/holidays	0730, 1200 hrs.

Return journey

Daily	0600, 1630 hrs.
Sunday/holidays	1630 hrs.

One-way fare 500 drs; duration 3 hrs.

Mitilini to Skala Sikamias

Daily	1315 hrs.

Return journey

Daily	0630 hrs (next day).

Mitilini to Museums of Theophilus & Teriad (*See* Places of Interest.)

Monday to Friday	0700, 0740, 0800, 0900, 1000, 1100, 1200, 1300, 1350, 1500, 1610, 1700, 1800 hrs.
Saturday	as for weekdays but no 1800 hrs bus.
Sunday/holidays	0800, 0900, 1010, 1100, 1200, 1310, 1500, 1600, 1700, 1800 hrs.

Note the Museums are closed on Monday.

CINEMAS Sappho Cinema faces the Country Bus terminal (*Tmr* 27B/C3/4) and is flanked by a supermarket on one side, and on the other, a one-time cinema converted into a now failed supermarket.

COMMERCIAL SHOPPING AREA There is not a specific market building but then with the Ermou Street Market there's no need. This 'Market St' is excellent stretching from almost the centre of the town, at the south end, all the way to the northern harbour. Most of its length is lined with shops, stalls and stores selling almost every conceivable requirement and, whilst open, the street is crammed with jostling humanity. The southern portion of Odhos Ermou is the most modern and is 'cheek by jowl' with fish shops on the Ag. Therapon Church side; the middle is the busiest, with many of the side lanes, including Odhos Basou, also crammed with shops, and the northern section, beyond the junction with Odhos Mitropoleos, is almost medieval in character.

The Country Bus terminal (*Tmr* 27B/C3/4) sports a small fruit and vegetable market on its edge. Opposite, across Odhos Smyrnis, is a large supermarket. In fact there are a number of quite large, 'proper' supermarkets. 'Proper' in that they are run and operated similar to their western European counterparts and are not simply Greek stores 'updated' by being renamed 'supermarkets'.

On the left of Odhos Konstantinou Kavetsou, south from the junction with Smyrnis St, is a row of smart shops including a pharmacy.

General Store Ermou/Prokymaia Streets
Directions: A rather narrow shop situated to the left (*Fsw*) of the National Bank (*Tmr* 8B/C2/3), and also spanning the block between the Esplanade and Ermou St.

An indispensable general store. The goods are piled high and apparently in some confusion – well at least that is to the customer. The owner seems to know where everything is and there are precious few items he does not sell from cheese to drink. Although the shop may appear to be closed it is worth trying the door – it is often open in the evenings when all others are closed.

Siesta is slavishly observed and on a number of evenings the Market St shops do not reopen, so get supplies in during the morning session. On the other hand Friday night bubbles away. There are rather unique signs on some of the side-turnings indicating businesses (and their names) that are located in the individual streets.

DISCOS: Yes, including the one referred to under **Banks**.

FERRY-BOATS Unfortunately for travellers, and the opportunity for Lesbos to be a pivotal junction, several ferry-boats terminate their Aegean journeys at Mitilini.

The **FB Skopelos** is a neat, very clean, two-thirds size ferry. There are reclining seats in a separate lounge compartment in which the television set is actually turned off at night! The galley opens for a disappointingly short time.

Ferry-boat timetables

Day	Departure times	Ferry-boat	Port/Island of Call
Monday	2230 hrs	Kyklades	Limnos, Kavala (M).
Tuesday	1600 hrs	Sappho	Chios, Piraeus (M).
Wednesday	0530 hrs	Kyklades	Chios, Samos (Vathy), Ag. Kirikos (Ikaria), Leros, Kalimnos, Kos, Rhodes, Chalki, Diafni (Karpathos), Karpathos, Kasos, Sitia (Crete), Ag. Nikolaos (Crete), Anafi, Thira (Santorini),

			Folegandros, Milos, Piraeus (M).
	1600 hrs	Nissos Chios	Chios, Piraeus (M).
	2130 hrs	Skopelos	Ag Estratios, Mirina (Limnos), Kavala (M).
Thursday	1600 hrs	Sappho	Chios, Piraeus (M).
Friday	1600 hrs	Nissos Chios	Chios, Piraeus (M).
Saturday	0700 hrs	Sappho	Thessaloniki (M)
Sunday	0900 hrs	Omiros	Limnos, Kavala (M).
	1700 hrs	Sappho	Chios, Piraeus (M).

One-way fare to Limnos 1110 drs; duration to: Ag Estratios 6 hrs, Limnos 7½ hrs, Kavala 12 hrs. There are trip boats to various island coastal destinations (*See* **Places of Interest**).

FERRY-BOAT TICKET OFFICES Despite the apparent number of firms spread along the Harbour Esplanade, it may prove difficult to track down the office selling tickets for a particular ferry-boat. This was especially so in respect of the **FB Skopelos** during 1986. The agent (*Tmr* 28C2) was tucked away in the far corner of that part of the Esplanade 'barrack square' Park behind the fairly permanent looking temporary Post Office (*Tmr* 24C2). Between this ticket office and Odhos Hiou is a branch of the National Bank.

Three offices (*Tmr* 29C2/3) are bunched together on the east Esplanade, Akti Kountourioti.

MEDICAL CARE
Chemists & Pharmacies. Sufficient, especially along the Market St (Odhos Ermou).
Hospital, Vostaneion. On the right of Odhos Vostani, the Chalikas road out of Mitilini Town.

OTE (*Tmr* 30B3) Open seven days a week between 0600 – 2400 hrs.

PETROL There is a friendly station at 'Five Ways' (*Tmr* 31B3), another (*Tmr* 31B4) on Odhos Konstantinou Kavetsou and one (*Tmr* 31C3) close to the Ferry-boat quay.

PLACES OF INTEREST
Museums
Archaeological Museum (*Tmr* 32C/D2/3) An interesting collection housed in a once private and still imposing mansion. Exhibits include mosaics from the nearby excavated *House of Menander*. Many of the larger items are littered about the front lawns.

Teriad Museum & Library. Situated in the village of Akrotiri, four kilometres south of Mitilini (*See* ROUTE ONE). Teriad, born locally, became a noted Parisian art critic/collector in the 1920s and the patron of a local artist Theophilus.

Teriad also founded the :-

Theophilus Museum. Close to the Teriad Museum. Theophilus was a colourful primitive who the art critic met only six years before the end of the painter's life. Teriad managed to put on an exhibition of the artist's work in the Louvre but this patronage occured too late to save Theophilus from dying in poverty.

Castle (*Tmr* 33C/D1) A very large fortress capping the northern city headland, the walls of which are in a relatively good condition. Probably Byzantine in origin, the Genoese made additions and the Turks erected a number of buildings, considerably strengthening the structure.

Churches There are a number of interesting Churches of which Ag. Therapon (*Tmr* 34B3) and Ag. Athanasios (*Tmr* 35C2), at the opposite ends of Odhos Ermou, are the best examples. On the right of Ermou St, beyond Ag. Athanasios and towards the northern harbour, is a ruined mosque (*Tmr* 36C2) that was the subject of an Orthodox 'conversion job', but is now in a parlous state.

Traditional House (*Tmr* 37C2) Situated on Mitropoleos St. The ground floor is a family home arranged to represent a 19th century interior.

Theatre, Ancient (*Tmr* 38A2) Overlooking the northern part of modern day Mitilini, dating from the 3rd century BC, and which supposedly inspired the Roman General Pompey to order a replica to be constructed in Rome.

Trip Boats There are a number of Inner Harbour-based craft that ply to and from various seaside destinations. These include the **FB Eresseos** to, surprise, surprise, Skala Eressou. Details are available from the Travel Agents situated around the Esplanade.

POLICE
Port (*Tmr* 39C2).
Tourist (*Tmr* 2C3). Already written about at some length, *See* **The Accommodation**.
Town (*Tmr* 40B3).

POST OFFICE (*Tmr* 41B3). A large office on the right (*Sbo*) of Odhos Vournazon. Apart from the more traditional facility there is a semi-permanent 'porta-cabin' (*Tmr* 24C2) on the northern Esplanade 'barrack square', close to Sappho's statue.

TAXIS A number of ranks around and about the spread of the central park and the inner harbour (*Tmr* T).

TELEPHONE NUMBERS & ADDRESSES
Bus offices:Town (*Tmr* 5C2)	Tel. 28725
Country (*Tmr* 27B/C3/4)	Tel. 28873
Hospital	Tel. 28457
Olympic Airways (*Tmr* 18B4)	Tel. 28659
Tourist police (*Tmr* 2C3)	Tel. 22776
Taxi ranks (*Tmr* T)	Tel. 28496/23345

TOILETS (*Tmr* 42B/C3) In a small park between two public buildings on Odhos Konstantinoupoleos.

TRAVEL AGENTS In the main, an unexciting, even a motley bunch. To name but two there are **Kronos Travel** (*Tmr* 43B/C2/3) and **Congolidas Travel Services** located to the north of the Trapeza Bank, (which itself is north of 'Omega Arcade') on the Esplanade. It was the latter office that was observed to be charging in excess of twice the usual going rate for a tourist map!

ROUTE ONE
To Ag. Ermogenis & back to Mitilini via Loutra – a circular route
(26 km). The road, surfaced only as far as the Airport, runs along the sea's edge almost at sea-level, as far as Kratigos. The shore is an unbroken, unshaded strip of gravel and sharp sand but is not really suitable for swimming or sunbathing, apart from one or two sand spits beyond the Airport.

For the first three or so kilometres there are some lovely, old, three storey houses and gardens, edging the inland side of the road after which bamboo takes over. Most of the villages marked on the tourist maps that this road is supposed to pass through are figments of someone's imagination.

After about 3½ km there is a turning to the right to:-

AKROTIRI (4 km from Mitilini) The whereabouts of the Museums of Theophilus and Teriad (*See* **Places of Interest, A to Z, Mitilini**).

Beyond Akrotiri the road forks right to the hamlet of **Taxiarches** and left to the village of **Ag. Marina**.

Back on the main road and south of the Airport (7½ km), the route commences to rise into the low mountainsides at **Kratigos** (11 km), beyond which take the right-hand fork overlooking 'Church Cove'. This is signed *OTE* after which the unsurfaced road is signposted:-

CHARAMIDA (17½ km from Mitilini) Two large coves with dirty and stony foreshores. One cafe-bar, several new houses and a skeletal building, possibly an embryonic hotel. The road rises out of the hamlet and winds into an area of olive groves.

An acute left-hand turning indicates a track, set in pine trees, down to:-

AG. ERMOGENIS (13 km from Mitilini) The track sharply and steeply decants on to an irregular earth square. Below, on the right-hand is a pretty cove, one of the two that make up the bay. On the right (*Fsw*) is a taverna, heavily tree shaded by, amongst others, a large fig tree. A sign indicates a couple of changing cubicles and a washroom, diagonally across the square and quite high on the tree planted slopes of the left-hand hillside. Steps lead down to the grey sand, small pebble and shale beach which is cleaned regularly and edges a pebbly sea bottom. To the left is the Chapel Ag. Erogenis set on rocks which form the left horn of this cove. Very much a Greek seaside spot and it gets rather crowded.

Back on the 'main track', the route advances to:

LOUTRA (7½ km from Mitilini) A pleasant, large village. There is a sign to a beach from alongside a large olive oil factory. Petrol is available and the main road is beyond the village. At the junction with the main road right makes back to Mitilini and left to:

SKALA LOUTRON (8 km from Mitilini) Actually a branch turning off the main road which leads to a large commercial quay set on the heavily indented bay. There is also an oil tanker depot and a number of ships for scrap.

The road on from the Skala Loutron turning terminates at:

KOUDOUROUDA (8½ km from Mitilini) A fishing hamlet set round a very small quay with a taverna to each side and, for a place as small as this, a rather incongruously large hotel. There is no sea-shore, only rocks. Koudourouda is connected to Perama, across the narrow neck of the Gulf of Yera, by a small cabin boat which runs a shuttle passenger ferry service.

On the route back to Mitilini the road runs along a hillside of massed olive trees and, at one spot, overlooks banks of wild hollyhocks. The large cove of Akothi is set in the crook of a bay of turquoise sea lanced by a sand spit. There is a view all the way along the shoreline to the tree edged sea-shore close by the hamlet of:

PYRGI (8 km from Mitilini) Not on the main road, but along a track off to the left which continues on to connect with the Mitilini-Keramia road. Despite signs to the contrary there are no *Seaside Rooms*. On the other hand there are **Rooms** in one or two of the substantial homes scattered about the sloping hillside. These houses are set in groves of olives at least 500m from the rocky water's edge and the small, caique harbour formed by a stone breakwater.

Back on the main road, the final approaches to Mitilini are rather unsatisfactory, passing through areas of quarrying and rubbish disposal. The ridge from which the route descends, and the squalor starts, is marked by a solitary kafenion/taverna.

ROUTE TWO
To Skala Sikamias via Mandamados (47 km) The road north out of the city, almost as far as the branch road to Moria, is rather unpleasant. There are a number of factories scattered about the countryside in various states of dereliction. Industries include olive oil processing and tanneries, with foul smelling goatskins hanging out to dry, as well as the island's Generating Station.

MORIA (6 km from Mitilini) The village is about 5 km down a left-hand turning off the main road. It is noted for the section of Roman aqueduct (AD 3rd century) left standing to the west of the settlement, which was part of a system that brought water from some twenty six kilometres away. There are further remains at Lampou Milli to the west-north-west.

PANAGIOUDA (6 km from Mitilini) A dusty, scrubbly, small port at which accommodation is available (Tel. 31274), as is petrol.

PAMFILLA (7 km from Mitilini) Tel. prefix 0251. A large olive oil factory is prominent and petrol available.

PARALIA THERMIS/(Lower Thermi) (11 km from Mitilini) The main road bypasses this pretty fishing port as far as the north end of the village. Here the road curves towards the seafront, forming an irregular square with the junction of the road on up to Thermi (which branches off to the left). There are some hot spring baths straight ahead and on the right a sprawling restaurant/taverna.
    To the right of the harbour (*Fsw*) is a small cove with a gritty sand, kelp strewn, narrow foreshore and large pebble, slimy seabed. This is a Greek holiday village set in green, pleasant, flower and tree planted surroundings, which is perhaps why the one or two old mansions have been supplemented by modern day villa development. It is a pity that the foreshore is not really suitable for swimming because I do not think I have ever seen so many **Rooms** available in one place.

UPPER THERMIS (12 km from Mitilini) More hot spring baths with the ability to cure 'most known medical complaints', which is why the place is renowned. Past glories include a Neolithic settlement added to which the area is supposed to have had some 160 medieval towers dotted about, but the few remaining look more like private houses to me.

PETALIDI (12 km from Mitilini) A small pebble, kelpy cove, despite which there is the *Hotel Petalidi*.

MISSTEGNA (16 km from Mitilini) A right-hand track sallies forth through olive groves to the 'one-eyed' port of Skala Misstegnon. The harbour is to the left (*Fsw*) and there is a long, curving, kelp covered pebble foreshore to the right. Rather a disappointment.

SKALA NEON KYDONION (19 km from Mitilini) Compared to Skala Misstegnon, a very nice spot. The large bay is divided up by a low taverna topped, rocky bluff. The track enters at the left of the bay (*Fsw*) passing several tavernas and a small fishing boat harbour. To the right of the bluff is a stony foreshore and a narrow strip of kelpy beach but the sea is very clear and clean, inviting a bathe.

XAMPELIA (20 km from Mitilini) No more than a large cove overlooked by the road as it sweeps past and on the edge of which a possibly misguided entrepreneur has constructed a Pension/Taverna. I write misguided because the stony pebble foreshore is very dirty being covered with sea driven plastic and other debris, as well as kelp.

ASPROPOTAMOS (27½ km from Mitilini) A large, grey, semicircular bay, in which are set a number of islets, edged by a narrow beach, spoilt by seaborne rubbish and kelp. The bay is backed by a large, saucer shaped plain, thickly planted with olive groves in amongst which are set a scattering of habitations.

From Aspropotamos the road climbs inland across rather boulderous moorland countryside, but still supporting olive trees.

MANADAMADOS (36 km from Mitilini) Tel. 0253. Not a very pretty settlement but renowned for the miracle working patron saint, Archangel Michael, commemorated by the Church of the Taxiarchi. This is to the right of the village and is a repository for the sacred icon fashioned from blood and clay. Petrol is available here.

It might well be worthwhile making the trek to the hamlets of **Palios** (8 km) and **Limani** (6 km), both on the eastern coast.

The moorland scenery continues on to:

KAPI (40 km from Mitilini) A pretty village beyond which, in a north-easterly direction, are dramatic vistas of the plunging, mountain scenery of the Capes of Faros and Korakas. It is possible to traverse the mountain range west of Kapi, to the main Kalloni-Molivos road, on a track via the villages of **Pelopi, Ipsilometopo** and **Stipsi**. The more convenient route is from:

SIKAMIA (46 km from Mitilini) The village, which hangs on the precipitous sides of Mt. Lepetimnos, is only some two kilometres above the very steep, winding, mountainside road to:

SKALA SIKAMIAS (48 km from Mitilini) Tel. 0253. The final approach to this most attractive fishing boat port is bordered by one or two modern buildings. The dusty, irregular main square, ringed by cafe-bars and taverna/restaurants, edges the small, almost enclosed harbour around which the buildings crowd. To the left (*Fsw*) is a narrow, stony foreshore and to the right, beyond the harbour entrance, a small cove rimmed by a narrow, grey sand, gravel beach or, more correctly, foreshore. The Chapel of our Lady the Mermaid (Panagia Gorgona), perched on a rock outcrop from which the harbour wall stretches, is lovely enough to have inspired a book title.

Accommodation is available at one or two private houses as well as the *Pension Niki, Pension Gorgona* and above the *Restaurant* ΨΑΡΟΠΟΥΛΑ, on the far right of the Main Square/harbour wall.

A very, very picturesque spot, so much so that it is surprising that, to date, there's only one 'arty' type shop and Skala Sikamias is not even passingly referred to in most guide books.

From Sikamia a wide, unsurfaced track loops around the north of Mt. Mirivilli. This proceeds via the villages of **Lepetimnos, Argennos** (almost a look alike for a Greek garden city and which, despite the grid layout of the streets, seems to have little purpose, centre or places of entertainment) and **Vafios** to emerge on the main Kalloni to Molivos road. (*See* ROUTE FOUR.)

ROUTE THREE
To Plomari, Vatera & back to Mitilini via Polychnitos & Agiassos
(120 km) From Mitilini the road winds up over the crest of a hill and down the other side to the shore of the Gulf of Yera, all the while passing through massed olive groves.

Prior to the hamlet of **Kedro** a track branches off to the left to Pyrgi (*See* ROUTE ONE). The road undulates parallel to the water's edge passing the very smart *Hotels Silver Bay* and *Mitilini Village*. They are both B Class and are rather stuck out in the middle of nowhere, with only the shelving, rocky foreshore of the nearby Gulf as an attraction.

At about seven kilometres the shoreline is hidden from the view of the road by a bamboo swamp and scattered along the roadside are a house with **Rooms**, a taverna and petrol station.

At 9 km a road branches off to the right to **Moria**, one kilometre after which is a major fork. Right advances to Kalloni and left, on round the top of the Gulf of Yera, to Plomari. Taking the left-hand turning leads across a lovely (French looking) agricultural plain, complete with a river and roadside poplars to:

NTIPI (14 km from Mitilini) Not a lot but a seed oil factory as well as a pleasant 'lakeside' taverna nestling alongside a small benzina harbour formed by a low, rock breakwater.

PIGADAKIA & KATO TRITOS (15 km from Mitilini) Actually more an area rather than a settlement. Alongside the road on the waterside is the small *Taverna Pigadakia & Rooms.*

Some three kilometres beyond Kato Tritos, the main road turns inland passing through **Palaiokipos** (22 km), west of which are the remains of a Middle Ages castle (Palaiokastro), **Plakados** (23 km) and **Pappados** (24 km), with a Turkish fountain dating back to 1795.

Back at the three kilometre mark on from Kato Tritos, a wide, reasonably well surfaced track runs parallel to the shoreline of the Gulf of Yera. This narrow foreshore has 'hints and smidgens' of sand here and there. The track passes through the chalet development of **Evriaki** to:

PERAMA (23 km from Mitilini) A rather industrial settlement. There are a number of factories with tall chimneys, most of which are part of a large tannery complex, and a commercial port. There is an OTE, a Post Office and a number of cafe-bar/tavernas, spread around the Main Square, as well as a petrol station and a resident pelican. The latter appears to be a bit of a nuisance to the shopkeepers who spend some of the day repelling the waddling bird from their premises.

A track leads on down the coastline of the Gulf for about five kilometres to the fishing harbour hamlet of **Pyrgi** – yes another Pyrgi close to which is a pleasant beach.

A road from Perama returns to the main road, just beyond **Pappados**, and close to the crossroads is a petrol station. The surface of the thoroughfare deteriorates very quickly becoming nothing more than a wide rubble. Four kilometres along the route to Plomari and a 4 km track to the left sheers off to the coast at:

TARTI (32 km from Mitilini) Again an area rather than a place but well off the beaten 'road'; if you see what I mean.

The route passes through **Playia** (37 km), where there is a petrol station, and slopes down to:

AGIOS ISIDOROS (38 km from Mitilini) A pleasant seaside resort with a long, clean beach, mainly composed of small pebbles but with some sand. There are litter bins ranged along the backshore, beach showers, changing rooms, beach umbrellas to hire and a firm renting out cars, motorbikes and bicycles. Naturally there are restaurant/tavernas and a number of houses with *Rooms*, telephone numbers for which include: 32252/32170/32071/32886.

On the west side of the village is a disco and, about one kilometre further along the road, an ouzo factory which manufactures the highly regarded, local 'Plomari brew'. The last section of the ride is high up on the edge of a cliff-face, overlooking a rocky shore. Just before the old port of Plomari is a 'bit' of sand set in a sea of shelving biscuit rock, after which commences the descent to:

PLOMARI (42 km from Mitilini) Tel. prefix 0252. Now the comparatively large fishing port and commercial town doubles up as a summer holiday resort with an increasing percentage of package holiday-makers. One of the most attractive features of the location must be that the heart of the town is still firmly entrenched in the past. There are tree shaded squares, pretty back streets and narrow lanes intriguingly climbing and winding past busy, bustling shops (including a baker, cafe-bars and kafenions) only to mysteriously run out on the hillside amongst a maze of stone built animal sheds and enclosures. Mark you there is plenty of new development. The focal point of Plomari is the large, irregular Main Square edged by a Bank (there are three in all), an OTE (open daily 0730-2100 hrs), a Post Office and petrol station. On the port side of the Main Square is an informal 'back-of-a-lorry' market and the Public toilets.

Behind the Main Square the old world Chora claws up the steep hillside. To the right (*Fsw*) of the Main Square, across a 'back street' river bridge, is the tiny, pebble cove of Amoudili beach.

There are any number of tavernas and restaurants, one at least which offers a breakfast of bacon and eggs. Souvlaki pita is available.

Accommodation includes the:
Hotel Oceanis (Class C)   Tel. 32469
A single room en suite costs 1000 drs and a double room 1500 drs.

There are *Rooms*, telephone numbers for which include: 32073/32093/32380/ 32933/31033/32158/32368/32413.

The car and scooter hire on offer is very competitive and is certainly cheaper that that available in Mitilini. There are taxis for hire and the town's services include Town police (Tel. 32222) and a doctor (Tel. 32288).

Continuing on the circular route the road climbs steeply out of Plomari, the last part of which is on an unmade surface despite being detailed as an asphalted road, to a fork after four kilometres. To the right climbs over the mountains passing by the turning to the village of **Megalochori** (birthplace of Benjamin, a local wise man) to Agiassos (*See* later details in this ROUTE description). Left at the fork makes off for a voyage of discovery in lovely, wooded, cultivated and olive tree planted mountain countryside. A drawback is that the signposting is non existent. On either side of the track are the small, pretty villages of **Kournella, Palaiochori, Neochori, Akrasi** (beyond which are the few habitations at **Drota** and the possibility of beaches suitable for swimming), pretty **Ambelikon, Stavros** and **Kato Stavros**. At the Stavros hamlets the road runs close by the large, stony bed of the River Vourkos all the way down to the coast, some 3½ km east of:

VATERA (54 km from Mitilini) The grey sand, shingle and pebble beach is in excess of four kilometres long. It stretches from where the track turns at right-angles to run along the edge of the beach, all the way past the main Polychnitos road as far as Cape Ag. Fokas. The backshore is tree lined in the centre of this straggling hamlet from whence the beach, spreading to the west, is dirty. There are a number of pensions, **Rooms** and tavernas. The coast is backed by a narrow plain and low, rolling hillsides make up the surrounding countryside.

From Vatera the asphalted road heads north towards Polychnitos. After two kilometres there is a petrol station on the right (the owner of which takes a long afternoon siesta) and a turning into the pretty, traditional village of:

VRISSA (52 km from Mitilini) By-passed by the main road, the gently winding High Street is lined by family houses, as well as a number of kafenions and tavernas where a wholesome, simple meal can be obtained.

POLYCHNITOS (46 km from Mitilini) Tel. prefix 0252. Possesses hot springs and, unofficially, the worst signposting on the island. Once enmeshed in the back streets it can prove very difficult to find a way out without local help.

From Polychnitos a road descends to the coastline of the Gulf of Kallonis and:

SKALA POLYCHNITOS (49 km from Mitilini) The port is to the left (*Fsw*) and a long, narrow, grey, sharp sand beach stretches away to the right. The backshore is lined with young, scrawny tamarisk trees. The foreshore is kelpy and the shallow seabed weedy and muddy with some rubbish, including the occasional bicycle frame and chair, thrown in the shallows. There are two beach showers. The straggling village is dusty and unfinished with a pension, tavernas, restaurants and one or two, once grand, houses.

A track makes off west to the coastal hamlet of **Nyfida** and the 'rumour' of a beach.

Back at Polychnitos the main road proceeds east towards:

VASSILIKA (40 km from Mitilini) From the village an unsurfaced road wanders the five kilometres down to **Skala Vassilikon** where legend has it that a boat bearing St. Paul had to anchor up in a storm.

Two kilometres east of Vassilika on the main road and a five kilometre, unsurfaced road angles down to the coastal hamlet of **Achladeri**, beyond which are supposed to be, in the shallows, the earthquake damaged remains of the ancient city of Pira, destroyed in 231 BC.

From Vassilika all the way to beyond the turning off to Agiassos, the olive tree scenery gives way to massed, stately pine trees. In the mountain area a right-hand, unsurfaced track makes off to Ambelikon (*See* previous description of the ROUTE), beyond which is the main turning to:

AGIASSOS (27 km from Mitilini) A very pretty town built on the luxuriant, northern slopes of Mt. Olympos planted out with olive groves, orchards and forests.

The town is famed for the *Icon of the Virgin and Child*, purported to have been brought to the island from Jerusalem in AD803 with some other relics. To house these, in 1170, the Church of Our Lady was built. A replacement church was built in the early 1800s, which was itself replaced by another building in 1814. Not unnaturally, the Church is a famed place of pilgrimage, the major festival climaxing on the 15th August. Strangely enough the healing powers of this icon were not restricted to Greeks as a Turkish official was reported to have been cured by a miracle of the Virgin in 1700, which earned the village a respite from taxes for some eighty years.

Back on the main route, after two kilometres, the road's asphalt surface deteriorates (okay disappears) for a stretch. Beyond the village of **Keramia**, where petrol is available, the route rejoins the Kalloni-Mitilini road.

ROUTE FOUR
To Molivos (62 km). Due to the size of the island it is probably advisable, in order fully to explore Lesbos, to make for the north-west sector and set up an alternative base. Inland Kalloni is of course a possibility but travellers requiring a seaside site can choose from a number of suitable locations including Sigri, Skala Eressou, Anaxos Skoutarou, Petra or Molivos.

Those readers catching the Molivos bus should consider stocking up with emergency supplies as the journey can take quite an inordinate time, including a possible, unscheduled delay at Kalloni coupled with the prospects of a change of bus here (as well as at Petra) and a fuel 'pit stop'.

The route to Molivos takes in:
LAMPOU MILLI (18 km from Mitilini). Here are further remains of the great Roman aqueduct, referred to under Moria (*See* ROUTE TWO).

Close to the large salt pans, on the edge of the Gulf of Kallonis, is a right-hand turning (36 km) to:
AGIA PARASKEVI (40 km from Mitilini). A pleasant, old town around which are scattered a number of archaeological remains including an ancient temple dedicated to Apollo. Apart from the 'standard' town church, there is the Chapel of Ag. Paraskevi located in a cave. Perhaps the town's most interesting feature is the 'Festival of the Bull'. This is celebrated on the last Sunday in May when a bull is ritually sacrificed followed by a 'meal of bull' and amateur horse races in the evening.

From Agia Paraskevi an unsurfaced road advances to the hamlet of **Napi**, some three kilometres away. Along this road, after about one kilometre, a track makes off to the left, in a general north-west (Lafionas village) direction. After some four kilometres in total, the River Tsiknias is spanned by the 'Hanging Bridge', a large, hump backed construction.

N.E. LESBOS
KALLONI (40 km from Mitilini) Tel. prefix 0253. A well spread out village set in a large, fertile, agricultural plain north of the Gulf of Kallonis and a 'way station' for the bus service. Travellers on public transport may well experience long delays here as well as changes of bus, often for no apparent reason.

Accommodation includes the *Hotel Kalloni* (Class C, tel. 22147), and a number of **Rooms** at Skala Kallonis, about four kilometres distant. There are two Banks, an OTE, a Police station, Post Office and a doctor.

The roads in and out of Kalloni are rather muddling and what signposting there is adds to the confusion.

The road northwards ascends, at first gently, out of the village past:
Myrssiniotissas Convent. Founded in 1487, the nuns ran a *Krifo Scholio* – an illegal, 'underground' school where Greek children were taught in the traditional Greek Orthodox ways during the Turkish occupation.

The route now climbs more steeply up and over the heavily wooded Mt. Skoteino. Prior to the Stipsi turning (*See* ROUTE TWO), is the memorial celebrating the Battle of Klapados, where the Turks were finally beaten in 1912, and, a little further on, a building where the surrender was formalised.

The road descends to the coastal plain and:
PETRA (55 km from Mitilini)
Tel. prefix 0253. The main road forms a junction with the Molivos road to the right and the Petra waterfront Esplanade to the left. This untidy junction cum square marks the

right-hand limit (*Fsw*) of Petra's development. There is a petrol station at the junction and a number of the houses, even at this far flung end, are rented to various package holiday companies that have taken over Petra (as well as Molivos, Skala Eressou and Plomari).

The holiday development spreads along the asphalted Esplanade bordering Petra's splendid beach. The foreshore is sandy, the middle and backshore a fine gritty gravel but it is a pity that there are few trees, and thus shade from the pitiless, midday sun. The land side of the Esplanade is lined by a spaced out mix of private houses, gift shops, **Rooms**, restaurants and the *Hotels Petra* & *Ilion*.

The road ends up on the Main Square of the old village, the streets of which approximate to a grid layout. The buildings scramble up the hillside which is topped off by the Church of Panagia tis Glykofilousa (or Our Lady of the Sweet Kiss) impossibly balancing on a pinnacle of rock. The building of this church was inspired by yet another 'mobile' icon, in this case one which refused to stay on a ship. The icon was found on the rock pinnacle for a number of consecutive nights, despite being returned to the boat each time, so the hint was taken and the church constructed on the spot.

Another church, dedicated to St. Nicholas, possesses some truly marvellous 16th century wall paintings completed during the Turkish occupation. There are a number of rather grand houses with large, dressed stone walls and first storey wooden balconies. The grandest of these is the *House of Vareltzidainas*, now fully restored and notable for an interior rich with frescoes, panelling and carved wooden ceilings.

The Main Square is edged by the Esplanade on the sea side, where the taxis rank. On the far side is a taverna/snackbar on the left of which (*Sbo*) a 'character' serves breakfast, and dispenses information including details of **Rooms** from a shed-like periptero. On the near, right-hand corner, where the buses turn round, stands a periptero along from which is the office of the:

Womens Agricultural Tourist Co-operative   Tel. 41238
Directions: As above.

This organisation (also to be found on Chios) is to all intents and purposes, an NTOG office run by Greek 'suffragettes'! The good ladies also run a restaurant/ taverna which is reputed to serve excellent food and therefore should be patronised.

Beyond the co-operative, off to the right from the Main Square, is Ermou St on which are a number of shops, a pharmacy, a foreign language bookshop and a clinic, outside which the waiting patients squat on the pavement. There is a baker and, on the left of the street that leads off the bottom right-hand corner of the Main Square, an OTE and Post Office, side-by-side. The OTE is open weekdays 0730-1510 hrs.

THE ACCOMMODATION & EATING OUT

The Accommodation Do not forget that the Womens Co-operative, on the Main Square, is probably the best bet for locating **Rooms**.

Rooms 'Clean & Furnished'   Tel. 41284/41443
Directions: Located over the pharmacy on Ermou St.

Hotel Petra (Class C)   Tel. 41257
Directions: Situated on the Esplanade.

A single room, en suite, costs 1800 drs and a double room 2500 drs.

The other hotel is the *Ilion*.

One establishment worth a mention is that owned by George Seretis, the:

Indernational (sic) Restaurant & Hotel Tel. 41488
Directions: On the side of the Esplanade road, across from where the tree and oleander edging to the backshore of the beach ends.

Chatty George and his wife spent some of their life in Australia. They serve up a splendid, well cooked, 'English' breakfast. A plateful of bacon, eggs, tomatoes accompanied by toast, butter and two large cups of coffee, costs 550 drs for two. The presence of package tourists booked into their accommodation pushes up the price of a double room, with en suite bathroom, to 2000 drs in mid-season.

To sum up, Petra is certainly a more representative Greek village than its near neighbour Molivos, and does possess a super beach.

From Petra the seven kilometre road proceeds quite close to the coast before dropping down to pass through those olive groves left standing by the builders of the two or three very smart hotels on the left. Beyond the hotels, the road climbs gently to the informal Bus turn-round point (*Tmr* 1B6) on the edge of:

MOLIVOS (Mithimnia, Mythimna): holiday village & port (Illustration 25).
Tel. prefix 0253.

FIRST IMPRESSIONS
Cats; cobbled streets; an unwhitewashed Lindos (Rhodes island); the castle; moni-pos (horse drawn carriages) complete with stereo radio!

SPECIALITIES
Package holiday-makers.

GENERAL
The main cobbled lanes (or 'High Streets') of Molivos, resembling the shutes of the old fashioned, penny slot machines, zig-zag up and down the very steep sides of the castle topped, cone shaped hill. The lanes may not be whitewashed, as are those of other tourist popular seaside resorts, but they are, for long stretches, prettily shaded by a thick matt of trellis supported vines and wisteria. Incidentally the cobbles are very uneven so high heels should be left at home. Due to the steepness of the by-ways and alleys, those with a weak heart should consider other venues.

THE ACCOMMODATION & EATING OUT
The Accommodation Visitors arriving by bus are beseiged and harried by 'landladies' as they disembark. Unfortunately choice is not only potluck in respect of a room's price and condition but more importantly position, as accommodation accepted might well be one of those tucked in way up at the foot of the Castle walls foundations. However there is the:
Municipal Tourist Office (*Tmr* 2B5) Tel. 71313
Directions: On the left (sea to the left), a stride or three beyond the Bus turn-round junction and alongside Odhos Parodos Possidonos that slopes down to the waterfront.

Apparently funded by the worthy citizens of Molivos. The titular head appears to be the oft present mayor, Costas Doukas, but the driving force is the efficient and smart Maria, who speaks excellent English. She will, in an atmosphere of comparative peace, locate rooms and place enquirers. Maria takes the job very seriously and callers who have not used the office's accommodation services may well be gently 'grilled' as to where they are staying. This is probably only a harmless check on 'moonlighting' landladies! The clean, spartan office is a single storey building. One of the wall posters is rather forceful (forceful that is to the normal male chauvinist pig)

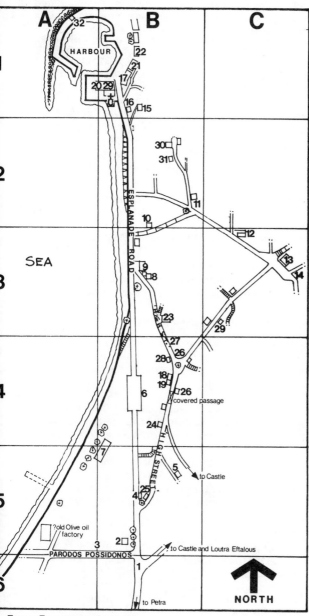

Tmr

1 Bus turn-round B6
2 Municipal Tourist office B5
3 Guest house Poseidon A/B5/6
4 Rent-A-Scooter B5
5 Nasos Guest House B5
6 Coach Park B4
7 Hotel Molyvos A/B4/5
8 Virginia's Rooms B3
9 Bank B3
10 Bike Hire – Powered B2/3
11 Rooms B2
12 Rooms C2/3
13 Bakers C3
14 Rooms C3
15 Youth Hostel Pension B1
16 Restaurant/Rooms B1
17 Hotel Sea Horse B1
18 Restaurant TO ΜΟΥΛΑΡΙ B4
19 OTE B4
20 Kafenion/Taverna A/B1
21 To Limani B1
22 Port police B1
23 Ο'ΝΑΣΟΣ B3
24 Galaktopoleio B4
25 Just Rent A Bike B5
26 Butchers B4
27 Vegetable shop B3/4
28 Cigarette shop B4
29 Pharmacy C3
30 Town police B2
31 Post Office B2
32 Public toilets A1

Tmr = Town map reference
Fsw = Facing seawards
Sbo = Sea behind one

Illustration 25 Molivos Village & Port

226

depicting a purposeful, chin-jutting lady representing all those Greek women who clandestinely fought for the nation's release from Nazi domination. Damned uncomfortable really! The office opens daily between 0900 - 1330 & 1400 - 1700 hrs until the height of season, when siesta is skipped. A most laudable institution.

For those who want to have an indication of what is on offer, the following provides a guide and only represents the tip of the 'domatio' available. Many likely looking places are increasingly let to package holiday firms and English companies predominate. Prices for accommodation are on the high side even for the N.E. Aegean, on the other hand the standards are good to excellent. For instance mid-season double room rates average between 1000-1200 drs and 1350-1500 drs.

On the approach to Molivos are the very smart hotels, the *Delfinia* (Class B), and the *Ariana*. They are followed by the *Pansion Garden* (sic) on the right (from the Petra direction) and situated in a large, tree planted garden prior to the Sikamia country track joining the road.

Guest House Poseidon (*Tmr* 3A/B5/6) (Class B) 2 Parodos Possidonos Tel. 71570
Directions: Along the street that branches off towards the sea from close to the Bus turn-round (*Tmr* 1B6), and on the right.

All rooms have en suite bathrooms with a single costing 1400 drs a night and a double 1700 drs rising to 2100 drs and 2500 drs respectively (1st July - 15th Sept). A continental breakfast costs 180 drs.

Back on the main Esplanade and alongside the Rent-A-Scooter building (*Tmr* 4B5), one of the 'High St' lanes that steeply angles up the hillside, climbs to the right.

Nasos Guest House (*Tmr* 5B5)
Directions: As above, first turning off to the right and on the left.

From the Bus turn-round (*Tmr* 1B6), the main road or Esplanade parallels the seashore all the way to the Harbour Square. It climbs gently upwards to a point significantly above sea-level and then slopes gently down to the harbour. On the first stretch and below the road, to the left, is the:

Hotel Molyvos (*Tmr* 7A/B4/5)   Tel. 71386/71534
Directions: As above. Beyond the massive Coach Park (*Tmr* 6B4) that has been carved out of the hillside, are, on the left, backward angled steps down to a path that tracks along parallel to the sea. The hotel is set close to the backshore of the narrow, pebble beach.

A single room en suite costs 1800 drs and a double room 2400 drs rising respectively to 2250 drs and 3230 drs (1st July - 15th Sept).

Readers planning to telephone, and requiring a seafront location, must ensure that this *'Hotel Molivos'* is the one alongside the beach as there are two hotels with this name under the same ownership.

Virginia's Rooms (*Tmr* 8B3)   Tel. 71281
Directions: Close to the apex of the Esplanade rise and on the right. The house is flanked by a large tree and a Bank (*Tmr* 9B3), and is at the outset of a major lane, or 'High Street', that angles back up the hillside, linking up with the other primary 'High St'.

This is the dwelling of Virginia Milonas, set in a small, pretty garden. Virginia lived in the USA with her family for some years so speaks English, if hesitantly. She selects her guests and, although the bathroom is not en suite, as she only lets out one room at a time this does not prove much of a problem. The bath and shower water is hot and the bedroom is very comfortable with an exceedingly pleasant balcony looking out over the Esplanade and the sea. On the other hand the charges are not inexpensive at 1500 drs mid-season, rising to 2000 drs.

Proceeding on from the Bank (*Tmr* 9B3) the next (stepped) lane on the right of the Esplanade and signposted *We Rent Bicycles*, scrambles up the hillside from alongside a restaurant/taverna. Prior to the junction with another lane climbing up from the Esplanade, there is a Bike Hire outfit (*Tmr* 10B2/3), almost next door to which are two houses in which accommodation is available.

Further on up the incline is:
Rooms (*Tmr* 11B2)
Directions: At the junction of the two lanes rising up from the Esplanade, described above, down the hillside a step or two and in the lane branching off to the right (now *Fsw*). On the right is the large, Palladian fronted house.

Back to the climb up the steep gradient and on the left is:
Rooms (*Tmr* 12C2/3)   Tel. 71403 *Directions:* As above.
   Nikolaos Prokopiou is the proprietor and his house is set in a lovely, walled courtyard.

Rooms (*Tmr* 14C3)
Directions: Further on up the lane is an irregular square with a Bakers (*Tmr* 13C3) on the left. The accommodation is a pace or three from the square and on the left.

Back on the Esplanade, which now commences to slope down towards the harbour, is the:
Youth Hostel Pension (*Tmr* 15B1)
Directions: Not actually on the side of the Esplanade but along a track off to the right indicated by painted signs, in four languages, on a static, wrecked green car. The track leads through tall gates, becoming a rough path, all the way up to the front porch. Inside the open sided porch is a plethora of authoritative information should the owners be absent. This includes a schematic layout of the house with the price of each room (between 975-1350 drs for a double room) and how many nights are available, all in three languages. The owners operate an informal book swap scheme.

Continuing on towards the harbour from the Youth Hostel track and the Esplanade passes, on the right, the:
Restaurant/Rooms (*Tmr* 16B1)
Directions: As above.
   The accommodation is on the first floor over a snappy and rather expensive restaurant, conspicuous by a caged, noisy Mynah bird.

The Esplanade winds down through a terrace of houses and opens out on to the pretty harbour quay square.

Hotel Sea Horse (*Tmr* 17B1) (Class B)   Tel. 71320
Directions: As above and on the right. A smart hotel despite which it is in keeping with the other quay-side buildings and, perhaps even more pertinently, does not overshadow them.
   A splendid location which is reflected in the en suite room rates of 2000 drs for a single room and 2400 drs for a double room rising to 2350 drs and 2850 drs (1st July - 30th Sept). An English breakfast can be ordered by non residents but the service ends at 0930 hrs. A couple of Nes meh ghala (70 drs each) and an ouzo (60 drs) costs 200 drs. It is a pity the management see fit to block off the swallow/house martins nests, rather than place a box beneath them, as do the villagers on Chios.

For further details of accommodation *See* **Beaches, A to Z.**

The Eating Out. Considering the number of tourists it is not surprising that

there are a large number of eating places but sadly few that are fully satisfactory. Some serve poor food, some are extremely expensive and some suffer from both drawbacks. Once a choice is made diners should arrive early because the popular places get crowded out.

An example of the lacklustre is the:

Restaurant To ΜΟΥΛΑΡΙ (*Tmr* 18B4)

Directions: Close to the OTE (*Tmr* 19B4), on the 'commercial stretch' of the southern 'High St'.

The owner finds it very difficult to raise any enthusiasm even out of the height of the season. The food is usually, if not always, served cold at both midday and evening sittings. This is a pity as the menu includes briam and 'giants' (beans). A meal here for two of a plate of pistachio (192 drs), a helping of briam (145 drs), beans (125 drs), a bottle of retsina (67 drs) and bread (20 drs) costs 549 drs.

Apart from the general attractiveness of the location, the most reasonable establishments are gathered round the harbour quay and include the:

Kafenion/Taverna (*Tmr* 20A/B1)

Directions: On the far left of the harbour (*Fsw*), close to the rather narrow harbour entrance. The tables and chairs are spread along the quay wall.

Not a wide variety but the food is freshly cooked daily. A meal for two, in splendid surroundings, varies in cost between 600 and 1000 drs. For instance 2 spaghetti bolognese, a Greek salad, a bottle of retsina, a beer and bread costs 660 drs. Nine hundred and fifty drachmae purchases 2 plates of grilled liver (185 drs each), a plate of white beans (110 drs), patatas (60 drs), 2 bottles of retsina (68 drs each), a beer (70 drs), 2 Nes meh ghala (100 drs), 2 Greek coffees (68 drs) and bread (16 drs).

To Limani (*Tmr* 21B1)

Directions: Not far to go from the establishment above as the taverna is next door to the *Hotel Sea Horse*.

This restaurant is so popular that the *cognoscenti* form queues early in the evening. The narrow fronted building, with a glass display cabinet on the left as clients enter, is across the way from the tables and chairs edging the harbour wall. The *To Limani* opens at lunchtimes. Interestingly enough the restaurant serves a 'new' dish to me, namely 'Zucchinni Pie' – a look-alike for a quiche made of zucchinis. A plate of stuffed zucchini, complete with lemon sauce and meat (yes meat filling, 194 drs) a Greek salad (167 drs), bread for two (16 drs) and 2 beers (74 drs) costs 525 drs. A zucchinni pie (245 drs), meat balls (145 drs), beans (194 drs), Greek salad (167 drs), a bottle of retsina (72 drs) and bread for two (8 drs*) costs 831 drs.

I know, I know it should be 16 drs so the bill would total 839 drs!

Continuing on round the harbour quay are two other tavernas on either side the office of the Port police (*Tmr* 22B1).

Back towards the centre of Molivos, up the southern 'High Streets' is:

Ο ΝΙΣΟΣ (*Tmr* 23B3)

Directions: Halfway up the 'High St' lane at the outset of which is situated *Virginia's Rooms* (*Tmr* 8B3). Ο ΝΙΣΟΣ is two doors before (or beyond, depending on the direction of travel) the *Spaghetti Marinara* (which is fitted out with ghastly, white topped tables and benches).

Mine host speaks good English and the popular restaurant is noted for it's vegetarian dishes. There is a wide range of meals and vegetables on offer with budget meals as well as the to be expected, expensive fish dishes.

Galaktopoleio (*Tmr* 24B4)

Directions: On the southern 'High St' lane, down the slope towards the Bus turn-round, beyond the OTE (*Tmr* 19B4) and on the right.

Outwardly a normal Galaktopoleio but clients who bother to wander through the shop find a pleasant surprise out the back – a small, shaded balcony terrace. This is suspended high up on the steep, almost vertical cliff-face looking out over the Esplanade, coastline and the sea. The proprietors serve a very good cup of coffee (55 drs) and loukoumades (80 drs) as well as a continental or eggs breakfast (served on a 'silver' plate). Down a flight of spiral steps, inside the shop, is a 'super loo' and shower.

THE A TO Z OF USEFUL INFORMATION

BANKS. There is one, the **National Bank of Greece** (*Tmr* 9B3) on the Esplanade. Usual hours.

BEACHES. A narrow, large pebble beach stretches from about the middle of the village to the left (*Fsw*) all the way on past a spit of land in the distance. The foreshore is grey shingle and the first metre or so of the gently shelving seabed is made up of pebbles which happily changes to grey sand. The sea is clear but the beach gets littered with some wind blown bits and pieces which rather surprisingly are left where they land, even in the vicinity of the *Hotel Molyvos*. Close to the old olive factory(?) (*Tmr* A5), the hyperactive are catered for with the provision of water-skiing, parascending and surfboards. To the right of the *Hotel Molyvos* (*Fsw*) are changing rooms and a beach shower, beyond which is a beach taverna. On a note of warning, there is a band of sea urchins easily visible on the sea bed which it is best to locate in order to remember their position.

Beyond Molivos, branching off the Castle road, is an unmade track stretching along the coast for some six kilometres to **Loutra Eftalous**. This track passes three coves, around the first two of which are some smart hotels. Only the last two coves are suitable for swimming but the beaches are definitely substandard being narrow and made up of grey, gritty sand with some rubbish. The third or last cove is hemmed in by the walls of old buildings, two of which are thermal establishments. More hotels would appear to be in the planning stage along this backwater.

BICYCLE, SCOOTER & CAR HIRE Car hire can be arranged through one of the offices of the various package holiday firms. They are present to look after their clients' well-being, and are conveniently located on the side of the Esplanade, between the Municipal Tourist office (*Tmr* 2B5) and the Coach Park (*Tmr* 6B4).

Scooter and motorbike hire is expensive and available from a number of firms including:
Just Rent-A-Bike (*Tmr* 25B5)
Directions: Located on the left, at the outset of the southern 'High St' lane, up the hillside from the area of the Bus turn-round (*Tmr* 1B6).

The office is run by a superior young lady, teutonic in character but Dutch by birth! The apparent efficiency is rather offset by the mechanic allowing scooters to go out on hire with malfunctions. A Vespa costs 1500 drs a day and the firm accepts payment by *Carte Bleu*.

Rent-A-Scooter (*Tmr* 4B5).
Directions: The house containing the office is on the corner site formed by the Esplanade and the southern 'High St' lane, next door to **Just Rent-A-Bike**. They hire out motorbikes as well as scooters.

Another firm (*Tmr* 10B2/3), labelling itself *Bike Hire – powered/State of Life*, is tucked away on the stepped lane off the Esplanade, from which it is signposted.

BREAD SHOPS There is a baker (*Tmr* 13C3) up the steep lane from the Esplanade signed *Police, Post*. The shop also sells yoghurt and some other dairy products but the opening hours are rather a mystery. They certainly open for an hour or two early in the morning.

BUSES Pull up and turn-round on the informal square (*Tmr* 1B6) at the entry to the village, where the Castle road circles off to the right of the hill.

For details of the schedules *See* **Bus timetables, A to Z, Mitilini**. But the best source of information is the Tourist office (*Tmr* 2B5). It is worth noting that as far as the worthy citizens of Molivos are concerned the last bus back to Mitilini (except perhaps during the height of the season months) is at 1300 hrs and not the 1600 hrs.

COMMERCIAL SHOPPING AREA Most of the village shops line the two 'High St' lanes that 'junction' on the hillside. Both lanes start off on the Esplanade, one angling up from close by the Tourist office (*Tmr* 2B6) and the other from close by the Bank (*Tmr* 9B3). The shops, which are concentrated towards the junction of the ways, are interspersed by gift shops, the odd boutique and eating establishments. They include two butchers (*Tmr* 26B4), a 'front room' vegetable shop (*Tmr* 27B3/4) and a shop selling cigarettes (*Tmr* 28B4).

MEDICAL CARE
Doctor *See* **Telephone Numbers & Addresses.**
Pharmacy (*Tmr* 29C4). On the right of the steep, shaded lane that continues up from the 'High St' 'junction of the ways'.

NTOG. *See* **The Accommodation** for details of the excellent Tourist office (*Tmr* 2B5).

OTE (*Tmr* 19B4). Certainly open weekdays between 0800-1200 hrs with a possibility of opening between 1600-2000 hrs.

PETROL *See* **Petra.**

PLACES OF INTEREST
The Castle. Genoese built, in the 14th century, on the top of the hill, and around the western flanks of which the village is draped. The hilltop was the site of an ancient acropolis. Probably worth the climb if only for the exercise. The walls are lit at night time, during the summer, and present a marvellous sight.

POLICE
Port (*Tmr* 22B1) Not unnaturally, on the harbour quay.
Town (*Tmr* 30B2) The hill climbing lane off the Esplanade is signposted *Police, Post*. Turn left along the second street and their office is to the left of a neglected square, beyond the Post office (*Tmr* 31B2) and a Turkish fountain. The building blocks off the end of the passage.

POST OFFICE (*Tmr* 31B2). *See* **Town police** for directions. The office is housed in a 'dinky' little building, almost dwarfed by the nearby Turkish fountain. There is a post box on the side of the *Hotel Sea Horse* (*Tmr* 17B1).

TAXIS *See* **Telephone Numbers & Addresses.**

TELEPHONE NUMBERS & ADDRESSES

Doctor	Tel. 71333
Police (*Tmr* 30B2)	Tel. 71222
Taxis	Tel. 71285, 71322

TOILETS A small, eye watering, 'Richter Scale 10', Public toilet block (*Tmr* 32A1) on the far edge of the harbour wall. *See* **Galaktopoleio** (*Tmr* 24B4), **The Eating Out** for a centrally located facility.

TRAVEL AGENTS Naturally the Municipal Tourist office (*Tmr* 2B5), detailed under **The Accommodation**, supplies much information.

The couple of very active tour offices representing the various package holiday companies ensure that their clients enjoy a fun packed itinerary of delights, including trips, expeditions and excursions. I was not sorry, in 1986, to have missed the *Darts Competition Night Out at the Castro Bar*, but there you go.

ROUTE FIVE
To Skala Eressou via Kalloni, Parakila & back via Eressos & Antissa (circa 140 km).
The first part of the route has been discoursed upon under ROUTE FOUR. After Kalloni (22 km from Molivos), the road proceeds in a southerly direction to the coast bordering the Gulf of Kalloni. Keeping to the left leads through the hamlets of **Kerami** and **Papiana** to:
SKALA KALLONIS (27 km from Molivos). The small fishing port hamlet of Kalloni.

It is possible to cut across from Papiana to the Kalloni-Parakila road or keep right at the fork, where a track branches off to the left to the hamlet of **Ariana.**

The main road skirts the Gulf, crossing a wide, marshy area either side of a low bridged river and yet another bridge over the River Potamia. The coastline becomes rocky but is very pretty. Prior to the road striking inland, there are a couple of small coves, one with a beach taverna.

PARAKILA (34 km from Molivos) A rural, tree shaded village. From hereon the road surface is unmade and the countryside barren and stony.
After about ten kilometres, to the left, is a lovely view down over the fishing hamlet of Apothikes, a small islet and the far side of the Gulf of Kalloni, the neck of water being quite narrow here. A very rough track bumps down to the fishing hamlet of:
APOTHIKES (46 km from Molivos) Depending on one's viewpoint either a dump with chickens scratching about the unmade pathways, or an unspoilt, rustic, traditional fishing village with one or two kafenions.

The unsurfaced road climbs up the valley, past a 'false trail' turning off to the left, before winding up into the large, mountainside village of **Agra** (52 km from Molivos). The other side of Agra, the road passes through a small forest and then breaks out on to rather arid mountainsides before dropping down and bypassing:
MESSOTOPOS (60 km from Molivos) This village is situated some 200m above sea level. A track winds the four or so kilometres down to the seaside hamlet of **Tavari** (64 km from Molivos) where there is supposed to be a worthwhile beach, but I doubt it.

From Messotopos the road bumps on ten kilometres or so to a junction with the main Antissa-Skala Eressou road. Right leads to the inland village of **Eressos**. To the left a section of the road passes through a lovely avenue of lime trees to the seaside village (and port for Eressos) of:
SKALA ERESSOU (74 km from Molivos) Tel. prefix 0253. Rather reminiscent of Kardamena (Kos island in the Dodecanese) but suffering less tourist exposure, to

date. The magnificent, wide sweep of sandy beach, some two and a half kilometres long, edging the clear blue sea ensures that Skala Eressou will become ever increasingly popular with the tour operators.

The streets of the narrow village follow a grid layout with an annoying one-way system which finally allows a traveller to decant on to the beach-fronting Main Square. The back of this large square is lined with restaurant/tavernas. An Esplanade, sketchily edged by the occasional gift shop, bar or cafe, stretches away to the left (*Fsw*) after crossing a dry river-bed. There are a couple of abandoned changing cubicles on the backshore of this section of the beach.

Pedaloes and windsurfers are hired out and there is a 'free-entrance' disco which, I am reliably informed, hots up as the night wears on.

Accommodation includes the *Hotel Sappho The Eressia* (Class C, tel. 53233), the:
Hotel Alkeos (Class E)   Tel. 53311
Rooms are complete with en suite bathrooms. A single room costs 1500 drs a night and a double room, 2000 drs.
and the:
Hotel Minavra (Class E)   Tel. 53202
Only double rooms sharing the bathroom which cost 900 drs rising to 1300 drs (16th May - 15th Oct).

Rooms available include those of *George Cordoutis* (Tel. 53322); *Rooms* (Tel. 53276) to the right on the way into the resort and *Rooms*, one back from the waterfront by the **Just Scooter** office. There are more ***Rooms*** advertised at the **Gift Shop Lukas** which edges the backshore, around the corner to the right from the Main Square (*Fsw*). Further information of ***Rooms*** is available at the Main Square periptero.

The impecunious sleep out on the beach at night, a number that increases greatly during the height of season months. I am advised that a high percentage are 'camps' of lesbians. This perhaps explains the preponderance of 'butch' ladies carrying out 'meaningful' heart-to-heart conversations with their female companions, night and day at the waterfront taverna/restaurants.

Shopping is catered for by one mini and two supermarkets (really large general stores). The first supermarket, passed on the way into Skala, sells fresh bread daily and possesses a metered phone. There is another pay phone in a private house (somewhere!).

A mobile bank bus is scheduled to arrive at 1000 hrs daily during the summer months. The doors are thrown open for one hour, and one hour only, after which they clang shut leaving the often long queues to disperse. Those 'caught short' then have to revert to the change facilities offered by many of the local cafe-bars. For postal and OTE services it is necessary to go to Eressos village.

There is a track from Skala Eressou around to Sigri (*See* ROUTE SIX) but it is extremely rocky at the Sigri end and should only be undertaken by intrepid travellers. More importantly, if mounted in or on transport, it is essential that there is no chance of having to settle the damage claims which will (note, not may) be incurred.

The asphalted road from the village of Eressos to the main Kalloni road climbs up through lovely countryside edged by 'rivers' of oleanders that fill the gorges and river-beds. For the rest of the journey *See* ROUTE SIX.

ROUTE SIX
To Sigri via Skoutaros, Skalochori & Antissa (137 km) From
Molivos proceed to Petra (*See* ROUTE FOUR) where take the Esplanade road along the waterfront and keep going past the Main Square. The road surface is unmade all the way to Skalochori.

ANAXOS SKOUTAROU (11 km from Molivos) The scrubbly hamlet of Anaxos is the antithesis to Petra, from which it could be a million miles away – not four kilometres. A track leads down to a beach of coarse sand with pebbles edging a steeply shelving seabed. Three rustic tavernas are spread along the backshore and there are beach showers and changing huts.

SKOUTAROS (14 km from Molivos) Keep to the right at this large village. The surfaced section of road prior to Skoutaros is only there to deceive as the stretch of flint and boulder between Skoutaros and Skalochori, laughingly referred to as a road, is probably the second worst I have ever travelled on any Greek island (Karpathos in the Dodecanese taking the 'Golden Unasphalted' award). Apart from the appalling surface, or more correctly lack of surface, there are a number of very, very dangerous concrete culverts sticking up proud of the road, which if driven over at any speed resembles running into a brick wall.

Heralding the approach to Skalochori is the unusual sight of a sizeable pond set in a large rock surround to the right, soon after which is:

SKALOCHORI (30 km from Molivos) A pleasant agricultural village where thankfully a junction is made with the main Kalloni-Sigri road. Petrol is available.

The route passes through the village of **Vatoussa** (39 km) and off to the right, the:
Monastery of Perivolis (about 45 km from Molivos) Built in the 16th century, the building possesses a number of murals dating back to the foundation.

Two kilometres prior to Antissa, an initially asphalted branch road, which deteriorates into an unsurfaced track at about half distance, runs down through olive groves to the coastal fishing port of:

GAVATHAS (50 km from Molivos) The track joins the semicircular bay at the right-hand side (*Fsw*) and, turning left, runs along the scrubbly backshore of a broad, sandy beach. The beach becomes very kelpy towards the dusty, unimpressive, hill peninsula mounted settlement. The village overlooks the surprisingly large harbour, built into the crook of the land, and a church topping a rock bluff. There is a rather deserted feel to the location.

Some two kilometres down the Gavathas road a track makes off to the right to the site of the ancient town of Antissa.

Back on the main road is:
ANTISSA (48 km from Molivos) A large prosperous village, built on the mountainside, which took it's name from the ancient coastal town, some eight or nine kilometres to the north. Petrol is available and there is an E class hotel, the *Athina* with single rooms costing 600 drs and double rooms 1500 drs, both sharing the bathrooms.

About two kilometres beyond Antissa the left-hand road progresses down to Skala Eressou (*See* ROUTE FIVE) and the right-hand turning leads across the now rolling, mountain moorland countryside on a saddle of land. Three kilometres further on and a path climbs up to the mountain top sited:
Monastery Ipsilou (53 km from Molivos) Founded in the 9th century AD by St. John the Sigrian and rebuilt in the 12th century. The monastery was the final objective, over the centuries, of plundering raids but was restored in 1971. On show are the 'usual' mixture of icons, manuscripts, stone encrusted crosses, saints' reliquaries (a *nom de plume* for bits of knuckles, fingers and other bones) as well as a number of gold objects and embroidery.

The moorland road, high on the side of Mt. Ordymnos, finally tops a crest by some farm buildings on the left, to look out over the indented coastline, the inshore island of Megalonissi with its accompanying islets and the port and village of:

SIGRI (66 km from Molivos) Tel. prefix 0251. The road joins the coast to the right of the bay on which Sigri is located and proceeds into 'town'. The road passes on the left, a ('dead'?) Information office and a hotel/restaurant prior to spilling on to an irregular square at the outset of the village. To the front is a pleasant cafe-bar/taverna, which serves a nice line in octopus snacks. To the right is a small craft harbour, beyond which is a wasteland area edged by a quay wall. This is obviously destined to be the subject of extensive civil engineering works at some time in the future. Quite often a Naval vessel moors up against the far quay. To the left is the Main Square, the right-hand side (*Sbo*) of which is edged by the High Street.

At the top of the Square is the *Restaurant Australia*, no doubt run by an islander who has returned to his home island after a sojourn 'down under'. The High St rises up the low hill on which Sigri stands, leaving, to the right, a ruined Turkish Castle built in 1757. The High St proceeds on through the centre of the village over to a neat, tree lined, semicircular cove which is rimmed by a grey sand beach. Although the beach is rather dank in the middle it is super at both ends where it broadens out to become banked, sandy sections. This is a most pleasant spot with the additional luxury of changing cubicles.

There is a Post Office, a baker, plenty of kafenions, cafe-bars and tavernas. Accommodation is available at the *Restaurant Macedonia*, a number of **Rooms** as well as the:

Hotel Nisiope (Class B)   Tel. 22340
Really a pension. Single rooms start at 900 drs, sharing a bathroom, double rooms 1500 drs sharing and 1700 drs en suite. These rates rise to 1100 drs for a single and 1800/2100 drs for double rooms. (1st July – 30th Sept).

If all the above were not enough to make Sigri a 'find', a super spot with not a package hotel in sight, there are further delights even if they do require a few kilometres travel. Prior to the main road reaching the coast, a flat, dirt track makes off to the right, in a northerly direction parallel to the seashore past the site of an old Castle (Palaikastro). A left-hand path branches down to the coast and a wild cove, part of a large bay. To the left are rocky outcrops and to the right, towards a high rock bluff, is a sandy beach with a foreshore of tiny pebbles. The rock outcrop has a platform on the far side making an ideal spot for large picnic parties. The rest of the magnificent, large bay opens out on to a very sandy, broad beach with a gritty foreshore. In the middle of the bay's backshore is the small Chapel of Our Lady of Revelation, set on a small hillock.

A river still trickling for most of the summer runs out on to the sands of the beach. The tree shaded river-bed is well worth a stealthy investigation for it is a wild life sanctuary. Tiny turtles breast stroke about the still pools over which dart and colour-flash large kingfishers.

Over the mountainsides stretching north and south of Sigri are the scattered remains of a large, petrified forest resulting from volcanic action in prehistory. Few of the stumps are left standing, most of the remaining trunks lying on the ground. It is pro-bably best to observe these phenomena where they are displayed, which includes Sigri, rather than tramp the countryside.

A most fitting location at which to end the description of an island of such wide contrasts.

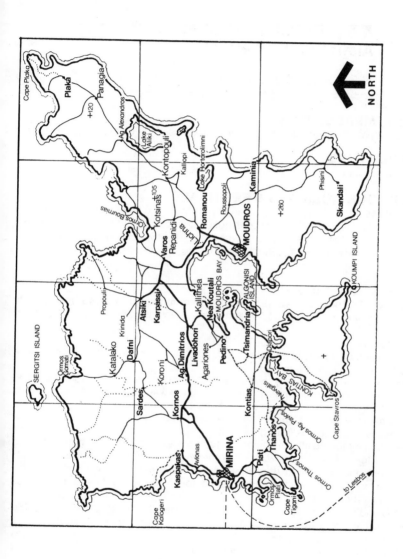

Illustration 26 Limnos island

16 LIMNOS (Lemnos)

& Ag. Estratios (Evstratios, Aistrates, Efstratios)

Mirina port & surrounds ★★★★★

Rest of island ★★★

★★

N.E. AEGEAN ISLANDS

FIRST IMPRESSIONS
Golden wheat; cows; horses; prairies; wind; poor roads; tortoises; Army; water short.

SPECIALITIES
Red & white wine.

RELIGIOUS HOLIDAYS & FESTIVALS
include: 21st April – Horse races, Kalliopi; 21st May – Pig fair, Pamanou; 20th July – Festival of Profitis Helias, Kornos; 26th July – Festival of Ag. Paraskevi, Thanos; 6th August – Festival of Sotiras, Plaka; 23rd August – Festival of Panagia, Kornos; 23rd August – Festival of Panagia, Repanidi; 30th November – Festival of Ag. Andreas, Kornos.

VITAL STATISTICS
Tel. prefix 0254. The island is approximately 60 km from side to side, 46 km from north to south with an area of 475 sq km and a population of some 16,000.

HISTORY
The mythological associations are much more interesting than the recent history, recent that is in historical terms.

The island was supposedly the home of Hephaistos or Vulcan, God of fire and metal workers. Perhaps far more riveting (!) is that he was also the patron of cuckolds because his wife, Venus (or Aphrodite), was having it away with Mars! Nudge, nudge, wink, wink. The worthy citzens of Limnos were supposed to have softened the fall of Hephaistos, when he was hurled from Mt Olympos by Zeus, thus he only broke his leg. Another intriguing little mythological footnote is that Limnian women killed their husbands for mass infidelity, not taking other men to their beds until the Argonauts put into port. Maybe this was the origination of the old, catchy song 'All the nice girls love a sailor'? Or on the other hand, maybe not. Certainly the deed of muder was encapsulated in the saying 'Limnian deeds' to indicate barbarous actions.

The island's culture and development was closely tied in with that of Troy. The Athenians held sway over the island off and on for some five or six hundred years, with Rome interfering every so often. After the lawlessness of the 4th – 6th centuries AD,the Byzantine empire ruled , a suzerainity interrupted by Venetian dominance for 70 or 80 years. The Venetians were followed by the Genoese who spent a few years in occupation only to be supplanted by , successively, Venetian, Turkish and Venetian forces. In 1478 the Turks settled the matter and did not yield until Limnos was united with Greece in 1912. The island was used during the First World War as a staging post for the ill-fated Allied Expeditionary Forces assault on the Dardanelles. Mark you the hidden hand of Turkish influence still dominates Limnos to this day because of the position of the island in relation to the Straits of Dardanelles.

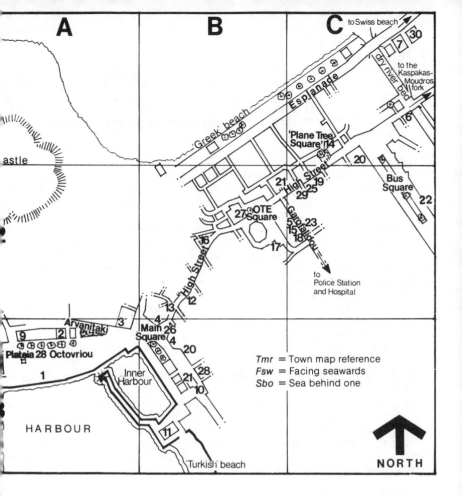

Ferry-boat quay A3
Hotel Limnos A3
Hotel Aktaion A2/3
Kafenion/Cafe-bars B2/3
Hotel Sevdalis B/C2
Pension Tsakiris C1
Hotel Castro Beach C1
Taverna Avra A3
Taverna Ackoali A3
Fish Taverna Lakis B3
Fish Taverna O Glaros B3
Zacharoplasteion 'Loukoumades' B2
Turkish fountain B2/3
Taverna Ο ΠΛΑΤΑΝΟΣ C1
Airline office & terminus B/C2

16 Bank B2
17 OTE B2
18 Post Office B/C2
19 Rent A Car Lemnos/Petridou Tours C1/2
20 Bookshops
21 Bread shops
22 Bus office C2
23 Cinema C2
24 General store/drink shop B/C2
25 Grocer C1/2
26 Supermarket B2/3
27 Greengrocer B2
28 Ferry-boat ticket office B3
29 Dry cleaners B/C2
30 Museum C1
31 Port police & Customs A3

Illustration 27 Mirina Town & Port

238

GENERAL

A lowland island hardly posses :ing a decent hill let alone a mountain, with an abundance of farm animals and wheat fields. This is despite Limnos being drier than its lush, southern neighbours in the N.E. Aegean chain. The lack of water causes the yellowy-brown colour of the summer countryside. Whatever minor disruptions might be caused by the water shortage, nothing can detract from the excellence of the beaches, more especially those adjacent to the port and capital of Mirina. Added to this Mirina Town has the advantage of being more intimate, rather Cycladean in layout, than the other capitals of the larger islands in the group. First impressions include the picturesque inner caique harbour and a medieval fort encasing the hill overlooking the port. The visual impact is strengthened by the pleasant mix of old and new dwellings edging the commercial High Street, that snakes the length of the town.

The dearth of good roads and the lack of attractive villages throughout the island is matched by a public transport system that hardly inspires travel. But why bother travelling to far flung locations as long as the nearby villages and beaches of Plati and Thanos and the large expanse of beach at Nevgatis are visited? For those with adventure in mind, the walk north of the port through and beyond Kaspakas round some five or six bays and coves will not disappoint.

Ignore the denigrators who insist otherwise, this is an island that must not on any account be left off the schedule but note that only the months of July and August are regarded as the 'proper' holiday period.

Here, as in Lesbos, German is the commonest foreign language.

MIRINA (Myrina, Kastron): capital town & main port
(Illustration 27)
Of all the N.E. Aegean ports this is certainly the most picturesque and intimate, especially to visitors who arrive by Ferry-boat.

A pleasant evening spectacle is to watch the fishermen rowing out to sea in their 'sardine' benzines (small boats), over the stern of which are suspended very large, multi-lamps lit once the fishing grounds are reached. The light attracts the sardines and, hey presto, they are netted.

ARRIVAL BY AIR
The airport is set in a large agricultural plain, much of which is planted out to wheat. That which isn't hosts a number of Army camps which are dotted about the landscape. The island's airfield, dominated by the Airforce, is some nineteen kilometres distant from Mirina. Naturally an Olympic bus is available to make the connection.

ARRIVAL BY FERRY
The Ferry-boats moor up (*Tmr* 1A3) on a section of the large commercial quay edging the main harbour. The area, named Plateia 28th Octovriou, is the least attractive of the port.

Buses do not park up on the quay but 'terminus' at the far end of the town on an elongated rectangular Square (*Tmr* C1/2). However for reasons that will become plain this does not matter overmuch.

Due to the small number of **Rooms** available, incoming Ferry-boat travellers are not exactly overwhelmed by eager, anxious owners of accommodation.

THE ACCOMMODATION & EATING OUT

The Accommodation. For such a large island, it is difficult to get used to the fact that there are comparatively few tourists. That is apart from those corralled at the *Akti Marina*, a specialist facility of which more later. The lack of visitors is not a bad thing as it is necessary to accept that there are few **Rooms** available and hotels are rather expensive.

Hotel Limnos (ΛΗΜΝΟΣ) *(Tmr* 2A3) (Class C) Plateia 28th Octovriou   Tel. 22153
Directions: A large, modern hotel, across the broad square from the Ferry-boat quay.
   There are rumours that the moral horizons of some of the female residents of the hotel are not all that they should be... Probably it depends on one's viewpoint! A single room sharing a bathroom costs 1500 drs, a double room 2000 drs and an en suite room 2300 drs.

Hotel Aktaion *(Tmr* 3A2/3) (Class D) 2 Arvanitaki   Tel. 22258
Directions: From the Ferry-boat quay (*Tmr* 1A3) turn right along the harbour wall. The hotel is in a block, opposite the north corner of the pretty inner caique harbour, on the edge of the Main Square.
   A single room sharing a bathroom costs 1200 drs, a double room 1800 drs sharing and 2200 drs en suite.

Also in this block, around the corner facing the Main Square, is a greengrocer with a notice *Room to Let, Tel. 23261.*

From between the two lively, local kafenion/cafe-bars (*Tmr* 4B2/3) the High Street charmingly wanders off winding through the town. Beyond 'OTE' Square (*Tmr* B2) and off to the right is Garofalidou St, whereon are two modern hotels, one the 'dead' *Astron*, opposite which is the:
Hotel Sevdalis (*Tmr* 5B/C2) (Class C) 6 Odhos Garofalidou.   Tel. 22691
Directions: As above and on the right.
   A single room sharing a bathroom costs 1260 drs and en suite 1860 drs, whilst double rooms are only available sharing a bathroom at a cost of 1960 drs per night. Rates rise to 1450/2150 drs and 2225 drs respectively (1st July - 31st Aug).

Back on the 'whimsical' High St, it is now almost arrow straight only to jink at the elongated 'Bus' Square (*Tmr* C1/2) after which, prior to a summer dry river-bed, is the:
Pension Tsakiris (*Tmr* 6C1)   Tel. 22929
Directions: On the right in an unprepossessing building.
   Stelios Tsakiris is one of the few owners of accommodation who doggedly meets all the ferry arrivals, including the early morning and 'late at night' boats. As his only sojourn abroad was as a German prisoner of war, it is in that language that Stelios attempts to communicate. He is persuasively dismissive in respect of questions regarding price and distance. But it is essential to establish the daily rate which, early to mid-season, should be about 1000 drs for a double room. Apart from a vagueness, quite possibly deliberate as it turns out, Stelios leads his 'captives' on a long walk to the pension. Strangely it is not directly up the High St, but by a most circuitous route. Of course new arrivals will not be aware of this peculiarity which, mindful of the general lack of accommodation, seems most unnecessary. It is not as if the High St is bristling with alternatives.
   The oldish house with high wooden ceilings has three double rooms on the first floor and one rather antediluvian bathroom on the ground floor. The water is often turned off in the evening, so shower early. Stelios and his wife are most solicitous which makes it that much more of a shock when he presents a daily rate bill for 1100

drs plus taxes which increases the indicated price by up to some 243 drs a night. Forewarned is forearmed so do not let him work this 'sleight of calculation'.

Left of the High St from the *Pension Tsakiris*, along the river-bed, here covered by a massive sheet of concrete to form a car park, leads to an Esplanade backing one of the town's three main beaches, the 'Greek' Beach. On the right is the modern, plush and very expensive:

Hotel Castro Beach (*Tmr* 7C1) (Class B) Tel. 22772
Directions: As above.

To list the prices almost hurts but single rooms start at 2200 drs and doubles 3400 drs. Ouch!

Not all is lost as there is a middle of the road alternative available, the excellent:
Hotel Afroditi (Class C) Tel. 23489
(Athens Address: 6 Katsimpin St, Papagoy Te. 6524022)
Directions: By road, proceed up the High St, crossing over the river-bed bridge close to *Pension Tsakiris*, beyond which take the left-hand turning for Kaspakas at the major fork in the road. The next main turning left progresses towards the 'Swiss' Beach, from which the hotel is some two plots back. Those on foot should follow the Esplanade along the backshore of the 'Greek' Beach. At the far end walk up past the Army camp, on to the road paralleling the backshore of the 'Swiss' Beach. The flower covered hotel is to the right.

The hotel's pamphlet lists the beautifully appointed, two bedroom suites, complete with self catering facilities and a fridge, as 'discouragingly' starting off at 3200 drs per day. The owner, energetic Panayiotis Papasotiriou, may well lower the rates to 2000 drs a day for early season lets. The official, height of summer charge (1st June - 31st Aug) is 4500 drs but, assuming he has space, these may well be negotiable. He is aided in the orderly running of the almost obsessively neat establishment by Aphrodite, his pretty and determined wife. There is an informal book exchange as well as the opportunity to make use of the hotel's speed boat and a large caique – rates to be negotiated. Panayiotis also exchanges foreign currency. A super hotel close by a super beach.

Mark you the 'ultimate of ultimates' must be the:
Akti Myrina Tel. 22681/5
Directions: The complex occupies a portion of the far end of the 'Swiss' Beach. The development was financed by Swiss funds, which is why I gave the beach the sobriquet. The hotel represents the quintessence of total and absolute luxury. Guards keep intruders at bay (or the inmates in?).

Double room chalet rates start off at 11,000 drs a night (yes, eleven thousand drachmae) so I will not continue with mouth watering descriptions.

Camping. There are no official sites and random camping is discouraged on the three main town beaches, but for alternatives *See* **Beaches, A to Z.**

The Eating Out There are no souvlaki pita bars but there are some 'fast food' shops, a 'fast food' van, that often parks up on the 'OTE' Square, as well as a number of galaktopoleio and zacharoplasteion. Mirina also has a quantity of acceptable and recommended tavernas and restaurants. At the far end of Plateia 28th Octovriou is the:

Taverna Avra (*Tmr* 8A3)
Directions: In the far corner of the Harbour Square, Plateia 28th Octovriou.

The large number of seats and tables outside, under the extensive canopy, masks the large interior. Plates of starters are lined up on the wide counter inside and, at 48 drs, must be one of the best value courses I have 'encountered'. The changes are rung every evening but these dishes include octopus, anchovies, tzatziki and garlic flavoured mashed potatoes. I very nearly renamed the place *Taverna Chaos*, due to the enjoyable antics that are enacted as the night wears on. It is best to arrive early which allows maximum enjoyment of the long leisurely evening ahead. It also ensures that diners will be able to 'pull up their trotters' at 'the trough', in an orderly fashion. Mind you, whatever time clients sit down, it is unlikely that they will escape being caught up in the confusion that evolves. The menu is rather limited. A meal for two of anchovies (48 drs), beans (48 drs), a souvlaki (282 drs), half a split roasted chicken (270 drs – a real plateful, with a whole chicken priced at 370 drs), a Greek salad (good and reasonably priced at 134 drs), a bottle of retsina (67 drs) and bread cost 732 drs. I am aware that the separate items total more than the whole but that is only one of the evenings surprises.....! It may take up to an hour to get the bill and a similar amount of time to get one's money accepted. A 'blow-out' meal of octopus, garlic potato, 2 helpings of meat balls and chips, a Greek salad, 3 bottles of retsina and 3 cups of Nes meh ghala costs 1088 drs.

Plateia 28 Octovriou 'harbours'(!) another eatery, the:

Taverna Ackoali (*Tmr* 9A3)
Directions: Along the edge of the Square, from the *Avra*, in the direction of the *Hotel Limnos*.

Very well spoken of with the chef Panayiotis especially recommended.

A number of fish tavernas cluster around a square edging the far, south-east side of the inner harbour. A Greek naval officer, met on Psara island, was most laudatory in respect of the *Fish Taverna Lakis* (*Tmr* 10B3) whilst the *Fish Taverna O Glaros* (*Tmr* 11B3) is prettily situated on the water's edge with the 'Turkish' Beach to the left (*Fsw*). About halfway round the 'Turkish' Beach is the:

Lobster Taverna
Directions: As above.

The establishment's fame is based on the fact that clients can select their lobster 'from the tank'. Rather disappointingly these are not glass fronted tanks but large fibreglass jobs plonked on the concrete floor with various, no doubt vital, pipes snaking across the premises and beach to the sea's edge.

Next door is an *Air Force Club*, 'Members Only'.

Zacharoplasteion 'Loukoumades' (*Tmr* 12B2)
Directions: On the right of the High St, beyond the Turkish fountain (*Tmr* 13B2/3), which incidentally is still much in daily use.

Super loukoumades but rather expensive – two helpings with honey and 2 Nes meh ghala costing 400 drs.

Taverna Ο ΠΛΑΤΑΝΟΣ (O Giorgos) (*Tmr* 14C1).
Directions: Further on up the High St, beyond the 'OTE' Square and the garish, out of place *Dagri's Pizzeria* and off to the left, on the far side of the small 'Plane Tree' Square. This plateia is attractively and abundantly shaded by two large trees.

The patron prepares a meal of the day and the establishment would be more correctly titled a restaurant as it is open midday, closing at about 1550 hrs until 1900/1930 hrs, when it opens for the evening session. A meal of spaghetti bolognese (very meaty and large), a plate of meat balls with a few chips, fried aubergines, an excellent Greek salad, bread and a kortaki retsina costs 735 drs; a splendidly prepared plate of moussaka, a meaty stifado, with boiled onions, gravy, herbs and tomatoes, a Greek salad, bottle of retsina and bread is charged at 695 drs. Meals are sometimes served on the 'cold side'.

There are two *kafenion/cafe-bars* (*Tmr* 4B2/3), one either side of the entrance to the High Street, at the harbour end. They cater for those in need of liquid refreshment and are extensively used by the locals. My own preference is the one on the right (*Sbo*) but this recommendation could be labelled prejudice. A beer, large brandy and bottle of limon (sic) cost 200 drs as do 2 Nes meh ghala and a large ouzo.

THE A TO Z OF USEFUL INFORMATION

AIRLINE OFFICE & TERMINUS (*Tmr* 15B/C2) On Odhos Garofalidou, which side street gets a bit crowded when hotel and airline buses clutter up the place. The office opens daily in the summer, between 0700-2030 hrs. The extensive presence of the Armed Forces results in airline seats being booked up, sometimes up to two or three weeks in advance.

Aircraft timetable

Limnos to Athens

Daily	2010 hrs.
up to 14th June additionally	
Tuesday, Thursday, &	
Saturday	0715 hrs.
From 15th June additionally	
Daily	0715 hrs.

Return

Daily	1845 hrs.
up to 14th June additionally	
Tuesday, Thursday &	
Saturday	0550 hrs.
From 15th June additionally	
Daily	0550 hrs.

One-way fare 2580 drs; duration 45 mins.

Limnos to Mitilini (Lesbos)

Monday, Wednesday, Friday	
& Saturday	1050 hrs.

Return

Monday, Wednesday, Friday	
& Saturday	1200 hrs.

One-way fare 2600 drs; duration 50 mins.

Limnos to Thessaloniki (M)

Monday, Wednesday, Friday	
& Saturday	1310 hrs.
Tuesday, Thursday,	
Sunday	0900 hrs.

Return

Monday, Wednesday, Friday	
& Saturday	0920 hrs.
Tuesday, Thursday &	
Sunday	0730 hrs.

One-way fare 3080 drs; duration 1 hr 10 mins.

BANKS One on the High Street (*Tmr* 16B2) and another, the **National Bank** next door to the OTE (*Tmr* 17B2). Note that here, as well as elsewhere, the **Post Office** (*Tmr* 18B/C) changes travellers' cheques and Eurocheques.

BEACHES Would that the main port of other N.E. Aegean islands could be blessed with say one beach to the Limnos standard but three is just a bit 'OTT'. In commenting on the beaches the reader must bear in mind that one beach (the 'Swiss') is absolutely super but must be the benchmark to which the others are compared.

Beach 1 To the left of the harbour (*Fsw*) and known as the 'Turkish' Beach. 'Bottom of the class' with a scrubbly backshore and some rubbish in the sea and on the beach.

Beach 2 Named the 'Greek' Beach, it is located around the Castle topped, large volcanic rock headland. The Esplanade and backshore of the beach approximately parallels the High St. Whereas the 'Turkish' Beach is set in a gently curving cove, the 'Greek' Beach is a straight strip of not completely clean sand with a band of small, seabed pebbles to be negotiated. Some 30m out to sea is a submerged bar of sand. The beach is edged by a wide swathe of land planted with trees as well as a children's playground and chairs and tables of various restaurants. The Esplanade is lined by a row of old, balconied houses, one of which the Army has requisitioned for an HQ.

Beach 3 The gently curving 'Swiss' Beach is beyond the Army camp occupied, rocky outcrop that marks the end of the 'Greek' Beach. I have designated it 'Swiss' for the reasons spelt out under **The Accommodation.** The beach and seabed is lovely sand which very slowly shelves beneath the sea, even rising for a section. The backshore is edged by a band of olive trees. Naturally the location is extremely popular with both locals and visitors.

There are two further coves, beyond the headland, at the far, south end of the 'Turkish' Beach. The track climbs up past a large water fountain bordering the shore, through trees and bears away to the left looking down on the first cove, most of the shore of which is taken up by a boat repair yard. The second cove is pleasant with a small, sandy beach and can be requisitioned for unofficial camping. A farm is set back from the land skirting the cove. Campers should take fresh water.

BICYCLE, SCOOTER & CAR HIRE Scooters cost 1500 drs a day but the real surprise is that car hire is comparatively inexpensive. Well at least the daily rate of 4000/4300 drs is only subject to a 10% tax with unlimited daily milage.

Scooters are hired from a shop next door to the *Hotel Aktaion* (*Tmr* 3A2/3), close to the inner harbour. Cars and motorbikes are available from the smartish office of **Rent-A-Car Myrina** situated on the harbour side of *Zacharoplasteion Loukoumades* (*Tmr* 12B2), on the right of the High St.

My personal choice for car hire is:
Rent A Car Lemnos (*Tmr* 19C1/2)
Directions: On the right of the upper end of the High St, close to the small 'Plane Tree' Square. The office also doubles up as Petridou Tours who run excursion buses around the island at the height of the season. The owners are pleasant, obliging and wish to please – such a change.

There is a sign on a tree across the Esplanade from the *Hotel Castro Beach* (*Tmr* 7C1) that proclaims *Rent Honda/Moto Vespa to Post Office near* (sic). I must confess to not unravelling the mystery of this exciting information!

BOOKSELLERS Two shops stock foreign language books. One (*Tmr* 20B3) is alongside the small square to the left (*Fsw*) of the Main Square and the other (*Tmr* 20C1/2), a good shop, is on the edge of the large, rectangular 'Bus' Square.

BREAD SHOPS One in a building (*Tmr* 21B3), on the far side of the small elongated square to the left (*Fsw*) of the Main Square. There is another (*Tmr* 21B/C1/2) on the left of the High St (*Sbo*).

BUSES The buses park up at the upper end of the High St (*Tmr* C1/2) on an elongated, rectangular Square. The Bus office (*Tmr* 22C2) is on the far left-hand side (the High St behind one) of the 'Bus' Square. The 'ticket wallah' speaks no English and the timetable is totally undecipherable. Local buses return the same day but buses to the further destinations come back the next day. One thing I can say is that despite the very poor state of many of the island's roads, buses depart daily to almost every village and hamlet.

Bus timetable
I have to own up, partly for the reasons above, to not being able to decipher, translate or quarry out the details.

CINEMAS (*Tmr* 23C2) One on the left of Odhos Garofalidou.

COMMERCIAL SHOPPING AREA The whole length of the High St, all the way up to the 'Bus' Square, is lined with shops of all shapes and sizes, with a number of older buildings on the left, prior to the 'Plane Tree' Square. Recommended shops on or close to the High St include a greengrocer on the right of the Main Square, in the same block as the *Hotel Aktaion* (*Tmr* 3A2/3); a general store/drinks shop (*Tmr* 24B/C2); a grocer (*Tmr* 25C1/2) who speaks some English; a supermarket (*Tmr* 26B2/3); a greengrocer (*Tmr* 27B2), and a shoe repairer on the right of the High St, across the road from the Turkish fountain (*Tmr* 13B2/3). Siesta is strictly observed, starting early (1330 hrs) and ending early (1600/1630 hrs).

FERRY-BOATS Once again, as elsewhere in the N.E. Aegean, the opportunity has not been grasped. Limnos could be a pivotal port but no, there are only connections to Kavala (M), Ag. Estratios, Lesbos and Skopelos. That is if the perambulations of the **FB Kyklades** are ignored. The old stager calls in once a week. Despite the location and the lines optimistically drawn on some maps, there are no ferry-boat connections with the islands of Thassos or Samothraki and the only boat that takes in most of the N.E. Aegean islands is the unforgettable **Kyklades.**

Ferry-boat timetables

Day	Departure time	Ferry-boat	Ports/Islands of Call
Tuesday	0500 hrs	Kyklades	Kavala (M).
	2300 hrs	Kyklades	Mitilini (Lesbos), Chios, Vathy (Samos), Ag. Kirikos (Ikaria), Leros, Kalimnos, Kos, Rhodes, Chalki, Diafni (Karpathos), Karpathos, Kasos, Sitia (Crete), Ag. Nikolaos (Crete), Anafi, Thira (Santorini), Folegandros, Milos, Piraeus (M).
Wednesday	0030 hrs	Skopelos	Kavala (M).
	1330 hrs	Skopelos	Ag. Estratios, Mitilini (Lesbos).
Thursday	0700 hrs	Skopelos	Kavala (M).
	2100 hrs	Skopelos	Ag. Estratios, Skopelos.
Sunday	0700 hrs	Aegeus	Kavala (M).
	1900 hrs	Aegeus	Ag. Estratios, Kimi (Evia).

One-way fare to: Ag Estratios   515 drs; duration: 1½ hrs.
Kavala (M)   1113 drs;   5 hrs.
Mitilini (Lesbos)   1087 drs;   6 hrs.
Skopelos   1106 drs;   5 hrs.
Kimi (Evia)   1064 drs;   7 hrs.

FERRY-BOAT TICKET OFFICES There is only one active firm, the:
Ticket office (*Tmr* 28B3)   Tel. 22820
Directions: To the left (*Fsw*) of the Main Square and on the left, in the narrow part of the street. The owner Aris, or his father who often stands in, sells tickets for the **Skopelos** and **Aegeus**. The office hours remain a mystery but it appears to open twice a day, in the morning and early evening.

A likely looking establishment on the right (*Fsw*) of the Main Square, in the same block as the *Hotel Aktaion* (*Tmr* 3A2/3), turns out to be a Cargo office only. The proprietor is both disinterested and off-hand, which I suppose is understandable but not very helpful. On the corner of the same block is another ('dead'?) ticket office which appears to have been disenfranchised by **Loucas Nomicos**, the ship owners. The proprietor occasionally opens the door but seemingly not for business.

LAUNDRY There is a dry cleaner's (*Tmr* 29B/C2) on the right of the High St.

MEDICAL CARE
Chemists & Pharmacies A number including one on the left and across the High St from the 'OTE' Square; two, one either side of Odhos Garofalidou, on the right, and another on the right of the High Street, beyond 'Plane Tree' Square.
Hospital Along Odhos Garofalidou, past the Olympic office (*Tmr* 15B/C2) and, towards the far end, the Police station after which follow the street round to the left.

OTE (*Tmr* 17B2). A modern office on the far side of the 'circular' Square, off the High St. Open weekdays 0730-2100 hrs.

PETROL There are a couple of petrol stations on the main road out of Mirina and the bypass that circles the port.

PLACES OF INTEREST
The Castle This Venetian fort, which gives Mirina its other name, Kastron, is draped over the volcanic rock outcrop that dominates the port and town. The Castle is now in ruins, so much so that the walls are quite difficult to discern from sea-level, but it is worth the climb if only for the sake of the views.

Museum (*Tmr* 30C1). On the far side of the *Hotel Castro Beach* with many exhibits from archaeological sites around the island.

Statue On the edge of the 'Greek' Beach is situated a striking memorial to an Unknown Soldier/Sailor to commemorating the island's Second World War dead. This and some of the murals and carvings in the Cathedral were executed by Theo Carradeos, an 84 year young sculptor/painter. He is a native of the island who became a professor in the USA but decided to return to Limnos in 1937....Bad timing! It is a pleasure to chat to Theo, a delightful man, who is usually to be found in the area of the High St, close to the 'Plane Tree' Square. His only latter-day regret is that the Mayor would not co-operate and commission a five metre Statue of Poseidon that is a 'twinkle in his minds eye'.

POLICE
Port (*Tmr* 31A3) The Port police and Customs occupy a large office on the edge of Plateia 28th Octovriou.
Town On the right, at the far end of Odhos Garofalidou from the High St.

POST OFFICE (*Tmr* 18B/C2). On the right of Odhos Garofalidou beyond the Olympic office. Travellers' and Eurocheques are exchanged. There is a post box conveniently situated at the outset of the High St, where it opens on to the Main Square.

TAXIS Rank on both the 'OTE' & 'Bus' Squares.

TELEPHONE NUMBERS & ADDRESSES:
Hospital	Tel. 22203
Police	Tel. 22200

TOILETS Between the *Taverna Avra* (*Tmr* 8A3) and the office of the Port police (*Tmr* 31A3), is a flight of steps, through ever open wrought iron gates, which climb to the Public Toilets.

TRAVEL AGENTS
Petridou Tours (*Tmr* 19C1/2)   Tel. 22039
Directions: From the same office as the Rent-A-Car business (*See* **Bicycle, Scooter & Car Hire**). Helpful but rather short on English.

ROUTE ONE
To Cape Kalogeri (10 km). This is a short but lovely route along the west coast, north from Mirina. The road rises up into the low hills at the far end of the 'Swiss' Beach and breasts the summit to reveal a splendid view over:
AVLONAS (2 km from Mirina). A natural, rather wild bay and hill-locked plain. The shoreline is rocky with a sand/pebble beach and lone fisherman's cottage. The hillsides are rock covered but the small, tree lined road leads down to fields of wheat and grazing for cattle and horses – yes horses.
   At the far end of this bay, and well set back, is the island's Generating Station beyond which the road rises to pass high above the indented coast before reaching the inland, hill-hugging village of:
KASPAKAS (6 km from Mirina) A meeting of the ways with roads to the villages of Kornos and Kalogeri. The village streets are winding and narrow but for Kalogeri follow the signs to Ag. Giannis.
   The very rough road makes a lovely walk but a bumpy ride, bending round the back of the village towards the coast and:
SKALA KASPAKAS (7 km from Mirina). My own nomenclature for this sea edging, 'doo-hickey' hamlet with a row of fishing boat sheds on a spit to the left (*Fsw*). The road runs along the narrow, pebbly foreshore to:
AG. GIANNIS (7½ km from Mirina). Dominated by a large, rather strange volcanic rock outcrop that dips its toes in the sea, dividing the bay, and is most unexpectedly topped off by a tiny chapel. At the height of the summer months a taverna operates from the foot of the convoluted rock. On the far side is a cove with a pleasant, sandy beach backed by pebbles. The bay is exposed to the prevailing wind and the shore is often subject to breakers.
   Over the headland is a small, kelpy harbour followed by another sweeping, sand/kelp/pebble beach and a hamlet. There are a pair of changing rooms.
   The track, which from hereabouts is in an appalling condition, finally ends on the far side of:
CAPE KALOGERI (10 km from Mirina). A lovely, moorland cove edged by fields of wheat with a relatively sheltered sand and pebble beach. At the end of the road, on the far side of the cove, is an attractive spread of single storey, stone, farm buildings.

ROUTE TWO
To Plaka via Kornos, Dafni, Atsiki, Varos, Kotsinas, Repanidi & Kontopouli (some 90 km).
The route is chosen to aid description of Limnos and should rid the idly curious of any wish to travel negligently the inner recesses of the island. Possibly nowhere else, size for size, of all the Greek islands are so many roads in the course of reconstruction, coupled with an alarming lack of signposting. Most of the villages (unless otherwise stated) are dusty, uninteresting and lack any coherent layout or focal point, added to which they rarely seem to have any notable tavernas. (Oh dear!) *See* ROUTE ONE for details of the road to Kaspakas.

The dusty wide track from Kaspakas passes a huge, sprawling Army Ordnance depot before reaching the village of **Kornos** (7 km from Mirina). About one kilometre beyond Kornos, on the Sardes road, a very promising asphalted road branches off northwards signposted **Vigla**. The mountainous nature of the countryside is attractive and typically 'island'. Whoopee, but don't count your asphalt..... In the far distance is one of those strange, monster balls associated with a nation's defence system. Sure enough the curious are turned back long before the coast is reached as the whole of this stretch is taken over by the Armed Forces.

Back on the route from **Sardes** village (11 km from Mirina) a track makes off northwards to:
KATALAKO (15 km from Mirina). This settlement is highly recommended as the best village on the island. One of the maps details an unmade road on from Katalako down to **Gomati Bay** but do not believe that. Various tracks in this area are not only 'doubtful' in respect of the surface but also direction.

Beyond **Dafni** (15 km from Mirina) the asphalted road deteriorates en route to the village of **Atsiki** (22 km from Mirina). Despite the beguiling temptation provided by the indication of little tracks off to the coast in a north and north-easterly direction, ignore them. The hamlet of **Krinida** is deserted, **Propouli** nearly so and the paths do not reach the coast.

Proceed on the asphalted road to:
KARPASSI (21 km from Mirina) This village is on the edge of the vast civil and military airfield complex that fills the large agricultural plain to the south. Petrol is available here.

The road westwards skirts the aforementioned airfield all the way to:
VAROS (22 km from Mirina) By Limnos standards this is an attractive village.

It is possible to head off on the now familiar, dusty, flinty track to the coast at the Bay of Bournias and:
KOTSINAS (24 km from Mirina) Despite some maintaining that this is a picturesque village with a fine beach and pretty cafes, or words to that effect, I must advise readers differently. Kotsinas is a particularly uninspiring, 'donkey dropping' of a house or three on a kelp edged, badly polluted stretch of beach. On the other hand there is one taverna that might or might not surface at the height of season as well as, the *Video Disco Vampire*. Oh goody! The disco's presence is no doubt to assuage the desires of the nearby Armed Forces but I hope the chaps do not mind dancing with each other because I have no idea where the girls are going to spring from.

Back at Varos the main road towards Moudros skirts the airport complex and an unattractive part of the large Bay of Moudrou. The road system hereabouts is particularly messy. Most maps detail a road to the south of the airport, along the top of Moudrou Bay, in the direction of Livadohori village. Forget these siren calls, it does not exist.

At the large fork in the road, beyond the branch off to the hamlet of **Lichna**, take the turning to:

ROMANOU (27 km from Mirina). A large, reasonably attractive village with a shop, kafenion and taverna or two.

Those heading for Plaka must search out the blue sign hidden amongst the tree lined, unsurfaced road heading off to the right, on the approach to Romanou. This route now arrows on up the land mass past the villages and hamlets of **Repanidi, Kontopouli**, the large, inland, salt **Lake Aliki, Ag. Alexandros, Dimosia** and:

PANAGIA (42 km from Mirina). Almost lively with two tavernas and a petrol station.

It is only 3 more kilometres on to:

PLAKA (45 km from Mirina). So often on the Greek islands this name signals an attractive area or village but this Plaka may well be a letdown. There is the hint of attractiveness in the whitewashed church at the entrance to the village, but most of the settlement is dusty and unlovely, based on a sterile grid layout.

One other general point is that frequently, where a map indicates this or that coastal village is some distance from the sea, thankfully this is not the case. Plaka is an exception to this empirical formula as the village is at least one kilometre off the coast, built on a low hill, overlooking the peninsula and two large, lifeless bays to the east. The left-hand bay (*Fsw*) has a little harbour and both possess a small foreshore of pebble and kelp with some sand. Quite frankly neither the journey nor the ultimate destination are worth the effort.

ROUTE THREE
To Moudros & Skandali (about 90 km) *See* ROUTE TWO for the roads to the Romanou village junction.

MOUDROS (28 km from Mirina) An unlovely town, dominated by a twin domed church, a grey concrete Army barrack block and the *Hotel Xenia*.

The village's one-way system is a bit of a brute, the small, boulder surrounded port is set in low lying land and the foreshore is rocky and muddy. Frankly Moudros, the second largest port and village of Limnos, is unmemorable, if not totally forgettable. Petrol is available.

The large bay hosted the First World War fleets prior to the infamous attacks on the Dardanelles and there is a British cemetery to the east of the village.

One of the island maps details a road of 'moderate passability' from Moudros round the edge of the bay in an anti-clockwise direction to the village of Skandali. Do not believe it as this is a cartographer's dream and a wheeled transport nightmare. Indisputably an unsurfaced road makes off eastwards from Moudros across prairie like land to the village of **Roussopouli** (33 km from Mirina). From this hamlet turn right at the 'T' junction, on across pretty agricultural countryside through the village of **Kaminia**, past the archaeological site of **Polichni** and the hamlets of **Ag. Sofia** and **Phisini** on to:

SKANDALI (46 km from Mirina). An attractive village in pleasant surroundings with friendly inhabitants.

There is a monastery at Ag. Sozon, to the south-east of Phisini, and, reputedly, some pleasant beaches in the area. I repeat the road does not continue on round and back to Moudros.

ROUTE FOUR
To Plati, Thanos, Diapori, Pedino, Livadohori & back to Mirina (circa 50 km). South of Mirina the road starts to climb into the hills. After one

kilometre there is a yellow sign **ΣΤΡΑΤΟΠΕΔΟΝ**, indicating a dirt track that leads up and over the hillside, through an Army camp, to the nearside of Plati Bay.

This diversion saves winding through:
PLATI (2½ km from Mirina). This pretty village is draped over a hill but the narrowness of the winding streets makes navigation very difficult especially when the way is blocked by 'loaded and parked' donkeys. There is a sign *Rooms for Rent with own fridge, toilet & bath Phones 24211, 23545. We speak English*. It's a nice change to all the signs in German!

Below the village, down a steep path, is the lovely sweep of sandy beach that fills the bay. There is some seaborne debris. The backshore of sand dunes is backed by a speckling of private dwellings, there are a few changing cubicles but no beach showers, probably due to the general water shortage. In the centre of the backshore is the *Taverna O Grigoris*. Towards the far, south end of the bay, prior to a benzina harbour, is a 'dead' holiday complex of African huts and small chalets – some misguided entrepreneur's dream. Even in mid-season there is unlikely to be anyone in sight.

Continuing south towards Cape Tigani leads, at the base of the mountainside, to:
PLAGISOS (4 km from Mirina). There is a house or two on the surrounds of this nice cove but the sand beach is littered with kelp, tar and rubbish and the seabed is made up of stones.

From Plati village it is a hard slog up and down the mountain to the old village of:
THANOS & THANOS BEACH (5 km from Mirina). To locate Thanos Beach ask the way at the Main Square, as below the village is a maze of contradictory, uneven tracks. No one should imagine that, without luck, they will be able to find their own way unaided.

The first, almost circular, large cove is rimmed by a truly amazing golden sand beach, perhaps one of the finest, most beautiful, small beaches in the Aegean. The occasional nudists sunbathe in amongst the rocks, away to the right, and there are two tavernas. Prejudiced as always I can only nominate:
Taverna O Nikos   Tel. 22787
The single storey building is sited dead centre of the beach backshore, with a large, formal, vegetable plot to the fore. Nick spent 20 years 'Down Under' and thus speaks, and understands, Australian very well. The taverna is famed for its fish dishes, so much so that we actually ordered one, a rare occasion due to the normally high cost. A meal for two of 5 fish, a Greek salad, retsina and bread cost 1000 drs – well 1028 drs, but we were let off the 28 drs. A beer and a limon cost 100 drs. For the 1987 summer season Nick may well be able to offer **Rooms** as the foundations and groundworks are now completed. The winter of 1985/86 was the first time that he did not return to Australia to help out his son and he is planning to finish off the additional building works in the 1986/87 winter but, who knows......?

To the left (*Fsw*) is a second bay, a total contrast to the first, with a stony foreshore and fishing boats moored up. On the left is a terrace of simple, old and uninhabited fishermen's cottages.

About three kilometres from Thanos village, the now unsurfaced road almost touches the shore of the Bay of St Pavlos. To reach the seashore the easiest path is a short trek alongside a river course. During the summer the river becomes a stagnant stretch of water with tiny terrapins swimming about, and in the banks of which sand martins nest. The area is a nature watcher's paradise. The summer weak river falters on the edge of a super, big, broad, sandy beach. There are occasional bands of kelp and the sea gently breaks on the water's edge.

KONTIAS (24 km from Mirina). From this village it is possible to drive south-east to the coastal hamlet of:

DIAPORI (29 km from Mirina). Located on the Bay of Kontias but probably (no definitely) not worth the trip unless interested in the old, ethnic Greece. This really is a 'doo-hickey' slum (to the power of 10) of a 'way port' on a muddy creek. Two kafenions, one with an antediluvian telephone switchboard, edge the muddy backshore. A small, wobbly pier accommodates the infrequent, large cargo caique that docks and a very narrow, sandy but dirty foreshore stretches away to the right (*Fsw*).

From Diapori the unsurfaced road turns northwards through the villages of **Tsimandria** and **Pedino**, past a petrol station, to:

NEA KOUTALI (18 km from Mirina). Part of the village of Pedino almost joins up with Nea Koutali. Both have experienced much rebuilding due to an earthquake in 1968 but the resultant new bungalows, arranged along a grid system of streets, are not very attractive. The creek-like foreshore has a small pier and a fair number of fishing boats moored up in the bay. Nea Koutali fishermen are famed for their sponge diving exploits and supposedly rival the Kalimnos men. (Don't tell the Kalimniots!).

The road makes a junction with the main Mirina/Airport road close to the village of **Livadohori** (15 km from Mirina) where petrol is available. To the right is the route to the airport. The asphalted, wide road to the left returns to Mirina Port, passing through ugly **Ag. Dimitrios** but very pleasant countryside set in low mountains. Six kilometres out of Mirina are, on the left,. the now abandoned but once renowned baths and hot springs of **Therma**.

EXCURSION TO AG ESTRATIOS (Evstratios, Aistrates, Efstratios) ISLAND

FIRST IMPRESSIONS
Ruined old port; horseflies; 'Soweto' style prefabs; oak trees; animals quartered in old buildings.

VITAL STATISTICS
The almost triangular island has an area of 44 sq km and a population of about 270.

GENERAL
The N.E. Aegean group has a few 'off the mainstream' islands, of which Ag. Estratios is the least visited. This is not entirely surprising as ferries cannot dock due to supposed underwater obstructions. It is necessary for the Ferry-boat that do call to heave-to in the exposed bay and connect with passage-boats. The exposure to westerly winds can make this an interesting experience, or even cause ferries to steam on if conditions are deemed too rough, especially as the boats used for the 'water taxi' ride are very small.

The port is the only settlement and the islanders are slow to warm to visitors, although a day or two makes a world of difference. The island was a place of exile and as recently as 1954 there were 1250 policemen looking after 5000 prisoners. Goodness only knows where they were all coralled? Perhaps this past concentration of lawlessness is reflected in the presence, even now, of three policemen which seems an inordinate number for such a small island.

If the difficulties of actually getting to the island were not enough, the port had the misfortune to suffer a calamitous earthquake as late as 1968. This destroyed nine tenths of the original, attractive buildings which used to stretch up the northern

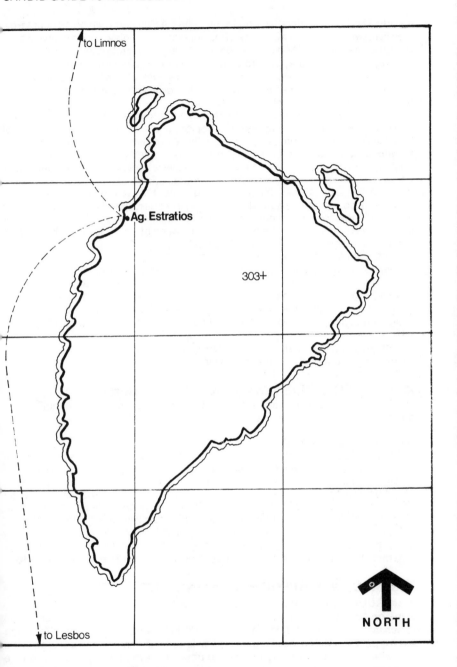

Illustration 28 Ag. Estratios island

hillsides. The solution decided upon to mitigate the disaster, in which 48 people lost their lives, was to build a new village in the adjacent river valley. Speed may well have been a prime consideration but the concrete taverna, concrete church and unlovely stereotyped, single storey concrete housing blocks laid out on a grid road system rather resembles a 'Soweto' style settlement. This redevelopment, coupled with the remnants of the old village strewn about the hillside and the massive concrete lining of the river-bed does not make a pretty sight.

To see how attractive the location was, prior to the disaster, it is only necessary to pop into the *Kafenion* (*Tmr* 2A2/3) across from the boat quay, and have a good look at the sepia photographs on the wall. One of these details not only the old village but six windmills either side of the hill top chapels. Alternatively walk a couple of hundred metres up the river-bed, past the soulless concrete streets, to the valley which is a fertile maze of smallholdings, orchards and agricultural plots. Another of the photographs shows the once magnificent beach which, despite the occasional contemporary guide book singing its praises, is unhappily no more. The major construction works necessary to alleviate the effects of the earthquake intruded on to the centre of the once splendid sweep of sand. (*See* **Beaches, A to Z** for more gruesome details!). *Costas' Taverna* (*Tmr* 3A/B2/3) also has a picture of the front cover of a local book depicting the old port.

Despite the various shortcomings the island is an ideal spot for travellers who simply wish to immerse themselves in a very Greek island way of life, who have a well stocked store of paperbacks and do not easily get bored. Furthermore the immediate countryside is rewarding, the valley smallholdings and orchards a delight and on the east coast, some two hours walk, is a long, volcanic, black sand beach.

Even Ag. Estratios is touched by the current Turkish situation and acts as host to a miniscule camp in the hills, manned by three soldiers.

AG. ESTRATIOS: the (only) village & port (Illustration 29)
The introductory remarks set the scene. The villagers become very friendly after a day or two but some Greek is a distinct advantage, if not a necessity.

ARRIVAL BY FERRY
The few ferries a week that do stop in the bay set down and take off passengers from local boats. Bearing in mind the possibility of adverse weather conditions it is a pity that the craft used are not substantial caiques but small, outboard motor powered, glassfibre rowing boats. The fare for the passage boat is rather expensive at 200 drs per head – the locals are charged 100 drs. Travellers are deposited on the quayside (*Tmr* 1A3) inside the harbour and are met by an inquisitive crowd of villagers. Very, very few of these worthies are much good to the first time visitor looking for a room – if only because there is only one pension – yes one, and there are even snags regarding the availability of rooms in this establishment (*See* **The Accommodation**).

THE ACCOMMODATION & EATING OUT
The Accommodation: A choice of one; the
Pension Galanakis (*Tmr* 4C/D1)   Tel. 93202
Directions: From the landing point (*Tmr* 1A3) turn right, walking past the raised 'Municipal Precinct' on the left. Take the first left after the church and proceed to the end where the street turns right, inclining upwards beyond the 'Old Clinic', on the right, and then angles sharply backwards still climbing. The pension is on the right.

The square, two storey house is one of the few old buildings still standing and has a total of eight or nine rooms. The landlady, who once lived in the African Congo,

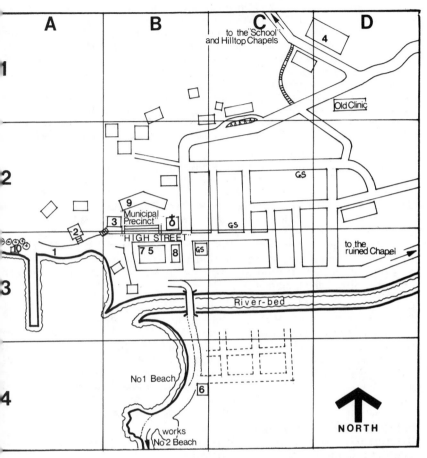

1 Boat quay A3
2 Kafenion A2/3
3 Costa's Cafe-bar Taverna A/B2/3
4 Pension Galanakis C/D1
5 Snackbar/Kafenion B3
6 Beach Kafenion/Taverna B/C4
7 Ferry-boat ticket office B3
8 Police station B3
9 Post Office B2
10 Public Toilets A3
G.S. General stores

Tmr = Town map reference
Fsw = Facing seawards
Sbo = Sea behind one

Illustration 29 Ag Estratios Village & Port

speaks some French and has an air of sophistication. Her husband, Dimitrios Galanakis, is the Mayor. But travellers have a problem – namely that, certainly during the week, most of the beds are taken. For some reason the authorities have chosen the island as one of the places to manufacture the reinforced concrete, four stump breakwaters that resemble giant knucklebones. The idea may of course have been to boost local employment but as with many such centralised, contrived bureau-cratic decisions, the very reverse would appear to be the result as most of the construction workers commute from the mainland! Naturally they require digs...so Madam Galanakis' pension is ordinarily very nearly full. One double room is usually available and the landlady may force two more beds into the room, if absolutely necessary. The shared bathroom has a cold water shower and charges are 500 drs per head.

A visitor intending to stay for a more extended period than say a week may well be able to rent one of the 'prefabs', many of which are empty due to absentee owners.

The Eating Out Well there are more possibilities than there are places of accommodation but...Incidentally, unless specifically ordered, fish is not readily available as a dish contrary to oft stated beliefs. In fact it can only be hoped that visitors enjoy souvlaki on a stick! The island supplies, including food, are very dependent upon the Limnos mail/provending boat being able to make its sche-duled calls. The usual charge for a beer is 65 drs, a bottle of retsina 65 drs, a Nes with dried milk 50 drs and a brandy 20 drs.

Costas' Cafe-bar/Taverna (*Tmr* 3A/B 2/3)
Directions: On the left of the 'High Street', on the edge of the 'Municipal Precinct'.

A large, soulless, single storey building in and around which the locals gather Costas, his wife and family have to work pretty hard to keep pace with the custom at peak periods of demand. The basic comestible is the ubiquitous stick souvlaki but subject to suitable supplies being available, there is more often than not a 'meal of the evening'. A dinner of 3 souvlaki sticks, a Greek salad, a bottle of retsina and bread costs about 300drs per head. The taverna is 'very shut' for siesta. Tucked in a corner of the building is a 'shack-like' hut with a metered telephone.

Snackbar/Kafenion (*Tmr* 5B3)
Directions: On the right of the 'High Street', opposite the 'Municipal Precinct', in the 'shopping arcade' row of 'doo-hickey' lockups.

Guess what? They serve up souvlaki cooked on a very smoky, half-drum type barbecue that lurks at the front of the snackbar.

Beach Kafenion/Taverna (*Tmr* 6B/C4)
Directions: Take a turn over the river-bed bridge and stroll along the backshore of the first, nearest beach. The hut-like taverna is on the left, slightly set back from the path

If advance notice is given it is possible to share in a lunchtime meal of the day which the construction workers whistle up during the week. Closes for the after-noons.

Quayside Kafenion (*Tmr* 2A2/3)
Directions: Across the quay from the harbour in a small area of rickety, ruined houses still left standing, if drunkenly, after the earthquakes.

The usual drinks only, but do not miss the photographs.

THE A TO Z OF USEFUL INFORMATION
BANKS. None but there is a Post Office (*Tmr* 9B2) that will perform basic transactions.

BEACHES Apart from the depredations of the earthquake and the necessary reconstruction works that started the destruction of the beach, other factors have conspired to further the ruination. For instance the huge piles of gravel and aggregate necessary to construct the breakwater 'knucklebones' are dumped on a flattened area separating the two beach coves. The workings in this area have certainly not helped keep the surrounds clean and wholesome.

The first beach was sand but it has suffered from continual excavation which, coupled with the construction of the harbour pier, has left more pebbles than sand.

The building of the islands Generating Station against the backshore of the second, mainly pebble beach cove is, as it were, the 'final stone'. There is a sandy outcrop towards the far end.

Both beaches are rather messy with seaborne rubbish. Perhaps to encourage *les autres* (all right, hordes of tourists), sometime in the past an optimist has erected beach showers and laid down sunbathing platforms.

There is reputedly a marvellous volcanic beach, complete with small inshore islet, on the east side of the island. This is some two/two and a half hours walk across the island, along the road close to the right side of the 'ruined chapel' hill.

BICYCLE, SCOOTER & CAR HIRE/BUSES/PETROL/TAXIS. None, although one comparatively recently returned islander has shipped in his car. This can only be to ease the strain of walking the 300/400 or so metres of the port's streets that make up the total of the island's road system. On the other hand it may have been to impress his fellow men!

BREAD SHOPS/COMMERCIAL SHOPPING AREA There are no bakers or bread shops. Yoghurt is not usually available but there are three stores (*Tmr* GS) scattered about the streets and, amongst general goods, they sell packets of rusks – a bread substitute. Siesta is strictly observed. Supplies arrive on the mail boat which sails from Limnos two or three times a week, weather permitting.

FERRY-BOATS Much of the harbour quay is obscured by the giant, metal moulds and ancillary equipment which are used to make the breakwater 'knucklebones'. Rumours that interisland ferries cannot dock in the harbour due to an underwater obstruction must be regarded with some doubt when it is possible for large cargo vessels to pull up alongside the harbour wall.

Mention of the mail boat here and there prompts me to remind readers that, despite locals murmurings to the contrary, unless in exceptional circumstances or well out of season, passengers are not allowed to catch this boat. There is no connecting Piraeus ferries, it being necessary to pick up connections at Kavala (M), Limnos, Skopelos (Sporades) or Evia island.

Ferry-boat timetable

Early and mid-season, sailings that incorporate the island in their schedules number some two or three a week and these often make the 'bay stop' during the hours of darkness. Ferry-boats include an 1830 hrs departure from Limnos on Sundays, that takes about two hours, and a Tuesday night boat that stops off at about 2200 hrs and goes on to call at Limnos and Kavala (M).

Day	Departure time	Ferry-boat	Ports/Islands of Call
Tuesday	2215 hrs	Skopelos	Mirini (Limnos), Kavala (M)
Thursday	0415 hrs	Skopelos	Mirini (Limnos), Kavala (M)
	2230 hrs	Skopelos	Skopelos island (Sporades)

| Sunday | 0415 hrs | Aegeus | Kavala (M) |
| | 2030 hrs | Aegeus | Kimi (Evia island) |

One-way fares: Limnos 516 drs;   duration 1½ hrs.
              Kavala (M) 1115 drs; duration 7½ hrs.

FERRY-BOAT TICKET OFFICES Only one (*Tmr* 7B3) on the 'High Street', which opens up prior to a Ferry-boats arrival.

MEDICAL CARE Best not to be ill as it is necessary to catch a Ferry to the nearest and most convenient neighbouring island.

OTE *See Costas' Taverna* (*Tmr* 3A/B 2/3)

PLACES OF INTEREST
The port is overlooked by two chapels on a small oblong plot, enclosed by a wall, that tops the northern hill up which the village used to spread. Inside one are the 'graves – actually labelled tin boxes piled one on top of the other.

The old school, shattered by the earthquake but still standing, is on the way up to the two chapels. It is well worth a look over as the erstwhile magnificence and size seems totally out of place for such a small and depopulated island. It only goes to show what a thriving place Ag. Estratios was in the past. Now one of the old classrooms has been requisitioned as a donkey stable!

Prominent are the remains of another chapel on the low hill to the east of the port, set in between the valley surrounds, situated well back from the bay. The hill has oleander filled river-beds to either side. In an inland direction the countryside is very scenic with, rather surprisingly, groves of oak trees – reminiscent of Kea island and oringinally grown for the same reasons – to support the once thriving, tanning industry. It is said that much of the port's development in years gone by spread over the hill slopes to the rear of this chapel. A stone slab close to the chapel ruins is supposed to be the grave of a Second World War German soldier. He was rumoured to have been killed by the opportunist shot of a British submarine captain whose vessel was cruising on the surface when the human target presented itself, probably outlined against a dusk or dawn skyline.

The slash of track zig-zagging up the mountainside over to the right (*Sbo*) clambers up to the islands mountain top.

POLICE The office (*Tmr* 8B3) is at the end of the 'Arcade' on the right of the 'High St' (*Sbo*). Perhaps recalling the islands importance as a large concentration camp for exiles, there are the staggering number of three policemen to ensure that the present day population does not run riot or endanger the Greek constitution. There is another office/jail in the angled 'Municipal Precinct' on the left of the 'High St'.

POST OFFICE (*Tmr* 9B2) In the 'Municipal Precinct'.

TOILETS (*Tmr* 10A3) A 'eye watering' little number over the other side of the harbour wall.

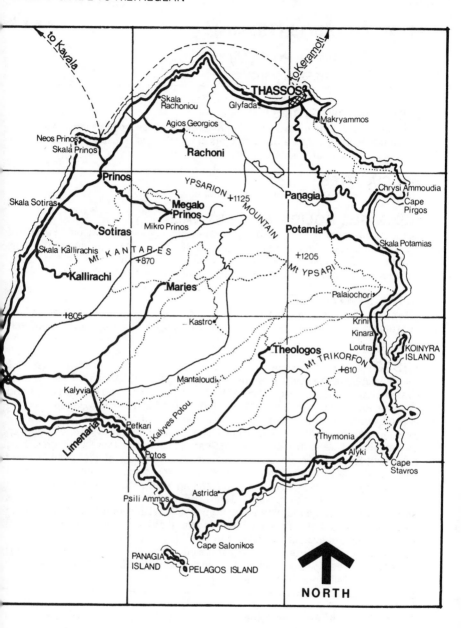

Illustration 30 Thassos island

17 THASSOS (Thasos)
& Kavala Port (M)
N.E. Aegean Islands

FIRST IMPRESSIONS
Pine trees; marble; beaches; asphalted roads; brightness; crickets; turquoise seas; few churches, chapels, cats, dogs, soldiers or wild flowers; unusually shaped house roofs of slate; German spoken.

SPECIALITIES
Loukoumades; meals of goat at Limenaria; olives; honey.

RELIGIOUS HOLIDAYS & FESTIVALS
include: 18th January – Festival of Ag. Athanasios, Limenaria; 23rd April – Festival of Ag. Georgios, Limenaria & Prinos; 29th June – Festival of the Marriage of Thassos, Theologos; 30th June – Festival of Ag. Apostoli, Prinos; 27th July – Festival of Ag. Panteleimon, Prinos; 26th October – Festival of Ag. Demetrios, Theologos.

VITAL STATISTICS
Tel. prefix 0593. Almost circular in shape, being 26 km from north to south and 22 km from east to west with an area of 379 sq km and a population of between 13,000 and 16,000.

HISTORY
An unexceptional history, that is unexceptional for the N.E. Aegean. There was the overall wealth attributable to mining activities in general, and gold in particular, and the consequences of an eighteenth century quirk when the Turks bequeathed the island to the then Turkish governor of Egypt. He was one Mohammed Ali who was a local lad really, having been born at Kavala on the adjacent mainland and bought up on the island. Due to this 'nepotism'(?) Thassos became almost a self governing outpost of Egypt with many advantages. This halcyon state of affairs deteriorated after the benefactor's death to such an extent that the islanders eventually implored the Turks to re-establish their authority. Needing no second bidding the Turks took over in 1902. The Germans organised a major mining company in the next few years and the island gained independence from their Turkish overlords in 1912. During the Second World War German occupation was taken over by the Bulgarians who in their turn were relieved of control by the Allied forces in 1944.

Prospecting found Greece's only offshore oil in the waters close by Thassos. This discovery may have sparked off the Turkish boundary disputes of 1973. The oil well platforms are brilliantly lit at night.

GENERAL
An island of massed pine forests and olive grove covered, marble hills and mountains. The extent of the pine and marble can be measured by the fact that they are respectively and comprehensively forested and quarried for shipping throughout Greece.

The other growth industry is human, the tourist industry. Years ago the Germans discovered the ease with which they could motor down through Europe to the delights of Thassos. These original camping forays are slowly but surely being

259

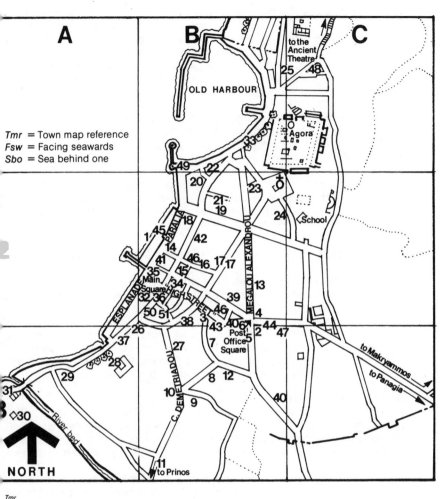

Tmr = Town map reference
Fsw = Facing seawards
Sbo = Sea behind one

Tmr

1 Ferry-boat quay B2
2 Thespina's Rooms B2/3
3 'Turkish Fountain' Square B2
4 Post Office & 'Post Office' Square
 & crossroads B2/3
5 Rooms B3
6 Hotel Akropolis B2/3
7 Naxos Pension B3
8 Hotel Vicy
9 Pension Aristotle B3
10 Pension Arion B3
11 Pension Victoria B3
12 Pension Archimedes B3
13 Hotel Lido B2
14 Hotel Akti/Commercial Bank B2
15 Rooms B2
16 Hotel Dionysos B2
17 Rooms B2
18 Forestry office B2
19 Agricultural Bank B2

20 Hotel Astir B1/2
21 Rooms B2
22 Customs office B1/2
23 Museum B2
24 Rooms B/C2
25 Rooms B/C1
26 Hotel Aktion A/B2/3
27 Pension Dafni B3
28 Talk of the Town Disco A3
29 Hotel Xenia A3
30 Hotel Laios A3
31 Restaurant Akrogiali A3
32 Cafe-bar A/B2
33 Kafenion B1
34 Souvlaki snackbars B2
35 National Bank B2
36 Gregory's Souvenir Shop B2
37 Thoma Tsipou A/B2/3
38 Billy's Scooter hire B2/3
39 Tony's Budget Bikes B2

40 Bakers
41 Bus office B2
42 OTE B2
43 Greengrocers
44 General store B2/3
45 Ferry-boat ticket office/Port police B2
46 Laundries
47 Clinic B/C2/3
48 Temple of Dionysos C1
49 Public toilets B1/2
50 Thassos Tourist Services A/B2/3
51 Drink shop B2

Illustration 31 Thassos (Limenas) Town & Port

260

extended to package holidays. Nothing intrusive but increasingly apparent. A welcome by-product is that there are probably more **Rooms**, campsites and restaurants than elsewhere on the Greek islands. It has to be admitted that the restaurant signs are all in German and the menu offerings, in the main unimaginative. One drawback is that overall prices are just that little bit more expensive than elsewhere in the N.E. Aegean. On the other hand Germans require excellence and generally the service is startlingly, almost confusingly, efficient in comparison with most other Greek islands. 'You pays your money and makes your choice.'

The beauty of the landscape is matched and possible excelled, if that is possible, by the majesty of one or two of the truly golden, almost white sand beaches and the turquoise seas which edge them. Admittedly those staying at the capital and second port of Thassos have to travel to reach these beaches. Moreover the closest is (monstrously) expensive to gain access.

The size of the beaches and the low number of tourists, except in the 'lemming-like' months of July and August, ensures plenty of room for everyone, despite there being few towns or, for that matter, seaside villages. Historically an island of gold, now a green and golden, sun-kissed holiday paradise.

THASSOS (Limenas): capital town & second port (Illustration 31)

The capital is rather attractive but despite being a port, rather than a distant mountain topping Chora, this function is subsidiary to unattractive Skala Prinos, some eighteen kilometres to the west.

I rarely advocate ferry-boat travellers to proceed directly to the capital of this or that island on landing. However that must be the advice for those disembarking at Skala Prinos which is simply a commercial Ferry-boat concrete quay with a miniscule strip of beach and few shops. On the other hand Thassos Town is reasonably large, agreeable, pleasing and interesting with a pretty, old harbour.

ARRIVAL BY FERRY

It is possible to catch a direct Ferry-boat, or more correctly the short haul, landing craft 'look alikes' that ply these waters, from Keramoti port on the mainland. They dock bow on to the long quay (*Tmr* 1B2) stretching along the Esplanade. One Ferry-boat a day makes the journey between Thassos port and Kavala, on the mainland, via Skala Prinos.

The ferries are crowded with locals and, during the season, Germans in cars, motor caravans or astride large, black motorbikes. A drink of Nes on board is damned expensive at 100 drs and the boats are not met by owners of accommodation.

THE ACCOMMODATION & EATING OUT
The Accommodation There are a lot of **Rooms**, in the main set someway back from the waterfront. There are also a large number of pensions, masquerading as hotels, and a lot of hotels. Prices, as for all other services, are on the costly side, no doubt pushed up by the high spending German tourists. Readers must not consider this conclusion as yet another example of my intolerance – it is axiomatic that prices in those holiday areas preferred by the Germans and Scandinavians (and Greeks) are higher than those of island resorts that are more the preserve of the (tight fisted?) English and French.

Thespina's (*Tmr* 2B2/3)   Tel. 22698
Directions: From the Ferry-boat quay (*Tmr* 1B2) cross over the Esplanade and the Main Square (*Tmr* A/B2), wind up the rather nebulous High Street, past the tree

shaded Turkish fountain (*Tmr* 3B2) on the right, to the 'Post Office' crossroads/square (*Tmr* 4B2/3). The accommodation, on the left-hand side of the road to the right, is reached up a flight of external stairs.

This pristine house is owned by smiley Thespina and her husband Elias who live on the job, as it were. The pension has the advantage of a communal dining room alcove and kitchen as well as a washing line. The shared shower bathrooms are extremely clean. A double room in mid-season, costs 1200 drs.

Almost opposite are **Rooms** (*Tmr* 5B3) and in the High St, immediately before the crossroads and on the right (*Sbo*), is the:
Hotel Akropolis (*Tmr* 6B2/3) (Class D) 62/63 Gallikis Archaeologikis Scholis
Tel. 22488

Directions: As above.

An older, classic building which makes it more of a pity that the hotel does not open until the height-of-season, if at all!

Back at 'Turkish Fountain' Square (*Tmr* 3B2), dominated by the very old and hollow tree, a narrow lane to the right (*Sbo*) leads past a number of pension/**Rooms** including the *Olympus, Naxos* (*Tmr* 7B3) and *Apollo*, all on the left.

At the next junction, the street to the right leads past the:
Hotel Vicy (*Tmr* 8B3) (Class D)   Tel. 22314
Directions: As above.

Rooms share the bathrooms with a single room costing 1000 drs per night and a double room 1200 drs, rising to 1250 drs and 1500 drs respectively (1st July - 31st Aug).

On along the street, at the next junction, are the *Aristotle* (*Tmr* 9B3) in the street to the left and the *Arion* (*Tmr* 10B3) across the road, the main Prinos road. Further up the Prinos road are the *Victoria* (*Tmr* 11B3), the *Adonis* and, in a street to the right, the *Hermes*.

The street, on the side of which is the *Aristotle* (*Tmr* 9B3), runs out into countryside surrounding the town and an area rich with accommodation including the *Plato, Goddess, Venus, Helios, Delphi, Meteora, Minerva, Immortality* and *Parthenon* – they almost sound like a range of Japanese saloon cars!

By not turning to the right beyond the *Naxos* (*Tmr* 7B3), and the *Apollo,* but continuing straight on, the street leaves the *Archimedes* (*Tmr* 12B3) on the right, the *Zeus* on the left and the *Socrates* on the right.

From the 'Post Office' Square (*Tmr* 4B2/3) Odhos Megalou Alexandrou angles down towards the Old Harbour.

Hotel Lido (*Tmr* 13B2) (Class C) 12 Megalou Alexandrou   Tel. 22929
Directions: As above and on the right-hand side of the street.

A single room en suite starts off at 1500 drs rising to 1900 drs (15th June - 15th Sept) whilst double rooms sharing the bathroom cost 1650 drs and en suite 1750 drs, rising to 2050 drs and 2200 drs.

Further on again, on the right, is the:
Hotel Lena (Class E) Megalou Alexandrou   Tel. 22793
Directions: As above.

All rooms are en suite with a single costing 1850 drs and doubles 2200 drs.

Along the waterfront to the left of the Ferry-boat quay (*Tmr* 1B2) (*Sbo*), edging the Esplanade and side-by-side, are the:
Hotel Akti (*Tmr* 14B2) (Class D) Paralia   Tel. 22326
Directions: As above and over the Commercial Bank.

Despite the position, relatively inexpensive. All rooms share the bathrooms with a single room costing 1200 drs and a double room 1400 drs, rising to 1400 drs and 1600 drs (1st July - 31st Aug).

Hotel Timoleon (Class B) Paralia   Tel. 22177
Directions: Next door to the *Hotel Akti*.
Rooms are en suite, as one would expect at these rates, with a single at 1850 drs and a double 2450 drs.

Pension Possidon (Class B) Paralia   Tel. 22690
Directions: Beside the *Hotel Timoleon* (which is next door to the *Hotel Akti*).
All rooms are en suite with singles starting off at 1600 drs and doubles 1800 drs, rising respectively to 2150 drs and 2500 drs (1st July - 15th Sept).

A lane at right angles off the street behind the *Akti* (*Tmr* 14B2), *Timoleon* and *Possidon* leads past a narrow alley to the right, on which are **Rooms** (*Tmr* 15B2) to the left, and further on the:
Hotel Dionysos (*Tmr* 16B2) (Class D)   Tel. 22198
Directions: As above and on the left.
All rooms share the bathrooms with a single room nightly charge of 1335 drs and a double room fee of 1600 drs, rising to 1460 drs and 1750 drs (1st July - 31st Aug).

The next street at right angles contains two **Rooms** (*Tmr* 17B2) to the left, diagonally across the street from each other. The one on the right is rather hostelish in appearance.

Further along the Esplanade, beyond the *Hotel Akti* and the Forestry office (*Tmr* 18B2), a soulless street off to the right advances past the Agricultural Bank (*Tmr* 19B2) to the:
Hotel Mary (Class B)   Tel. 22257
Directions: As above and on the left of the road.
Classified as a pension, all rooms have en suite bathrooms with singles costing 1665 drs and doubles 2000 drs.

In the crescent behind the Esplanade, which bends on to the near side of the Old Harbour, is the:
Hotel Astir (*Tmr* 20B1/2) (Class D)   Tel. 22160
Directions: As above and on the left.
Rooms share the bathrooms with a single costing 1125 drs and a double 1350 drs.
Just before the *Hotel Astir*, an alley branches off to the right and there are **Rooms** (*Tmr* 21B2) on the right.

Hotel Angelika (Class C) Paralia   Tel. 22387
Directions: In the same area as the *Hotel Astir*, around the corner, on the junction of a narrow lane and the Esplanade.
All rooms are en suite. Single rooms start off at 1250 drs (1st Sept - 31st Dec), rise through 1350 drs (1st Jan - 30th June) to 1665 drs (1st July - 31st Aug). Double rooms advance from 1500 drs, to 1650 drs and then 2000 drs.

In the triangular shaped block, housing the Customs office (*Tmr* 22B1/2), are three houses with **Rooms**.
At the bottom of the Old Harbour, a street edges the near, south side of the Agora through parkland, past the Museum (*Tmr* 23B2) and a church proceeding towards the Primary School. In this very pleasant spot, on the right, are **Rooms** (*Tmr* 24B/C2).
Further on round the Old Harbour, and prior to the attractive row of dilapidated two storey houses, a street marked by a sign to *The Theatre,* leads past a lane off to the left.

On the right of this lane are **Rooms** (*Tmr* 25B/C1).

Back at the Ferry-boat quay (*Tmr* 1B2) and to the right (*Sbo*), in the street one back and parallel to the Esplanade, is the *Hotel Aktion* (*Tmr* 26A/B2/3). The side street prior to the *Hotel Aktion* rises quite steeply off the Esplanade, curving round to the left (*Sbo*). At the first junction, keeping to the right on the Prinos road progresses past the *Mykonos* and *Dafni* (*Tmr* 27B3) on the left and the *Midas* and the *Arion* on the right.

South-west along the Esplanade, beyond the Talk of the Town disco (*Tmr* 28A3), and on the left is the defunct (defunct that is in 1986) *Hotel Xenia* (*Tmr* 29A3). The street to the left joins up with the Prinos road at a triangular junction in the vicinity of which are the *Hermes, Adonis* and *Victoria*. Further along the Esplanade is the *Blue Sea* and over the river-bed the *Diamand, Crete, Lesbos* and the:

Hotel Laios (*Tmr* 30A3) (Class C)   Tel. 22309
Directions: As above, beyond the *Restaurants Aphrodite* and *Akrogiali* (*Tmr* 31A3).

All rooms are en suite with the single room rate commencing at 1850 drs and double rooms 2200 drs, rising to 2100 drs and 2500 drs (1st July - 31st Aug).

Camping there are a number of sites on the road between Thassos Town and Neos Prinos.

The Eating Out
Those who enjoy cafe or more correctly kafenion/cafe-bar society will (or should) be appalled at the prices.

For instance the:
Cafe-Bar (*Tmr* 32A/B2)
Directions: On the right of the Main Square (*Sbo*), sandwiched between a periptero and the *Little Coffee Bar*, with red, moulded seats and a few kiddies' 'ride-on' animals.

Two Nes meh ghala (80 drs each) and an ouzo (70 drs) totals 230 drs. Ouch!

A less expensive establishment, across the quay road from the Old Harbour, is the:
Kafenion (*Tmr* 33B1)
Directions: As above and set in very attractive surroundings, shaded by ancient, very large plane trees.

A pleasant situation in which to while away an hour or three. A beer and limon costs 120 drs.

There are any number of restaurants spaced out along the length of the waterfront but, as is often the case, the general mediocrity of the offerings is widespread. If readers are prepared to spoil themselves I can recommend the:
Restaurant Akrogiali (*Tmr* 31A3)
Directions: At the far right-hand end of the Esplanade (*Sbo*).

Rather expensive but the service is excellent and the establishment's large patio is attractively situated across the road, close to the water's edge under a large awning. A meal for two of mussel soup (330 drs – I know, I know, very expensive but worth the price), a stuffed tomato and pepper (200 drs), 2 plates of kalamari (227 drs each) a plate of beans (costly at 180 drs), bread (30 drs) and a bottle of retsina (65 drs), totals some 1260 drs. Best not to order the beans and why not leave out the mussel soup?

There are a couple of *souvlaki snackbars* (*Tmr* 34B2) at the junction of the High Street and the Main Square.

Taverna ПНГН
Directions: Up the High St from the Main Square and on the edge of the 'Turkish Fountain' Square (*Tmr* 3B2).

Gourmets might gag on some of the offerings but an acceptable meal can be obtained, the prices are certainly reasonable (for Thassos that is), added to which Greeks patronise the place – always a good sign. A meal for two of macaroni in the bowl (350 drs), a Greek salad (140 drs – preprepared but not bad), a plate of fassolakia freska (green beans, very reasonably priced at 82 drs), a bottle of retsina (65 drs), bread and service charge (20 drs) costs 1007 drs. For the cost conscious an alternative choice might be the spaghetti bolognese (233 drs), galeos (a fish – 203 drs), patatas (cold and 53 drs), 'giants' in a sauce (beans at 140 drs), two bottles of retsina (65 drs each) bread and service (a small amount of bread – 20 drs) costs 779 drs.

There are a lot of 'sticky bun' shops, some honey shops and an interesting, small high-bodied, yellow van labelled ΜΠΟΥΓΑΤΣΑ which parks close to the Ferry-boat quay very early in the morning. The proprietor sells cream, apple and cinammon 'slices' at a 100 drs for a 200 gm slice, as well as cheese pies.

THE A TO Z OF USEFUL INFORMATION

BANKS. The **National Bank** (*Tmr* 35B2) is on the left corner (*Sbo*) of the Main Square. The **Commercial Bank**, which exchanges Eurocheques, is located in the ground floor of the *Hotel Akti* (*Tmr* 14B2). Other banks include the **Agricultural Bank** (*Tmr* 19B2). *See* **Gregory's Souvenir Shop** (*Tmr* 36B2), **Commercial Shopping Area.**

BEACHES. There is a pleasant, if smallish, sandy town beach beyond the caique repair yard, at the far end of the Old Harbour (*Tmr* B1). The sea's edge is dotted with some seaweed and broken tile. The first portion of the backshore is tree planted.

At the other, south end of the waterfront, opposite the Talk of the Town Disco (*Tmr* 28A3), is a very small, sandy, 'pocket handerchief' of beach.

BICYCLE, SCOOTER & CAR HIRE Scooter hire is extremely expensive and car hire is the usual costly exercise. There are a couple of island 'scooter peculiarities'. Scooters have to be returned every night, which is not such a bad idea as maintenance can be carried out overnight, and the petrol tank filled. Additionally the police demand that crash helmets are in evidence. The observant will note 'in evidence' not 'worn' as it is enough to have them 'on show'. Most hirers strap them to the parcel bracket!

Thoma Tsipou (*Tmr* 37A/B2/3)
Directions: Sited on the street one back and parallel to the Esplanade, south or to the right (*Sbo*) of the Ferry-boat quay and, as his card announces, *Next Door To The Paper Shop*!

The daily hire rate for 2/3 days is 1750 drs per day BUT, before the screams of anguish and indignant bellows gather force, this includes a daily tank of petrol, and the necessary number of crash hats. The owner and his wife are very helpful but rather short of English.

Incidentally a tankful will just transport two-up right round the island.

If Thoma seems expensive it is enough to say that **Budget**, diagonally across the street from the Agricultural Bank (*Tmr* 19B2), charges 2500 drs for one day and 4500 drs for two days. Other scooter hire firms include **Billy's** (*Tmr* 38B2/3) – rather a ragbag assortment of vehicles – and **Tony's Motor Bikes For Hire** (*Tmr* 39B2), quite close to the 'Post Office' Square.

Car hire is available from **Rent-A-Car Thassos** and **Budget**, both on the same street as the Agricultural Bank (*Tmr* 19B2).

BOOKSELLERS. Only an 'International' paper shop next door to Thoma Tsipou Scooter hire (*Tmr* 37A/B 2/3), although one or two shops around the Main Sq/High St have a few 'airport' paperbacks. *See* **Gregory's Souvenir Shop, Commercial Shopping Area.**

BREAD SHOPS. There is a baker (*Tmr* 40B2/3) on the right of the High St, halfway between 'Turkish Fountain' Sq (*Tmr* 3B2) and 'Post Office' Sq (*Tmr* 4B2/3). This shop, unusually, also opens up in the evenings. Another baker (*Tmr* 40B3) is located towards the outskirts of the town, on the road that branches off to the right of the 'Post Office' Square (*Sbo*).

BUSES A good service that allows access to almost the whole island. Mind you, absurdly, there are no services all the way to the town's closest beach (Makryammos), thus keeping the taxi proprietors financially sound! The Bus office (*Tmr* 41B2) is across the Esplanade from where the buses pull up against the railings of the Ferry-boat quay.

Bus timetable
Thassos Town to Panagia * (& on to Potamia & Skala Potamias)†.
Daily   0730, (0930), (1045), (1200), (1300), (1400), (1600) hrs.
* *It is necessary to walk on down to Chrysi Ammoudia (Avlakia).*
† *The buses in brackets proceed on to Skala Potamias.*
Thassos Town to Prinos (& on to Limenaria)†.
Daily   (0640), (0815), (0945), 1030, (1150), 1230, (1445), (1645), 1740, (1830) hrs.
Return journey (from Limenaria).
Daily   0620, 0800, 1020, 1215, 1430, 1630, 1730, 1845 hrs.
One-way fare to Prinos 90 drs.
† *The buses in brackets proceed on to Limenaria.*
Thassos Town to Alyki
Daily   0640, 1300, 1600 hrs.
Thassos Town to Theologos
Daily   0945, 1150, 1445, 1645 hrs.
Thassos Town to Rachoni & Kallirachi
Daily   1450 hrs.
Thassos Town around the island
Daily   0640, 1300, 1600 hrs.
Note this is a mid-season schedule.

COMMERCIAL SHOPPING AREA. No central area, market or market street. The shops are dispersed throughout the town and include a butcher, close to the OTE (*Tmr* 42B2), drink shop (*Tmr* 51B2), greengrocers on the right (*Sbo*) of the High Street (*Tmr* 43B2/3), and a general store, labelled *Supermarket* (*Tmr* 44B2/3), east of the 'Post Office' Square, as well as a number of specialist honey shops.

Gregory's Greek Folk Art (*Tmr* 36B2).   Tel. 22634
Directions: On the corner of the High St and the Main Sq.
I rarely list souvenir shops – the last being, I think, an art shop on Paros, in the Cyclades, but there must be exceptions to any rule. Not only does the shop exhibit an exceptionally wide range of reasonably priced goods for sale but they operate a book swap scheme, change currency and gratuitously dispense advice. This is a family business. The Papa wanders around supposedly masterminding matters but probably has nowhere else to go and rather disconcertingly uses a spitoon. The mid 40s, bearded son actually runs the show, speaks good English, and is ably assisted by George, again in his mid 40s.*En passant*, I might treat readers to a glass of retsina who, on first acquaintance, realise George is not British, his command of the English language is so good. The team is completed by a disinterested, 'luckless-in-love' grandson who spends his waking hours contemplating methods of trapping female

tourists. Generally siesta is at the usual hours but Gregory's store stays open late into the evening, which is very useful for those who require to change money out of hours.

DISCOS. There are a number including the previously referred to **Talk of the Town** (*Tmr* 28A3), located in a rather grand building, set back from the Esplanade.

FERRY-BOATS. An excellent service from the town to the rather 'off the beaten track', mainland port of Keramoti.

One boat a day makes a dog-leg via Skala Prinos to Kavala. It is of course little hardship to take a bus to Skala Prinos and catch a ferry-boat direct to Kavala (M).

Ferry-boat timetables

Day	Departure time	Ferry-boat	Ports/Island of Call
Daily	0615 hrs		Keramoti (M).
	0615 hrs.		Skala Prinos (Thassos), Kavala (M).
	0730, 0830, 0930,		Keramoti (M).
	1130, 1230, 1330,		
	1430, 1530, 1730,		
	1830, 2030 hrs.		

Return
Daily from Keramoti: 0730, 0830, 0930, 1030, 1230, 1330, 1430, 1530, 1630, 1830, 1930, 2130 hrs.
Daily from Kavala: 2100 hrs.
One-way fares: to Keramoti 202 drs.
to Kavala via Skala Prinos 240 drs.
Duration: to Keramoti 45 mins.
to Kavala via Skala Prinos 1 hr 45 mins.

FERRY-BOAT TICKET OFFICES. There is a small office (*Tmr* 45B2) 'en suite' with the single storey Port police office on the Ferry-boat quay. The ticket office is often 'dead' but tickets can be purchased on board the ferry.

LAUNDRY Several (*Tmr* 46B2 & 46B2/3).

MEDICAL CARE
Chemists & Pharmacies. There is one in the street parallel to the Esplanade, behind the block in which is situated the Bus office (*Tmr* 41B2), and another on the right (*Sbo*) of the High St.
Clinic (*Tmr* 47B/C 2/3). Nicely referred to as a *Health Station*. The clinic is on the right of the High St, east of the 'Post Office' Sq (*Tmr* 4B2/3) and down a short alley.
Doctors. One advertises his presence on the first floor of a building opposite the pharmacy, in the street parallel to the Esplanade, behind the block in which is situated the Bus office (*Tmr* 41B2).

NTOG. There is a defunct information office in the Port police/Ferry-boat ticket office building (*Tmr* 45B2). *See* **Travel Agents.**

OTE (*Tmr* 42B2) The office is in a street behind the Esplanade block containing the *Hotel Akti* (*Tmr* 14B2). Open weekdays only, between 0730 – 1510 hrs.

PETROL. There are some petrol pumps on the Esplanade, to one side of the Bus office (*Tmr* 41B2), as well as a number of petrol stations on the main Thassos Town to Prinos road.

PLACES OF INTEREST:

The Agora (*Tmr* B/C1). Similarly to the Kos Town (Dodecanese), this Agora is sited alongside one side (the north) of the town. It is rather regrettable that the excavations have been permitted to become overgrown or, as my notes record, 'the ruins have been allowed to go to ruin'! Oh dear!

The Old Harbour. (*Tmr* B1) Now a fishing and trip boat harbour with a number of very large, tall plane trees ranged around the nearside perimeter, but once the site of the island's ancient naval port. About centre of circumference is a row of old, pleasant but run-down, two storey houses none of which are now used for human occupation. One or two have been pressed into use as stores and another is nothing more than a very large pigeon loft.

Museum (*Tmr* 23B2) South of the Agora in a pleasant park. Naturally exhibits include many of the finds made around the island. That is those items that were gratuitously left by the jackals, no hush my mouth, the curators of other more influential establishments. For example the management did contrive to hang on to the 6th century BC Kouros*, the oversized Kriophoros of Thassos. Closed Tuesdays.
**A Kouros is a stylized statue of a young god.*

Theatre, Ancient. Initially signposted from the Old Harbour but, confusingly, further directions cease. Turn left up the lane at the division of the ways, that is around the **Temple of Dionysos** (*Tmr* 48C1). The lane soon becomes a flight of long steps that clambers up the steep hillside. The smallish, 3rd century BC amphitheatre is extensively tree shaded, but rather disappointing. The modern-day wooden seating planks are in poor condition.

Trip Boats. A number of craft moor up stern on to the Old Harbour quay. Destination, itineraries and prices are chalked on boards propped up on the after decks.

Wall, Ancient. Vestiges of the wall and gates that encircled the ancient city are visible in places but the only outstanding structural remains are those of the **Gate of Silinos** fenced in and close to the junction of the Makryammos and Panagia roads.

POLICE
Port (*Tmr* 45B2) Where they should be, alongside the Ferry-boat quay. The officers are helpful and there are various timetables stuck up on the windows of the small building.

Town A modern office on the left of the main Esplanade (*Sbo*), close to the Forestry office (*Tmr* 18B2).

POST OFFICE (*Tmr* 4B2/3). Towards the top of the 'High Street'.

TAXIS Rank by the Ferry-boat quay railings on the Esplanade.

TELEPHONE NUMBERS & ADDRESS.

Clinic (*Tmr* 47B/C2/3)	Tel. 22190
Doctor	Tel. 22663/22184
Ferry-boat ticket office to: Kavala	Tel. 22426
Keramoti	Tel. 22694
Police, Town (*Tmr* 18B2)	Tel. 22500

TOILETS (*Tmr* 49B1/2) On the nearside of the Old Harbour, but they are 'squatties' and not very pleasant.

TRAVEL AGENTS
Thassos Tourist Services (TTS) (*Tmr* 50A/B 2/3)   Tel. 22041
Directions: On the street behind the Esplanade, south of the Main Square, and boxed in by the *Restaurant T Asteria* and across the road from which is the *Cafe Pizza Roma.*

An efficient office run by an efficient American girl, in an efficient, if rather impersonal manner. There are racks of useful information including leaflets detailing bus and ferry-boat timetables. They also have a very helpful sheet setting out how to get to Istanbul (Turkey) by public transport in one day, if necessary, for a cost of about 1600 drs one-way. This is very public spirited if one considers that the firm runs a four day tour to Istanbul at a fee of some 12000 drs, excluding the cost of meals, entrance fees and ferry-boat fares. The various leaflets are charged at 25 drs each but their Town plan is not worth the outlay (!) as most island maps incorporate a more detailed plan.

For 'unofficial' advice why not pop along to Gregory's? *See* **Commercial Shopping Area.**

ROUTE ONE
To Limenaria & on back to Thassos Town, a circular route clockwise round the island (about 99 km). The east coast is majestic, mountainous and wooded whilst the west coast is very much less dramatic, with olive trees replacing the pine trees and a mainly sea-level road.

At the outskirts of Thassos Town, by the Gate of Silinos, a turning left off the main road proceeds to:
MAKRYAMMOS BEACH (2 km from Thassos Town). A splendid, sandy beach set in lovely, low, tree covered hillsides on to which have been built discreet, luxurious holiday bungalows. The oversight that allowed any development of this once beautiful and deserted spot is compounded by the necessity for outsiders to pay to gain entrance. The extortionate fees amount to 120 drs per head, and a further 200 drs to park a vehicle, despite which many Thassos Town based tourists taxi out here for the day. (Not the author who strongly objects to paying for that which should be free.)

The main road from Thassos Town towards Panagia village makes a steep climb through massed pine forest covered mountainsides, in which are dotted about a number of marble quarries. On the other hand... From close by Makryammos Beach a very rough, mountain track skirts the coastline at quite a height along the side of the tree clad, precipitous slopes. This route is not for the nervous as the surface is almost non-existent in places. After about four kilometres the track drops down to a fabulous, white, marble pebble beach cove. A track makes off in an inland direction up the towering mountainside to rejoin the main road. By keeping around the edge of the cove to the left, through dumps of quarried materials, the coastal route continues on past very extensive quarry works. The track once again climbs high on to the side of the mountain range, past another lovely cove way down below but backed by a goat herd's dwelling and curtilage.

The stony surface curves round the large horn of the headland of Cape Pirgos down to Chrysi Ammoudia (Avlakia).

But I race ahead of myself so back to the main road whence:
PANAGIA (7 km from Thassos Town). A pleasant and pretty but not outstanding look-alike for an Alpine village, with a fountain in the Main Square and summer running streams. Quite a number of unusually roofed houses, for which Panagia is noted, shops, two bakers, a number of kafenions, cafe-bars and restaurant/tavernas.

Two coffees at the Main Square restaurant cost 140 drs. Hotels and pensions include:

Pension Chrissaphis (Class B)   Tel. 61451
A single room en suite costs 1600 drs per night and a double room 1900 drs.

Golden Sands (Class D)   Tel. 61471
En suite rooms with singles from 1460 drs and doubles 1750 drs, rising to 1920 drs and 2300 drs (1st July - 31st Aug).

Theo (Class D)   Tel. 61284
A single room en suite costs 1300 drs, a double room sharing the bathroom 1350 drs and a double en suite 1500 drs.

Helvetia (Class E)   Tel. 61231
Rooms share the bathrooms with a single costing 900 drs and double rooms 1080 drs.

There are a number of **Rooms** scattered throughout the village.

From Panagia a road winds and descends steeply to:
CHRYSI AMMOUDIA (Avlakia) (14 km from Thassos Town). The name means golden beach and that's no misnomer. There are some three kilometres of sweeping, golden sand beach edging the clean sea, with a gently shelving seabed, set in a backdrop of pine clad mountains. At the far, east end the road terminates up against Cape Pirgos headland where the track round from Makryammos Beach tumbles down on to the edge of the bay. Here are a few, acceptably priced, backshore restaurant/tavernas, shaded by very tall plane trees, and a small quay to which tie up the trip boats. Otherwise almost the entire sweep of the gently curving bay is devoid of any buildings. There are a number of **Rooms**, an official campsite, wind-surfing and some pedaloes. Chrysi Ammoudia is very popular with both Greeks and Germans, and no wonder.

Back on the main road and the next village is **Potamia** (10 km from Thassos Town). There is a petrol station beyond the village after which the following two kilometres of road is edged by dozens of houses with **Rooms** – so many in fact that it would be easier to list the houses that do not have accommodation.

At about fourteen kilometres a turning edges off to the left to:
SKALA POTAMIAS (Chrysi Akti) (14½ km from Thassos Town). A busy little fishing boat harbour/holiday resort with a small 'cove end' of golden sand beach. Several mini-markets and shops as well as scooters for hire. The friendly young lady at the *Cafe-bar Alexandros* speaks English.
   The foreshore stretching away to the left (*Fsw*) becomes stony before joining up with the southern end of Chrysi Ammoudia beach. To the right is a harbour breakwater beyond which is a large, square stone building.

The coastal main road is paralleled, after three kilometres, by an unsurfaced road connecting the hamlets of **Palaiochori** and **Krini** and a track leads off to the first named. There are also tracks back to Potamia and down to the inland village of Theologos.

KINIRA (22 km from Thassos Town) An old, headland hamlet with a small pebble beach. About one and a half kilometres offshore is the pretty islet of Koinyra. There are two hotels including the *Hotel Gerda* (Class C, tel. 31278) which only has en suite double rooms starting off at 1800 drs and rising to 2200 drs (1st July - 31st Aug). **Rooms** are available in the hamlet.

South of Kinira the road passes a sandy beach with a pebble backshore set in surrounds of thickly planted olive groves, with the Koinyra islet still clearly visible. One and a half kilometres from Kinira and the main road passes through **Loutra.** After an additional 1 ½ km, a track descends steeply through pine forests to an idyllic looking, long, sandy stretch of shore some way below the road and tantalizingly glimpsed through the trees.

Beyond Cape Stavros the countryside is planted out with groves of olive trees until: **ALYKI (33 km from Thassos Town).** The road swings past a very attractive, small, stony cove tucked into the nearside or east of the Aliki headland. This was once the site of an ancient 7th century BC shrine and there are still remains of a terrace and collonades. But this pretty location is only a precursor, an appetiser, to the far side of the small headland where a path wanders down to the edge of a cove set in the west side of the promontory. This is a picturesque, 'artists' colony', a tiny hamlet of square, stone clad, white slate roofed cottages that circle the edge of the small bay. The 'U' shaped inlet is snuggled in hillside jaws of marble to the right (*Fsw*) and rock to the left, both pine tree clad. The sandy beach has a stone backshore and a narrow band of pebbles about a metre into the sea. At the far end is a small, simple taverna that serves up good quality but basic fare.

To the right of the path down to the beach, a lady has a **Room** which costs 1100 drs per night but it will accommodate a large family as she allows up to five or six to squeeze in. All facilities are outside including water and lavatorial arrangements – some take to the hedges!

About one kilometre further along the road, set on a cliff face to the left and overlooking the sea is the:
Monastery of Archangelou. The buildings appear almost new, such is their state of repair and upkeep which, combined with a high perimeter wall, gives an impression of sanitised ugliness. Archangelou is in fact a convent, an outpost of one of the Mt. Athos monasteries. Visitors must be conservatively dressed. Below the convent is clearly visible a small, stony beach, not sandy as is occasionally suggested.

From here onwards the countryside is drier with less forest, becoming more a granite/marble landscape on which grows low trees and gorse. The coastline appears to be made of marble.

Beyond the spur road to **Astrida (Astris)** and Cape Salonikios, off which are two islets, is a small modern development. Out of the height of the season the place seems to be abandoned. There is an air of quiet desertion overlaying the two small hotels (with a new one under construction), the **Rooms** and restaurants. The sandy beach has a pebble band and the sea bottom rafts of sand divided by stripes of weed and rock.

Another 1 ½ km west along the main road is the sandy cove of **Psili Ammos** which is on the day boat trip schedules. The bare hills in this area are lower, and have suffered much forest fire damage in recent years.

POTOS (54 km (or 46 km in anticlockwise direction) from Thassos Town). Now a modernish, unpicturesque resort, rather reminiscent of the Spanish Costas in the 1960/70s. The main road, on which the traffic whizzes past, bypasses the settlement. There are hotels, **Rooms**, a supermarket, baker and restaurants. The beach is sand and pebble with more pebble. There are a couple of other beaches to the right of the rocky mole (*Fsw*) as well as a campsite. Potos is not a place about which I can enthuse.

On the modern bypass is a petrol station and, at the crossroads, a road to the right climbs the eleven kilometres up to:

THEOLOGOS (64 km from Thassos Town). This village took over from Kastro as the capital of the island, reaching its zenith in the 19th century. A pleasant, large settlement stretching the length of the High Street and rich in springs, rivulets and streams. One of the houses has been converted into a Folk Museum.

PEFKARI (44 km now in an anticlockwise direction from Thassos Town). More pleasant than Potos despite a number of two storey hotels and restaurants. There are **Rooms**, camping, beach showers and changing cubicles. The nice cove is hemmed in by pine trees but the sandy beach has a swathe of pebbles at the sea's edge. The sea bottom is mainly rock and weed but there is a wide spur of sand out to sea.

On the approach to Limenaria, the main road passes a small cove backed by pine trees in which are set down a number of ruined buildings once owned by the German mining company.

LIMENARIA (42 km from Thassos Town). On the approach to this large seaside town is a large church and an iron bridge over the slip road to the Esplanade. To the left is an 'out of place', chateau style building topping a high headland. This was once the headquarters of the German company that operated here at the turn of the century.

The curious ambience about this bustling, provincial resort must be entirely due to the once, all pervading presence of the Germans. Limenaria certainly does not evoke the usual Greek atmosphere. Lowenbrau is the local beer, with hardly an Amstel to be found, which is acceptable if you are a wealthy German.

Many hotels and restaurants, interspersed by large Victorian seaside houses, line the town's Esplanade, hotels to the right and restaurants to the left (*Fsw*). There are shops, greengrocers, an OTE, Post Office, a bank that changes Eurocheques and a petrol station.

The long, large pebble beach improves in quality towards the far right-hand end of Limenarion Bay.

Hotels include the: *Menel* (Class C, tel. 51396) – single rooms 1250 drs, doubles from 1500 drs; *Sgouridis* (Class C, tel. 51241); *Giorgos* (Class C, tel. 51413) – single rooms start at 800 drs and doubles 900 drs; *Theodora* (Class D, tel. 51251) – singles from 600 drs, doubles from 1010 drs; *Molos* (Class D, tel. 51389) – singles cost from 900 drs, doubles from 1200 drs; *Asterias* (Class E, tel. 51497) – singles start at 900 drs, doubles 1200 drs; *Ralitsas* (Class D, tel. 51578) – doubles only at 1600 drs; *Thalassies* (Class D, tel. 51163) – single room en suite costs 1500 drs and an en suite double 2000 drs; *Papantoniou* (Class E, tel. 51363) – en suite rooms only with singles from 1150 drs and doubles 1250 drs; *Hatzichristos* (Class E, tel. 51567) – only en suite rooms with singles costing 1000 drs and doubles 1600 drs and the *O Ilios* (Class E, tel. 51512) – on the main road with en suite singles 1700 drs and en suite doubles 2000 drs. Phew!

Buses depart for Thassos Town at 0620, 0800, 1020, 1215, 1430, 1630, 1730 and 1845 hrs.

An unpaved road (not the asphalted road to Kalivia) climbs inland the ten or so kilometres towards:
KASTRO (52 km from Thassos Town). The pinnacle topping, medieval Chora was abandoned in favour of Limenaria but now some of the derelict dwellings have and are being restored. There are rumours of simple accommodation and a taverna.

Beyond Limenaria the main road roughly parallels the coastline before shooting past the unmade track to:

SKALA MARION (31 km from Thassos Town). Do not simply drive on, but make the small detour to this sleepy, colourful and charming fishing village. The track to the village passes a lovely fjord like inlet with a sandy beach, some weed in the water and beach showers. Beyond this the unmade road drops down on to the central foreshore at the bottom of a broad 'U' shaped bay around which the settlement is wrapped. The sandy beach of the foreshore is lined with old fashioned, vertical post windlasses and littered with thin pole, boat beaching frames. The windlasses became redundant, in the main, when Greek fishermen fitted power takeoffs to their marine engines to drive the line haulers. This enables them to simply shackle a block to any convenient fixed point and pull the craft up on the beach using the winch.

There are one or two small hotels, a few **Rooms** and an excellent baker. The *Aggelos Fish Taverna* is on the far side of the village quay and the proprietor is a very pleasant man. A meal for two of a Greek salad, 2 omelettes, 2 beers and bread costs 600 drs.

The road continues on out of the village in a northwards direction. It progresses by a small cove with a scrubbly backshore and a pleasant, coarse sand beach edging the seabed which has a scattering of pebbles. A few boats are pulled up on the shore.

The west coast of Thassos is much less dramatic than the east. The road edges the mild coastline just above sea level with an inland vista of gently undulating countryside, thickly planted with groves of olive trees.

Some seven kilometres on is:

SKALA KALLIRACHIS (24 km from Thassos Town). Prior to the village the road is bordered by a 'doo-hickey' straggle of tin and asbestos roofed dwellings lining the narrow, pebbly foreshore. The centre of the village is equally 'doo-hickey' but does thicken out to line both sides of the route. To the left of the Main Square is an apparently disproportionately large quay for such a 'one-eyed' place. There are a few **Rooms**, restaurant/tavernas and a petrol station.

A three kilometre road makes off to the hamlet of **Kallirachi**.

Another three kilometres along, the coastal road progresses to:

SKALA SOTIROS (21 km from Thassos Town). Similar to Skala Kallirachis but neater with less shoreline and an equally large quay. Petrol is available.

It is 2½ km to the inland village of **Sotiras**, which is small but attractively original, set on a steep hillside and possessing a well regarded taverna. Both Skala Kallirachis and Skala Sotiros are ports of call for tramp cargo vessels loading logged wood which must account for the massive quays.

Further on the number of villages with the nomenclature Prinos is definitely confusing and island maps appear not to agree as to titling. The main route passes through **Prinos** where there is a branch road off, in an inland direction, to **Megalo Prinos** and **Mikro Prinos**. About ¾ km beyond Prinos is the junction with the road down to the Ferry-boat harbour of:

SKALA PRINOS (Ormos Prinos): (19 km from Thassos Town) main port (Illustration 32)

Note that **Neos Prinos** is a hamlet beyond Skala Prinos which is itself often referred to as Neos Prinos – perplexing!

Skala is an unattractive 'way station', well all right a Ferry-boat 'way station'. This makes it even more extraordinary that the place should attract so many German and English package holiday-makers.

The narrow strip of development that stretches along the waterfront is a loose mix of the occasional hotel, some **Rooms**, a few restaurant/tavernas, cafe-bars and gift

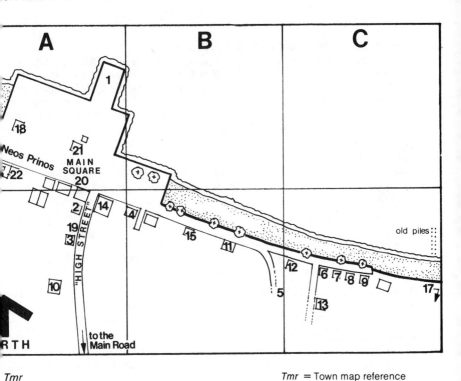

Tmr

1 Ferry-boat quay A1
2)
3)
4)
5) Rooms
6)
7)
8)
9)
10 Hotel Patra A2
11 Hotel Prinos B2
12 Hotel Filippidis B/C2
13 Hotel Xanthi C2
14 Restaurant Vasilis A2
15 Motorbike hire B2
16 Supermarket A1
17 Disco C2
18 Ferry-boat ticket office A1
19 Petrol A2
20 Taxis A1/2
21 Travel agent (dead) A1
22 Katha Travel A1

Tmr = Town map reference
Fsw = Facing seawards
Sbo = Sea behind one

Illustration 32 Skala Prinos Port

274

shops. Pedaloes 'bask' on the beach.

THE ACCOMMODATION & EATING OUT
The Accommodation. There are plenty of **Rooms** (*Tmr* 2A2, *Tmr* 3A2, *Tmr* 4A/B2, *Tmr* 5B/C2, *Tmr* 6C2 (tel. 71305), *Tmr* 7C2, *Tmr* 8C2, *Tmr* 9C2). The three at the far left-hand (*Sbo*), or east end, are just across the narrow, backshore edging street from the beach. There are shower heads hanging over the road, presumably so clients can wash off before tramping all that nasty, dirty sand into the landladies nice, clean house. Sounds more like Margate to me.

Hotels include the:
Hotel Patra (*Tmr* 10A2) (Class E)   Tel. 71401
Directions: To the right of the 'High' St that takes off from the Main Square.
   Only double rooms available with en suite bathrooms which cost 1250 drs rising to 1500 drs (1st July - 31st Aug).

Hotel Prinos (*Tmr* 11B2) (Class E)   Tel. 71327
Directions: To the left (*Sbo*) along the waterfront from the Ferry-boat quay.
   Single rooms sharing a bathroom start off at 1000 drs and 1100 drs en suite. Double rooms sharing cost 1100 drs and en suite 1160 drs. Charges rise to 1200/1300 & 1400/1450 drs (16th June - 31st Aug).

Hotel Filippidis (*Tmr* 12B/C2) (Class E)   Tel. 71563
Directions: Through the covered patio of the *Cafe* ΕΛΓΚΡΕΚΟ.
   Only double rooms en suite at a cost of 1600 drs per night.

Hotel Xanthi (*Tmr* 13C2) (Class E)   Tel. 71303
Directions: Beyond the *Hotel Filippidis* and on the left of the track to the right.
   Only en suite doubles starting off at 1115 drs rising to 1335 drs (1st July - 31st Aug).

The Eating Out
Restaurant Vasilis (*Tmr* 14A2)
Directions: On the junction of the 'High' St and the Main Square.
   Inviting, being situated in a converted and attractive old house.

THE A TO Z OF USEFUL INFORMATION
BANKS. A sign indicates *Prinos Post Office For Change*, so those in need will have to travel the two kilometres or so although one of the hotels will probably change travellers cheques and currency.

BEACHES. A very narrow strip of sand, with some kelp, to the left of the waterfront (*Sbo*).

BICYCLE, SCOOTER & CAR HIRE. One motorbike rental firm (*Tmr* 15B2).

BOOKSELLERS. Another sign advises that Prinos is the place for foreign news-papers so best to tie in money changing with paper purchasing.

BREAD SHOPS/COMMERCIAL SHOPPING AREA. Well there is a supermarket (*Tmr* 16A1).

BUSES. *See* **Thassos Town.**

DISCOS (*Tmr* 17C2). Opposite the old wooden piles at the far left-hand end of the waterfront (*Sbo*).

FERRY-BOATS *See* **Thassos Town.**

Ferry-boat timetables
Boats only arrive from and depart to Kavala (M).
Daily departures: 0545, 0615 (on from Thassos Town), 0715, 0915, 1100,
 1300, 1600, 1800, 1930 hrs.
One-way fare 202 drs; duration 1hr.
For the return times *See,* **Ferry-boat timetables, A to Z, Kavala.**

FERRY-BOAT TICKET OFFICES. There is an office (*Tmr* 18A1) on the Ferry-boat quay but, if this is not open, tickets can be purchased on the boat.

PETROL (*Tmr* 19A2). On the right (*Sbo*) of the 'High' Street.

TAXIS (*Tmr* 20A1/2). Rank on the waterfront road close to the junction with the 'High' Street.

TRAVEL AGENTS. One 'dead' office (*Tmr* 21A1) and one 'alive', **Katha Travel** (*Tmr* 22A1) which opens weekdays 0900-1300/1730-2030 hrs and Sundays 0900-1300 hrs.

To the right of Skala Prinos (*Sbo*), a waterfront track edges along the seashore past a foreshore yacht, caique and small ship repair yard to the hamlet of **Neos Prinos**. To the left the coastline is made up of a scrubbly but sandy foreshore for some three kilometres.

Back on the main road, after three kilometres a track branches off towards the coast past:
Camping Ioannidis Tel. 71377
A pleasantly disorganised site set in old olive groves
and the:
Room Hotel Hara Tel. 71296
Only en suite double rooms costing 1600 drs per night.
 To the right (*Fsw*) the foreshore becomes seaweedy.

Just under one kilometre further along the main road from the Ioannidis track and, in the vicinity of a petrol station, a road branches off to the right through **Ag. Georgios** to **Rachoni** (16 km from Thassos Town).

SKALA RACHONIOU (12 km from Thassos Town) A bit of a dump with a large quay, ***Rooms*** and a scrubbly, narrow, sand and grit foreshore. The two storey *Hotel Argiros* is just beyond the hamlet.

A further kilometre on from Skala Rachoniou is a very pleasant sweep of sandy beach with a scattering of weed on the immediate foreshore. There is a taverna, some pedaloes scattered about and informal camping amongst the pine and olive trees, despite a sign forbidding the same.

GLYFADA (2½ km from Thassos Town) Really only a very steep track down from the main road to a narrow but sandy cove, hedged in by pine trees and dominated by the large package holiday booked *Hotel Glifada.* Ordinary mortals are not really encouraged!
 A short distance beyond Glyfada (½ km), a short track leads down to an even more attractive bay with sand beach edged by pine trees but cut off from easy access by

the *Hotel Villa Nisteri* which commands the heights, as it were.

The main road curves past a private block of flats and, about one kilometre out of Thassos Town, a track branches down to the coastline and the *Taverna Vournelis Beach*. Rather a 'hillbilly' setting, close by the plane tree edged, narrow, sandy but messy beach. There is a certain amount of seaweed and pebbles for the first metre of the sea bottom.

KAVALA: mainland ferry-boat port. (Illustration 33)
Tel. prefix 051.

This is a large, busy, attractive ferry and fishing boat port, built on low hillsides and dominated by a Byzantine Castle on the right-hand headland (*Sbo*). More importantly Kavala allows for Ferry-boat connections to the islands of Thassos, Samothraki and Limnos.

There is an airport and the nearest main railway station is Drama, some thirty seven kilometres away.

ARRIVAL BY AIR
Only connections to and from Athens. The airport bus links with the town's Olympic office (*Tmr* 3A/B2).

Aircraft timetable
Athens to Kavala
Daily   0645 hrs.
Up to 14th June additionally
Daily except Thursday   2015 hrs.
After 15th June additionally
Daily   2015 hrs.
Return
Daily   0825 hrs.
Up to 14th June additionally
Daily except Thursday   2155 hrs.
After 15th June additionally
Daily   2155 hrs.
One-way fare 3510 drs; duration 1 hr.

ARRIVAL BY BUS
The long distance buses park up on Plateia Hrissostomou (*Tmr* 4A/B2) and the Bus office is sited on a corner of the same square (*Tmr* 5B2). The local buses line up on the Esplanade or Erithrou Stavrou (*Tmr* 6B2) where, as a dual carriageway, it edges the harbour wall.

Bus timetable
Kavala to Athens
Daily   0915, 1915 hrs.
Return journey
Daily   0730, 1915 hrs.
One-way fare 2670 drs; duration 11 hrs.

ARRIVAL BY FERRY
Ferries connect separately with the islands of Thassos, Samothraki and Limnos (from whence there are links to other N.E. Aegean islands). Note the word separately despite the evocative lines drawn on various maps depicting this or that ferry-boat 'ghost' trip. It is difficult to understand why the Thassos Ferry-boats do not proceed on to Samothraki but..... It is necessary to reconnect with the mainland to journey

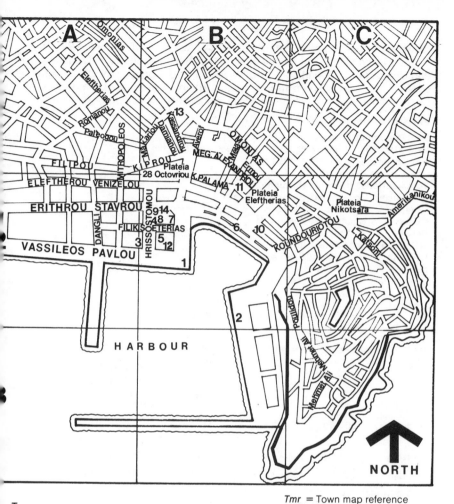

Tmr

Tmr = Town map reference
Fsw = Facing seawards
Sbo = Sea behind one

1 Thassos ferry-boat quay B2
2 Main ferry-boat quay B2
3 Olympic office & terminus A/B2
4 Plateia Hrissostomou/Country buses A/B2
5 Bus office B2
6 Local buses B2
7 Cafe-bar B2
8 Cafe-bar/Soup kitchen B2
9 Cafe-bar B2
10 Market building B2
11 NTOG office B1/2
12 OTE B2
13 Police offices B1
14 Post Office B2

Illustration 33 Kavala Mainland Port

278

between one island and the other – shades of Kea and Kithnos in the Cyclades.

Thassos ferries depart from the east quay part of the port (*Tmr* 1B2). Samothraki and Limnos ferries depart from the other side of the harbour (*Tmr* 2B2). It is a five to seven minute walk between the two departure points. The Thassos quay has a small, usually unmanned ticket office but tickets for all boats can be purchased on board.

Ferry-boat timetables

To Skala Prinos (Thassos Island).
Daily 0730, 0845, 1100, 1400, 1600, 1745, 1930 and 2100 hrs
(this last boat goes on to Thassos Town).
One-way fare 202 drs; duration 1 hr.

To Kamariotisa (Samothraki island)
Mid-season: Once a week, Saturday 0900 hrs.
Height of   Wednesday 1300 hrs &
season: Saturday 1000 hrs.
Return
Mid-season: Once a week Friday, 1800 hrs.
Height of   Wednesday 0800 hrs &
season: Friday 1300 hrs.
One-way fare 1030 drs; duration 4 hrs.

General Day	Departure time	Ferry-boat	Ports/Island of Call
Tuesday	1030 hrs	Kyklades	Limnos, Mitilini (Lesbos), Chios, Samos (Vathy), Ag. Kirikos (Ikaria), Leros, Kalimnos, Kos, Rhodes, Chalki, Diafni (Karpathos), Karpathos, Kasos, Sitia (Crete), Ag. Nikolaos (Crete), Anafi, Thira (Santorini), Folegandros, Milos, Piraeus (M).
Wednesday	0800 hrs	Skopelos	Mirina (Limnos), Ag. Estratios, Mitilini (Lesbos).
Thursday	1300 hrs	Skopelos	Mirina (Limnos), Ag. Estratios, Skopelos.
Sunday	1300 hrs	Aegeus	Mirina (Limnos), Ag. Estratios, Kimi (Evia).

One-way fare to: Limnos   113 drs;   duration 5 hrs.
                 Ag. Estratios 1113 drs; duration 7½ hrs.
                 Lesbos   1805 drs; duration 12 hrs.
                 Skopelos   1555 drs; duration 12 hrs.
                 Kimi (Evia)   1727 drs;

ARRIVAL BY TRAIN
The Athens train stops at the main railway station of **Drama** from whence daily buses connect with Kavala.

Train timetable
Drama to Athens
Daily 0310, 0934, 1215, 1605, 1855 hrs.
Return
Daily 0600, 0700, 1425, 2110, 2310 hrs.
One-way fare 1440 drs; duration 12 hrs.

THE ACCOMMODATION & EATING OUT
The Accommodation. Edging the broad dual carriageway of El. Venizelou
are the:
Hotel Panorama (Class C) 32c El Venizelou   Tel. 224205
Singles from 1500 drs and doubles 1980 drs.
the:
Hotel Acropolis (Class C) 53c El Venizelou   Tel. 223543
Singles start off at 1000 drs and doubles 1485, rising to 1200 drs and 2160 drs
respectively (16th June - 30th Sept).
and the:
Hotel Galaxy (Class B) 51 El Venizelou   Tel. 224521
Singles from 1780 drs and doubles 2490 drs, rising to 1928 drs and 2695 drs (1st
June - 30th Sept).

Cheaper hotels are located in the streets behind the Esplanade including the:
Hotel Attikon (Class D) 8 Megalou Alexandrou   Tel. 222257
Doubles only sharing the bathroom start at 1160 drs, and rise to 1295 drs (16th June
- 30th Sept).

Hotel Paggeon (Class E) 12a K. Palama   Tel. 223689
All rooms share bathrooms with single rooms costing 650 drs and doubles 940 drs,
increasing to 780 drs for a single and 1125 drs for a double (16th June - 30th Sept).

The Eating Out The usual range of eating places, most of which are spread out
along and around Erithrou Stavrou, the municipal Squares of Eleftherias and 28th
Octovriou, the Market Street of Odhos Koundouriotou and Plateia Nikotsara.
   The Thassos quay side of the harbour (*Tmr* 1B2) has a *Cafe-bar* (*Tmr* 7B2), from
which it is convenient to keep an eye open for the ferry-boats. In adjacent Odhos
Eterias is a small *Cafe-Bar/Soup Kitchen* (*Tmr* 8B2) and around the corner, on the long
distance Bus Square of Hrissostomou, is a *Cafe-bar* (*Tmr* 9B2) that serves pies.

THE A TO Z OF USEFUL INFORMATION
BANKS Any number including the **Commercial Bank** and the **Ionian and
Popular,** looking out over the harbour, on Erithrou Stavrou. The **National Bank** is on
the corner of K. Palama and Mela Streets.

COMMERCIAL SHOPPING AREA At the Samothraki/Limnos quay end of the
Esplanade is a **Market Building** (*Tmr* 10B2) and **Market Street**, Odhos Koun-
douriotou, at the top of which can be observed the rather unexpected arches of a
Turkish built aqueduct.

NTOG There is a single storey, prefabricated style office (*Tmr* 11B1/2) on Plateia
Eleftherias. This opens six days a week during the season: Monday to Friday 0730-
1300 hrs & 1730-1930 hrs, Saturdays 0730-1300 hrs and closes Sundays.

OTE (*Tmr* 12B2) Vassileos Pavlou. On the corner of the buildings facing the Thassos
ferry quay. Open daily between 0700-2400 hrs.

POLICE (*Tmr* 13B1) All the police offices are lumped together on Omonias St.

POST OFFICE (*Tmr* 14B2) Plateia Hrissostomou.

USEFUL TELEPHONE NUMBERS & ADDRESSES

ELPA, Dangli St/Plateia Filikis Etairias — Tel. 229778
NTOG, (*Tmr* 11B1/2) 2 Filellinon St/Plateia Eleftherias — Tel.228762/222425
Police, tourist, (*Tmr* 13B1) 119 Omonias St. — Tel. 222905

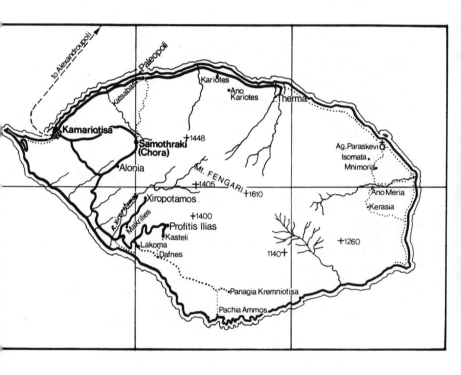

Illustration 34 Samothraki island

18 SAMOTHRAKI (Samothrace)
& Alexandroupoli (M)
N.E. Aegean Islands

The port   ★
The countryside   ★★★
The beaches (a minus!)

FIRST IMPRESSIONS
Dust; flies; horses; lack of beaches; (inopportune, optimistic) aluminium beach huts scattered about; pebbles; prairie fields; commercial fishing; large trees, marvellous archaeological site.

SPECIALITIES
Not a lot but lovely countryside.

RELIGIOUS HOLIDAYS & FESTIVALS
include: 20th July – Festival of Ag. Profitis Ilias, Profitis Ilias; 26th July – Festival of Ag. Paraskevi, Perashata; 9th August – Festival, Therma.

VITAL STATISTICS
Tel prefix 0551. The island is oval in shape, some 23 km from east to west and 14 km from top to bottom, covering an area of 178 sq km. The population is down to some 2,800 (having been 4,260 as recently as 1951).

HISTORY
It is difficult to imagine, viewing the Samothraki of today, that in the 6th century BC, the island was powerful and rich enough to have territory on the mainland, an independent Naval fleet and a Mint. If this were not enough there was the truly magnificent site of the Sanctuary of the Gods as evidenced by the remarkable archaeological excavations at Paleopoli. Despite becoming a satellite of various overlords, the religious importance of the island did not diminish until the 4th century AD, when the Romans imposed Christianity as the official religion. The decline was hastened by a 6th century AD earthquake which 'rubbled' the various buildings at the Sanctuary.

    The usual train of Genoese and Venetian overlords were followed by the Turks (1457 – 1912).

GENERAL
Ferry-boat visitors will, at first sight, and from a distance, be impressed by the almost disproportionately tall mountain peaks of Mt Fengari (1611m). The God Poseidon is reputed to have watched the seige of Troy from these heights.

    Samothraki was so named because in historical times the citizens of Samos colonized the island, naming it Son of Samos. Be that as it may...Most island chains have in their midst one that is a disappointment, a bad apple in the basket, a 'runt of the litter' and Samothraki must collect the N.E. Aegean wooden spoon. Not that the general countryside isn't very attractive, the landscapes are some of the most appealing in the group; not that the interesting Chora and few outlying villages aren't quite acceptable but at this point the plaudits must cease. Apart from anything else almost the whole of the island's foreshore is made up of large, grey pebbles.

    The port and main village, Kamariotisa, is dusty, gritty, flyblown and unattractive. It is the sort of place where watching horseflies climb windowpanes can become the

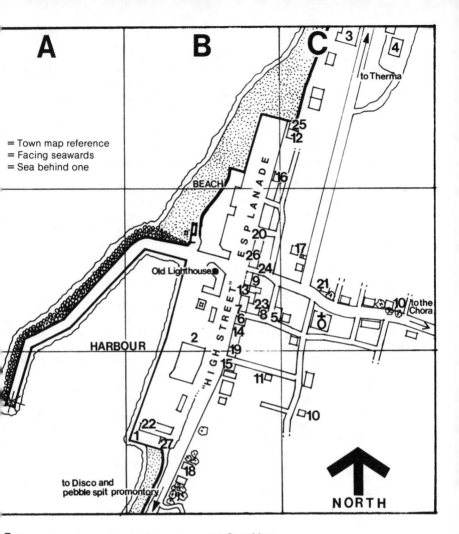

= Town map reference
= Facing seawards
= Sea behind one

Tmr

1 Ferry-boat quay A/B3
2 Bus terminus/park B2/3
3 Hotel Elnikh C1
4 Hotel Aiolos C1
5 Koula's Pension & Taverna B/C2
6 Cafe-bar B2
7 Souvenir/gift shop B2
8 Snackbar Carolina No 2 B2
9 Rooms/National Bank B2
10 Rooms
11 Baker B3
12 Kafe Estiatoria Kyma/Rooms B/C1
13 Souvlaki snackbars
14 Snackbar
15 Kafenion
16 Cafeteria/Snackbar Scorpio's B/C1/2
17 Scooter hire C2
18 Motorbike hire B3
19 Bus office B2/3
20 Port & Town police B2
21 Shop C2
22 Passenger shed B3
23 Ferry-boat ticket office B2
24 Chemist B/C2
25 Navy outpost B/C1
26 Petrol pumps B2
27 Public toilets B3

Illustration 35 Kamariotisa Village & Port

high spot of this or that hour. If this were not enough the proximity to the mainland ensures that the island is a Greek resort. These 'homegrown' visitors are topped up by a (surprising) number of tourists, mainly German, thus ensuring that Samothraki is not even an isolationist's dream. Added to this the natives are reserved. No let's be truthful, they are rather unfriendly, with a large proportion of cold-eyed young people aimlessly slumped on the patio of this or that record-thumping cafe-bar.

At least the island's name, Samothraki, has a poetic ring which may be why those that visit do so...! Similar in a way to the tourists who clatter down to Milos in the Cyclades, probably with Venus in mind, only to be disappointed.

KAMARIOTISA: capital village port (Illustration 35).

Really one of the most contrasting Greek ports I have visited, almost a total conundrum. Nowhere else can there be such a long (dusty, messy, unmade) Esplanade/High Street for such a lowly populated settlement. Nor can there be so many 'smarty' cafe-bars scattered along a waterfront's length. There have been and still appear to be ambitious plans for the Esplanade and beach area but they seem to founder on the twin reefs of ineptitude and time. Once one project has finally been completed it has usually taken so long that other pieces of the development jigsaw are falling apart. A good example must be the large, formal paved square on the edge of the beach backshore. This still unfinished and grandiose scheme has suffered the ravages of wear, tear, redesign and vandalism. For instance the large grids that should have been fitted over the drain sumps are not, lying about unfitted. One sump that lacks a grill hosts an upturned forty gallon drum stuck in the hole, looking rather like a nose diving submarine. No doubt the (toxic) wastes, once drum bound have now drained elsewhere! A formal traffic island, close to the Bus park (*Tmr* 2B2/3), has had smart lamp clusters fitted. Not only are they totally out of place and do not work but the 'grass' has become a weed infested mess.

There are no old buildings and some of the development is ugly, very ugly. The harbour is extremely large. For once in a while this size is not due to some obscure bureaucratic decision but because the local fishing fleet is probably one of the largest in size and number in the N.E. Aegean. Not only are there big, middle distance boats but any number of sardine caiques with their distinctive, large stern hung lamps. These latter craft are towed off towards the far, night time horizon by the larger boats in strings that sometimes number up to ten.

ARRIVAL BY FERRY

There is a minimum of a once-a-week service to and from Kavala on the mainland. Kavala is a most convenient port as it allows travellers to link up with a ferry-boat service to the island of Thassos and seperately to the islands of Limnos, Ag. Estratios and Lesbos. It is only a pity that these connections are so limited. The other, main Samothraki ferry-boat hook-up is to mainland Alexandroupoli, almost at the eastern end of Greece and the second to last major station on the railway line. From there it is up an eighteen hour train journey (if lucky) or fifteen hours on the bus to Athens. Why oh why is Samothraki not directly coupled to Thassos and why are these islands not linked to the rest of the N.E. Aegean without having to make a mainland call?

The exposed postion of Samothraki sometimes results in delayed and or 'hairy' docking procedures.

THE ACCOMMODATION & EATING OUT

The Accommodation. Yes, well. The number of **Rooms** are very restricted but there are two good hotels. The *Hotel Elnikh* (*Tmr* 3C1) is almost at the far left end of the port (*Sbo*). The other side of the road, on an embankment and overlooking the

Elnikh, is the *Hotel Aiolos* (*Tmr* 4C1).

Pension Koula's (*Tmr* 5B/C2)   Tel. 41587
Directions: From the Ferry-boat quay (*Tmr* A/B3) turn left (*Sbo*), walk along the High St/Esplanade past the first side street and on to the second. This is flanked by a record-thumping *Cafe-bar* (*Tmr* 6B2) and a Souvenir Gift shop (*Tmr* 7B2), next door to Niki Tours. Turn up this side street and the next turning on the left, beyond the *Snackbar Carolina No.2* (*Tmr* 8B2), leads to *Koula's Taverna* on the ground floor of the accommodation building. The entrance to the pension is on down the original side street.

Koula, an ample, smiling, freckle-faced lady meets the ferry-boats, usually 'accosting' clients in the area of the Bus park (*Tmr* 2B2/3). The pension is certainly the sleaziest I have ever stayed in especially considering the comparative modernity of the building. Some of the rooms are absolutely awful, some bearable and most unfurnished. All are linked by a first storey, vine draped and entwined balcony, giving access to the shared bathrooms which are of questionable construction and cleanliness. It must not be thought that the balcony is a continuous assembly. Oh no. It is necessary, halfway along the front of the building, to scramble up some stacked bricks, through folded back wire and cross over a yawning gap. Double rooms are charged at 1000 drs per night. But if Koula's does not appeal to a reader all is not lost.

Rooms (*Tmr* 9B2)
Directions: Over and behind the National Bank. The house is approached through the smoked glass door in the corner, to the right (*Sbo*) of a long, narrow fronted, cafe-bar. The entrance door gives on to a passageway, off which stairs rise to the first floor.

The clean rooms, which cost 1200 drs mid-season, share a bathroom, complete with a (short) bath and shower.

There are other **Rooms**. One house (*Tmr* 10C2) is on the left of the Chora road; another is up the first side street off the Esplanade from the Ferry-boat quay, beyond the baker (*Tmr* 11B3), right at the 'T' junction and on the left (*Tmr* 10C3); and yet more neat looking **Rooms** over the *Kafe Estiatoria Kyma* (*Tmr* 12B/C1).

Eating Out. A number of souvlaki snackbars, a couple of which are excellent, including one (*Tmr* 13B2) close by the informal taxi rank. This is actually a mini-taverna serving good value, inexpensive snacks. A souvlaki pita with all the bits and pieces costs 60 drs.

On the other hand the *Snackbar* (*Tmr* 14B2) further to the right (*Sbo*) serves up souvlaki in rolls, a bad habit.

Generally it is unfortunate that only small bottles of Amstel are available but Heineken can be purchased on draught. I say unfortunately because the 'stubby's' do not cost commensurately less, being charged at 60/70 drs.

Some of the cafe-bars masquerade as 'rock-bars', and are frequented by faintly menacing youngsters, whilst other cafe-bars are unfriendly, somewhat piratical and very ethnic.

The *Kafenion* (*Tmr* 15B3) on the corner of the first side lane off the High St (from the Ferry-boat quay) is run by a friendly man. Two Nes meh ghala and an ouzo cost 170 drs.

Koula's Taverna (*Tmr* 5B/C2)
Directions: As for the Pension. *See* **The Accommodation.**

Actually classed and probably licensed as a Galaktozacharoplasteion but has obviously widened its horizons. So what's in a name? Although the establishment might well be nominated for a 'greasy spoon' award, some good, hot food issues forth from the kitchen. Enough to say it is one of the few places where I have eaten meat balls! There are tables and chairs across the alley from the taverna which the locals make a habit of frequenting. The range of fare is limited but not preprepared. Sample offerings include 2 plates of fish (large sardines – 160 drs per person), a Greek salad (140 drs), a plate of patatas (50 drs), a bottle of retsina and bread for 610 drs (but should have totalled to 600 drs); two plates of meat balls (titled 'beef steak' – 180 drs each) fassolakia freska (green beans, rather cold – 120 drs), patatas (50 drs), a beer (50 drs), a bottle of retsina (70 drs), and bread (10 drs), cost 680 drs – I know, 10 drs adrift somewhere!; 2 spaghetti bolognese (unimaginative – 180 drs), a Greek salad (incorrectly charged at 50 drs), a plate of loukoumades (80 drs), 2 bottles of retsina (70 drs each), and bread was charged at 660 drs which is obviously too little but with reference to the other meals it's swings and roundabouts...It's not a bad place for breakfast either serving mugs of Nes, boiled eggs and bread. The only snag is that the taverna, being on a closed alley, is shut off from the waterfront views and any gongoozling...!

At the other end of the 'plate', as it were, is the:
Cafeteria/Snackbar Scorpio's (*Tmr* 16B/C 1/2)
Directions: Along the Esplanade, to the left (*Sbo*), and almost opposite the far end of the very large, paved backshore Square.

Extremely chi-chi which can be equated to gross overcharging. The management encourage the waiters to be supercilious, mistaking this for smart international elegance, sometimes with disastrous results. Any attempt to speak Greek is dismissed but the misconstrued translation of English and the resultant items served often bear little relationship to the original order. You have been warned!

Establishments that do deserve a mention include:
Snackbar Carolina No. 2 (*Tmr* 8B2)
Directions: On the left of the lane leading towards *Pension & Taverna Koula's* (*Tmr* 5B/C2). This snackbar thinks it's a swinging 'clip joint' but serves a very inexpensive 'tost' ham sandwich for 50 drs.

Cafe-bar
Directions: A narrow fronted building, alongside the National Bank (*Tmr* 9B2).

Run by a pleasant lady but the opening hours are indeterminate. 2 Nes meh ghala costs 130 drs, a beer and orangeade 90 drs.

THE A TO Z OF USEFUL INFORMATION
BANKS
National Bank (*Tmr* 9B2). Changes travellers cheques and foreign currency.

BEACH. As pointed out in the introduction, it is unfortunate for Samothraki that here, as elsewhere, the long port shoreline to the left of the harbour (*Sbo*) is a continuous belt of large and small, grey pebbles. Despite this the locals resolutely lie out on the shore. As if to promote and encourage the illusion of a desirable beach there is a shower head and changing cubicles adjacent to the paved Square. The aluminium framed compartments are deteriorating.

To the right of the harbour (*Sbo*), a track makes off past a disco and restaurant, set back on the flat countryside, towards the tip of the large, remarkable spit that shields the port from southerly winds (but not unfortunately westerlies). Even this initially inviting landmark is nothing more than a promontory almost entirely made up of large pebbles and set in which is an inland pond. The whole resembles a moonscape, land infill scheme.

BICYCLE, SCOOTER & CAR HIRE
Scooter Hire (*Tmr* 17C2) This business shares an office with a papershop on the first street that branches left off the Chora road. The short steps down pass the various machines, stored under cover. Hire is expensive at 1500 drs a day for a Honda type machine but the parners are amiable.

Motorbike Hire (*Tmr* 18B3) The shed is set to the side of the track to the right of the Ferry-boat quay (*Sbo*).

BREAD SHOPS. One baker (*Tmr* 11B3) His shop is on the right on the lane that branches off the Esplanade, opposite the Bus park.

BUSES. Park up on the widened section of the High St/Esplanade (*Tmr* 2B2/3) whilst the Bus office (*Tmr* 19B2/3) is across the road.

Bus timetable
Kamariotisa to the Chora (Samothraki)
Daily 0800, 1000, 1230, 1300, 1600, 1830, 1930 hrs.

Kamariotisa to Therma (Loutra)
Monday, Tuesday, Sunday

	0900, 1300, 1500, 1700 hrs.
Wednesday, Friday	0900, 1300, 1500, 1700, 1830 hrs.
Thursday	0615, 0900, 1300, 1500, 1700 hrs.
Saturday	0900, 1300, 1500, 1700, 1930 hrs.

Kamariotisa to Profitis Ilias
Monday, Tuesday, Thursday 0615, 1030, 1330 hrs.
& Sunday

Wednesday, Friday	0615, 1030, 1330, 1830 hrs.
Saturday	0615, 1030, 1330, 1930 hrs.

COMMERCIAL SHOPPING AREA. None but there are a sufficiency of shops and stores. These include a supermarket next door to the Port and Town police office (*Tmr* 20B2); two rather 'doo-hickey' general stores cum greengrocers side-by-side behind the Esplanade petrol pumps (*Tmr* 26B2); a shop (*Tmr* 21C2) on the Chora road and a souvenir/gift shop (*Tmr* 7B2), next door to Niki Tours. This latter emporium is run by a rather bored lady who possibly considers the whole business beneath her station in life, probably because she is the wife of the owner of Niki Tours.

Siesta is the customary hours but unusually for an island where there is not exactly a glut of tourists, or islanders for that matter, the shops all open on Sunday evening.

DISCOS. One on the track south from the Ferry-boat quay out to the promontory.

FERRY-BOATS. An excellent daily service to Alexandroupoli (M) and at least one boat a week to Kavala (M) which, incidentally, is the most convenient, sensible and only (?) mainland port from which to make connections with the rest of the N.E. Aegean islands. That is apart from Piraeus based ferries and the occasional Thessaloniki boat.

The **F.B. Arsinoi**, which plies the two routes, is a pleasant, small, stern-loading craft, small that is compared to the large, modern day Aegean ferries. It is difficult to find peace and quiet in the thru' deck lounge but the snackbar is clean and well run. A coffee costs 80 drs as does a 'tost' sandwich.

The harbour's exposure to bad weather can cause troublesome docking procedures – well in fact quite a 'to-do'. Waiting passengers may languish in the shade of a quay-side shed (*Tmr* 22B3).

Ferry-boat timetable

Day	Departure time	Ferry-boat	Ports/Island of Call
Monday, Tuesday	1800 hrs	Arsinoi	Alexandroupoli (M)
Wednesday (height of season)	0800 hrs	Arsinoi	Kavala (M)
Thursday	0800 hrs	Arsinoi	Alexandroupoli (M)
	1800 hrs	Arsinoi	Alexandroupoli (M)
Friday	1200 hrs	Arsinoi	Alexandroupoli (M)
	1800 hrs*	Arsinoi	Kavala (M)
Saturday	1400 hrs	Arsinoi	Alexandroupoli (M)
Sunday	1800 hrs	Arsinoi	Alexandroupoli (M)

Height of season this departure time is 1300 hrs which must affect the earlier sailing time.....!

One-way fare: to Alexandroupoli 660 drs; duration 1 hr 50 mins.
to Kavala 1030 drs; duration 4 hrs.

FERRY-BOAT TICKET OFFICES
Niki Tours & Travel The office is next door to the Souvenir/Gift Shop (*Tmr* 7B2). They handle the **FB Arsinoi** as well as Olympic Airlines and double up as a travel office. The owner wears a disinterested, world-weary air. The office is open daily, 0900-1200 & 1700-1800 hrs.
Ferry-boat ticket office (*Tmr* 23B2). 'A.N. Other' office but I'm not sure which craft they represent as there is only the **FB Arsinoi**.

MEDICAL CARE
Chemists & Pharmacies. One (*Tmr* 24B/C2) in the street one back and parallel to the Esplanade.

NAVY The Armed Forces are represented by an 'outpost' office, a sort of small, wooden shed shore establishment (*Tmr* 25B/C1), on the far side of the *Kafe Estiatoria Kyma*.

OTE. The island's OTE is up at the Chora but there is a metered phone inside the shop (*Tmr* 21C2) on the left of the Chora road, opposite the large church.

Incidentally close to this church, an old boy sits out in the shade of a tree with all his shoe shining tackle laid out on the ground. I'm not sure where the customers pop up from and I must sadly observe that I have never seen him actually reach 'in anger' for one of the 'light bulb' topped jars.

PETROL. There are petrol pumps on the High St (*Tmr* 26B2), in front of the two 'side-by-side' general stores.

POLICE
Port & Town (*Tmr* 20B2).

POST OFFICE In the Chora.

TAXIS. Rank on the High St/Esplanade in front of the souvlaki snackbar (*Tmr* 13B2), almost opposite a small 'look-alike' for a now defunct lighthouse(?).

TELEPHONE NUMBERS & ADDRESSES
Clinic   Tel. 41217/41376
Ferry-boat office   Tel. 222425

TOILETS A 'loo-block' (*Tmr* 27B3) is sited at the Ferry-boat docking point end of the quay.

TRAVEL AGENTS. *See* **Ferry-Boat Ticket Offices.**

ROUTE ONE
To the Chora (5 km). This route passes through lovely, rolling, rich agricultural countryside with large fields of wheat dotted with trees, but no hedgerows.

THE CHORA (Samothraki, Samothrace).
This is the old time capital where islanders retreated from marauding pirates. Despite which the village is not entirely hidden out of sight from the sea and in fact from one vector is rather prominent. The main port road spills on to and forms part of an unlovely Square on the edge of which is a monument and a kafenion, all dominated by a ruined Castle topping off a pillar outcrop of rock on the left.

The rest of the not unattractive village is layered up the hillside in the style of a Greek Odeion. On the left, as the street climbs to the right up and out of the Square, is a modern 'block of flats' and **Rooms**. The street then curves left round into the 'Chora proper' which bubbles away with busy activity, even on Sundays. The ever narrowing lane becomes cobbled and decants on to another smaller Square. On the left is the OTE, open on weekdays 0730-1510 hrs, beyond which the lane curves right passing the Bank of Greece (Exchange and Eurocheques) and then left on to another irregular Square. On the right is a Post Office, below and to the left of which is a large paved Square with formal park bench seats. On the far side is a baker and the lane winds on past another old fashioned baker on the right. Mark you the whole of the 'High Street's' length is lined with busy little shops and kafenions.

The relatively modern Church of the Assumption, built in 1875, is the repository for the skulls of the 'Five Martyr Saints' of Samothraki.

The village is the recognised base camp for an assault on the heights of Mt Fengari (1611m). As the paths are poorly marked it is a sensible idea to ask around for the assistance of a local 'sherpa' for the five hour trek.

The map shows that a road continues on through the Chora to the large village of Alonia and on to the Lakoma road. But the way through the Chora is rather difficult to find, to say the least, so it is best if contemplating a circular route to approach from the direction of Alonia.

ROUTE TWO
To Profitis Ilias (13 km) The initial stages of the route pass the junction to the

Chora (*See* ROUTE ONE) and the turning (at 3¾ km) off to:
ALONIA (5 km). The road climbs towards the village, through the outskirts and on to the Chora.

Back on the main route, which is some distance above and from the coastline, the road progresses through lovely countryside, full of olive groves. There are tantalising glimpses of the shore here and there.

The road finally drops to sea-level in the valley of the River Xiropotamos and swings inland.

At this point a track heads off for the coast. Perhaps an idyllic, sand blessed, sea and sun kissed hamlet of a port? Forget it! Certainly the wide path, once having reached the shoreline, angles left and runs parallel to the sea-shore but it is a shadeless, narrow shore of shingle and pebbles with a large pebble seabed. The path ends up, after some 1¾ km, at a small, dusty bluff topped by a kafenion which is more often closed than open. Incidentally, for some obscure reason, this track is being surfaced. There are a number of benzinas pulled up on the very messy shore which is littered with rubbish, donkey droppings and tar. If that were not enough, there are masses of tiny flies and it smells, so there! A small rivulet and fountain sustains the weary traveller and a path heads off inland towards the village of Lakoma.

Back on the main route, after a total of nine kilometres, the road forks, left to:
XIROPOTAMOS (8 km from Kamariotisa). A pleasant and well watered, mountain-side village.

The right fork passes the turning down to:
LAKOMA (11 km from Kamariotisa) A small and uninteresting village but from whence a 7½ km path makes off towards the Church of Panagia Kremniotisa. Prior to the church the bed of the River Amos tumbles down to the coast and supposedly a sandy beach at a spot named **Pachia Ammos.** I must own up to never having made the trek.

The main thrust of the right-hand road climbs up to:
PROFITIS ILIAS (13 km from Kamariotisa). A pleasant village with running streams and a taverna or two.

The road does continue on for a short distance, steeply dropping down to the hillside hugging **Kastelli** which in actuality is only three humble cottages, one of which hosts a viciously barking dog.

ROUTE THREE
To Therma (Loutra) (13 km). This route proceeds along a lovely sea-level road edging an almost continual sea-shore made up of large pebbles. To landward are low hills alternatively wooded or sprouting waist high scrub. On the side of the road is the occasional accommodation, with a taverna and two **Rooms** at:
PALEOPOLI (5 km from Kamariotisa). The site of a once ancient city complete with the ruins of some medieval defensive towers and a broken quay but it is not for these that one visits Paleopoli. Oh no. On the far side of the roadside taverna a track bears off in an inland direction. A path to the left advances to the *Xenia Hotel* (Class B, tel. 41230). Double rooms sharing a bathroom cost 1800 drs. The track proceeds to a tiny, large tree-shaded hamlet dominated by the single storey building of the:
Museum of the Sanctuary of the Great Gods. Naturally the museum displays the finds that the original excavators, the French, kindly left behind. The pillage of artifacts cannot be better illustrated than by the fact that the world famous, headless statue of the winged *Victory of Samothrace (the Nike),* unearthed in 1863, resides in the Louvre. The one on display in the museum is a copy 'thoughtfully' gifted by the

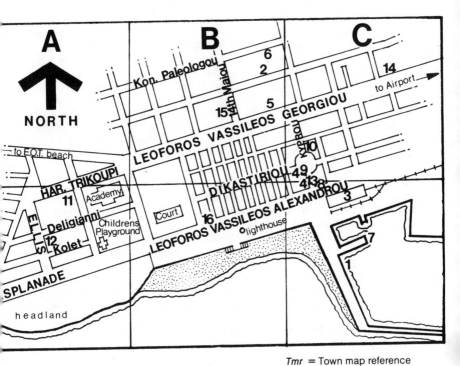

Tmr = Town map reference
Fsw = Facing seawards
Sbo = Sea behind one

Tmr

1 Ferry-boat quay C2
2 Bus station B1
3 Railway station C1/2
4 Rooms
5 Hotel Alex B1
6 Hotel Lido B1
7 Ferry-boat quay Taverna C2
8 Souvlaki/fast food snackbar C1/2
9 Taverna C1
10 Taverna C1
11 Pizza restaurant/taverna A1/2
12 Olympic Airline office A2
13 Ferry-boat ticket office C1/2
14 National Bank C1
15 OTE B1
16 Main Post Office B2

Illustration 36 Alexandroupoli Mainland Port

French. Fortunately the last excavators of the site were American archaeologists who caused the Museum's exhibits to be labelled in English and wrote a guide to the site. The Museum is open daily between 0845-1500 hrs and 0930-1430 hrs on Sundays and holidays. Entrance is a rather steep 150 drs but this covers both the museum and the excavations. On the way to the fenced site the path dips past a super toilet block and then up to the gate. At the entrance is a very useful annotated plan of the magnificent:

Sanctuary of the Great Gods. Set in a pretty hillside cleft and dates back to the 6th century BC. The original Kabeiroi cult, of which little is known, was absorbed by the Greeks and the Romans only for the Sanctuary to be destroyed by an earthquake in the 6th century AD. Despite this the remains are very interesting and the rebuilt columns of the Heraion dramatic.

Back on the coast road are **Rooms** close to the short branch track to the hamlet of:
KARIOTES (9 km from Kamariotisa). Kariotes is set on a scrub plain that runs up to the foot of the steep mountainside dominating the mass of the island.

The main route passes a pleasant but still pebbly stretch of shore complete with the 'standard', aluminium framed, changing cubicles. Beyond a large taverna, and opposite a small quay, the road turns sharply right up a sloping, wide street, almost of avenue proportions, flanked by enormous, sodium light lamp standards, leading to:
THERMA (Loutra) (13 km from Kamariotisa). The present spa village is a comparatively modern, messy and ugly development that straggles up the extensively tree shaded river valley. The restaurants are crammed with Greeks compulsively 'digging in at the trough' and here for the curative waters. To the left, on entering the village, a track leads to the fairly new **Hotel Kaviros** (Class B, tel. 41577).

Those seeking more homely accommodation can find simple **Rooms** towards the top end of the village costing about 880 drs a night.

An uneven, stony track continues on parallel to the coastline, from the point where the main road angles up to Therma. This sallys forth right round to the east end of the island. Not far along the stony track, paths wander through the woods, on the left, to an unofficial campsite set in the sylvan glades on either side of a swampy, summer dry river-bed which runs out on the still large pebble shore.

Before a kilometre is up, a path branches off to the right towards **Rooms**.

ALEXANDROUPOLI: mainland port. (Illustration 36)
Tel prefix 0551.

A very large, busy, bustling seaside resort and town with a large harbour and a contrasting mixture of old and new.

The old port and town is at the right-hand end of Alexandroupoli (*Sbo*). Hereabouts are the railway terminus, Bus depot, Ferry-boat quay, the more provincial hotels and a number of restaurant/tavernas.

The railway is to the east of the road that descends to the Ferry-boat quay (*Tmr* 1C2). To the left (*Sbo*), beyond the prominent, Esplanade mounted lighthouse, the wide waterfront road, Leoforos Vas Alexandrou, passes along a development that is increasingly holiday resort in nature and edges a very sandy beach. The spread out town is wearisomely large.

ARRIVAL BY AIR
Ostensibly a convenient airport but due to the presence of the Greek Armed forces it is often difficult to book a flight. The Olympic Airline office (*Tmr* 12A2) is rather inconveniently situated in Odhos Ellis, way down to west along the Esplanade.

Aircraft timetables
Alexandroupoli to Athens
Daily   1930, 2255 hrs.
Up to 14th June additionally
Monday, Thursday, Friday   0835 hrs.
After 15th June additionally
Daily except for Tuesday   0835 hrs.
Return
Daily   1755, 2120 hrs.
Up to 14th June additionally
Monday, Thursday, Friday   0700 hrs.
After 15th June additionally
Daily except for Tuesday   0700 hrs.
One-way fare 3390 drs; duration 55 mins.

ARRIVAL BY BUS
The bustling, crowded Bus station (*Tmr* 2B1) is several blocks back from the Old Town waterfront.

Bus timetable
Alexandroupoli to Athens
Daily   0800, 1530, 1900 hrs.
Return journey (from Larissis Railway Station Terminal, Athens).
Daily   0630, 1500, 1800 hrs.
One-way fare 3430 drs; duration 14½ hrs.

ARRIVAL BY FERRY
The harbour is muddling and large with the Ferry-boat quay (*Tmr* 1C2) tucked away on the left-hand side (*Sbo*) of the facility. A wide concrete road climbs up the hillside from the harbour leaving the railway station to the right.

There is a Ferry-Boat Ticket Office (*Tmr* 13C1/2) on the left (*Sbo*) of Odhos Kyprou.

Ferry-boat timetable

Day	Departure time	Ferry-boat	Ports/Island of Call
Monday, Tuesday	1000 hrs	Arsinoi	Samothraki
Wednesday	1600 hrs	Arsinoi	Samothraki
Thursday	1400 hrs	Arsinoi	Samothraki
Friday	0800, 1600 hrs	Arsinoi Arsinoi	Samothraki Samothraki
Saturday	1700 hrs	Arsinoi	Samothraki

ARRIVAL BY TRAIN
The station (*Tmr* 3C1/2) is a branch line terminus with a ticket office, waiting room and toilets. The ticket clerks are most helpful, luggage can be left in the waiting room and the lavatories made use of but due to the massed flies and mosquitoes it is not a pleasant location. Across the road from the terminus is a convenient if rather sleazy, late night cafe-bar.

Train timetable
Alexandroupoli to Athens, via Thessaloniki
Daily   0600, 1151, 1502, 2256 hrs.
Return
Daily   0700, 1425, 2110, 2310 hrs.
One-way fare 1705 drs*; duration 15½ hrs†.
It may well be worth travelling first class for 2560 drs especially considering the increased comfort and the length of the journey.

† *An anguished* cri de coeur *from Anne's husband, who was stationed at Alexandroupoli, points out that a minimum of 18 hours must be allowed, that is unless "delayed even longer"! I can confirm that my last journey on this line took some 21 hours due to a railway carriage catching fire.*

THE ACCOMMODATION & EATING OUT

The Accommodation There is any amount of accommodation, varying from one A class, three B class, eight C class, four D class and two E class hotels. Odhos Kyprou, the street branching off from the Esplanade, across from the way up from (or down to) the Ferry-boat quay (*Tmr* 1C2), connects with the town's main thoroughfare, Leoforos Vas. Georgiou, which runs parallel to the Esplanade. On the left of this side street are two 'provincial' hotels, the:

Hotel Tourist (Class D) 7 Kyprou   Tel. 26403
Directions: As above.
   All rooms share the bathrooms with a single room costing 650 drs and a double room 900 drs.
and the:
Hotel Metropolis (Class D) 24 Kyprou   Tel. 26443
Directions: As above.
Rates and standards as for the *Hotel Tourist.*
   There are also **Rooms** (*Tmr* 4C1/2).

Hotels in this area and convenient to the Bus, Ferry and Train termini include the:
Hotel Alex (*Tmr* 5B1) (Class C) 294 Vassileos Georgiou   Tel. 26302
Directions: From the Esplanade, adjacent to the Ferry-boat quay, proceed up Odhos Kyprou to Leoforos Vas. Georgiou. The hotel is across the avenue and to the left.
   All rooms have an en suite bathroom. A single room costs 1200 drs and a double room 1750 drs, rising, respectively to 1350 drs and 1900 drs (1st July - 30th Sept).

Hotel Lido (*Tmr* 6B1) (Class D) 15 K. Paleologou   Tel. 28808
Directions: From the junction of Odhos Kyprou with Leoforos Vas. Georgiou, a street branches off from the other side and to the right of Leoforos Vas. Georgiou. The second turning off to the left is Odhos K. Paleologou and the hotel is on the left.
   A single room sharing a bathroom costs 800 drs and a double room sharing 1175 drs. Double rooms with an en suite bathroom are available for 1460 drs.

The Eating Out There are any amount of eating places ranged along the Esplanade. Convenient for ferry-boat arrivals is a recommended *Taverna* (*Tmr* 7C2) at the end of the Ferry-boat quay.
   At the top of the Ferry-boat quay approach road, at the outset of Odhos Kyprou is a good *Souvlaki/Fast Food Snackbar* (*Tmr* 8C1/2). Further along Odhos Kyprou, on the left of the 'circular square', is a *Taverna* (*Tmr* 9C1). Diagonally across the street is an excellent *Taverna* (*Tmr* 10C1). Turning left on Leoforos Vas. Georgiou and continuing along on to Har. Trikoupi leads past the Academy. On the left, in the next block, is an excellent *Pizza Restaurant/Taverna* (*Tmr* 11A1/2).

There is a National Bank (*Tmr* 14C1) on Leoforos Vas Georgiou, an OTE office (*Tmr* 15B1) on Odhos 14th Maiou and the main Post Office (*Tmr* 16B2) on the Esplanade, Leoforos Vas. Alexandrou.
It may be worth noting that Alexandroupoli hosts an annual wine festival between mid July and mid August. Take the NTOG Beach road. Entrance costs 150 drs but that allows participants to drink as much of the twelve or so different wines available from the barrel as they can consume. The event is staged in a park with two eating places and includes displays of Greek dancing. The atmosphere is very nice and the 'happening' is well worth visiting. The only drawback is the universal Alexandroupoli curse – mosquitoes.

INDEX